Money in a Human Economy

The Human Economy
Series editor:
Keith Hart, University of Pretoria

Those social sciences and humanities concerned with the economy have lost the confidence to challenge the sophistication and public dominance of the field of economics. We need to give a new emphasis and direction to the economic arrangements that people already share, while recognizing that humanity urgently needs new ways of organizing life on the planet. This series examines how human interests are expressed in our unequal world through concrete economic activities and aspirations.

Volume 1
People, Money and Power in the Economic Crisis
Perspectives from the Global South
Edited by Keith Hart & John Sharp

Volume 2
Economy For and Against Democracy
Edited by Keith Hart

Volume 3
Gypsy Economy
Romani Livelihoods and Notions of Worth in the 21st Century
Edited by Micol Brazzabeni, Manuela Ivone Cunha and Martin Fotta

Volume 4
From Clans to Coops:
Confiscated Mafia Land in Sicily
Theodoros Rakopoulos

Volume 5
Money in a Human Economy
Edited by Keith Hart

Money in a
Human Economy

Edited by
Keith Hart

berghahn
NEW YORK · OXFORD
www.berghahnbooks.com

First published in 2017 by

Berghahn Books

www.berghahnbooks.com

© 2017, 2019 Keith Hart
First paperback edition published in 2019

All rights reserved. Except for the quotation of short passages for the purposes of criticism and review, no part of this book may be reproduced in any form or by any means, electronic or mechanical, including photocopying, recording, or any information storage and retrieval system now known or to be invented, without written permission of the publisher.

Library of Congress Cataloging-in-Publication Data

Names: Hart, Keith, editor.
Title: Money in a human economy / edited by Keith Hart.
Description: New York : Berghahn Books, 2017. | Series: The human economy ; Volume 5 | Includes bibliographical references and index.
Identifiers: LCCN 2017013681 (print) | LCCN 2017021938 (ebook) | ISBN 9781785335600 (eBook) | ISBN 9781785335594 (hardback : alk. paper)
Subjects: LCSH: Money–History. | Foreign exchange.
Classification: LCC HG231 (ebook) | LCC HG231 .M5864 2017 (print) | DDC 332.4–dc23
LC record available at https://lccn.loc.gov/2017013681

British Library Cataloguing in Publication Data

A catalogue record for this book is available from the British Library.

ISBN 978-1-78533-559-4 hardback
ISBN 978-1-78920-505-3 paperback
ISBN 978-1-78533-560-0 ebook

Contents

Part I. Introduction

Introduction. Money in a Human Economy   3
 Keith Hart

Chapter 1. Capitalism and Our Moment in the History of Money   15
 Keith Hart

Part II. Thinking About Money

Chapter 2. Money is Good to Think: From "Wants of the Mind" to Conversation, Stories, and Accounts   43
 Jane Guyer

Chapter 3. The Shadow of Aristotle: A History of Ideas about the Origins of Money   61
 Joseph Noko

Chapter 4. Luxury and the Sexual Economy of Capitalism   81
 Noam Yuran

Part III. The Evolution of Money Today

Chapter 5. The Future of Money is Shaped by the Family Practices of the Global South   103
 Supriya Singh

Chapter 6. Remittance Securitization in the Hemisphere of the Américas: From Wall Street to *Calle Principal* and Back   128
 David Pedersen

Chapter 7. Cross-Border Investment in China   147
 Horacio Ortiz

Chapter 8. Value Transfer and Rent: Or, I Didn't Realize My Payment Was Your Annuity   167
 Bill Maurer

Chapter 9. Bitcoin as Politics   189
 Nigel Dodd

Part IV. Money in Its Time and Place

Chapter 10. A South Asian Mercantile Model of Exchange: Hundi during British Rule   209
Marina Martin

Chapter 11. Money and Markets For and Against the People: The Rise and Fall of Basotho's Economic Independence, 1830s–1930s   229
Sean Maliehe

Chapter 12. Gender and Money in the Argentinian *Trueque*   250
Hadrien Saiag

Chapter 13. An Imaginary Currency: The Haitian Dollar   270
Federico Neiburg

Index   291

Part I

Introduction

Introduction
Money in a Human Economy

KEITH HART

This book is the third in a series of volumes (Hart and Sharp 2014; Hart 2015) exploring the idea of a human economy as a way of thinking about a better world. These first two chapters explore the tension between money as a human universal and its historical manifestation as capitalism. Inevitably, conceiving of money in abstract and general terms lends a more benign perspective to it, whereas capitalism offers a more divisive and critical perspective. Our aim is not to choose one over the other—a move that is commonplace in ideological conceptions of money—but rather to keep a dialectical focus on both poles, to keep two ideas in our head at once. For if any topic resists reductive treatment, money's essence lies in movement between the extremes that constitute its character.

We tend to think of money as one thing, akin to the national monopoly currency we are familiar with. It is the same with theories of money. Most people stick with their favorite, to the exclusion of all others. But this monolithic assumption concerning money is losing its power in our time. Singular conceptions of money are giving way to plural versions not just of money but of the kinds of society that it supports. This raises the question of how our various concrete examples relate to "money," whatever that may be.

We could make of money an analytical construct with some pretension to being money—debt, for example. But then money as the object of our common inquiries would be lost. Once we accept that many thousands of social things can be money, the pursuit of a solid middle ground becomes increasingly implausible. We must admit therefore that each case bites off a chunk of money that combines general and particular dimensions of the enquiry that we share. We must then add the historical complexity of modern money, which is global in scope and goes by the name of capitalism. Finally, as our title indicates, we do have an analytical take on money—its place in something we call "a human economy." This is what readers will get from this book: a wide-ranging and open-ended set of particular inquiries into money as a feature of the human economy. It doesn't get more specific than that.

Money is, with language, one of humanity's two great means of communication. Take a look again at the preceding paragraphs and substitute "language" for every incidence of "money." The presumption of unity in the case of money is replaced by one of diversity. This is our method. We take something assumed to be generically the same and explore its diversity.

For many, the idea of money in a human economy makes no sense, for what could be more inhuman than money? On the whole, money gets a bad press. Why? For thousands of years property in money fought property in land, and most often the latter was politically dominant (Hann and Hart 2011; Hart and Sharp 2014). Markets and money were denigrated as antisocial elements in economic texts written by supporters of the military-agrarian complex. The poor have had little love for the rich through the ages and several world religions make a point of stressing this. The idea has entered the modern era in the form of socialist or communist thinking, most strikingly in the Soviet anti-market economy inaugurated by the Bolshevik revolution and later by Mao's Cultural Revolution. There have also been countless utopian experiments that were aimed at making money marginal to their societies. Intellectuals habitually join this chorus, as they have little money and resent having less public influence than those who do have it. The popular saying "money is the root of all evil" has deep cultural resonance, both ancient and modern. Finally – and less pejoratively – money was an impersonal instrument and therefore, in a way, inhuman. It had to be impersonal in order to reach people faraway whom the sender didn't know and so it stood for the opposite of humanity, even as it served wider human purposes.

In order to identify money's human side, we must decide what an "economy" is. Is it a species of rationalism, as the economists claim, or a social object as featured nightly on the national news? It is both, a subject-object relationship that takes the form of a strategy meant to guide the behavior of a class opposed to other classes. Thus the Greek military aristocracy fought the great trading cities in the name of *oikonomia* – economy as household management. Political economy, the opposite of its ancient domestic rival, argued that economic growth required the diversion of funds from land rents to commercial profit. National economy and urban economy unified classes against "the world." The recent idea of "world economy," however, has so far disguised highly unequal interests, mainly European and North American to date. Humanity's task in the twenty-first century is to make a more equal version, but its contours are still vague.

The principles of an economy, conceived of as a specific strategy, must be discovered, articulated, and disseminated. To be useful, an economy should be based on general principles that guide what people do. It is not just an ideology or a call for realism. The social and technical conditions of our era – urbanization, fast transport, and universal media – must underpin any inquiry into the principles of human economy. We do not assume that people know best, although they usually know their own interests better than those who presume to speak for them.

In origin, "economy" privileged budgeting for domestic self-sufficiency; "urban economy" represented the collective interests of a city's population; "political economy" promoted capitalist markets over military landlordism; "national economy" sought to equalize the chances of a citizen body. Perhaps "human economy" could be a way of envisaging the next stage, linking unique human beings to humanity as a whole by articulating a sequence of social extension, involving its principal predecessors, "house-city-market-nation-world."

So a human economy is, lest we forget, an economy. But what makes it human? First, it engages with human beings in their everyday lives. As such it feeds off the ethnographic impulse to join people where they live in order to find out what they do, think, and want. Everyday life consists of many small-scale activities, a plethora of economic enterprises and institutions. Economic analysis, moreover, should aim to reach people in ways that make sense to them.

All of this is consistent with a humanist view of the economy. It must be so, if the economy is to be returned from remote experts to the people who are most affected by it. But humanism by itself is not enough. To be human also involves participating in the widest circles of humanity, in world society. So a human economy must seek to build bridges between different levels of association. This is a process of extension and it is closely linked to markets and money, which are an intrinsic part of the human economy. The social dimension of human economy therefore lies not in local and global spheres considered separately, but in movement between them. It must be informed by an economic vision capable of bridging the gap between everyday life (what people know) and humanity's common predicament, which is inevitably impersonal and lies beyond the actor's point of view (what they don't know).

Emergent world society *is* the new human universal – not an idea, but the fact of our shared occupation of the planet crying out for new principles of association. We urgently need to make a world where all people can live together. Small may be beautiful and a preference for initiatives grounded in local social realities is essential, but large-scale bureaucracies are also necessary if economic democracy is to embrace the movement of the world we live in.

Since 1800, energy production has grown at twice the rate of the population. Many people now live longer, work less, and spend more than they did before. But the distribution of this extra energy has been grossly unequal. A third of humanity still works in the fields with their hands. Americans each consume four hundred times more energy than Ugandans. This hectic dash of humanity from the village to the city is assumed to be driven by an engine of economic growth and inequality known as "capitalism." But several social forms have emerged to organize the process on a large scale: empires, nation-states, cities, corporations, regional federations, international organizations, capitalist markets. We need more effective social coordination at the global level and the drive toward local self-organization is strong everywhere. Progressives denigrate the dominant bureaucratic institutions while tending to promote small-scale self-organized groups and networks. Yet no future society could dispense with the principal forms that have brought us to this point. So we need to work out how states, cities, and big money might be selectively combined with citizens' initiatives to promote more democratic societies at every level. A first step would be to stop viewing the economy exclusively in national terms.

Many progressives, not to mention more radical groups, would not consider working with states and firms. Yet the French revolution was backed by the slaving shippers of Nantes and Bordeaux, the Italian revolution by the industrialists of Milan and Turin. You need a lot of money to raise an army and rich backers whose interests coincide with the revolution are hard to find. Kenya's world-leading experiment in mobile money, M-Pesa, was launched by a subsidiary of Vodacom. Hewlett-Packard has developed research stations in outlying areas to make computers accessible to the world's "poorest four billion." The notion of a "popular economy" has emerged in Latin America since the 1990s, bringing new coalitions (peasants, urban informal workers, unions) into an alliance with progressive governments. Brazil under Lula introduced a community banking system combining microfinance and complementary currencies. The government of Uruguay sponsored a "3C" alternative circuit for SMEs based on unpaid invoices as currency. South Africa is speeding up SMEs' access to liquidity through a Validation Clearing Bureau.

This dialectic of small-scale humanism and large-scale institutions is central to any version of human economy with a constructive purpose.

Given our preference to anchor economic strategies in people's everyday lives, aspirations, and local circumstances, the focus must be on extension from the local toward the global. We can't arrive instantly at a view of the whole, but we can engage more with less familiar worlds. Humanity has developed three preeminent means of moving continuously between extremes of scale and register: music, math, and money. Money and markets are intrinsic to our human potential, not antihuman. Of course they should take forms that are more conducive to economic democracy. It helps to recognize that they span the extremes of human existence: they link us to the universe of our social relations and give precise definition to our most intimate circumstances. As Simmel (1978 [1900]) suggested, money reflects our human potential to make universal society.

What then is money? It is a universal measure of value, but its specific form is not yet as universal as the method humanity has devised to measure time around the world. It is purchasing power, a means of buying and selling in markets. It counts wealth and status. It is a store of memory linking individuals to their various communities, a kind of memory bank (Hart 2000) and thus a source of identity. As a symbolic medium, it conveys information through a system of signs that relies more on numbers than words. A lot more circulates with money than the goods and services it buys.

Huon Wardle has this to say about "drop pan," a Jamaican numbers game played daily for money:

> Under modern conditions, Simmel (1900) argues, money becomes the most objective gauge of human relationships; and control over money is the chief marker of the self's ability to validate its existence in a shared social framework of space and time. . . . To play drop pan is to search for signs which connect the immediate and utterly contingent elements of Creole experience within an ordering of meaning which, nonetheless, is itself gauged against the shifting evaluations of money as a social principle. Lévi-Strauss describes totemism as a concrete vehicle for understanding abstract relational systems. Simmel's analysis of money reverses this. Money is a (relative) abstraction, which works because it is able to encompass concrete human connections. Drop pan is a game of concrete symbols played against the abstract master index, money. (2005: 88–89).

Money—the main device in capitalist societies for making social relations objective—is at the same time a benchmark for concrete narratives of subjective attachment. That is why, in far-reaching conflicts like divorce, the argument often focuses on money as a proxy for personal pain. Money's power lies in this synthesis of impersonal abstraction and personal meaning, objectification and subjectivity, analytical reason and synthetic narrative. It comes from the fluency of its mediation between infinite potential and finite determination. Money has some of the qualities of religion in this regard, the aspiration and ability to link inner subjectivity to the object world that we all share (but would like to establish a meaningful connection with). Once we are open to the possibility, we will discover a number of money's redemptive features, while recognizing that none of them is more intrinsic to money in isolation than its characterization as "the root of all evil."

Finally, the human economy idea clarifies a vexatious political issue of our times. Ronald Coase (1937) asked why, if markets are efficient, any self-employed person would choose to work in a collective rather than outsource what they can't do themselves. Oliver Williamson (1996) takes what is internal and external to the firm to be entirely flexible and extends this idea to relations between corporations and governments. The Fordist phase of internalizing transaction costs is over, not least because the digital revolution has cheapened the cost of transferring information reliably. This does not mean that corporations have ceased to be large and powerful. Of the one hundred largest economic entities on earth, two-thirds are corporations and one-third are governments, half each if national economies are included. All but one of the top 150 firms are financial. Moreover, we are witnessing a drive for corporate political independence that would leave the corporations as the only citizens in a world society made to suit their interests. This is the logical conclusion of the collapse of the difference between real and artificial persons in law, granting business corporations the legal standing of individual citizens (Hart 2005). Thomas Jefferson identified commercial monopolies ("pseudo-aristocrats") as a powerful threat to democracy—mere human beings cannot compete with organizations of their size, wealth, reach and longevity.

Coase and Williamson imagine a world where companies control the marketing of their brand, outsource production, logistics, and much else, and internalize government. Why rely on nation-states for conflict resolution? After all, corporations also have to handle conflicts internally. Why have more state-made and international laws, when what the world needs most is moral law? Corporate Social Responsibility (Salmon 2010) is a major field for negotiating changes in the relationship between firms and society. What kinds of political mobilization could challenge the power of corporations at every level from the local to the global?

The human economy idea may have its origins in small-scale informal activities and a humanist ideology, but effective resistance to a corporate takeover will require selective alliances between self-organized initiatives on the ground and large-scale public and private bureaucracies. It will also require the development of global social networks. There are powerful anti-humanist forces in the world we share. So we must build bridges between local actors and the new human universal, world society. To be human is to depend on and make sense of impersonal social conditions in order to act effectively. Individual rational choice does not come close to approximating this situation.

Human beings need to feel "at home in the world." The twentieth century opposed state and market as two principles that came into ruinous conflict, whereas they are indispensable to each other, even if they leave out people much of the time. "Society" bridges these extremes and, following Marx, people, machines, and money matter most in our societies, even if the order of their priority is the opposite of what is desirable. Money buys the machines that control people's access to work. Humanity's task is to reverse that order.

Money in Society

At the University of Pretoria we have organized a research team to develop a "human economy" approach to development (Hart et al. 2010; Hart and Sharp 2014; Hart 2015). As we have seen, this starts from an ethnographic approach that addresses the variety of particular institutions through which most people experience economic life. We aim to promote economic democracy by helping people to organize and improve their own lives. Our findings must therefore be presented to the public in a spirit of pragmatism and made understandable for readers' own practical use. The human economy must also be informed by a vision capable of bridging the gap between everyday life and our common predicament. For this purpose a variety of methods might be drawn from philosophy, world history, literature, and grand social theory. Initiatives grounded in local social realities are unchallengeable, but large-scale bureaucracies are also essential if we are to embrace the movement of the world we live in.

In defending ourselves from corporate domination, we need to be very sure that we are human and they are not. The drive for economic democracy will not be won until that confusion has been cleared up.

Money, much as Durkheim (1912) argued for religion, is the principal means for us all to bridge the gap between everyday personal experience and a society whose wider reaches are impersonal. It is often portrayed as a lifeless object separated from persons, whereas it is a creation of human beings, imbued with the collective spirit of the living and the dead. Money, as a token of society, must be impersonal in order to connect individuals to the universe of relations to which they belong. But people make everything personal, including their relations with society. This two-sided relationship is universal, but its incidence is highly variable (Hart 2007). Money in capitalist societies stands for alienation, detachment, impersonal society, the outside; its origins lie beyond our control (the market). Relations marked by the absence of money are the model of personal integration and free association, of what we take to be familiar, the inside (home). People want to integrate division, to make some meaningful connection between their own subjectivity and society as an object. It helps that money, as well as being the means of separating public and domestic life, was always the main bridge between the two. That is why money must be central to any attempt to humanize society. It is both the principal source of our vulnerability in society and the main practical symbol allowing each of us to make an impersonal world meaningful.

The reality of markets is therefore not just universal abstraction, but this mutual determination of the abstract and the concrete. If you have some money, there is almost no limit to what you can do with it, but, as soon as you buy something, the act of payment lends concrete finality to your choice. Money's social power comes from the fluency of its mediation between these extremes. To turn our backs on markets and money in the name of collective rather than individual interests reproduces the bourgeois separation of self and society. It is not enough to emphasize the controls that people already impose on money and exchange in their personal practice (Parry and Bloch 1989; Zelizer 1994). That is the everyday world as most of us know it. We also need ways of reaching parts of the macro-economy that we don't know, if we wish to avert the ruin it could bring down on us all.

It is, however, no longer obvious, as it was for Mauss, Polanyi, and Keynes, where the levers of democratic power are located, since the global explosion of money, markets, and telecommunications has severely exposed the limitations of national frameworks of economic management. Before long, a genuine revival of Keynesian redistributive politics is inevitable. But the imbalances of the money system are global.

Money opens up local societies to interdependence with foreigners, but the pressure to reassert local control persists. Hence the internal and external dimensions of economy are often in conflict. National capitalism turned away from the world in an era of war and disruption of trade into an aspiration to self-sufficiency whose symbol was national currency (Hart and Padayachee 2013). On a much smaller scale, community currencies of the LETS type (Blanc 2010) reject money's capacity to link us to universal society in favor of local restrictions on exchange. Even Simmel believed that the dematerialization of money would reveal to us our dependence on society. Yet the economy is global and lawless, while national capitalism is on the slide.

Neoliberal privatization and the invasion of money into public and domestic life continue unabated (Maurer, this volume). The penetration of finance into everyday reproduction poses problems that should be addressed through developing alternative approaches to money, not by denying its central role in the organization of complex societies (Singh and Pedersen, this volume). The attempt to separate spheres of paid and unpaid labor ("the market" vs. "home") was always utopian and is in any case negated by money's indispensability to both.

Money is a great equalizer, but it also fuels inequality. This is related to its ability to mediate the extremes of human experience. Money as memory links individuals and their community; past, present, and future; fact and fiction; local and global (Hart 2000). Indeed, the word "money" comes from the Roman goddess of memory and the mother of the muses, who were custodians of the arts and sciences of civilization. We must resist the temptation to perch on one pole of these paired categories, learning rather how to think dialectically through them and to work out practical ways of combining them socially.

The two great memory banks are language and money. Humanists have paid much attention to the first, which divides us more than it brings us together, but not to money where the potential for universal communication is less ambiguous, in addition to its well-advertised ability to symbolize differences between us. Exchange of meanings through language and exchange of commodities through money are now converging in a single network of communication, the Internet (Hart 2000). We must learn how to use this digital revolution to advance the human conversation about a better world. Our political task is to make a world society fit for all humanity. Money is how we learn to be truly human.

The extension of society to a more inclusive level has some positive features and, before we demonize money and markets, we should try to turn them to institutional ends that benefit us all. More effective regulatory frameworks need new principles of political association. This means addressing squarely the combinations of money, machines, and people emerging today. For this, however, we need to be weaned from old social structures and habits of mind that have not yet been destroyed, as they would be by a general war of the sort that has accompanied all the major revolutions of modern history.

Money in This Collection

The Cold War pushed the opposition between states and markets to the edge of nuclear annihilation, yet the coin's two sides demonstrate their interdependence, in money at least (Hart 1986). Even so, state and commodity theories of money are both impersonal. We have seen, however, that human beings habitually bring a personal dimension to their engagement with society, however remote and impersonal it may be (Neiburg and Saiag, this volume). Moreover, despite the common belief that we are oppressed by money's impersonality, money mediates the poles of our existence, offering a means of communication between them. The human economy approach suggests one way that money might provide a synthesis of our existential divisions, between self and world. That is its institutional capacity to serve the interests of people rather than just impersonal states and markets, to help and not hinder our attempts to build bridges between personal experience and the implacable forces of the wider society.

This book explores "money in a human economy" in thirteen chapters, most of them based on invited contributions to a conference, "Money in the Making of World Society," held at the University of Pretoria.[1] Their range is very wide, reflecting the human economy approach's double roots in anthropology and an interdisciplinary approach to development. The authors assembled here include six anthropologists, two sociologists, two economic historians, two heterodox economists, and one independent scholar. Their professional status ranges from distinguished, middle-rank, and starting professors to postdoctoral researchers, a graduate student, and no academic status at all. The countries they are from and/or study include Lesotho, Zimbabwe, India, China, Argentina, Haiti, El Salvador, Brazil, Israel, Australia, Britain, France, and the United States. Half the chapters attempt global comparison; while the rest focus on one country each, within a context of wider history to a varying degree.

Obviously this collection is not a coordinated exercise pursuing a shared analytical agenda, even less a particular paradigm, whether familiar or new. Some readers may feel, given the subject matter—gender, postcolonialism, and finance, for example—that we have neglected important bodies of literature. Moreover, there is a definite bias toward "Dead White European Males" (DWEMs), a bias that marked my book on money (Hart 2000). I felt then and now that the classical canon offers rich material for exploring issues like the human economy, money, and the Internet. The authors most cited for that book were Locke, Marx, Keynes, Weber, and Mauss. Later perhaps we can narrow down the focus and bring it up to date; but for now we do not apologize for the idiosyncratic mélange of case studies, each in its own way exploring the relationship between money and human economy.

The text is divided into four parts. Part 1 introduces money as a central feature of the human economy, followed by an overview of money in its historical form as capitalism. Why should we consider our time to be a decisive moment in the history of money? Part 2 takes as its theme "thinking about money." Jane Guyer's chapter, "Money is Good to Think," combines some unusual and revealing sources for reflection; Joseph Noko explores the origins of money from Aristotle to Ancient Egypt; and Noam Yuran provides an extraordinary revival of Sombart's theory of the origins of capitalism—not in hard work and rational accumulation, but in a new market for luxuries linked to sexual freedom.

Part 3 brings together a number of examples of the speed and variety of developments in the money form today. Supriya Singh sees banking the unbanked poor as a central policy for their emancipation, whereas David Pedersen offers a more jaundiced perspective on global finance. Horacio Ortiz offers rare insight into China's financial relations with the West in the field of cross-border investment. Bill Maurer offers a remarkable survey of the US payments industry, while Nigel Dodd reveals the subterranean politics of bitcoin. This section offers some justification for the eclectic assemblage of these chapters. They are all about money, but in a great variety of contexts.

Part 4 covers a wider range of time, including the traditional Indian financial instrument, hundi, under British colonial rule (Marina Martin) and the vagaries of markets and money in nineteenth-century Lesotho (Sean Maliehe) . We conclude with Hadrien Saiag's study of gender and money in Argentina and Federico Neiburg's examination of an imaginary currency, the Haitian dollar. Our larger aim, by casting our net so wide, is to expose the human economy idea to as wide a range of cases as possible.

Keith Hart is a well-known specialist in the study of money. He co-directed the Human Economy Program at the University of Pretoria from 2011–2018. He contributed the concept of an informal economy to development studies and has taught widely, notably at Cambridge. He is the author with Chris Hann of *Economic Anthropology: History, Ethnography, Critique* (2011).

NOTES

1. I am grateful to John Sharp, South Africa Director of the Human Economy Program, and the Andrew Mellon Foundation for making this conference possible.

REFERENCES

Blanc, J. 2010. "Community and complementary currencies." In K. Hart, J. Laville, and A. D. Cattani (eds.), *The Human Economy*. Cambridge: Polity Press, pp. 303–312.

Coase, R. 1937. "The nature of the firm." *Economica* 4(16): 386–405.

Durkheim, E. 1965 [1912]. *The Elementary Forms of the Religious Life*. Glencoe, IL: Free Press.

Hann, C., and K. Hart. 2011. *Economic Anthropology: History, Ethnography, Critique*. Cambridge: Polity Press.

Hart, K. 1986. "Heads or Tails? Two Sides of the Coin." *Man New Series* 21(4): 637–656.

———. 2000. *The Memory Bank: Money in an Unequal World*. London: Profile.

———. 2005. *The Hit Man's Dilemma: Or Business, Personal and Impersonal*. Chicago, IL: Prickly Paradigm.

———. 2007. "Money is always personal and impersonal." *Anthropology Today* 23(5): 16–20.

———. (ed.). 2015. *Economy For and Against Democracy*. New York: Berghahn Books.

Hart, K., J. Laville and A. D. Cattani (eds.). 2010. *The Human Economy: A Citizen's Guide*. Cambridge: Polity Press.

Hart, K., and V. Padayachee. 2013. "The history of South African capitalism in national and global perspective." *Transformation* 81/82: 55–85.

Hart, K., and J. Sharp (eds.). 2014. *People Money and Power in the Economic Crisis: Perspectives from the Global South*. New York: Berghahn Books.

Parry, J., and M. Bloch (eds.). 1989. *Money and the Morality of Exchange*. Cambridge: Cambridge University Press.

Salmon, A. 2010. "Corporate social responsibility." In K. Hart, J. Laville, and A. D. Cattani (eds.), *The Human Economy*. Cambridge: Polity Press, pp. 166–174.

Simmel, G. 1978 [1900]. *The Philosophy of Money*. London: Routledge.

Wardle, H. 2005. "A city of meanings: Place and displacement in urban Jamaican self-framings." In J. Besson and K. Fog Olwig (eds.), *Caribbean Narratives of Belonging: Fields of Relations, Sites of Identity*. Oxford: Macmillan, pp. 79–93.

Williamson, O. 1996. *The Mechanisms of Governance*. Oxford: Oxford University Press.

Zelizer, V. 1994. *The Social Meaning of Money*. New York: Basic Books.

CHAPTER 1

 # Capitalism and Our Moment in the History of Money

KEITH HART

According to writers as varied as John Locke and Karl Marx, ours is an age of money, a transitional phase in the history of humanity. Capitalism is the organization of society by and for money. Its historical mission is to bring cheap commodities to the masses and break down the insularity of traditional communities before it is replaced by a just society. It matters where we are in this process, but opinions about that differ widely. When a third of humanity still works in the fields with their hands, capitalism still has a way to go. The Victorians believed that they stood at the pinnacle of social evolution. I think of us as being more like the first digging-stick operators, primitives stumbling into the invention of agriculture. They had no idea that it would culminate in Chinese civilization and neither can we anticipate where the communications revolution will end up.

Money has called the present phase of world society into being and we must explore its potential to repair the damage it has caused. In the second half of the twentieth century, humanity formed a single interactive social network for the first time. Emergent world society *is* the new human universal—not an idea, but the fact that seven billion of us desperately need new principles of association. The task of building a global civil society for the twenty-first century is urgent. Certainly we have regressed a long way from the hopes for freedom and equality released by the Second World War and the anticolonial revolution that followed it. On the other hand, there is growing awareness of the risks for the future of life on this planet. The ecological ("green") paradigm—manifested as concern for global warming and for scarce food, water, and energy supplies—could replace market fundamentalism as the religion of this emergent world society. But we should beware of rejecting money and markets for the illusion of local self-sufficiency.

The Origins of Our Times

The 1860s saw a transport and communications revolution (steamships, continental railroads, and the telegraph) that decisively opened up the world economy. At the same time a series of political revolutions gave the leading powers of the coming century the institutional means of organizing industrial capitalism. These were the American civil war, Italy's *Risorgimento*, the abolition of serfdom in Russia, the formation of the Anglo-Indian super-state, Britain's democratic reforms, and Japan's Meiji Restoration. German unification spilled over into the 1870s through the Franco-Prussian War, the Paris Commune, and the French Third Republic. The First International was formed in 1864 and Karl Marx published *Capital* in 1867. The concentration of so many epochal events in such a short period would suggest that world society was quite well integrated even then. But in the 1870s, international trade accounted for no more than one percent of Gross National Product (GNP) in most countries and the most reliable indicator of Britain's annual economic performance was the weather at harvest time (Lewis 1978).

Capitalism has always rested on an unequal contract between owners of large amounts of money and those who make and buy their products. This contract depends on an effective threat of punishment if workers withhold their labor or buyers fail to pay up. The owners cannot make that threat alone: they need the support of governments, laws, prisons, police, even armies. By the mid-nineteenth century, it became clear that the machine revolution was pulling unprecedented numbers of people into the cities, where they added a wholly new dimension to the traditional problem of crowd control. The political revolutions of the 1860s and 1870s were based on a new and explicit alliance between capitalists and the military landlord class (who had been sworn enemies in the bourgeois revolutions, see below) to form states capable of managing industrial workforces and of taming the criminal gangs that had taken over large swaths of the main cities. Germany and Japan provide the clearest examples of such an alliance, which took a specific form in each country.

Before long, governments provided new legal conditions for the operations of large business corporations, ushering in mass production through a bureaucratic revolution (Hart 2005). The author of this new synthesis ("national capitalism") was Georg Wilhelm Friedrich Hegel, who argued in *The Philosophy of Right* (1821) that states, run by university-trained bureaucrats, should regulate capitalist markets with a view to containing their extreme consequences, while allowing their material benefits to accrue to all citizens. The national system became general after the First World War and was the dominant social form of twentieth-century civilization. Its apogee or "golden age" (Hobsbawm 1994) was in the period 1945–1979. This was a time of developmental states, economic growth, and redistribution, when, for the first and only time in history, the purchasing power of working people and the public services available to them were the principal goals of economic policy everywhere—in the Soviet bloc and postcolonial states, as well as in Western industrial societies. "Development" replaced colonial empire as the norm of relations between rich and poor countries. When, shortly before his downfall, Richard Nixon announced, "We are all Keynesians now," he was reflecting a universal belief that governments had a responsibility to manage national capitalism in the interests of all citizens.

The 1970s were a watershed. US expenditures on its losing war in Vietnam generated huge imbalances in the world's money flows, leading to a breakdown of the fixed parity exchange-rate system devised at Bretton Woods in 1944. The dollar's departure from the gold standard in 1971 triggered a free-for-all in world currency markets, leading immediately to the invention of money market futures. The world economy was plunged into depression in 1973 by the formation of the Organization of Petroleum-Exporting Countries and a hefty rise in the price of oil. "Stagflation" (high unemployment and reduced purchasing power) increased, opening the way for Reagan, Thatcher, and other neoliberal conservatives to launch a counterrevolution against social democracy in the name of "the market" rather than "the state" (Hart 1986). These events three decades ago and the policies pursued then find their denouement in the world's economic crisis today.

In the mid-1970s, all but a minute proportion of the money exchanged internationally paid for goods and services purchased abroad. Forty years later, these payments account for only a small fraction of global money transfers, the vast bulk being devoted to exchanging money for money in some other form (foreign exchange transactions alone reached daily turnover rates of $5.3 trillion in 2013). This rising tide of money, sometimes known as "the markets," represents the apotheosis of financial capitalism, with political management of currencies and trade virtually abandoned in favor of freeing up the global circuit of capital. As a result, we have lived through an explosion of money, markets, and telecommunications for more than three decades and are now experiencing the consequences.

This process of "globalization" represents a rapid extension of society to a more inclusive level than the twentieth-century norm, when society was identified with the nation-state. For us to live in the world together, we have to devise new ways of doing things for each other that go beyond the national ideal of achieving local self-sufficiency and the tradition of domestic economy before that (Hann and Hart 2011). Money, markets and communications are intrinsic to globalization. I follow here a number of writers—Marx, Simmel, Mauss, Polanyi, Keynes—who believed in money's centrality to the formation and maintenance of a better society.

The End of Something

Money is not just a means of exploitation; it also has redemptive qualities, particularly as a mediator between persons and society. Money—and the markets it sustains—is itself a human universal, with the potential to be emancipated from the social engines of inequality that it currently serves. In the late 1990s, I asked what future generations will be interested in about our times and settled on the development of communications linking all humanity. This has two striking features: first, it is a highly unequal market of buyers and sellers fueled by a money circuit that has become detached from production and politics; and second, it is driven by a digital revolution whose symbol is the Internet, the network of networks. I then explored how the forms of money and exchange are changing in this communications revolution (Hart 2000).

Money has acquired its contemporary preeminence because the economy has been extended rapidly from a national to a global level with much less social regulation than before. Of course, the specialists in money used their newfound freedom from postwar social democracy to loot the world in scandalous ways that we will have to repair, if we can. But, in addition to drawing people en masse into unsustainable credit schemes, they also began to put in place some of the institutional mechanisms that could make markets work for all of us and not just for those with lots of money. Capitalism clearly is instrumental in making world society. It will not be the basis for its stable functioning, but it does get us some of the way there.

It is always dangerous when the economy is temporarily extended beyond the reach of normal society, especially when social frontiers are pushed rapidly outward. Our times could be compared with previous episodes in the history of global capitalism, such as the dash to build continental railroads, the gold strikes in California, Alaska, and South Africa, or the wild rubber boom of the mid- to late-nineteenth century. Many analogous episodes may be found in the mercantilist economies of the period 1500–1800. The quick wealth and cowboy entrepreneurship we have just witnessed were made possible by the absence of regulation in a period of global economic expansion. We now have an opportunity to consider how world markets might be organized in the general interest.

The positive residue of previous booms and busts included transport and communication systems, a mildly inflationary gold standard, new industrial uses for rubber, stock markets, and banking regulations. All the founders of modern social theory believed that the extension of society to a more inclusive level has positive features. The world economy is more integrated than it was, but we need new forms of political association capable of administering more effective regulatory frameworks. Fragmentation would be a disaster, but some would say it has already begun. Clearly the political questions facing humanity today concern distributive justice above all. Western dominance of the world economy is coming to an end. New actors on the world stage will have their say about who gets what. Escalation of war and general fractiousness is quite likely under these circumstances. A focus on the socially redemptive qualities of money and markets might be quite helpful.

The current crisis of world economy is not merely financial, a phase in the historical cycle of credit and debt. The removal of political controls over money in recent decades has led to a situation where politics is still mainly national, but the money circuit is global and lawless (Hart 2015a). The crisis is rather an irreversible moment in the history of money, occasioned by the collapse of the money system that the world lived by in the twentieth century. This has been unraveling since the US dollar went off gold, a new regime of floating currencies emerged, and money derivatives were invented. As the need for international cooperation intensifies, the disconnection between world economy and national political institutions makes finding effective solutions very difficult.

We tend to see the potential disaster we are living through in economic rather than political terms. In this respect, neoliberalism's detractors often reproduce the free market ideology they claim to oppose. We need to ask not what is beginning, but what is ending. This is not straightforward. What is ending is "national capitalism," the synthesis of nation-states and industrial capitalism (Hart 2009). Its main symbol has been national monopoly currencies (legal tender policed by a central bank), the attempt to manage money, markets, and accumulation through central bureaucracy within a cultural community of national citizens. It was never the only active principle in world political economy: cities, regional associations, and empires are at least as old or much older. Nor has national capitalism run its course everywhere. The BRICS countries[1] are each giving the model a serious try, just as the world's nation-states seek mutual protection in regional trade federations. The point is rather that most nations have diminished influence over world economy and new principles of association must emerge soon.

People learn to understand each other as members of communities; they share meanings as a way of achieving their practical purposes together. Money is an important vehicle for this. Nation-states have been so successful in a relatively short time that it is hard for us to imagine society in any other way. Five different types of community came together in the nation-state:

- **political community:** a link to the world and a source of law at home
- **community of place:** territorial boundaries of land and sea
- **imagined or virtual community:** the constructed cultural identity of citizens
- **community of interest:** subjectively and objectively shared purposes in trade and war
- **monetary community:** common use of a national monopoly currency.

The rise and fall of single currencies is therefore one way of approaching national capitalism's historical trajectory. At present, national politics and media frame economic questions so narrowly that we find it hard to think about the world as a whole. But money is already global in scope and we urgently need to overcome these limits of imagination.

From Singular to Plural Monies

Mainstream economics says more about what money does than what it is. It is held to be a medium of exchange, a more efficient lubricant of markets than barter. Another school emphasizes money's function as a means of payment, especially of taxes to the government and hence of "purchasing power." It is a standard of value or unit of account, with the government establishing the legal conditions for trade; while John Locke (1690) conceived of money as a store of wealth, a new form of property allowing the accumulation of riches to escape from the limits of natural economy.

Karl Polanyi (1977 [1964]) argued that only modern money combines the four functions (payment, standard, store, and exchange) in a few "all-purpose" symbols, national currency. His approach offers profound insight into the causes of today's global economic crisis. We must conceive of society once more as plural rather than singular, as a federated network rather than a centralized hierarchy, the nation-state. The era of national monopoly currencies is very recent (from the 1850s); it took the United States, for example, half a century to secure an uncontested monopoly for "greenbacks," and "all-purpose money" has been breaking up for four decades now, since the dollar left gold.

Since the end of the Bretton Woods system of fixed parity exchange rates, world economy has reverted to the plural pattern of competing currencies that was normal before central banks learned how to manage national economies. The international rule system imposed after the Second World War was subverted by an offshore banking system that brought the informal economy to the heart of global finance (Shaxson 2012; Hart 2015a). The separation of functions between different types of monetary instruments was also crucial to money's great escape from the rules of the Keynesian consensus. Central bank control has been eroded by money being issued in multiple forms by a global distributed network of corporations of many kinds, not just governments and banks.

Georg Simmel (1900) considered money's twin anchors to be its physical substance (coins, paper, etc.) and the social institutions supporting the community of its users. He predicted that the first would wither away, making the second more visible. Simmel's prophecy has been realized to a remarkable degree, as the digital revolution accelerates and cheapens electronic transfers. But if the essence of money is its use in a community with shared social institutions, globalization has made national capitalism seem a lot less self-sufficient than it once did. Radical reductions in the cost of transferring information have introduced new conditions for engagement with the impersonal economy (Hart 2000, 2005). The replacement of single currencies by more specialized monetary instruments is one inevitable result of this (Dembinski and Perritas 2000).

We must therefore move from singular (national) to plural (federal) conceptions of society. The infrastructure of money has already become decentralized and global, so a return to the national solutions of the 1930s or a Keynesian regime of managed exchange rates and capital flows are bound to fail. But the extension of economy beyond national boundaries is fraught with danger. We need to extend systems of social rights to the global level before the contradictions of the market system collapse into world war – but local political organization resists such a move. Ours is becoming a multipolar world marked by a variety of political forms and an income distribution that is much less divergent than during the age of European imperialism.

We are witnessing a global power struggle of awesome consequences and we cannot afford to stand to one side. Money is at the heart of this struggle: the US dollar, currency wars, BRICS vs. the Bretton Woods institutions, the rise of China (Ortiz, this volume); but conventional economics does not help ordinary people grasp what is going on. By studying monetary relations on different geographical scales, from intimate encounters to foreign exchange markets, the contributors to this collection can help create new meanings and connections between everyday life and the human predicament as a whole.

Through the Internet or phone network, we can span the world and connect personally with people whom we will never meet. Humanity now has universal media for the expression of universal ideas. Money is essential to their dissemination. It is a constitutive part of our multiple-layered identities, from the most intimate relations to communities of exchange on a vast scale. Money allows us to express ourselves and indexes our place in hierarchies, solidarities, and enclosures (Hart and Ortiz 2014). Our identities expand, fragment, and recombine as we move from the most local transactions to national or regional currencies. Central banks, insurance companies, pension funds, global and local banks, savings clubs and other local credit schemes all shape the possibilities for our personalities to develop. We learn about politics and our membership in larger groups through our participation in monetary networks that exclude and entrap us even as they extend our horizons. As Marcel Mauss knew (2016; Hart 2014), the idea of society itself is reshaped by this multifarious expansion. If we hope for a more peaceful and integrated world society, money will certainly play an important role in its recovery from the present impasse.

The economy always has two faces, being pulled inward to secure local guarantees of a community's rights and interests and outward to engage with foreigners through the medium of money and markets of various sorts—not just the sort we are familiar with. We need to build an infrastructure of money adequate to humanity's common needs, although this agenda seems impossibly remote right now. One move in this direction goes by the name of "alter-globalization" (Pleyers 2010), and the idea of a human economy offers a bridge to that movement.

Capitalism and Inequality

Thomas Piketty's (2014) book on capital was the smash hit of our times, even though it weighed in at seven hundred pages. It was based on serious economics, up to two hundred years of national income accounting for a few rich countries, and it had an accessible literary style. An economist who can quote Balzac can't be all bad. The reasons for his success are several, but I would identify three in particular. First, Piketty brought inequality back onto the mainstream agenda, just as Occupy Wall Street did—"we are the 99 percent"—(Graeber 2013); this touched a nerve after three decades of neoliberal policies and government responses to the financial crisis that bailed out the rich and made the poor pay. Second, Piketty's argument rests on two simple equations describing the relationship between capital and labor over the last two centuries; he uses these to demonstrate that capital's share of national income must always increase. Third, instead of the widespread notion that capitalists make their money by producing competitively for profit, Piketty argued that property was still an important, even growing component of wealth; and that inheritance or rent is a neglected factor in distribution today.

These observations were significant and together justify the attention the book received. In what follows, I ask, what is capitalism? I next review the official story of the bourgeois revolutions that launched modern capitalism; then I ask whether the last two centuries constitute a Great Transformation. I identify a thread going back to Rousseau, "the anthropology of unequal society," whose most visible practitioner today is David Graeber (2011). The world revolution (social democracy) and counterrevolution (neoliberalism) of the last seventy years provide the historical context for discussing the relative significance of profit, rent, and interest in capitalism today. Finally, Piketty's method cannot capture the movement of world society, being tied to a national framework. I conclude therefore with some observations on global history.

What is Capitalism?

In the early nineteenth century the world's population was approximately one billion. At that time under 3 percent of humanity lived in cities. The rest lived by extracting a livelihood from the land. Animals and plants were responsible for almost all the energy produced and consumed by human beings. A bit more than two centuries later, the world population has reached seven billion. The proportion living in cities is now half. Inanimate energy converted by machines now accounts for the bulk of production and consumption. For most of this period, the human population has been growing at an average annual rate of 1.5 percent; cities at 2 percent a year; and energy production at around 3 percent a year. This last figure is double the rate of population increase, a powerful index of the economic expansion of the last two centuries. Many people live longer, work less, and spend more than before. But the distribution of all this extra energy has been grossly unequal. Americans each consume four hundred times more energy than the average Ugandan, for example.

This hectic dash of humanity from the village to the city is the most striking feature of our times. It is widely assumed that the engine driving this economic growth and the inequality it entails is "capitalism." So it is imperative to learn how capitalist growth occurs and how to make good the damage it causes. In the last half-century, the rich countries made a commitment of sorts to helping poor countries become richer. In the wake of the anticolonial revolution, such a commitment was real enough, even if the recipes chosen were often flawed. But after the watershed of the 1970s, this commitment has faded (Hann and Hart 2011: chapter 6).

What are the forms of society and technology organizing our hectic march from the village to the city and to a world economy? "Capitalism" was a term in public circulation by the 1850s, but it was not used by Marx and Engels and entered social theory a century ago through Werner Sombart (1928 [1902]) and Max Weber (2013 [1904–1905]). This combination of money and machines is often taken to drive the polarizing tendencies of our world. As a keyword of our civilization, capital reflects the contrasting ideologies that have arisen to represent it (Hann and Hart 2011: chapter 8). Marx and his followers consistently restrict the definition of capital to its form as money. Most economists, however, equate capital with the stock of goods that are used in production and are themselves produced.

Marx (1970 [1867]) viewed the piling up of riches by businessmen as a social relationship of exploitation that was mystified by equating capital with physical plant and profit with the reasonable income of its owners. For him, as for Locke (1960 [1690]), human labor was the source of wealth and the addition of machines to that labor only made it more productive. Economists, however, tend to stress the withdrawal of goods from immediate consumption and the enhanced productivity of factors other than labor in which the capitalist has invested. So that profit constitutes the reward for making the sacrifice. This argument makes sense in an industrial economy where money wealth flows most predictably if it is invested in mechanizing production. But many forms of capital accumulation need not involve physical plant (banking and trade, for example) and the broader usage tends to confuse money with machines by representing capital as a thing (that is, as *real*), thereby mystifying the social relations involved. The economists' definition cannot address the historical relationship between production and the circuit of money, as Marx's dialectic can.

Capitalism is thus that form of market economy in which the owners of large amounts of money direct the most significant sectors of production with a view to increasing the money they already have. For a time, the most reliable way of making money with money was to raise the productivity of labor through investment in machines. This is Marx's position. For him, modern capitalism was a form of making money with money where free capital was exchanged with free wage labor. He sought, therefore, to explain how people's capacity to work was freed from the legal encumbrances of feudal agriculture and funds were released for investment in new forms of production. He discusses this process of "primitive accumulation" at the end of the first volume of *Capital*.

Adam Smith (1961 [1776]) had related profit levels to reduced costs achieved through raising the efficiency of workers; he identified specialization and division of labor as the best ways of doing this. Marx's great discovery was that this logic led to the introduction of more and better machines to the production process. He held that wage slavery under capitalism was fundamentally similar to feudal serfdom. The most primitive type of industrial capitalism, therefore, is one where the feudal approach is transferred to the industrial system of wage labor. We might call this "sweatshop capitalism." He called it "absolute surplus value."

Max Weber (1961 [1922]) did not disagree with Marx's account—although for him property relations ("ownership of the means of production") were less important than the Marxists believed—he just felt that it did not go far enough. For Weber, capitalism was an economic system based on rational enterprise. Enterprise is something undertaken with a view to future profit. How could whole societies commit their livelihood to the uncertainties of enterprise? Enterprise commonly takes two forms. The first is speculative and involves people gambling on a hunch that they will win. Keynes (1936) saw these "animal spirits" as central to the dynamism of capitalist markets, leading to a cycle of booms and busts as herds of investors chase the latest chance for windfall profit. Weber was interested in the second form, one driven by a compulsion to eliminate the risks entailed in relying on uncertain futures. Rationality is the calculated pursuit of explicit ends by chosen means. Rational enterprise, according to him, rests above all on the entrepreneur's ability to calculate outcomes. For capitalism to take root, reliable calculation of the probabilities is essential.

This explains the paradox that, while capitalists celebrate the risks of competition, they will do everything in their power to avoid it in practice. Weber shows how the fledgling capitalist economy progressed by instituting the means of more reliable calculation. This meant improvements in bookkeeping, working practices, and technology. Above all the state had to be alert to the needs of enterprises, securing their property and profits in law and stabilizing the conditions of market economy. Weber did not think that mercantile colonialism was a sufficient explanation for the accumulation of a European capitalist fund. Rather, he believed (Weber 2013 [1904–1905]) that capitalism owed its specificity to developments in the sphere of religion. If Marx successfully linked capital accumulation to machines and the wage-labor system, Weber's emphasis on rationality and religion helps us to see developments in the system of money and markets as a cultural revolution.

Capitalism is always modified by the specific historical conditions in which it grows. Thus Italian capitalism is not Japanese capitalism; Brazilian capitalism is different again, and so on. The particular social realities revealed by ethnography and history should inform the search for general principles of economic organization in our world. For we need to explain not only the common form, but also its infinite variations.

The Bourgeois Revolutions

The economy, from its Greek origins, was identified with agriculture, but even when landlords ruled, mechanisms of exchange were a principal focus of theoretical attention (Hann and Hart 2011: Chapter 2). With the consolidation of the European empires as the first "world system," economy came to be increasingly identified with markets. These are networks constituted by acts of buying and selling, usually through the medium of money. Hitherto marginal to the mainstream institutions on which societies were built, from the eighteenth century markets came to be accepted as central to society. The political debate about the appropriate relationship between the two has been vigorous ever since. Adam Smith (1961 [1776]) provided a charter for "the market" (now often singular) to assume its place as the dominant institution of modern societies. Neither the breakthrough to industrial capitalism nor the consolidation of Britain's overseas empire could yet be envisaged.

All agrarian civilizations tried to keep markets and money in check, since power came from the landed property of an aristocratic military caste afraid that they might undermine their control over society. In stateless societies too, markets were usually kept marginal and subject to regulation by the agents of dominant social institutions. Colonial demand for export crops and wage labor meant that the market principle became more pervasive, undermining the existing authorities. Why are markets supposed to be subversive of traditional social arrangements? Because commerce knows no bounds – all markets are in a sense world markets—and this threatens local systems of control. Markets offer a potential means of escape to the dominated: serfs and slaves, ethnic minorities, young people, women. The power of long-distance merchants often modified the autonomy of local rulers.

So Smith knew what he was taking on when he proposed that society had nothing to fear from markets and indeed much to gain. As a moral philosopher, Smith did not celebrate the narrow pursuit of self-interest in market transactions; but he preferred to indulge this trait en masse rather than to concentrate economic power in the hands of an elite, however high-minded. He stopped short of claiming that society's interests as a whole were best served by free markets, without regard for what he called "sympathy" or "fellow-feeling"; but these reservations have largely been forgotten since. Modern economists glibly quote his invocation of the "invisible hand" without noticing that Smith was referring to the providential design of nature, not to an impersonal market mechanism. Rather than a unified world economy, he anticipated a plural world in which China might again surpass the fragmented national markets of Europe (Ortiz, this volume).

Political economy developed in the early nineteenth century as a discipline concerned with how the value generated by an expanding market economy might best be distributed in the interest of economic growth (Introduction, this volume). David Ricardo (1817) provided a more systematic account of its theoretical principles. He identified three types of resources, each thought to be endowed with the "power of increase": the environment (land), money (capital), and human creativity (labor). These were represented by their owners: landlords, capitalists, and laborers. The distribution of specific sources of income—rent, profit, and wages—contained the key to the laws of political economy. He took the main conflict to be between landlords and capitalists; the best policy was for the value of market sales not to be diverted from the capital fund to high rents.

Political economy held that competitive markets would lower the profit margins available to middle men and force capitalists to reduce their production costs through improved efficiency. This was achieved through economies of scale, division of labor, and ultimately the introduction of machines to factories. The productivity of labor rose, allowing the resulting profits to be ploughed back into an expanded level of activity. Society's manpower was thereby freed up for ever more elaborate forms of commercial production. The only threat to this upward spiral was if landowners raised their rents to take advantage of these newly profitable industries, diverting value into wasteful consumption. Worse, whereas the capital fund was inherently limitless, land was in limited supply. Economic expansion meant population growth, which would drive up food prices and squeeze the capital fund through wages. The solution was to expose Britain's landowners to competition with cheap overseas suppliers, and this made free trade the great political issue of the nineteenth century.

So the bourgeois revolutions were an attempt to replace rent with profit as the dominant principle of economy, a symbolic shift that also meant a move in emphasis from distribution to production. Capitalists assumed that their workers would benefit from victory over the landlords, not least because their food costs would be reduced. Karl Marx (1970 [1867]) set out to show that this proposed alliance was based on a false premise, since capitalists exploited workers whose interests were best served by opposing rather than identifying with them. Marx and Engels were convinced that Victorian capitalism was going to change the whole world. So they were almost as bullish about the triumph of industrial capitalism as the liberal political economists, but for different reasons.

Marx (1970 [1867]) distinguished between three forms of capital: financial, mercantile, and industrial. The first two were as old as civilization, making money through loans and buying cheap to sell dear; but industrial capital was recent and injected a new dynamic into economy. It was "industrial" because when labor of any kind, not just manufacturing, is bought as a commodity, it can produce more than its cost. Moreover, when people move out of peasant subsistence to work in the towns, they have to buy much more to live on—food, clothes, housing, etc.—thereby massively increasing the scope for markets. Marx acknowledged that finance and merchant capital persisted, alongside rent, but in Volume 1 he held that profit under industrial capitalism imposed its logic on the others. "Surplus value" is the share of the value of produced commodities retained by the capitalist and its three components for Marx were profit, rent, and interest. He claimed that rent and interest were now subsumed under the logic of profit. This remains a contentious issue.

The Great Transformation?

So the Marxists and the liberals agreed that a world change was taking place in nineteenth-century Britain. Hegel's (2010 [1821]) historical model was very different from Marx and Engels's idea of separate successive stages (feudalism to capitalism to socialism). His three phases were based on the family and the land, the market economy of urban civil society, and the modern state respectively. These now coexisted under the coordinating guidance of the state. But the most articulate case for irreversible change was made by Karl Polanyi (1944) in *The Great Transformation* (Hann and Hart 2009).

Polanyi argued that the elevation of the market (specifically, "the self-regulating market") to a position of social dominance in Victorian England meant that the economy no longer served the interests of society as a whole and indeed actively undermined it. He traced this historical process to specific legislation and institutional innovations—the gold standard, the liberal state, the international balance of power, and the notion that the market should be free from external intervention. As a Christian socialist, he did not buy the Marxist package; but he did have a class analysis of his own. The market economy detached many people from traditional mechanisms of social protection, but in a "double movement" specific classes retaliated and in the process represented wider social interests. Polanyi wrote during the Second World War, after three decades of political and economic disaster. For him this was a direct outcome of the social damage wreaked by markets in the previous century. He recognized that the decades leading up to the First World War had been driven by *haute finance* (mainly the Rothschild family), which played a coordinating international role. Indeed a major focus of his book is on money. His economic approach was plural, but he put considerable trust in social planning as a way of rebuilding the postwar economy.

The Great Transformation is persuasive, but Polanyi's political program and historical analysis leave some questions unanswered (Hart 2009). A major target was political economy as a doctrine. Then as now, the subordination of society to economy is more clear-cut in economic ideology that in social reality. Was the destruction of embeddedness a matter of propaganda or a social fact? Polanyi's "double movement" makes this even more obscure. Moreover, both he and Marx missed the revolutions of the 1860s and 1870s that installed a new class alliance in the leading countries, the partnership between capitalists and the traditional enforcers that I call "national capitalism." This new alliance soon spawned the legal conditions for modern corporations, as well as a massive expansion of state property and a bureaucratic revolution at all levels of the economy. The result was the birth of modern mass production and consumption. This new social form was also the engine of a world economy driven by financial imperialism, a process concluded by the First World War, after which several kinds of state aspired to world domination, while retreating behind national boundaries. So we have here radically different combinations of profit, rent, and interest and fluctuating relations between nation-states and the world economy. Neither Polanyi nor Marx help us to understand this phase of capitalist history.

The Anthropology of Unequal Society

Jean-Jacques Rousseau's *Discourse on Inequality* (1984 [1754]) launched anthropology as the critique of unequal society. Certainly Lewis Morgan (1964 [1877]) and Friedrich Engels (1972 [1884]) were heavily indebted to him when they reconstructed human history as the evolution of society from kinship to states based on class divisions. The decades after 1945 saw a revival of this genre by Claude Lévi-Strauss (1969 [1949]), Marshall Sahlins (1958), and Eric Wolf (1982). But today its main exponents are Jack Goody (2012; Hart 2011, 2014a, 2014b) and David Graeber (2011)

Apart from seeking to explain Africa's divergence from the agrarian civilizations of Eurasia, Goody has devoted much of his work to undermining Western claims to being uniquely superior to the main Asian societies, especially China. This means downplaying the industrial revolution that allowed Europeans to take over the world in the nineteenth century. Following Fernand Braudel (1975), Goody (2012) prefers to point to the similarities between industrial capitalism and the "merchant cultures" of preindustrial civilizations. He takes on Marx for misreading merchant capitalism, but does not address his arguments for the distinctive dynamics of industrial capital. Weber too gets short shrift for suggesting that modern capitalism differs from its predecessors. Goody's repudiation of the Great Transformation leads him to claim that the two "continents" making up Eurasian land mass have been more equal than was previously understood. Stressing their common origins in the Bronze Age urban revolution (Childe 1954), he points out that modern European capitalism diffused faster to Asia than the Italian renaissance to northwest Europe.

Despite a consistent barrage of propaganda telling us that we now live in a modern age of science and democracy, our dominant institutions are still those of agrarian civilization—territorial states, embattled cities, landed property, warfare, racism, bureaucratic administration, literacy, impersonal money, long-distance trade, work as a virtue, world religion, and the nuclear family (Hart 2002). This is because the rebellion of the middle classes against the Old Regime was coopted by the synthesis of industrial capitalism and the nation-state ("national capitalism"); and humanity's emancipation from inequality has suffered setbacks as a result. Consider the shape of world society today. A remote elite of white, middle-aged, middle-class men, "the men in suits," rule masses that are predominantly poor, darker, female, and young. The rich countries, which can no longer reproduce themselves, try to stem the inflow of migrants. Our world resembles nothing so much as the old regime in France before the revolution (Tocqueville 2004 [1859]), when Rousseau wrote his *Second Discourse*, in fact. So Goody may have a point in asking us to reconsider how exceptional our societies are.

David Graeber's *Debt: The First 5,000 Years* was published in summer 2011. In August–September that year he helped form the first New York City General Assembly, which spawned the Occupy Wall Street movement (Graeber 2013). He has been credited with being the author of that movement's slogan, "We are the 99%." He has drawn attention to debt as another neglected feature of modern capitalism. Much of the contemporary world revolves around claims we make on each other and on things: ownership, obligations, contracts and payment of taxes, wages, rents, fees, etc. Graeber aims to illuminate these questions through a focus on debt in broad historical perspective. It is a central issue in global politics today, at every level of society. The class struggle between debtors and creditors to distribute costs after the long credit boom went bust is universal.

The social logic of debt is revealed most clearly when money is involved. Indeed a powerful school of thought holds that "money is debt." Money was always both a commodity and a debt token, giving rise to much political and moral contestation, especially in the ancient world. Following Nietzsche, Graeber argues that money introduced for the first time a measure of the unequal relations between buyer and seller, creditor and debtor. Whereas Rousseau traced inequality to the invention of private property, he locates the roots of human bondage, slavery, tribute, and organized violence in debt relations. The contradictions of indebtedness, escalating class conflict between creditors and debtors fed by money and markets, led the first world religions to articulate notions of freedom and redemption, often involving calls for debt cancellation.

The book contrasts "human economies" (Hart 2015b) with those dominated by money and markets ("commercial economies"). Graeber shows what happens when human economies are forcefully incorporated into the economic orbit of larger "civilizations." He points out that these societies are not necessarily more humane, but "they are economic systems primarily concerned not with the accumulation of wealth, but with the creation, destruction, and rearranging of human beings" (2011: 130). They use money, but mainly as "social currencies" that maintain relations between people rather than being used to purchase things.

"In a human economy, each person is unique and of incomparable value, because each is a unique nexus of relations with others" (ibid.: 158). Yet their money forms make it possible to treat people as identical objects in exchange and that requires a measure of violence. Brutality is omnipresent. Violence is inseparable from money and debt, even in the most "human" of economies, where ripping people out of their familiar context is commonplace. This, however, gets taken to another level when they are drawn into systems like the Atlantic slave trade. Slavery and freedom – a pair driven by a culture of honor and indebtedness – culminate in the ultimate contradiction of modern liberal economics, a worldview that conceives of individuals as being socially isolated.

Graeber then organizes the world history of money in four stages: the first urban civilizations, the "axial age," the middle ages, and "the great capitalist empires," which ended when the US dollar left gold in 1971. Money oscillates between two broad types, "credit" and "currency or bullion" – that is, money as a virtual measure of personal relations, like IOUs, and as impersonal things made from precious metals. The recent rise of virtual credit money suggests the possibility of another long swing in money's center. Ours could be a multipolar world, more like the middle ages than the last two centuries. It could offer more scope for "human economies" or at least "social currencies." The debt crisis might provoke revolutions. Perhaps the institutional complex based on states, money, and markets (capitalism) will be replaced by forms of society more directly responsive to ordinary people and their reliance on "everyday communism." Graeber's historical vision does not hinge on a Great Transformation in the nineteenth century and so he has more in common with Goody than with the social theorists of modernity.

World Revolution and Counterrevolution

So there is not much agreement about what capitalism is, when it occurred, and what its relationship is to other economic forms. The last half-century has provided even more striking contrasts. After 1945, humanity embraced a radical departure from the old system. This hinged on developmental states set on controlling markets and money in the public interest. These were the welfare state democracies of the industrial West, the states produced by the anticolonial revolution in Asia and Africa and the forms of state socialism promoted in the Soviet bloc. What they had in common was an expanded commitment to public services, a focus on raising the spending power of working people, and a strong preference for state control of commerce and capital accumulation. All of these built on the forms of centralized command developed to manage the war. They varied in their methods and priorities, but this was nothing less than a world revolution—the only time in history that public policy, at least in principle, served the interests of ordinary people rather than the privileged few. It also generated the longest economic boom in world history, since expansion in one country could rely on synchronized expansion of the others. Income distribution was remarkably even during this period, in sharp contrast to the last few decades.

This period is sometimes seen as one of social democracy, especially when compared with what followed. Others insist that it was modified capitalism, with welfare states mollifying the continued dominance of capital. David Harvey (2005) prefers the term "embedded liberalism," the weak sister of Polanyi's disembedded liberalism in Victorian England. The 1970s saw fluctuating exchange rates, a global depression triggered by high oil prices, "stagflation," and sky-high interest rates. Neoliberal conservatives blamed Keynesian macroeconomics and state dominance for this instability. They advocated a return to "sound money" and low inflation driven by market imperatives. The dismantling of state power began in the 1980s through structural adjustment policies imposed on developing countries by the World Bank and the International Monetary Fund. But before long the recipe was applied everywhere in the interest of unrestricted global flows of money. Most national economies are powerless to influence "the markets" and money has become progressively detached from politics and trade, as we saw above.

Two features stand out in this process: the privatization of public interests and a shift from profit to rent as the main source of wealth. Politicians need money and moneymen need political cover. Central banking was invented to institutionalize their partnership. The Bank of England, Banque de France, and Federal Reserve are all private institutions given the appearance of public sponsorship in return for absorbing the "national debt," that is the debts of the king, Napoleon, and congress respectively. Official propaganda insists on the separation of public and private interests, but it has never been so. What is new in neoliberalism is not the privatization of public interests, but its promotion as an ideal, where before it was clandestine. The Gilded Age looks Leninist in comparison with today. In both cases the social contract between rulers and masses was torn up.

Yet there is something special about the plutocracy built up in recent decades. The rise of modern corporations comes from their being granted the rights of individual citizens by the United States Supreme Court in

1884 and they now combine those rights with their long-held special privileges (including limited liability for debt; Hart 2005). Even the Romans, not noted as champions of democracy, limited the spending of the rich in political campaigns. The US Supreme Court not long ago refused to accept any restriction on corporate political spending since it would infringe their "human rights."

These same corporations once built their wealth by producing industrial commodities for profit at prices cheaper than their competitors. Now they rely on extracting rents (transfers sanctioned by political power) rather than on producing for profit in competitive markets. Thus Big Pharma makes more money from patents granted by congress than the entire Medicare budget. Sony makes 75 percent of its revenues from DVDs that are reproduced almost without cost, from movies initially sold to the public as "bums on seats"; their duplication is called "piracy". Goldman Sachs used its friends at the US Treasury to retrieve at face value the $90 billion lost by insurance giant AIG in the 2008 crash. Yet these rent-seekers, far from being punished for stealing from the public, are bailed out by our taxes and held up as shining examples of super-rich consumption to be adulated by a public that has exchanged equal citizenship for bread and circuses. This is decadence, a repudiation of the values of modern civilization, and the result is an impasse: there are no longer any political solutions to our economic problems.

Marx's take on the Great Transformation of the mid-nineteenth century is potentially useful, despite its limitations. *Capital* is difficult to interpret since he decided for rhetorical and political purposes to accept a number of propositions of liberal economics so that he could reach the opposite, revolutionary conclusions on the basis of shared premises. The opening chapter of Volume 1 (Marx 1970 [1867]) is an egregious example. Even so the book is a critique of political economy and there is a lot there about the relationship between the three components of surplus value—profit, rent, and interest.

The idea of surplus value in turn rests on a homology between feudal and capitalist exploitation, which gives the lie to capitalism as the revolutionary negation of its precursor. Yet Marx held that capitalist profit subordinated rent and interest to its logic. This is why Marx and Engels thought that Victorian England was the future of the world economy. New phases of capitalist development and decline have been identified ever since. The American macroeconomist Dean Baker (2011) provides much insight into rentier capitalism today.

In *Grundrisse* (Marx 1973 [1859]) the introduction is particularly illuminating. Here Marx tackles relations between the main economic categories: production, distribution, exchange, and consumption. Of particular interest are his comments on production and consumption, on how distribution had been collapsed into exchange and why distribution never dominated production (the main idea of agrarian civilization or the old regime). There is an iron bond between Marx and Locke's (1690) labor theory of value: the way to rise in society was once to use political power to extort value from producers (if you want to get ahead, get a gun). But what if producers got to keep what they made rather than hand it over to bandits? Locke made no distinction between owners and workers in enterprises, while for Marx the difference was crucial. Yet he remarked famously that you couldn't steal from a nation of shepherds in the same way as from a nation of bankers. (The best way to rob a bank these days is to own one.) So the mode of production always conditions distribution.

The national system of capitalism became general after the First World War and was the dominant social form of twentieth-century civilization, especially after 1945. We all know what happened next. But neither Marx nor Polanyi (who had less excuse) saw the social consequences when the liberal revolution was transformed into bureaucratic capitalism based on an alliance between capitalists and the traditional enforcers. But Weber (1961 [1922]) did, with the alliance between the Prussian army and Rhineland capital under his nose. And Hegel envisaged it in *The Philosophy of Right* (2010 [1821]).

Capitalism's trajectory must be placed within a framework of world history. If rent-seeking in the West threatens to restore the old regime to societies that were built on its revolutionary overthrow, world society today cannot be reduced to this reverse. The BRICS countries are each engaged with national capitalism in ways reminiscent of Europe and North America after the war. They all face the challenge of providing social protection to the masses drawn into the cities in the boom years from the 1990s. They have to develop viable welfare states to cushion their populations from the vagaries of markets. No doubt each of them has its rent-seekers, but the overwhelming task of political economy there today is to avoid social catastrophe. Call it "embedded liberalism" if you like, but neoliberalism it is not.

Selling stuff for profit means adding value through production. As Marx insisted, there is nothing intrinsically productive about tangible rather than intangible commodities. Productive labor under capitalism is anything that generates surplus value for capital, which could be education (an example he uses). Rent-seeking is ". . . an attempt to derive economic rent by manipulating the social or political environment in which economic activities occur, rather than by adding value" (*Wikipedia*).

Marx claimed that in his time rent and interest (banking) took their scale, form, and function from industrial capitalist production for profit; and this could probably still be said of the main capitalist countries before the 1980s. No longer, however. Of course all three sections of surplus value coexisted both then and now. So has the focus of political economy tipped away from industrial production (in the broadest sense, not just manufacturing) toward rents derived from political privilege? It is hard to see how the richest one percent could have done so well in the last three decades otherwise, given the stagnation of production and real wages in this period.

The digital revolution in communications is highly relevant, since many intangible commodities can now be copied easily at no cost. If you steal my cow, I can no longer milk it, but no one loses out if I copy your song. The entertainment industry is the fastest-growing sector of the world economy after finance, so what happens there matters. A lot hinges on whether, under the stimulus of national capitalism amplified by imperialism, markets became more monopolistic before the First World War than in the mid-nineteenth century. What happened after that period ended is highly relevant to the economic crisis today. Crazy Digital Rights Management (DRM) regimes being installed around the world illustrate the centrality of political and legal coercion for the economy today. Rent-seeking now trumps value added by production in capitalism's Western heartlands. The war over intellectual property continues to escalate to ever-higher levels of absurdity; but when it comes to information technologies, a powerful competitive sector (the open source and free software movement) is based on principles diametrically opposite to those of corporate command and control. Like Marx and Engels I believe that the machine revolution can be a force for greater economic democracy.

World Society (1800–2100)

In conclusion, a tentative periodization of the modern era may be useful:

- 1776–1815   Age of war and revolutions
- 1815–1848   Industrial revolution
- 1848–1873   Origins of national capitalism
- 1873–1914   First age of financial globalization
- 1914–1945   Second age of war and revolutions
- 1945–1979   Golden age of national capitalism
- 1979–2008?   Second age of financial globalization
- 2008?–   Third age of war and revolutions

My story is essentially a play in three acts: the nineteenth, twentieth, and twenty-first centuries; and the drama is emergent world society. Is this a Great Transformation and what is capitalism's role in bringing it about? Has the world become more unequal or less so? Returning to Piketty (2014), what methodological conclusions may be drawn? Two to start with: it hardly seems likely that a simple formula could apply equally across the last two centuries – economic categories do not retain their meaning nor do they form stable sets over such a long period. More important, we are not talking about national trajectories here, but a world society that is already launched.

In the nineteenth century, European empires made world society in their own image as a racial hierarchy. The main event of the twentieth century was the anticolonial revolution, when peoples coerced into joining world society by European empires now sought to make their own independent relationship to it. World war was its catalyst. But this process had diverse results. Asian countries generally made the transition to national capitalism; Latin America's development was more uneven; and most African countries regressed economically for half a century. What does the twenty-first century hold in store? A central feature will be African demographic and economic expansion (Hart forthcoming).

In 1900 Europeans controlled 80 percent of the world's inhabited land mass; Europe itself accounted for a quarter of humanity, a figure that rose to 36 percent when the lands of temperate zone new settlement are included. At that time Africans accounted for only 7.5 percent of the world's population in a continent that has 14 percent of the occupied land. This was the context for the scramble for Africa. Africans have now doubled their share of world population since 1900 to 15 percent. UN projections predict that this figure will rise to 25 percent by 2050 and to 40 percent by 2100. Asia, which now accounts for 60 percent of world population, will then be 42 percent. The whole of the New World, Europe, Russia, and the Pacific will have 18 percent. Europe's share will be only 6 percent, a quarter of the 1900 figure.

So what kind of world would be peopled two-fifths each by Asians and Africans? The Asian manufacturers are well aware of the situation, since they know that Africans will contribute the main increase in consumer demand. For it seems likely that Africans' per capita disposable incomes will also grow. There is no shortage of academic naysayers – recent growth is a temporary and reversible effect of commodity prices; the GNP calculations are wildly inaccurate and disguise endemic inequality; dysfunctional politics will undermine development, as before.

Most Westerners think of Africa as a place for famine, disease, and war. Yet it is the only major region whose population is expanding (2.5 percent per annum), while everywhere else is aging. Africa's demographic rise and Europe's fall captures the threat to a racial order created by nineteenth century imperialism. Can Africans convert their prospective global weight into political strength? If they do, the racial assumptions of our unequal world will not last long in their present form.

Capitalism is often represented as an engine of inequality. Yet Western capitalism, especially in Europe, seems to be in decline, while the Asian masses have now been rising for several decades. Africans too have grounds for optimism in the coming century. There are many kinds of inequality and we should not oversimplify modern history, when the emphasis of political economy has varied so much over time. We should keep in mind world history as a whole. If nothing else, the period 1800–2100 is increasingly integrated, despite or because of the disruptions of world war. Many revolutions that once seemed irreversible are now palpably not so. Just think of the French, Russian, and Chinese examples. Is the old regime making a comeback at the expense of the bourgeoisie? After all, how does the pairing of George III and the East India Company differ from George W. Bush's relationship with firms like Halliburton?

The current global crisis is often compared with the 1930s, but the Great Depression was part of a sequence that began when three decades of financial globalization were interrupted by the outbreak of war in 1914.

NOTES

1. Brazil, Russia, India, China, South Africa.

REFERENCES

Baker, D. 2011. *The End of Loser Liberalism: Making Markets Progressive*. Washington, DC: Center for Economic and Policy Research.
Braudel, F. 1975. *Capitalism and Material Life*. New York: Harper Collins.
Childe, V. G. 1954. *What Happened in History*. Harmondsworth: Penguin.
Dembinski, P., and C. Perritas. 2000. "Towards the breakup of money: When reality, driven by information technology, overtakes Simmel's vision." *Foresight* 2(5): 483–496.
Engels, F. 1972 [1884]. *The Origin of the Family, Private Property, and the State*. New York: Pathfinder.
Goody, J. 2012. *Metals, Culture and Capitalism: An Essay on the Origins of the Modern World*. Cambridge: Cambridge University Press.
Graeber, D. 2011. *Debt: The First 5,000 Years*. Brooklyn, NY: Melville House.
———. 2013. *The Democracy Project: A History, a Crisis, a Movement*. New York: Penguin.

Hann, C., and K. Hart (eds.). 2009. *Market and Society: The Great Transformation Today.* Cambridge: Cambridge University Press.
———. 2011. *Economic Anthropology: History, Ethnography, Critique.* Cambridge: Polity.
Hart, K. 1986. "Heads or Tails? Two Sides of the Coin." *Man New Series* 21(4): 637–656.
———. 2000. *The Memory Bank: Money in an Unequal World.* London: Profile Books Ltd.
———. 2001. *Money in an Unequal World: Keith Hart and His Memory Bank.* New York and London: Texere.
———. 2002. "World society as an old regime." In C. Shore and S. Nugent (eds.), *Elite Cultures: Anthropological Perspectives.* London: Routledge, pp. 22–36.
———. 2005. *The Hit Man's Dilemma: Or Business, Personal and Impersonal.* Chicago, IL: Prickly Paradigm Press.
———. 2006. "Agrarian civilization and world society." In D. Olson and M. Cole (eds.), *Technology, Literacy and the Evolution of Society: Implications of the Work of Jack Goody.* Mahwah, NJ: Lawrence Erlbaum, pp. 29–48.
———. 2009. "Money in the making of world society." In C. Hann and K. Hart (eds.), *Market and Society: The Great Transformation Today.* Cambridge: Cambridge University Press, pp. 91–105.
———. 2014a. "Jack Goody: The anthropology of unequal society." *Reviews in Anthropology* 43(3): 199–220.
———. 2014b. "Marcel Mauss's economic vision, 1920–1925: Anthropology, politics, journalism." *Journal of Classical Sociology* 14(1): 34–44.
———. 2015a. "Human economy: The revolutionary struggle for happiness." In K. Hart (ed), *Economy for and against Democracy.* New York and Oxford: Berghahn Books, pp. 201–220.
———. 2015b. "How the informal economy took over the world." In P. Moertenboeck et al. (eds.), *Informal Market World Reader: The Architecture of Economic Pressure.* Rotterdam: NAI010 Publishers, pp. 33–44.
———. Forthcoming. *Africa 2100: A History of the Future.* (In preparation).
Hart, K., and H. Ortiz. 2014. "The anthropology of money and finance: Between ethnography and world history." *Annual Review of Anthropology* 43: 465–482.
Harvey, D. 2005. *A Brief History of Neoliberalism.* Oxford: Oxford University Press.
Hegel, G. 2010 [1821]. *The Philosophy of Right.* Oxford: Oxford University Press.
Hobsbawm, E. 1994. *Age of Extremes: The Short Twentieth Century, 1914–1991.* London: Michael Joseph.
Keynes, J. M. 1936. *The General Theory of Employment, Interest and Money.* London: Macmillan.
Lévi-Strauss, C. 1969 [1949]. *The Elementary Structures of Kinship.* Boston, MA: Beacon.
Lewis, W. A. 1978. *The Evolution of the International Economic Order.* Princeton, NJ: Princeton University Press.
Locke, J. 1960 [1690]. *Two Treatises of Government.* Cambridge: Cambridge University Press.
Marx, K. 1970 [1867]. *Capital: Volume 1.* London: Lawrence and Wishart.
Marx, K. 1973 [1859]. *Grundrisse.* New York: Vintage.
Morgan, L. 1964 [1877]. *Ancient Society.* Cambridge, MA: Belknap.
Piketty, T. 2014. *Capital in the Twenty-First Century.* Cambridge, MA: Harvard University Press.

Pleyers, G. 2010. *Alter-Globalization: Becoming Actors in a Global Age*. Cambridge: Polity Press.
Polanyi, K. 1964 [1977]. "Money objects and money uses." In *The Livelihood of Man*. New York: Academic Press, pp. 97–121.
———. 2001 [1944]. *The Great Transformation: The Political and Economic Origins of Our Times*. Boston, MA: Beacon.
Ricardo, D. 1817. *On the Principles of Political Economy and Taxation*. CreateSpace Independent Publishing Platform.
Rousseau, J. J. 1984 [1754]. *Discourse on Inequality*. Harmondsworth: Penguin.
Sahlins, M. 1958. *Social Stratification in Polynesia*. Seattle: University of Washington Press.
Schumpeter, J. 2010 [1942]. *Capitalism, Socialism and Democracy*. London: Routledge.
Shaxson, N. 2012. *Treasure Islands: Tax Havens and the Men Who Stole the World*. New York: Vintage.
Simmel, G. 2004 [1900]. *The Philosophy of Money*. London: Routledge.
Smith, A. 1961 [1776]. *An Inquiry into the Nature and Causes of the Wealth of Nations*. London: Methuen.
Sombart, W. 1928 [1902]. *Der moderne Kapitalismus*. Charleston, NC: Nabu Press.
Tocqueville, A. de 2004 [1859]. *The Old Regime and the Revolution*. Chicago, IL: University of Chicago Press.
Weber, M. 2013 [1904–1905]. *The Protestant Ethic and the Spirit of Capitalism*. CreateSpace Independent Publishing Platform.
Weber, M. 1961 [1922]. *General Economic History*. Piscataway, NJ: Transaction.
Wolf, E. 1982. *Europe and the People without History*. Berkeley: University of California Press.

Part II
Thinking About Money

CHAPTER 2

 Money is Good to Think
From "Wants of the Mind" to Conversation, Stories, and Accounts

JANE I. GUYER

This chapter takes up Keith Hart's suggestion (Introduction, this volume) that money and language have qualities in common: a diversity and communicative power that engage people in many arenas of their everyday lives. Hence the concept of the "human economy" is built through forms of participation that involve everyone. For long periods of history and over expansive regions, money and language were mediated face to face. People met in designated public spaces where varieties of goods and their specialists came together regularly, commented on the conditions of economic life, invented novel terms and commodities, and even novel modes of association and political expression. These were market-*places*, not markets in the sense that Polly Hill criticized economists for abstracting from their human-social instantiation: "Traditionally, economists have displayed little interest in market places, as distinct from market principles" (1989: 238). In her voluminous study of "the market" historian Laurence Fontaine argues, in similar terms, for a recuperation of the idea and participatory practice of "public space" (2014: 360) in economic and political life, taking "the market" in ever more inclusive directions, especially under the new conditions of a globalized monetary world. The marketplace of Ancient Greece, the *agora*, was this kind of inclusive public space where rhetoric, negotiation, and commentary all took place, and where even the concepts and practices of "democracy" developed.

Here, I build from Hart's observation about money, language, and the shaping of a "human economy" of communication that traverses the standard borders of nation, class, and monetary function. As we now meet, bargain, comment, complain, and generally engage language(s) with money(s), how does that occur, in an increasingly inclusive, though broadly varied, "human economy"?

The Other Side of the Coin

New works on the history of money and finance (Amato and Fantacci 2014; Desan 2015; Dodd 2014) take us back into the dynamics of the historical and philosophical nature of money. National sovereignty, the power of the state, and dominant political philosophies are prominent in reflecting and generally policing the material, political, and cultural forces that have come together in ever-changing systems of monetary valuation and payment, within complex administrative regimes. Noam Yuran (2014), for example, draws on Western social theory to explore the longing that drives money in motion. Influential and inspiring as these scholarly works have been, I miss from their accounts the trade monies that long mediated valuation across political and cultural boundaries outside the imperial and national powers that eventually claimed authority over them. These were commercially successful, multiple systems of valuation that flourished in non-state zones, such as the Hanseatic League of medieval Europe and later the Atlantic slave trade currency zone, which spawned many modern financial instruments like insurance contracts and company shares.

Thirty years ago, Hart drew attention to the long-term tension between the "two sides of the coin," the state and the market: "We need to know on what solid foundation money rests—on commodities or states or what?" (1986: 651). He focused on the formation of trust, particularly in trade. And his main example, the Trobriand *kula* and *gimwali* described by Bronislaw Malinowski (1922), was regional in its reach, extending beyond the islands and chiefly domains of its protagonists. This brings in the experience of "elsewhere", as Marcel Mauss suggested when he sought to understand contracts and rejected arguments made in terms of a "so-called necessary logic" claiming that "the point of departure lies elsewhere" (1990: 36). These practices of "elsewhere" find little place in contemporary approaches to money, which are dominated by Western philosophy and economic theory. However, Joseph Noko (this volume) goes beyond the recent European past, by reaching into the philosophy and practice of Ancient Greece, which we can then connect to the life of the *agora*, as well as tracing forward in the modern philosophy that indexes to Aristotle.

In the era of Western capitalism's hegemony it may make sense to focus on national monies, but for understanding valuation from below, and the daily interactions that sustain it, a focus on the political and administrative dynamics is limited if not examined in its relationship to everyday creativity. After all, the quantity theory of money, which was taken up again in neoliberal theory in the twentieth century, was first proposed in the sixteenth century by Copernicus, son of a Hansa merchant, for the king of a newly sovereign nation, Poland, with the aim of stabilizing monetary policy and national cultural values. He knew well enough from experience that nationalism would both contrast and interact with the "fictional units of account" (Einaudi 1953) that then constituted trade monies and were cleared in institutions such as the Hanseatic League's center for that purpose in Bruges. The hegemonic imposition of currency commensuration through imperialism is well known from ancient times (Graeber 2011). In our world, a measure of coherence is achieved through global financial institutions, monitored and adjudicated centrally by the International Monetary Fund. With all the currencies now competing in the world, with local (Peebles 2011) and digital (Maurer 2010) versions multiplying, with mobile populations earning incomes away from home and sending remittances back (Nyamunda et al. 2014; Bolt 2015) and with proliferating trade diasporas, there must be scope for practices of mediation arising from below to intersect with formal state institutions and International Financial Institutions (IFIs). People everywhere have to deal with an expanding range of commodities, shifting prices, multiple currencies, and fluctuating exchange rates.

Senegalese philosopher Souleymane Bachir Diagne prefers the French term *"mondialisation"* to "globalization". A globe is discrete and closed, while a world is open to creating a "unity whose true nature is to be made of additions and contributions rather than subtractions and evictions" (2011: 141). This implies localized working concepts, like the fictional units of account of the old merchant systems, perhaps within specific commercial networks; and in the physical context of market places where currency use and prices are always emergent, not fixed. Migrant farmworkers from Benin to Western Nigeria may be paid in kind, a motorcycle each at the end of the season, as a way of bypassing naira-franc CFA (*Communauté Financière Africaine*) exchange rate fluctuations (Guyer 2016). This could be described as a local "addition and contribution" backed by a discussion of life among all the parties to the deal: farmers, crew bosses, workers and motorcycle dealers in Nigeria, probably families and marketers at home, and possibly the whole border and customs infrastructure between the two countries. Imagine how many topics, other than money and price as such, underpin such a practice.

The title of the conference that generated this collection, "Money in the Making of World Society," draws us back into the wider world of people's monetary lives, lived in local spaces and moments of time, where multiple currencies, changing relationships, and many margins at play generate advantages to be created or lost: through exchange rates, differential costs of production and transport, financial mediation, and so on. I leave aside here how the encompassing order is "made", generally from above, in order to explore the other side of the coin: how a meaningful nexus might be made not only for trust, but also for understanding life across borders and margins. In *"mondialisation"* the monetary terms and numbers that depict transactions in the world may become our main common language. Hardly anything now falls completely outside the monetary nexus, even–and perhaps especially in the register of the everyday–gifts (Miller 1995: Chevalier 2014). And the forces of globalization–money markets, regular reporting of exchange rates, etc.–force everything into a commensurate interface with authority.

The terms for thinking and conversing about money may be becoming our common world language, incorporating–without submitting to–the religious and colonial languages that once took on the task of conversion and domination (Introduction, this volume). Gestures become widely recognizable, as they must have been in the earlier trading eras. Even if I speak no Polish, I can still bargain for something in a Warsaw market using objects, gestures, and fingers (Maurer 2010), starting and ending with conventions that are understood as such, even if the words themselves are incomprehensible. With money at the center, people can communicate affect, value, acuity, trust, and ignorance, and also maintain an archived account in their own minds, in their own and/or shared languages, without having exchanged comprehensible words. Then judgments arise based on familiar standards: a price is fair, ridiculous, dishonest, generous, and so on. The implicit standards that underpin daily accounts of money, economy, and life are both a conceptual issue and an important focus for our attention in the world. They bring "society", or more accurately "sociality" (James 2014), into central focus. Creole languages have been created out of long-term encounters of this kind: means and idioms for thinking about and discussing, in quantitative and comparative terms, every possible aspect of morality and materiality.

The rapidly expanding possibilities for people to make this kind of configuration of money, things, and relationships in a *tour du monde*, cheaply through the Internet, was highlighted by Hart in *The Memory Bank*: "somehow humanity is propelling itself to a new stage of global integration through the development of new communication systems, through markets and money as much as through the exchange of words and things" (2000: 320). Of course, since then monetization has invaded Internet communications as well. But this, too, provokes inquisitive thought and judgment: if someone, anywhere in the world, wants Internet access to a published article, what is the logic and practice of being charged thirty euros for a quick view of it? What do we "think" about "money in world society" at that moment? Undoubtedly, thought, conversation, and judgment are rapidly provoked by the common communicator that money is. Hann and Hart (2009), from engagement with Karl Polanyi's *The Great Transformation*, bring forward the concept of a "human economy" into new publications, including for the public (Hart, Laville and Cattani 2010; Hart and Sharp 2014). In the same volume, Stephen Gudeman highlights the "normative and social reformist concerns" (Hann and Hart 2009: 55) in Polanyi's idea of the economy being embedded in social relations. This focuses attention on terms, conversations, acts of coordination, and collaborative endeavors toward the future. It would make the second side of the coin yet more complex by seeing monetary transactions as socially and culturally inventive processes as well as a system of market prices.

The emergent standards and points of reference forming people's rapid and interactive configurations of monetary situations is surely a frontier in the creation of world society at this moment of rapid *mondialisation* and changing global hegemonies. The media and bureaucracy are creating "icons" and rankings for us, on vertical scales of monetary value. Politics is generating all kinds of monetary turbulence. But, beyond the money equivalent of hype about pop stars and catastrophes, the people must also be creating vernacular conversations for configured complexes of qualities that are relevant to their daily lives. As Hart writes elsewhere, money has "persuasive power" and becomes a language of expression and communication of "shifting meanings, identities and memories" (2009: 156). The mutual imbrication of number, money, and spiritual power is a European historical theme developed by Bruce Carruthers and Wendy Espeland (1991).

Money complexes provide compelling persuasive stimulation for people to think creatively and particularly to develop such powerful judgmental concepts as "worth." The next section, taking off from classical theory, is a thought experiment, a provocation toward seeing popular monetary thinking through ethnography, as revealed in "actual" moments of engaged configuration, both quantitative and judgmental.

Classical Inspirations

The vast capacity of money and commensuration to provoke thought and communication goes back to the beginning of economic theory. Aristotle evaluated monetary wealth in philosophical terms, as Noko (this volume) shows. The Bible makes a series of equations: between monetary land purchase and the specific rights of ownership, between personhood and contribution, and so on. Both have provoked debate and reinterpretation for thousands of years. By thinking about money's functions as a means of account, in the sense of stories as well as records, I privilege the classical function of money known as the unit of account. This expresses durably though time the comprehension, judgment, and basis for trust and projection to which Hart refers. Thinking ethnographically and historically about *how* money has the capacity to mediate and interpret the world, especially through engagement from below, I take inspiration from two classical sources for political economy and anthropology—Karl Marx and Claude Lévi-Strauss—to explore how judgments may be made without the parties to transactions sharing precision of either language or calculation and without one necessarily succumbing to the authority of the other. Indeed, exactness is unlikely when things, ideas, measures, and situations are brought together and recognition of this drives the creation of mediating languages and concepts. An account is not only a formalized list of numbers. It presumes a narrative and is thus an artefact summarizing the past and projecting the future. People's intellectual engagement with money may not be pleasurable or painful, but it must be intensely creative, however mundane the stakes. Their questions may be endless, especially concerning price and worth: between this and that object, from last year to this year, from franc to naira, between my own mind and yours, weighing responsibilities to oneself and others, choosing to accept the role of an authority in a transaction or to reject and evade it. And so on.

Right at the beginning of *Capital*, Marx inserts a footnote quoting Nicolas Barbon: "Desire implies want; it is the appetite of the mind, and as natural as hunger to the body. . . . The greatest number (of things) have their value from supplying the wants of the mind" (*Discourse on Locke, New Money Lighter*, 1696: 2–3; Marx 1977: 43n2). In his discussion of the commodity (43), Marx states that it "satisfies human wants of one sort or another. The nature of such wants, whether, for instance, they spring from the stomach or from fancy, makes no difference." It may be too restrictive to limit the domains of reference to material need and symbolic value. The whole range of commodities conceived of as "the greatest number of things" implies enormous comparative juggling across and within both domains and this too implies having to engage with an "appetite of the mind." If the appetites of the mind cover the whole process of recognition, triage, consideration, and decision, then which impulse is applied to which object, under what circumstances? And how are justifications between that "greatest number of things" made? Processes of "choice" may well be modeled in studies of economic budgeting, but there remains the fundamental question of how money judgments are made at all and whether indeed one of the joys of monetary mediation is the mental challenge that necessarily ends in an affirmation of one sort or another. Something like a particular appetite of the mind is implied here, and goes beyond mere "satisfaction."

From Lévi-Strauss, I juxtapose two quite different but complementary statements about thought. In *Totemism* (1962), he extracts from complex evidence the qualities that allow contrasting species to be assimilated into frames of thought where criteria of similarity and distinction can evoke relation and difference: "how to make opposition, instead of being an obstacle to integration, serve rather to produce it"; for this purpose, "natural species are chosen not because they are 'good to eat' but because they are 'good to think'" (1962: 89). All the rich observations that people bring to this process are turned into the logics of myth by bricolage through which "man has always been thinking equally well"; as well as in scientific mode, where the progress lies not in the mind itself but in "the discovery of new areas to which it may apply its unchanged and unchanging powers." (Lévi-Strauss 1963: 230). That orientation toward the ingenuity of bricolage, and its use to think within social processes, is one of Lévi-Strauss's deeper provocations. He forces us to ask how disparate qualities are brought together effectively, through a combination of intellectual processes and especially in an archive of narrative knowledge (*mythologiques*), insisting that no particular method is intrinsically superior to another, even less giving it the right to disqualify a rival. Narrative makes classification come alive and sharpens its relevance to living social life.

Monetization necessarily brings differences and resemblances together and this may be the one characteristic that permits people, objects, and qualities to be compared, and hence to be "good to think" in all the rich intellectual variety revealed by Lévi-Strauss. How people actually do this kind of comparison, as more and more items and qualities come under the monetary rubric, surely goes beyond the economists' reductive logic of "rational choice." It involves judgment in the broadest sense: not just a decision but a procedure, an engagement and a culmination in a discursive narrative. Here Marx offers further thought for thinking about money.

Worth as a Concept in Use

Soon after making his remark about appetites of the mind, Marx points us in another direction, again in a footnote: "In English writers of the 17th century we frequently find 'worth' in the sense of value in use, and 'value' in the sense of value in exchange. This is quite in accordance with the spirit of a language that likes to use a Teutonic word for the actual thing and a Romance word for its reflexion." (1977: 44n1). An ethnographer would set aside theories of value at first in order to focus on how "worth" is attributed "in use" through bricolage. It is remarkable how significant the concept of worth is in vernacular English, yet it is barely developed as an analytical term, when compared with the vast range of referents covered by the concept of value. I have yet to find a recent book on money where "worth" appears in the index. But English-speakers mobilize it as an implicit benchmark for the most complex of comparative gymnastics. Indeed, perhaps its vague inclusiveness makes it so applicable across value registers, including—if we could collect all the comparable vernacular terms—the emergent terminologies of the world of money that are currently being "made". "Worth" allows thought to expand beyond discrete variables, each of which is "maximized," to heterogeneous configurations —time, money value, social relevance for the future, cultural symbolism, etc.—which are complexly "optimized" (Monga 2015).

Worth is an Anglo-Saxon word depicting personal merit, even nobility, something always contextualized and implicitly comparative, indicating price and value only later, as material money was itself stabilized. We have many mundane formulations for the multiplicity of variables at stake in "worth." For example, pejoratively:

> "It's not worth the paper it's written on."
>
> "It's not worth it" (anything that is being compared: the price of one object against another, the effort of doing one thing over another, the time spent on something, including your time, that I might be wasting with my voice).

Worth is ironic and used for proverbial allusion.

> There is a cartoon from Punch in the nineteenth century where a small child is at the grocer's counter: "My Mum wants a ha'p'orth (halfpenny worth) of your best tea to poison the rats with."
>
> "Don't spoil the ship for a ha'p'orth of tar."

Looking for literature on worth, I ran across a paper by Maurice Godelier (2000) asking: "Is social anthropology still worth the trouble? A response to some echoes from America." More positively, we say, "it (and he or she) is worth its weight in gold." Worth can also be used to indicate the changing purchasing power of money: "it's not worth what it used to be." "It's worthless" is the opposite of "it's priceless."

And "worth" is a word used very often, occurring 64,000 times on the Amazon website, for example. Perhaps half are in authors' names and place names, reflecting a long social history of naming in English, returning us to the personal attribute that worth once was. Indeed, local leaders were sometimes called "worthies," qualifying them to function as witnesses, to sign documents and perform other roles implying veracity. In the eighteenth century, with the ascent of local worthies into the entrepreneurial bourgeoisie, we find monetary amounts being attributed to individuals, under the concept of "his worth," meaning the monetary value of his realizable capital. "Worth" may be combined with many other morphemes.

So "worth" emerges from configuring qualities and variables, not from calculation of singular scales of value. This breadth of allusion, to include personal qualities, is captured in the English translation of *grandeur* as "worth" in a book on "justification" by Boltanski and Thévenot (2006). At the same time, however, their concentration on personal qualities loses some of the vernacular breadth of daily applications by applying it to prominence in economic and managerial life rather than to ordinary mediations. Is it worth walking, if I save the bus fare? Noting the wide range of applicability of such words as "worth," we may ask whether the mental gymnastics intrinsic to money—in use, in marketplaces, among people, in the "making of a world" through the constant creation of narratives of judgment—evoke classic concepts and generate new ones, so that people may apply them to puzzling situations and juxtapositions, across registers, to provide a center of gravity or a focus for thought, for judgments that would otherwise appear bothersome or even intractable. Recall that the ancient Greek *agora* brought public life, debate, and the market into one place of assembly.

Some economic historians have recently developed a website called "Measuring Worth" to guide people through what they see as the "complicated" process of tracing money-object commensurations over time. They work with prices, but readily see that there is a moral and cultural component also at work. Their methods of calculation are revealed in questions such as, "A loaf of bread sold for seven pennies in 1915; what is its value today? Your great-grandfather's estate was $1000 or £200 in 1900; what is that worth today?"[1] The diffuse nature of these inquiries would be even greater if they crossed the world, across monies, and time periods. The question of worth opens up narrative compilation, political judgment, and much else.

A case that carries enormous moral gravitas, and exemplifies the complexity of the comparative criteria involved when "worth" is evoked comes in a book by Kenneth Feinberg (2005), administrator of the fund created by the US Congress to compensate the families of 9/11 victims. Its title is *What Is Life Worth? The Unprecedented Effort to Compensate the victims of 9/11*, and its chapter headings exemplify clearly the range of processes and terms that enter into debates and judgments of worth: "From Theory to Reality," "The Families Speak," "Struggling with the Incomprehensible," "Solomon's Choices." The appendices offer intricate tables and quantitative detail, while the final sentence expresses an ideology of national life: "the nation speaking with one voice and demonstrating the best of American character" (191). Remarkably varied monetary transactions and monetary amounts, from a bus fare to a life, may be dignified far beyond market price by being subjected to value considerations resulting in judgments of worth.

Every negotiation creates a story, a corpus from which an ethnographer could elicit much, starting with all its components, participants, concepts, judgments, and resolutions. While economic models preserve the starting point and the outcome, a "good to think" orientation would preserve the experience and the augmentation of knowledge that a negotiation brought, especially if it crossed previously unexplored boundaries. A short diversion into the mnemonics of monetary transactions illuminates Marx's emphasis on "in use."

Money and Narrative: An African Inspiration

I like provocative surprises and have found them most often in Africa (Guyer 2013). I was drawn to record keeping with respect to money: ranging from personal memory (Hart 2000) to written records, receipts, promissory notes, and the rest through which all modern debt systems function—the "actual", in other words. I have always been surprised by the complexity and sheer volume of West African regional trade, much of it recorded as oral history and preserved through techniques of the memory. I wonder, for example, whether the Ashanti gold weight system moved away from geometrical design to the figurative arts with trade expansion (Phillips 2010), because each transaction could then be embedded in a memory bank of narrative, proverbs, and perhaps jokes between the trading partners, as each brought their own weights to the bargain. This research would have to be done by someone with a sophisticated grasp of the Twi language and its narrative traditions, abetted by their own archive of comparative worth and concepts of number or measure and able to spin their own narratives provoked by the gold-weight figures.

I would like to curate images, words, social interactions, memories, and comparative configurations of "worth" within precise moments, in an archive. How then might instances within life-as-lived be identified? We are awash with monetary information, so we could choose almost any entry point. Ideally we could overhear observations, negotiations, and the settling of "accounts," in both the mathematical and narrative senses. My own experiments along these lines have been utterly mundane, with information contained in American and British daily newspapers as an example here.

Experiments with Money as Daily Food for Thought

When living in the West, we rarely meet in marketplaces to compare, trace out, complain, negotiate face to face, and generally converse about money, worth, and "what is to be done" about it. Except, perhaps, in crises. With regard to market behavior, the daily press may be the one meeting place where thought and commentary among strangers might be provoked. Out of curiosity to discover what aspects of money readers are exposed to on a regular, daily basis, I analyzed one day's edition of a popular newspaper. I examined juxtapositions, to see how articles brought money and worth into view, to identify narrative forms and to imagine what conversations might ensue: on the bus, around the table. Then, in order to compile a time series for one item over several months, I collected one advertisement in a national newspaper that appears daily in the same spot. My preliminary ruminations on "thinking about worth" follow, as a reader and member of the public, a witness of the "actual", infused as they are by assumptions and enactments of the presenter's notion of "worth". I felt free to say, as readers of the newspaper might do, "that's rubbish!" "not worth it', a "waste", or to add another perspective to an open discussion. My aim here is to illustrate the thought provoked by our daily "marketplaces" and to note that how they reach outwards into "making the world" would extend any study of "the other side of the coin" and its deployment in the world at large.

1. The Daily Mail: A Single Day (28 June 2014)

Almost forty of the articles mentioned "money," in 112 pages of text, and of course there are many advertisements. Almost the whole front page was devoted to money, in numbers: £16 (in an advertisement for wine), £15 (for holidays), and £15,000 (of accounts in an article on "savers" being put "in limbo" by banking delays). The last article sounds like the story of Noah's flood: "millions facing misery," "flagship," "launch," "fear," "deluge," "chaos," "black hole," and "struggle." Many pages juxtapose comparable amounts, such as "win £1,000" and "mortgage rates rise by £2,000"; the Church of England's £6 billion portfolio comes next to a report of a fall in Tesco profits to only £3.3 billion. One whole page reports Scottish referendum bribes and a story of a firm that charges three thousand pounds to get you onto the Queen's honors list. One page sports the headline "The 2.8m pound question facing judges: When is a cake not a cake?" since this determines the tax level and liability. Most are about scams and confusions in the formal sector, thefts, surprising prices, or prize money in sports and the amount at stake is usually in the headline. The sheer proliferation of bribes, prize money, bureaucratic confusion, and straight crime would offer a fine topic for conversations about standards in the world of money. Readers are invited into such a world where the amounts are very prominent but hardly explained. Thus how prices are made by markets would seem to be a compelling invitation to discuss how it all works; but no. The question "is it worth it?" may work subliminally, as when we are told that £15,000 a year is the "price of perfect skin" for a film star. Only one article mentions "worth" explicitly and that is when the recipient of an award is deemed "worthy," which harks back to the original Anglo-Saxon meaning. Rather, articles about money leave us—the reading public in all our diversity—to make commensurations, calculations, and judgments about worth, and discuss them with one another.

England now has an ethnically and linguistically varied population. What do we say to each other about all these stories of money making in our common world? Perhaps we throw the evidence in the bin, while remaining skeptical of all stories about money on a large scale and of their basis in *any* kind of truth that we can judge. Or we see the whole thing as the polemic of politicians. Or, more likely, we reconfigure our understanding about "society" itself as being riven with incongruities, frauds, failures, and foolishness—all itemized in great detail. Such conversations would be highly variable as well as comparative enterprises: "Isn't it the same where you come from?" The conversation then moves on to interpretations of global inequality, possible causes of inscrutable behavior, and other puzzles, all grounded in "the actual," and made possible by being expressed as amounts of money. These make "wants of the mind" about the world we live in more real and are perhaps even satisfied—for the moment anyway, until tomorrow's conversation.

2. Expensive Goods with Supposed "Use Value": What Are They Worth?

In another experiment over an extended period, I looked at a regular advertisement spot in the *New York Times* that features expensive objects for women purporting to be useful and not just decorative like traditional jewels. These included items such as shoes and handbags, which appear neither particularly useful nor beautiful to this pragmatic mind and frequently have negative worth, especially in action—some could be a positive nuisance. What distinctive features and categories would account for their price and perhaps for a buyer pondering whether to make a purchase (invoking Malinowski's "imponderabilia of actual life")? Judgments of worth made by buyers/consumers would indeed justify deep study.

I saved this advertisement for a total of eighty-three consecutive days and tabulate the contents below. How could a pair of shoes be worth more than advice when seeking a royal honor.

Footwear: 25
Average price $1,942
Range from $975 to $7,150.

Handbags: 26 priced, 6 unpriced
Average price $5,732
Range from $2,000 to $9,500

Other items were not priced.

Higher prices are associated with:

1. Composition: unusually wild skins, like python;
2. The prominence of the company logo;
3. The name given, e.g. *minaudière*: a small purse invented for a millionaire by Van Cleef and Arpels in Paris during the Great Depression! What does it signify? "According to fashion journalist Lloyd Boston, a *minaudière* constitutes an 'essential' part of an evening wardrobe, a small object with no limit to its usefulness and a 'fabulous character'" (Wikipedia, consulted August 2015), defined in English as "dainty" (etymology: "excellent," delightful, pleasing).

4. Some of these *minaudières* can only be "food for thought" and conversation, perhaps for withering arguments and judgments as well as puzzled amazement, as miniature versions of the most mundane containers: an egg box, a jerry can, a milk carton, and a pearl ball, into which almost nothing could conveniently fit, except perhaps a paper handkerchief. So much for "use value"!

This elaboration of such ordinary articles for fashionable purposes adds up to using money not to *buy* utility or honorable status, nor conventional "luxury" (the jerry can is made of gold with diamond studs, but could also be brass and glass). It may be for attention-getting and conversation-making. Noam Yuran (this volume) takes us deeper into the history of luxury in capitalism, where "excess", including sexual, may come closer to the impact of these advertisements than my pragmatist and class-conscious gaze can appreciate. He calls such objects "an entry ticket to society." My recent visit to the Coffin Works, a coffin museum in Birmingham, England also revealed the history of growth in demand among all social classes for brass coffin decorations after the elaborate funeral in 1861 of Prince Albert, consort of Queen Victoria. Clearly this had no material use, nor any current symbolic value except as a memento; so its cost may reflect what Yuran focuses on, but also an ostentatiously public way for the middle and lower classes to mark respect and spiritual connection within a particular community. The logic of Yuran's argument is now seen through the conversations, judgments and sexual attraction that these goods provoke, and especially in the huge demand for cheaper and more widely available copies. "A luxury industry that drove the economy from its traditional stable organization into an emergent capitalist form"- continues to "emerge".

Advertising of luxury items that were once "must-haves" only for the rich now perform the same kind of work for a wider public. The satisfaction afforded by conspicuous (literally, to be looked at attentively) consumption is thus social, not material or utilitarian. People take notice of it. When the goods are very expensive, idiosyncratic and in limited supply they are exclusively attached to one individual. Their acquaintances will ask about them, make comments to each other, build stories based on a mixture of curiosity and judgment, and then archive them for future reference. Scarcity allows for individuation, quite apart from the added value for producers and merchants. No wonder social commentators increasingly refer to "icons".

The prices of the goods advertised in my sample are well beyond the ordinary shopper's range. But it is interesting to speculate about how this all affects the "appetites of the mind" of wearers, escorts, rivals, critics, and observers alike. Stories about them grab the attention and provide points for memory in future, amplified by people who "matter"—media experts and peers within the wearer's class. We are obviously no longer buying cabbages in the marketplace here, but showing off at the opera, grand ball, banquet, Ascot races and other high-class occasions. Maybe the "worth" is of different kinds for buyers, sellers and the audience to the purchase or at the theatre. There may be a limit to how much conversation of this kind can take place and how long it will last in social memory.

So the worth of luxury goods attracts attention and produces talking points; this is surely why they are copied in cheaper materials for the popular market. Mind games and verbal gymnastics rule. Neither utility in use, nor the cost of production nor nobility of feature can account for the status of these luxuries. Some companies strictly limit production and maintain a long waiting list of clients, who may eventually sell them off to the "vintage" market, where they also demand high prices. This is bricolage by the very wealthy, reproduced on a smaller scale by the rest of us when we buy gifts for each other! We are still far from answering Shakespeare's question (in *The Merchant of Venice*): "Tell me where is fancy bred. Or in the heart or in the head?" But this elusive process provides grist for an inventive, mutual, sometimes poetic genre of communication. It is a genre replete with populist and creole categories, as well as hegemonic terms and conditions. And markets feed on its energies voraciously.

These daily provocations and conversations about money, stimulated by a plethora of advertisements, fill the memory banks of incremental social value This is one way we explore how money types and quantities become a medium of social understanding within a multiplicity of actual circumstances. This approach to social analysis could be extended to more populations and arenas (*agora*) worldwide.

My examples here are all denominated in single hard-money systems, such as pounds sterling and US dollars. But many of the participants, even in these systems, bring themselves and their goods from other currency zones. Beyond the exchange rates between these hard currencies, whose value fluctuates relatively narrowly (at least in the short run), there is a much more turbulent world of soft monies operating at interfaces with the hard currencies where most of the world's people live. What is the scope for the processes that I have described here when the stakes of worth and value often have more weighty implications for life itself?

Conclusion

Money is a pervasive topic for thought and discussion, a vernacular through which anyone may join a conversation about their "society" in the vast and constantly changing meeting place between states and markets that is the *agora*. Although everyone uses money as a medium of exchange, means of payment, and store of value, the sheer reach of monetization these days—daily exposure to the media, tracking and making sense of it all—surely is grounded in conversations, judgments, and stories archived in and retrieved from the banks of our social memory. So money, both as a unit of account and in accounts of life and worth, brings together the systemic and emergent processes that link all of us to society: structure and experience, storage and exchange, the 1% and the 99%, value and worth, narrative and scalar judgment, Lévi-Strauss's "good to think" and Malinowski's "imponderabilia."

My exploratory ethnography of worth has generated a set of vernacular experiments, a bricolage of comparative judgment with respect to things, numbers, and the archives of memory. Christine Desan (2015) is doubtless right that the crown's authority and its monopoly of universal equivalence for payment, purchase, and storing value, supported dependable money systems on which business calculation, investment, and state finance once rested. But we must revisit the sedimentary histories of monetary practice, and above all the commentaries and points of reference, through which people have made on-going assessments of life: numbers, optimal configurations, ethics, and temporal change. These are deep and complex topics, requiring an ethnographic sensibility that is ever more necessary for grasping the complexity of a rapidly commoditizing world market made up of so many competing currencies. The use of money as a unit of account, in all its sites and historical forms, in all the diverse money systems to which we are alerted by comparative history and by visions of money's future, is where we should look for glimpses into a vernacular *mondialisation* from below. The stories people tell about that world are stored in many memory banks. Language and money still converse with one another, and we still have unlimited face-to-face contexts and some limited concepts to encourage that conversation.

Jane I. Guyer became professor emerita of anthropology at Johns Hopkins University in 2015, after thirteen years, and earlier periods at Harvard, Boston, and Northwestern Universities. Her books include *An African Niche Economy* (1997), *Marginal Gains* (2004), and *Legacies, Logics, Logistics* (2016). She was elected to the US National Academy of Sciences in 2008.

NOTES

1. Quote from consultation, 25 June 2015. http://www.measuringworth.com/explaining_measures_of_worth.php.

REFERENCES

Amato, M.., and L. Fantacci. 2014. *Saving the Market from Capitalism: Ideas for an Alternative Finance*. Cambridge: Polity Press.
Bolt, M. 2015. *Zimbabwean Migration and South Africa's Border Farms: The Roots of Impermanence*. Cambridge: Cambridge University Press.
Boltanski, L., and L. Thévenot. 2006. *On Justification: Economies of Worth*. Translated by C. Porter. Princeton. NJ: Princeton University Press.
Carruthers, B., and W Espeland.1991. "Accounting for rationality: Double-entry bookkeeping and the rhetoric of economic rationality." *American Journal of Sociology* 97(1): 31–69.
Chevalier, S. 2014. "Turning commodities into presents." *Journal of Classical Sociology* 14(1): 54–64.
Desan, C. 2015. *Making Money: Coin, Currency and the Coming of Capitalism*. Oxford: Oxford University Press.
Diagne, S. B. 2011. *African Art as Philosophy: Senghor, Bergson and the Idea of Negritude*. Calcutta: Seagull Books.
Dodd, N. 2014. *The Social Life of Money*. Princeton, NJ: Princeton University Press.
Einaudi, L. 1953 (1936). "The theory of imaginary money from Charlemagne to the French revolution." In F. C. Lane and J. C. Riemersma (eds.), *Enterprise and Secular Change: Readings in Economic History*. Homewood, IL: Richard D. Unwin, pp. 229–261.
Feinberg, K. R. 2005. *What is Life Worth? The Unprecedented Effort to Compensate the Victims of 9/11*. New York: Public Affairs, member of Perseus Book Group.
Fontaine, L. 2014. *Le Marché. Histoire et usages d'une conquête sociale*. Paris: Éditions Gallimard.
Godelier, M. 2000. "Is social anthropology still worth the trouble? A response to some echoes from America." *Ethnos: Journal of Anthropology* 65(3): 301–316.
Graeber, D. 2011. *Debt: The First 5,000 Years*. Brooklyn, NY: Melville House.
Gudeman, S. 2009. "Necessity of contingency? Mutuality and market." In C. Hann and K. Hart (eds.), *Market and Society*. Cambridge: Cambridge University Press, pp. 17–37.
Guyer, J. I. 2013 "The quickening of the unknown': Epistemologies of surprise in anthropology." *HAU: Journal of Ethnographic Theory* 3(3): 283–307.
———. 2016. "Money in the future of Africans." In B. Goldstone and J. Obarrio (eds.), *African Futures. Essays on Crisis, Emergence, and Possibility*. Chicago, IL: University of Chicago Press, 63–76.
Hann, C., and K. Hart (eds.). 2009. *Market and Society: The Great Transformation Today*. Cambridge: Cambridge University Press.
Hart, K. 1986. "Heads or tails? Two sides of the coin." *Man* New Series 21(4): 637–656.
———. 2000. *The Memory Bank: Money in an Unequal World*. London: Profile Books.

Hart, K. 2009. "The persuasive power of money." In S. Gudeman (ed.), *Economic Persuasions*. New York: Berghahn Books, pp. 136–158.
Hart, K. and W. James (eds.). 2014. "Special Issue on Marcel Mauss: A living inspiration" *Journal of Classical Sociology* 14 (1): 3–131.
Hart, K., J.-L. Laville, and A. Cattani (eds.). 2010. *The Human Economy: A Citizen's Guide*. Cambridge: Polity Press.
Hart, K., and J. Sharp (eds.). 2014. People, Money and Power in the Economic Crisis: Perspectives from the Global South (The Human Economy). New York and Oxford: Berghahn Books.
Hill, P. 1989. "Market Places." In J. Eatwell, M. Milgate, and P. Newman (eds.), *The New Palgrave: Economic Development*. London and New York: W.W. Norton, pp. 338–342.
James, W. 2014. "Human Life as Drama: A Maussian Insight." *Journal of Classical Sociology* 14(1): 78–90.
Lévi-Strauss, C. 1962. *Totemism*. Boston, MA: Beacon Press.
———. 1963. *Structural Anthropology*, vol I. New York: Basic Books.
Malinowski, B. 1922. *Argonauts of the Western Pacific: An Account of Native Enterprise and Adventure in the Archipelago of Melanesian New Guinea*. London: G. Routledge & Sons.
Marx, K. 1977 [1954]. *Capital: A Critique of Political Economy*. Moscow: Progress Publishers.
Maurer, B. 2010. "Finger counting money." *Anthropological Theory* 10(1–2): 179–185.
———. 2012. "Mobile money: Communication, consumption and change in the payments space." Journal of Development Studies 48(5): 589–604.
Mauss, M. 1990 (1925). *The Gift*. Translated by W. D. Halls. London: Routledge and Kegan Paul.
Miller, D. 1995. "Consumption and commodities." Annual Review of Anthropology 24: 141–161.
Monga, C. 2015. "The Macroeconomics of Marginal Gains: Africa's Lessons to Social Theorists." Unpublished manuscript.
Nyamunda, T. 2014. "Cross-border couriers as symbols of regional grievance? The Malayitsha remittance system in Matabeleland, Zimbabwe." *African Diaspora* 7: 8–62.
Peebles, G. 2011. *The Euro and its Rivals*. Bloomington: Indiana University Press.
Phillips, T. 2010. *African Goldweights: Miniature Sculptures from Ghana 1400–1900*. London: W.W. Norton, Thames and Hudson.
Yuran, N. 2014. *What Money Wants: An Economy of Desire*. Stanford, CA: Stanford University Press.

CHAPTER 3

The Shadow of Aristotle
A History of Ideas about the Origins of Money

JOSEPH NOKO

Money in the conception of many is a singularity, one monolithic object defined by some primary objective function. What follows is a history of two thousand years of competing visions of this singularity, a history of reflections on the legacy of Aristotle, the first thinker to ponder seriously the problem of the origins of money.

His solution to this most vexing problem is pregnant with possibilities of a quite Darwinian nature: understanding the origins of money allows us to make a quantum leap toward grasping the nature and behavior of money. A lasting solution holds within it a greater understanding of money and of how it evolves; for this reason the greatest minds in the field, from time immemorial, have made it their task to answer that question.

Here I will draw on the examples of classical Greece and ancient Egypt to demonstrate that money does not have any one origin; rather, the perturbations and revolutions of history provide myriad means and reasons for money to have emerged; moreover, the birth of money is not the end of the story, for money continues to evolve.

Inhuman, bloodless, impersonal money animates and is animated by human society in all its forms. The upheavals and revolutions of society often find their cause in money and the new money they generate congeals the resulting relations of power. In such cases, money is a protagonist that preserves institutions, social hierarchies and modes of class relations. Without money, societies of any complexity collapse.

Today, as the world economy chokes on the fat of its own excess, we face a future of stagnation, racist-xenophobic politics, and creeping breakdown of the power of institutions that have for decades controlled the socioeconomic order and benefited most from globalization. So, for the second time in a century, globalization as the organizing force in world relations stands on the verge of collapse.

The age of empire and the following dispensation forged a single civilization (Wilkinson 1987; Wallerstein 1974) in which previous versions remained only as local expressions of the new one. The spoils of capitalism today have been dispersed along two lines: across global civilization according to a country's level of integration into the world system, with the United States at the core and the least integrated states forming a periphery with little influence; and within states by relations of power in the financial economy, with the manufacturing classes left devastated in even the richest nations (Hart, this volume).

Now is a turning point when global civilization will either become a caste-like system of limited opportunity and wholesale exclusion, or one where we can construct a human economy that is fairer, more just, and more equal, connecting people rather than separating them into gluttonous winners and poverty-stricken losers. Understanding the nature of money through the problem of its origins is an essential means to this end. Accordingly, we start at the very beginning, with Aristotle.

The Aristotelian Concept of Money

The dominant schools of thought on this subject have nearly all been influenced by what we might call the "Aristotelian concept of money." The genealogy of ideas concerning the origins of money may be traced back to the fifth book of Aristotle's *Nicomachean Ethics*, which deals with reciprocity as justice, a work we must read along with his *Politics*, for Aristotle's idea of money was intimately related to his ideas on the formation of society. In the Aristotelian scheme, ethical problems cannot be separated from politics and consequently, *Nicomachean Ethics* and *Politics* should be seen as different perspectives on a single totality.

One senses that the great ambition of economics is to establish the conditions for a Newtonian revolution of its own, to make a giant leap forward in scientific respectability by donning the laboratory coat of the scientist, to achieve rigor through *Bourbakianisme* (a species of formalism), to transfigure economics into a physics of economic problems. To what do we owe this tendency of economics to approach definite historical and dynamic problems with *ahistorical* and static tools? Nowhere is this more evident than in the literature on the origins of money: from Aristotle to the countless textbooks disseminated today, the story of the birth of money is told as if it were a myth based on nameless transactional archetypes, a simple model from which are revealed the mechanisms out of which money emerged.

"The most valuable insights are *methods*" (Nietzsche 1968: 260), and Aristotelian methodology was the groundwork upon which medieval Christian and Islamic scholastic thought were erected and propagated up until the seventeenth century. His illuminating genius shone everywhere; the first and greatest *uomo universale*, his importance to economics has been thoroughly under-appreciated: the basic ahistorical methodology of modern economics is the legacy of the Stagirite.

That great pessimist Oswald Spengler held that we see the world from one of two distinct perspectives: the world-as-history perspective, in which we feel ourselves "an element in a far wider life-course that goes on for hundreds and thousands of years" (Spengler 1926: 8), and the ahistorical perspective, in which one "conceives of [oneself] as something rounded off and self-contained"; it is into an ahistorical culture that Aristotle was born.

In the world-consciousness of the Hellenes all experience, not merely the personal but the common past, was immediately transmuted into a timeless, immobile, mythically-fashioned background for the particular momentary present; thus the history of Alexander the Great began even before his death to be merged by Classical sentiment in the Dionysus legend, and to Caesar there seemed at the least nothing preposterous in claiming descent from Venus (ibid.).

The student of classical literature cannot help but notice the peculiar difficulty the Greeks and the Romans had with non-contemporary history. Herodotus, Thucydides, Polybius, Livy, and Aristotle produced their finest historical work when dealing with the immediate past and yet, when these contemporary historians delved into the non-contemporary past, their efforts became ham-handed, lost, and confused. Incapable of critically interrogating older texts or of using non-narrative sources, they resorted to myth and bestowed upon economics an ahistorical approach to the study of the origins and nature of money.

The Origins of Money in Barter

Aristotle argued that a good had two uses, the intrinsic use for which it was intended, and its value in exchange;[1] and, as some men had a surplus of provisions and others a deficit, they exchanged goods. In the very beginning, however, in the time of "family societies" (Aristotle 1912), things were held in common; accordingly there was no barter exchange; and only as the family society grew and separated did barter trade arise.

But this barter introduced the use of money, as might be expected; for a convenient place from whence to import what you wanted, or to export what you had a surplus of being often at a great distance, money necessarily made its way into commerce; for it is not everything which is naturally most useful that is easiest of carriage; for which reason they invented something to exchange with each other which they should mutually give and take, that being really valuable itself, should have the additional advantage of being of easy conveyance, for the purposes of life, as iron and silver, or anything else of the same nature: and this at first passed in value simply according to its weight or size; but in process of time it had a certain stamp, to save the trouble of weighing, which stamp expressed its value. (Aristotle 1912)

According to Aristotle, money originally facilitated trade between communities.[2] However, the possibility of a causal connection between trade and the birth of money is denied by archaeology and numismatics: they were not in use in foreign trade (Cook 1958; Kraay 1964, 1976), and electrum coins circulated within close proximity of the Greek polis (Kraay 1964, 1976), including the earliest coinage of all, that of Ionia and Lydia.[3]

Society—an assemblage of differing skills, property, and services—is, in Aristotle's conception, an association for exchange based on the principle of proportionate reciprocity, secured, if justice prevails, by tit-for-tat, whereby evil is returned with proportionate evil, good with proportionate good and one quantity or quality of goods is proportionally reciprocated in exchange by another (Aristotle 1999). Without proportionate return, society unravels.

Money exists in the interstices between things, and arose to mediate in exchange and to make equivalent different and unequal things, which, given the presence of money, may be compared and exchanged. Allowing for equivalence in proportion generated the conditions for just exchange:

> It is for this reason that money has been introduced, and it becomes in a sense an intermediate; for it measures all things, and therefore the excess and defect of how many shoes are equal to a house or to a given amount of food. The number of shoes exchanged for a house (or for a given amount of food) must therefore correspond to the ratio of builder to shoemaker. For if this be not so, there will be no exchange and no intercourse. And this proportion will not be affected unless the goods are somehow equal. (Aristotle 1999: 79–80)

After this, Aristotle says something that has largely gone unnoticed and his supposed thesis on the origins of money out of law is very different when placed in the context of his work on reciprocation as justice:

> All goods must be measured by some one thing, as we said before. Now this unit is in truth *demand*,[4] which holds all things together (for if men did not need one another's goods at all, or did not need them equally, there would either be no exchange, or not the same exchange); but money has become by convention a sort of representative of demand; and this is why it has the name "money" (*nomisma*) – because it exists not by nature but by law (*nomos*) and it is in our power to change it and make it useless. (Aristotle 1999: 80)

The conventional interpretation of this passage zeroes in on the notion that Aristotle believed that money was created by law to be a medium of exchange, thereby overcoming the high transaction costs of barter exchange.

Elaborating on this line of thought, Julius Paulus Prudentissimus, a Roman jurist whose views on money are preserved in Justinian's *Digest*, expounded on some of the encumbrances inherent in barter and suggested that these difficulties could be removed by a public body that stamped an external nominal value on some substances (Cernuschi 1877; Menger 1892, 2007): "A substance was selected whose *public* evaluation exempted it from the fluctuations of the other commodities, thus giving it an always stable external (nominal) value. A mark (of its external value) was stamped upon this substance by society. Hence its exchange value is based, not upon the substance itself, but upon its nominal value" (Julius Paulus quoted in Menger 2007: 316).

In reviewing the evidence of these three great men, Carl Menger, who refined Adam Smith's theory, said:

> Summarizing the course followed by the investigations of these writers, they almost always begin by showing the difficulties to trade arising from pure barter. They next show how it is possible to remove these difficulties by the introduction of money. In the further course of their arguments, they stress the special suitability of the precious metals for serving as money, and finally, citing Aristotle, they reach the conclusion that the precious metals actually became money by the legislation of men. (Menger 2007: 317)

Julius Paulus noted that the axiom "money was whatever the state made money" (Del Mar 1900: 127) was a constitutional principle of Rome, and by the Middle Ages the "Aristotelian" position was accepted universally, while speculation focused on how precious metals became money (Menger 2007). This notion is inadequate, however. When there is a coincidence of wants, money allows different and unequal things to be measured and exchanged in proportion; without a mutuality of demand; "when men do not need one another" (Aristotle 1999: 80), there can be no exchange; when men need each other, they exchange; money mediates in that exchange and is "surety" that in future the seller has something he can exchange for whatever he wants. "Now the same thing happens to money itself as to goods; it is not always worth the same; yet it tends to be steadier" (Aristotle 1999: 80).

An alternative inference is that Aristotle uses the word "demand" here in a noneconomic sense, placing it within a historical, customary context. He seems to be referring to the use we make of things according to the customs of a place; for example, custom might dictate that a young bull be sacrificed as a burnt offering, and so there arises a demand for knives, bricks to make altars with, etc. Moreover, that demand remains steady over time, conditioned by custom and history. The demand for money, however, is even steadier, and when one understands the meaning of that key word, "*nomos*," the picture becomes even clearer: *nomos* refers not just to "law," but "anything assigned, a usage, custom, law, ordinance."[5] Therefore, Aristotle's famous line, "but money has become by convention a sort of representative of demand; and this is why it is the name 'money' (nomisma)—because it exists not by nature but by law (*nomos*) and it is in our power to change it and make it useless"—refers to more than just money as a creature of the law, but money also as a creature of custom or usage. These determine what is in demand, and so, when it becomes "customary" to listen to music on devices such as mobile phones or iPods, that customary usage creates a present and future demand for such devices. Custom, then, is the universal basis for measuring all things, the true begetter of money. "Now in truth it is impossible that things differing so much should become commensurate, but with reference to demand they may become so sufficiently. There must, then, be a unit, and fixed by agreement (for which reason it is called money); for it is this that makes all things commensurate since all things are measured by money." (ibid.)

Society, in the Aristotelian sense, is held together by customary demand, the mutual needfulness of man; bound together in an association of exchange. Society falls apart when men no longer need each other to meet their needs; and when exchange is no longer proportionate, it becomes unjust. Without exchange and money, there is no society. Society exists to meet the customary demands of man that allow him to live the good life and money is the vehicle through which an interlocking and mutual satisfaction of customary demands is achieved. It is said that "no man is an island," and in living together, we depend on each other to meet our customary demands, but this dependence can only become material and give birth to society through money, which interlocks our dependency in an association of exchange.

The connection between money and the making of society in Aristotle's thought is further highlighted in his *Politics*. Searching for the first elements of various forms of government in order to determine their nature and fundamental differences, Aristotle commences with the household, that form of society that exists to supply man with his daily succor, and therein discovers three implied relations: that of the father and child, husband and wife, and master and slave. The slave is defined as an "animated instrument," a form of property. Proceeding logically from this, he tackles the condition of slavery, the general question of property, and how it is obtained and used.[6]

The acquisition of property follows naturally from hunting, husbandry, etc., and Aristotle classes barter exchange as part of the natural process of acquisition. Then, there is acquisition through exchange with money as the medium. To this, he adds that there are limits to what may be acquired as property, but the acquisition of money is unlimited. The household economy differs from other forms of economy in that it is centered on the acquisition of property, whereas in a financialized world, which he considers unnatural especially in the it's the form of usury, the acquisition of money is paramount.

In his somewhat vulgar critique of Plato's ideal commonwealth, he comments on its homogeneity, arguing that extreme sameness would destroy society, which is built on interlocking and diverse demands. This distinction is further emphasized where he argues that Platonic communism would engender discord and a dilution of interest in what one meresharing.

Aristotle appears to claim that society exists because of private property and that society is held together by interlocking customary demand.

The Commodity Theory: Metalists, Law, Smith, and Menger

For the metalists, money was neutral, a veil over the basic role of barter in the economy, a medium of exchange lubricating markets and whose value is derived from its metallic content. John Law (1740) rebuffed the notion of money as an invention and institution of law, while demonstrating the special characteristics of precious metals, which led to their becoming money. It is from Law that Adam Smith (1904) took the view that not only did money emerge as a medium of exchange to overcome the high transaction costs of barter exchange, but money also evolved logically through the efforts of market actors to overcome these costs. The state's role was to standardize, mint, and stamp coinage, to tackle counterfeit and to bring order to coinage systems. Smith (1904) developed Law's theory and bequeathed to the world its most famous exposition of the origins of money: that a people who conducted little trade and whose division of labor was moderate, found that as division of labor became the organizing principle of society, barter exchange emerged to meet the diverse needs of society. However, barter exchange often proved to "have been very much clogged and embarrassed in its operations" (Smith 1904: 49) due to the difficulty of achieving a double coincidence of wants; and some commodity—iron, silver, or gold, or even cattle—became the first monies, to simplify barter exchange. This soon became the new orthodoxy in economics, so that Karl Marx (1909: 74) could say, "The difficulty lies, not in comprehending that money is a commodity, but in discovering how, why and by what means a commodity becomes money." The answer, typically, was that hoarding of the most exchangeable commodity propels it to become money in its fullest expression (Smith 1904; Menger 1892, 2007). Carl Menger (1892) provided the classic treatment of the theory of money's *logical* emergence from barter exchange. His thesis, deduced from typically Aristotelian principles, laid bare how, through the pursuit of liquid goods, a barter economy could settle on its most liquid good as money, with only a limited role played by the state.

Menger's theory of the origins of money is now generally accepted in mainstream economics, while Smith's theory is more famous. Menger's thesis is basically taken from Law's *Money and Trade Considered*: "Law, on the contrary, most decidedly repudiates the contractual theory, and recognizing, as no author before him, the special position of the precious metals among other commodities, he derives the genesis of the money character of the precious metals from their special characteristics. Thus he is the founder of the correct theory of the origin of money" (Menger 2007: 318).

Law made a decisive contribution to the barter theory by showing how money could arise from the interaction of market forces. Giving reasons for the peculiar attributes that made silver fit for use as money, he said, "Silver having these qualities, 'tis reasonable to think it was used as money, before it was coined; what is meant by being used as money, is, that silver in bullion was the measure by which goods were valued: the value by which goods were exchanged: and in which contracts were made payable" (1740: 8–100). Law added the proviso that Smith and Menger were took up later: "Silver being capable of a stamp, princes, for the greater convenience of the people, set up mints to bring it to a standard, and stamp it; whereby its weight and fineness was known, without the trouble of weighing or fining; but the stamp added nothing to the value.

For these reasons silver was used as money; its being coined was only a consequence of its being applied to that use in bullion, tho' not with the same convenience" (ibid.: 14).

With Law, commodity theory broke with the ersatz-Aristotelian tradition of ascribing the origins of money to law; rather the market developed money autonomously to purge itself of the high transaction costs inherent in barter exchange (Law 1740; Smith 1904). while the wheels of exchange turned in what was essentially still a barter economy (Samuelson 1948). Law (1740) propagated an approach to the ontology of money by arguing that precious metals became money because their intrinsic features accorded with the functional demands of money.[7] The break with the Aristotelean was not complete, however, since Law (1740) and Smith (1904) still granted a special role for the state in stamping coins to guarantee their weight and fineness, but this stamp was merely declarative, imparting no value to the coin.

Stanley Jevons (1876), in exposing the flaws of barter by analogy, became the chief modern propagandist of a negative theory of the origins of money. Robert Clower (1969) follows Jevons in arguing for the birth of money as a result of the high transaction costs of barter.

Menger (1892), however, made the decisive break with the contractual component in Aristotle's conception of money, completing the position of modern orthodoxy, with market forces taking credit for the emergence of money and for the selection of precious metals as money. The state often played a role that was usually denied by Menger's followers, but it was severely limited. Furthermore, an explanation based on the differing spread and liquidity of commodities was developed to show how a commodity might become money. The proof rests on a *circulus in probando*, whereby the liquidity of a commodity is held to be the cause of its liquidity. Thus Menger's fifth cause of liquidity is no more than a definition of liquidity.

Aristotle and Menger both arrived at their theory of money through deductive reasoning based on an assumption of a *definite* historical event which could be falsified factually regardless of how precise their logic might have been. Moreover, Caroline Humphrey (1985) has shown that historical barter economy has ever existed without the prior development of trade. Thomas Crump (1981) argues that, as control would have been exercised over the supply of money, a commodity frequently used in barter would not be allowed to morph into money. So the origins of money in primitive barter presuppose mature markets and a market mentality (Humphrey 1985). It has not been explained how frequency of use leads to the creation of money or, to paraphrase Geoffrey Ingham

(2004b), how inter-subjective hierarchies of value are produced from subjective preferences. The belief that money originated in barter led naturally to the view that money is primarily a medium of exchange and from this three inferences may be made: money is an exchangeable commodity; or it is a convertible note symbolizing such a commodity; or it is a *numeraire* of a commodity standard (Ingham 2004b). The question of how exchangeable it has to be in order to be money remains unanswered.

The Credit and State Theories of Money

Henry Dunning MacLeod made advances toward a credit theory of money by seeing money as a symbolic debt whose general acceptance was a sign of its transferable power (MacLeod 1893). Currency has no intrinsic value as paper money and, in the case of commodity money, its intrinsic value was secondary to the claim a currency had on goods and services, a notion that Bishop Berkeley developed in his theory of money as "tickets or tokens for conveying and recording such power" (1735). The credit theory of money shares with the state theory the view that money is a social relation that standardizes debt obligations (Mitchell Innes 1914; Graeber 2011). The key difference consists in credit theorists proposing that money cropped up at the social level before the emergence of the state; so that much of the discussion concerning credit in state theory is pertinent to the more general credit theory of money.

Andrew Mitchell Innes (1913, 1914) wrote what might be considered the founding texts of the credit theory. He summarized his thinking as follows:

> Shortly. The Credit Theory is this: that a sale and purchase is the exchange of a commodity for credit. From this main theory springs the sub-theory that the value of credit or money does not depend on the value of any metal or metals, but on the right which the creditor acquires to "payment," that is to say, to satisfaction for the credit, and on the obligation of the debtor to "pay" his debt and conversely on the right of the debtor to release himself from his debt by the tender of an equivalent debt owed by the creditor, and the obligation of the creditor to accept this tender in satisfaction of his credit. (1914: 152)

To the credit theorists, all money is debt and the banking system's function is to act as a clearing house, with each economic unit possessing the power to create credit (Mitchell Innes 1914; Mehrling 2000). Max Weber (1978) criticized the notion that each market participant is both debtor and creditor, this being no more than an accounting truism, the adoption of which in the economy would generate inflationary policies. Credit theories of money generally suffer from failure to appreciate that the lines between public authority and private enterprise were often blurred in ancient times (Graeber 2011) and that merchants were often palace or temple officials (Gardiner 2004). Though monetized credit may have the characteristics of money, there is no reason why they should not be classed as money-substitutes rather then as money.

We inherited the idea that money is a token for exchange created by the state from Plato (1892), but chartalism as a distinct school was the child of Georg Friedrich Knapp (1924) with roots in the Aristotelian tradition. To a chartalist, "money is a creature of the law" (Knapp 1924: 1) created by fiat to standardize debt obligations (Knapp 1924; Lerner 1947; Keynes 1930) and demand for it is created through the imposition of taxes payable in state money, which obliges citizens to seek out "tax-driven money," thereby creating and perpetuating demand (Mill 1909; Marx 1909; Polanyi 1966). The state does not choose the money-thing arbitrarily: chartalists, including Knapp (1924) himself, often forget his distinction between what is valuable and value. This leads them to overstate the state's role and to imply that private money either does not exist or is peripheral. The state does not add value where there was none before; it imparts value to money, but market interactions determine what money is worth. Thus when colonial governments in Africa imposed taxes payable solely in European currency they put pressure on Africans to produce cash crops and work for wages, in the process monetizing African societies and creating markets for European goods (Forstater 2003; Graeber 2011).

Geoffrey Gardiner (2004), however, points out with respect to the founding of the Bank of England, that it did not monetize government debt; rather, it took it out of circulation, converting short-term into long-term debt, by the extension of an extended loan by merchants to the government, in exchange for an irredeemable government annuity. This meant that Bank of England notes could only circulate if the government never repaid its debt, something that it has not done (Graeber 2011). The Bank of England was given the power to issue notes, whose primary purpose was to accumulate commercial bills of exchange from private individuals. Thus, the Bank of England's formation served to monetize private and not government debt. Furthermore, Bank of England notes could not meet the demands of the economy and had to be supplemented by bills of exchange in a system of free banking (Selgin 1988; Gardiner 2004). The state theory of money reaches its limits in cases such as those defined by Thiers' Law, where good money chases out bad money, as happens during the dollarization of a hyperinflationary economy (Noko 2011), when state acceptance in Zimbabwe was insufficient to maintain the national currency in circulation, since holders of the currency restricted their exposure to the point of sale, holding foreign currency and hard assets instead. Indeed, the state may forbid the circulation of foreign currency, but cannot prevent it, as shown when dollarization came in by the back door. At best, the state theory cannot account generally for the origins of money and, at best, it comes close to being empirically sound. The government may decree anything to be money, but the populace need not hold it.

Graeber (2011) has identified a difficult problem for the state theory of money: in many instances, money emerged where direct taxation was frowned upon and infrequent, as in classical Greece, or where there was no general system of taxation, as in Mesopotamia and Egypt, nor a unified state, something that was at one time near universal—rendering the concept of the state or even "society" useless—nor, as in the Islamic world during the Middle Ages, any state enforcement of contracts. In fact, the "state" often acted to cancel debts, as in Sumeria, Babylon, and Ancient Israel. Nevertheless, Norbert Elias (1982) showed how the evolution of early modern centralized states involved turning tribal arrangements into the payment of tributes, levies, and taxes. So, if we develop a more evolutionary conception of taxation, seeing tribute or the extraction of surplus produce for redistribution by the ruling class as an inchoate form of tax, then the difficulty disappears.[8]

Andrew Mitchell Innes (1913, 1914) and Philip Grierson (1977), among others, have advanced the *wergild* theory of the origins of money, in which it is seen as the natural outcome of ancient penal systems designed to prevent blood feuds by levying fines through public assemblies that transgressors paid to victims and their families (Tymoigne and Wray 2005). These were standardized through the creation of money. Eventually the payment of these fines was centralized in public authorities when egalitarian tribal societies had become stratified. In ancient Mesopotamia, the temples stored vast treasures and were centers of money lending—and in the case of the Jerusalem temple, imposed taxes on society (Sombart 2001). Michael Hudson (2003) advanced the view that the origins of money may be traced back to the Mesopotamian temples and palaces, where it served as a means for keeping account of their treasures and administering prices. Thus, for Hudson, money evolved not only through *wergild* practices,[9] but also through administration. Wergild fines, according to this theory, were succeeded by tithes and tributes when crimes against the people in general were added onto transgressions against victims and their families. Much later, these fines, fees, tithes, and tributes would be replaced by taxes, with England introducing taxes in the nineteenth century (Tymoigne and Wray 2005).

John Henry (2004) shows how the earliest ruling classes in prehistoric Egypt began as hydraulic engineers before becoming priests and operating a system of limited redistribution, then inventing money to account for payments of levies, foreign tribute, and tribal obligations to the king and priests.

A Potential Solution from Ancient Egypt

Examination of the historical record suggests another possibility that has been surprisingly neglected. The origins of money cannot be separated from the emergence of society; and how money emerges is strongly linked to structures of knowledge and power which of course vary from society to society. Ancient Egypt, where money emerged under very different conditions than in Greece, provides a striking example of how a revolution in knowledge or metaphysics may alter power relations and give birth to money. It was much the same in Greece, but this aspect was generally played down there.

Conditions favorable to the emergence of money in Ancient Egypt arose from increased solidarity among tribes as a result of intensification of the division of labor between them. A specialist class of knowledge workers was created committed to raising productivity; and this class instituted a management revolution. Creeping social stratification led to a unified and hierarchical super-tribal society with itself at the head. Money as a unit of account was the creation of this managerial class.

There is little evidence for large-scale migrations into Egypt during its formative period (Trigger 1982); and so, despite the diffusion of some cultural influences from elsewhere, Egyptian civilization is as close as we can get to the emergence of money in a society largely operating under its own steam.

Henry's (2004) study of the genesis of money in Egypt attempts to synthesize credit and state theories. He shows how the earliest ruling classes operated a system of limited redistribution and invented money to organize payments to the king and priests of levies, foreign tribute, and tribal obligations. Wergild fines were followed by tithes and tributes as crimes against the people were added to transgressions against victims and their families. Much later, fines, fees, tithes, and tributes would be replaced by taxes.

Intensification of the division of labor and increased specialization shifted the structure of work away from a simple gender basis, in the process creating the first class of what Peter Drucker (1986) calls "knowledge workers" known to history—the hydraulic engineers of the River Nile. Drucker believed that this class was a recent phenomenon; but their genealogy stretches back into the mists of time. All work is made productive through the application of knowledge, but the difference between manual labor and knowledge work is that manual labor requires no skill, as Taylorism proved. It is just a series of coordinated, simple, and repetitive motions whose productivity may be increased through scientific organization and simplification of the motions. The knowledge worker's mission is to raise his own or others' effectiveness and his tools for this are knowledge, ideas, and concepts. New versions of these are useless in themselves, but when work is collective, they must be realized by others through production.

The hydraulic engineers became detached from general labor, organizing workers to build hydraulic works and distributing food, clothing, tools, and other goods produced in the villages for use on work sites. Trade relations, in so far as they related to the hydraulic system, came under their supervision and they decided which goods could be exported. Trade with other parts of the eastern Mediterranean was under tight control and was usually carried out by foreign merchants; thus, in the regional division of labor of the time, Lebanese merchants exchanged their timber for Egyptian crafts (Curtin 1984). Curtin adds that trade to the south was undertaken by "government expeditions" up the Nile and along the Red Sea coast to the "Land of Punt".

As administrators whose justification was their knowledge, the reach of the hydraulic engineers went far beyond that of the villagers who made up Egypt's original tribal society with the inevitable result of escalating class stratification. Possessing knowledge that was closed to the rest, yet vital to their existence, the gains in productivity that the engineers made possible increased the centrality of agriculture. Henry adds that physical separation over long periods and monopoly of hydraulic knowledge combined to give to this new managerial class a much faster income growth than was normal for the average tribesman:

> All members would have seen a rise in their standard of living, but the engineers would have seen a relatively greater increase. It is very likely, and the evidence supports this, that in the early stages of this development, the difference in growth rates were minuscule. But, over centuries, even a .05% difference would result in clearly observable absolute differences by

the end of that time. This development would correspond to the Badarian period of 4400–4000. (2004: 85)

In time, the hydraulic engineers became the first large-scale administrators, doing what was needed to ensure the floodwater irrigation of crops throughout the Nile Delta, and eventually they assumed the role of a wealthy ruling class. A process of political unification followed, starting with the Amratian or Naqada I period (4,000–3,500 BC), through the Gerzean or Naqada II period (3,500–3,200 BC) and culminating in the proto-dynastic Semainian or Naqada III period (3,200–3,000 BC) when Egypt became unified.[10] The success of the hydraulic systems and floodwater irrigation of the Nile Delta created, according to Henry (2004), a pressing need to unify the tribes of the Nile Valley under some super-tribal authority, in order to regulate the flow of water in a more coordinated way, so that one tribe would not use the flow of the Nile for its own needs while depriving other groups downstream, so that the administrators became independent of any one tribe, holding authority over an area encompassing many tribal lands. In this way, their possession of unique and socially necessary knowledge placed them at the summit of Egyptian life, as plutocrats and administrators, creating a super-tribal society based on economic inequality out of what had been egalitarian societies. In the Semainian period, the slow stratification of society congealed into a permanent structure, held together by religion and a division of labor that had become by now accepted as divinely ordained. The ruling classes operated a system of limited redistribution of economic surpluses raised through taxes from the producing majority.

Henry (2004) concludes from the communistic way of life of prehistoric Egypt that society must therefore have been nonpolitical – since a political class separate from the populace could not exist – and egalitarian because decisions were taken consensually. Furthermore, in such a society, there could be no debt, for debt is a relation of inequality disguised as one of equality, in which creditors have power over debtors, but debtors are deemed equal to the task of paying the debt and therefore as equal partners in that relationship. The emergence of money in that context was inseparable from the hydraulic organization of a great river and could hydrot be attribute to some abstract propensities of decentralized exchange.

In the light of this Egyptian excursion, we should recall that coinage[11] was first created by the Greek polis to establish social justice and to affirm its role as arbiter of distribution and prosperity over the claims of the aristocracy (von Reden 2003 [1995]; Kurke 1999; Semenova 2011). The choice of silver for coins reflected the view that it symbolized the purity and worth of the citizens' qualities, unlike the "elitist hierarchy of values and spheres of exchange" (Kurke 1999: 305). Trevett (2001) argues that coinage was also needed to pay for performance of civic services, thus establishing a link between democracy, public pay, and coinage, a link that explains why an oligarchic polis like Sparta did not develop coinage (Semenova 2011). Money predates coinage by several thousand years and it is the same with writing—the earliest examples of writing are records of monetary debts (Tymoigne and Wray 2005).

A broad theory encompassing the Greek and Egyptian examples, would therefore link the origins of classes, and therefore of money, out of a revolution in ideas that changed the forms of social domination. Such a theory would shift the center of original power, not to control of the means of production, as Marx would argue, but to the ownership of vital knowledge which *led* to the ownership of the means of production. We should not, following Smith, ascribe the emergence of money to the division of labor as such, but to a knowledge-centered change in the mode of domination. Division of labor and mutual need may hold society together once it has reached a definite form, but a fundamental shift in social relations of knowledge and power was needed to arrive at a mode of domination that required money.

What if all these competing economic visions, these many singularities, are all correct? Could it be that for two thousand years everyone was right? When tested against the laboratory of political and monetary history, it doesn't seem impossible. Our main error has been to cling to a singular aspect of money and to elevate it above all others, rather than think of it as representing just a dimension or gradation of money that may help us to answer some questions, but not others, according to context. While some see money as credit generated by the private sector, others see it as a creature of the state, and to most economists it is simply a medium of exchange in a barter economy. Money is all of these things, combining a rank order that reflects power relations and inequality in society and gradations of liquidity. Not only this, but money takes many forms corresponding to particular institutional orders of rank and with different grades of liquidity.

Conclusion

From John Law's enunciation of what has become mainstream commodity theory today (that money emerged as a cost-saving mechanism in the struggle against the inefficiencies of barter trade) down to Knapp's notion of the birth of money through the will of the state and Mitchell Innes's vision of money as credit, Aristotelian thought has followed the movement of monetary theory like a shadow that never leaves, long after the fall of the classic Aristotelian formulation. The commodity theorists have struggled with the damning silence of history; and, although the chartalists have the weight of history on their side, the evidence suggests that "private acceptance" is an important missing link in their theories. The notion of money as debt is problematic and credit theories tend to underestimate the role of the state in the emergence of money, as in colonial Africa. A theory of the origins of money must embrace the Aristotelian position that the birth, existence, and evolution of society are accompanied at every stage by the evolution of money. In the end money mirrors the social order in its multi-dimensionality and sometimes is the main instrument for changing it.

Joseph Noko is managing director of Scallywag Mine, a small-scale gold mine in Gwanda, Zimbabwe. He researches monetary economics, the history of economic thought, and the use of machine learning as a means of forecasting economic events.

NOTES

1. Law (1740: 4–5) predates Smith (1904: 52–53) in discussing the paradox of value.
2. This position is in keeping with the views of Karl Polanyi (1957), who believed that long-distance trade was prior to the emergence of local markets.
3. Kraay (1964) allowed for the possibility that the thirst for seniorage played a part in the establishment of coinage.
4. Emphasis added.
5. *The King James Version New Testament Greek Lexicon.* Strong's Number: 3546.
6. Graeber (2011) notes that the very notion of absolute private property emerged from the grappling with the legal status of slaves: the Latin word *dominium*, or absolute private property, came about during the late Roman Republic, when Rome was becoming a slave society, and is derived from *dominus*, or master/slave-owner, and ultimately from *domus*, or house/household. Indeed, the word *familia* is derived from *famulus*, or "slave."
7. Tymoigne (2006) has since shown that the functionalist approach is problematic, and that there are essential properties that define money and monetary

systems, essential properties explored by Tymoigne and Wray (2005) and relating to debt, accounting, debt instruments, and their use.
8. I am indebted to John F. Henry for this and the following point.
9. Wergild is a term of Germanic law that can be loosely translated from Old English as "man price" and stems from *were*, or "man" and *geld*, or "payment or fee".
10. It was during this era of unification that the Egyptian language was first recorded in hieroglyphics, and as Graeber (2011) is quick to point out, the first hieroglyphics were debt contracts. This is also true of the first examples of Mesopotamian cuneiform.
11. We must not conflate coinage with money, since money existed before coins (Grierson 1977; Kim 2001).

REFERENCES

Aristotle. 1912. *Politics: A Treatise on Government*. London and Toronto: J. M. Dent & Sons Ltd., book 1, chapter VI. http://www.gutenberg.org/files/6762/6762-h/6762-h.htm.

———. 1999. *Nicomachean Ethics*. Translated by W. D. Ross. Kitchener, Ontario: Batoche Books.

Bell, S. 2001. "The role of the state and the hierarchy of money." *Cambridge Journal of Economics* 25: 149–163.

Berkeley, G. 1735. "The Querist containing several Queries proposed to the consideration of the Public". http://socserv2.socsci.mcmaster.ca/econ/ugcm/3ll3/berkeley/querist.

Cernuschi, H. 1877. *Nomisma or Legal Tender*. New York: D. Appleton and Company.

Clower, R. W. 1969. "Introduction." In Robert W. Clower (ed.), *Monetary Theory*. Harmondsworth: Penguin.

Cook, R. M. 1958. "Speculation on the origins of coinage." *Historia* 7: 257–262.

Crump, T. 1981. *The Phenomenon of Money*. London, Boston, MA, and Henley: Routledge & Kegan Paul.

Curtin, P. 1984. *Cross-Cultural Trade in World History*. Cambridge: Cambridge University Press.

Del Mar, A. 1895. *History of Monetary Systems*. Chicago, IL: Charles H. Kerr & Company.

———. 1900. *The Middle Ages Revisited*. New York: Cambridge Encyclopaedia Company.

Drucker, P. 1986 *The Frontiers of Management: Where Tomorrow's Decisions Are Being Shaped Today*. New York: Truman Talley Books.

Elias, N. 1969. *The Civilizing Process*, vol. 1: The History of Manners. Oxford: Blackwell.

———. 1982. *The Civilizing Process*, vol. 2: State Formation and Civilization. Oxford: Blackwell.

Forstater, M. 2003. "Taxation: A Secret of Colonial Capitalist (So-Called) Primitive Accumulation." Centre for Full Employment and Price Stability, Working Paper No. 25.

Gardiner, G. 2004. "The Primacy of Trade Debts in the Development of Money." In L. R. Wray (ed.), *Credit and State Theories of Money: The Contributions of A. Mitchell Innes*. Cheltenham and Northampton, MA: Edward Elgar, pp. 128–173.

Graeber, D. 2011. *Debt: The First 5,000 Years*. Brooklyn, NY: Melville House Publishing.

Grierson, P. 1977. *The Origins of Money*. London: Athlone Press.

Hart, K. 2005. "Notes towards an anthropology of money." *Kritikos* 2. http://intertheory.org/hart.htm.

Henry, J. F. 2004. "The Social Origins of Money: The Case of Egypt." In R. Wray (ed.), *Credit and State Theories of Money: The Contributions of A. Mitchell Innes*. Cheltenham and Northampton, MA: Edward Elgar, pp. 79–98.

Hudson, M. 2003. "The creditary/monetary debate in historical perspective." In S. Bell and E. Nell (eds.), *The State, the Market and the Euro*. Cheltenham and Northampton, MA: Edward Elgar, pp. 39–76.

Hume, D. 1978. *A Treatise of Human Nature*, 2nd ed. Edited by L. A. Selby-Bigge, revised by P. H. Nidditch. Oxford: Clarendon Press.

Humphrey, C. 1985. "Barter and Economic Disintegration." *Man* 20: 48–72.

Ingham, G. 2004a. "The Emergence of Capitalist Credit Money." In L. R. Wray (ed.), *Credit and State Theories of Money: The Contributions of A. Mitchell Innes*. Cheltenham and Northampton, MA: Edward Elgar, pp. 173–222.

———. 2004b. "The Nature of Money." *Economic Sociology* 5: 18–28.

Jevons, W. S. 1876. *Money and the Mechanism of Exchange*. New York: D. Appleton and Company.

Keynes, J. M. 1930. *A Treatise on Money*. London: Macmillan.

Kim, H. S. 2001. "Archaic coinage as evidence for the use of money." In A. Meadows and K. Shipton (eds.), *Money and Its Uses in the Ancient Greek World*. Oxford: Oxford University Press, pp. 7–23.

Knapp, G. F. 1924. *The State Theory of Money*. London: Macmillan & Company.

Kraay, C. M. 1964. "Hoards, small change and the origin of coinage." *The Journal of Hellenistic Studies* 84: 76–91.

———. 1976. *Archaic and Classical Greek Coins*. New York: Sanford J. Durst.

Kurke, L. 1999. *Coins, Bodies, Games, and Gold: The Politics of Meaning in Archaic Greece*. Princeton, NJ: Princeton University Press.

Law, J. 1740. *Money and Trade Considered: With a Proposal for Supplying the Nation with Money*. Glasgow: R. & A. Foulis.

Lerner, A. P. 1947. "Money as a Creature of the State." *The American Economic Review* 37: 312–317.

MacLeod, H. D. 1893. *The Theory of Credit*. London: Longmans, Green and Co.

Marx, K. 1909. *Capital: A Critique of Political Economy*, volume I: The Process of Capitalist Production. Chicago, IL: Charles H. Kerr and Co.

———. 1973. *Grundrisse der Kritik der Politischen Okonomie*. Harmondsworth: Penguin.

Marx, K., and F. Engels. 2002. *L'idéologie allemande*. Quebec: Bibliothèque Paul-Émile-Boulet de l'Université du Québec à Chicoutimi.

Mehrling, P. 2000. "Modern Money: Fiat or credit?" *Journal of Post Keynesian Economics* 22: 397–406.

Menger, C. 1892. "On the Origins of Money." Translated by C. A. Foley. *Economic Journal* 2: 239–255.

Menger, C. 2007. *Principles of Economics.* Auburn, AL: Ludwig von Mises Institute.

Mill, J. S. 1909. *Principles of Political Economy with Some of Their Applications to Social Philosophy,* 7th ed. London: Longmans, Green and Co.

Mitchell-Innes, A. 1913. "What is Money?" *The Banking Law Journal* 30: 377–408.

———. 1914. "The Credit Theory of Money." *The Banking Law Journal* 31: 151–168.

Nietzsche, F. 1968. *The Will to Power.* London: Weidenfeld and Nicolson.

Noko, J. 2011. "Dollarization: The Case of Zimbabwe." *Cato Journal* 31: 339–365.

Plato. 1892. *The Republic.* Translated by B. Jowett, in *The Dialogues of Plato,* 3rd ed. Oxford: Oxford University Press.

———. 2008. *Protagoras.* http://www.gutenberg.org/files/1591/1591-h/1591-h.htm.

Polanyi, K. 1957. *The Great Transformation.* Boston, MA: Beacon Press.

———. 1966. *Dahomey and the Slave Trade: An Analysis of an Archaic Economy.* Seattle: University of Washington Press.

Samuelson, P. A. 1948. *Economics.* New York: McGraw-Hill.

Selgin, G. A. 1988. *The Theory of Free Banking: Money Supply under Competitive Note Issue.* Lanham, MD: Rowman & Littlefield.

Semenova, A. 2011. "The Origins of Money: Evaluating Chartalist and Metallist Theories in the Context of Ancient Greece and Mesopotamia." Unpublished PhD dissertation, University of Missouri–Kansas City.

Smith, A. 1904. *An Inquiry Into the Nature and Causes of the Wealth of Nations* (Cannan ed.), vol. 1. London: Methuen.

Sombart, W. 2001. *The Jews and Modern Capital.* Kitchener, Ontario: Batoche Books.

Spengler, O. 1926. *The Decline of the West: Form and Actuality.* New York: Alfred A. Knopf.

Trevett, J. 2001. "Coinage and democracy at Athens." In A. Meadows and K. Shipton (eds.), *Money and Its Uses in the Ancient Greek World.* Oxford: Oxford University Press, pp. 23–34.

Trigger, B. G. 1982. *The Rise of Civilization in Egypt.* Cambridge: Cambridge University Press.

Tymoigne, É. 2006. "An Inquiry into the Nature of Money: An Alternative to the Functional Approach." The Levy Institute of Economics, Working Paper No. 481.

Tymoigne, É., and L. R. Wray. 2005. "Money: An Alternative Story." Centre for Full Employment and Price Stability, Working Paper No. 45.

Von Reden, Sitta. 2003 [1995]. *Exchange in Ancient Greece.* London: Gerald Duckworth & Co. Ltd.

Wallerstein, I. 1974. *The Modern World System: Capitalist Agriculture and the Origins of the European World Economy in the Sixteenth Century.* New York, San Francisco, and London: Academic Press.

Weber, M. 1978. *Economy and Society: An Outline of Interpretive Sociology.* Berkeley and Los Angeles: University of California Press.

Wilkinson, D. 1987. "Central Civilisation." *Comparative Civilisations Review* 17: 31–59.

CHAPTER 4

 Luxury and the Sexual Economy of Capitalism

NOAM YURAN

Is there such a thing as "capitalist money"? Is money in capitalism the same kind of thing as in precapitalist economies? Marx and Weber have shown that capitalism is distinguished by new ways of using money: new ways of organizing production according to money-related considerations. But as Keith Hart argues in this volume, the question of what money does is not the same as what it is. In order to inscribe the historical specificity of capitalism on the thing it uses as money, this chapter turns to another genealogy of modern economy, Werner Sombart's *Luxury and Capitalism*. In this often-neglected thesis Sombart traces the origin of capitalism to a deep transformation in relations between the sexes. The secularization of love in the renaissance, he argues, brought on the emergence of a semi-formal class of "concubines" and "courtesans." This new class of women triggered the demand for luxury gifts, and as it spread by imitation to the broader circles of high society, it gave rise to a luxury industry that drove the economy from its traditional stable organization into an emergent capitalist form.

Sombart's thesis can be easily dismissed as a misogynistic expression of fear over the spread of consumerism. Nonetheless, it may deserve a charitable reading because it offers two interrelated possibilities to historicize money: first, through its relation with objects, as apparent in its emphasis on luxury goods, and second, through its entanglement in relations between subjects, its place in a human economy, evident in the role of luxury gifts in concubinage.

First, by exploring capitalism from the perspective of consumption, rather than the more familiar perspective of production, Sombart lays the ground for an understanding of how capitalism is embedded in goods. He turns our attention not only to how goods are produced in capitalism, but also to how they confront subjects in everyday life. Focusing on luxury as a typical capitalist good has two theoretical advantages. Luxury is one way to historicize money, as it demands conceptualizing the relation between money and goods beyond the ahistorical economic paradigm of means-end relation. Indeed, money is used to purchase luxury goods just like any other type. Yet in the case of luxury, money is not reducible to a means of purchasing goods (see Guyer, this volume). It also qualifies goods, since money price renders a good luxurious. Following Thorstein Veblen's concept of "pecuniary canons of taste," the means-ends relation between money and commodities may be inverted in the case of luxury. When "the marks of expensiveness come to be accepted as beautiful features of the expensive articles" (Veblen 2007: 88), luxury goods assume the role of means in relation to money. They are the means to display the possession of money.[1] Identifying luxury with the origin of capitalism has a further advantage, since luxury goods are necessarily entangled with subjective attitudes. The relation to luxury is never neutral. It always invokes a complex fusion of attitudes: fascination, jealousy, righteous contempt. For that reason luxury objects can be seen as a horizon of the subject, mixed with moods, expectations, desires. Luxury goods can be seen as objects that partake in fashioning subjectivity. Viewing luxury commodities as paradigmatic to capitalism allows us to conceive of capitalism as a system that produces subjects in producing objects.

Second, by tracing the origin of the demand for luxury to gifts characteristic of extramarital relations, Sombart opens the way to considering capitalism as a unique form of sexual economy. The renaissance cult of love, he argues, arose through an opposition to the conception of marriage as an economic exchange. The luxury gift that later on became associated with it marks concubinage as a unique economy, organized around the formal exclusion of gender relations from the sphere of exchange. It can be seen as symptomatic of capitalism if we keep in mind that, in contrast to traditional societies, in capitalist societies the possibility that marriage involves an exchange is considered highly obscene. But the fact that it is obscene attests that while formally banished from reality it is still present in substitute practices and economic imagination. This possibility has much to do with capitalist money. A society where marriage is conceived as an exchange, maybe as a purchase of a wife, is obviously utterly different from ours. It goes without saying that its conception of gender relations is different from ours, and maybe even its notions of gender itself. What should be added, though, is that its money and its forms of ownership are different from ours. Money that can be associated with a gender exchange is not the same kind of thing as money that precludes that possibility. Here lies a way to historicize capitalist money in spite of its apparent universality. Capitalist money, I will argue, is unique in that it is not a universal. Its role in capitalism is related to an exception to its universality, epitomized in gender relations. Capitalist money is distinguished in being related, among other things, to what should not be bought.[2]

Sombart's Thesis

Let us quote the last sentence of Sombart's book: "Luxury, then, itself a legitimate child of illicit love, gave rise to capitalism" (1967: 171). He begins his historical narrative with the secularization of love from the eleventh century onward. In the Middle Ages sexual love was subordinated to a religious cosmic order, either through a diversion of love to heavenly goals (Mariology) or through the sacrament of marriage. The minnesingers and troubadours began to separate love from religion and a cult of sensual, earthly love, which he terms "the emancipation of the flesh," arose. He traces this emancipation from the timid attempts of the troubadours, which strike the modern eye as false and stilted, to its maturation in the thirteenth century, which reached a "firm ground of natural sensuality," and culminated in a "refinement which approaches perversion" in eighteenth-century France (1967: 47–48).

This historical transformation opposed free love to marriage. "What free love ... could never become reconciled to was the institutionalization of love by marriage" (ibid.: 48). Sombart demonstrates this antagonism through derision of marriage in Boccaccio and in Montaigne's view of love and marriage as mutually exclusive. "Love loathes anything which deals with other matters and shuns every relation contracted for other reasons, such as marriage, where connections and wealth are at least as important as charm and beauty" (ibid.: 49). This emerging opposition between love and marriage took on some practical forms. Sombart notes how in Petrarch's days it became "good form for a young man to seduce a married woman," and princes ceased to be embarrassed about their illegitimate offspring and began to boast about them. He further notes the large numbers of prostitutes in the big cities at the close of the Middle Ages (ibid.: 51). Most important was the emergence of a new class between respectable women and prostitutes, known by many names: *courtisane*, concubine, *maîtresse*, *grande cocotte*, and more. With these women, Sombart claims, love itself becomes semi-institutionalized. After being first freed from religion, it becomes an "art of love," that "emerges again from the dilettantism of the preceding centuries," with its own female masters "devoting their whole life to its practice" (ibid.: 51).

Sombart then links the emergence of this class to a growth in the demand for luxury goods and in the luxury industry. From economic records he traces an immense increase in expenditure on luxury goods in European courts, from the fifteenth century, and attributes it to the "endless pursuit of love of women" by kings. The most famous example of this is the Versailles palace that Louis XIV built for his mistress, Louise de la Vallière. The desire for luxury spread from the court to the nobility and high society. Sombart recounts in this context the influence that women such as Madame de Pompadour had in shaping the tastes and fashions of society. A contemporary observes that "we live now only by Mme de Pompadour; coaches are à la Pompadour, the color of dresses is à la Pompadour; we eat meat stews à la Pompadour, and in our houses we have mantelpieces, mirrors, tables, sofas, chairs, fans, boxes, and even toothpicks à la Pompadour" (ibid.: 73). From the aristocracy the desire for luxury spread by imitation to the nouveaux riches and parvenus.

Economic history provides a good reason for considering luxury production as the source for capitalism. Capitalism is usually linked to an increase in production, which necessitated or enabled greater investment in labor power and the rational management of labor. This increase may be attributed either to mass production of the same goods or to the production of new types of goods that employ more labor. Given the stable pattern of production and consumption in medieval societies, the rise of luxury may be a cause pushing the economy away from its traditional pattern (ibid.: 118–119). To take one example, the rapid growth in specialized retail trade in London from the early eighteenth century replaced traditional wholesale and retail business. These specialized shops required a greater variety of goods. Their rise was accompanied by a new sensibility for elegant display, testified by contemporary witnesses ("they look more like palaces and their stocks are of exceeding great value") (ibid.: 134). In economic terms, more capital was needed for the establishment and maintenance of such shops. Sombart cites from Daniel Defoe's *The Complete English Tradesman*, a story about a merchant who for two hours presented to a certain lady merchandise worth £3,000 without her buying anything (ibid.: 135). Note how this example connects different orders of social and economic reality: commercial practices that require more capital involve new types of goods, a new phenomenology of commercial space, new types of interactions, and new subjective attitudes. The retail shop displays a wider variety of objects, but it also implies the emergence of the customer as connoisseur.

Here lies a reason to return to Sombart's thesis. By associating capitalism with a specific type of consumer good, it allows us to consider how capitalism is embedded in the objects it produces. To follow through on this possibility, it is useful to read Sombart alongside another genealogy of capitalism, related to the same intellectual circle of the German Historical School of Economics, namely Max Weber's *The Protestant Ethic and the Spirit of Capitalism*.

A Macroeconomics of Morals

At first sight, Sombart's and Weber's genealogies of capitalism appear as mirror images of each other:

- Secularization vs. sacralization. While Sombart focuses on the liberation of love from its religious context, Weber traces the origin of the capitalist spirit to a religious dogma that extended itself into formerly profane matters. The idea of work as a vocation, according to Weber, results from changes in religious dogma characteristic of the reformation, but it also contains the germ of capitalist business for its own sake.
- Hedonism vs. asceticism. While Sombart saw the sensual, obscene pleasures of illicit love as propelling economic change, Weber emphasizes "this-worldly asceticism" in generating capital—religious practice directed toward this world. The combination of work as a vocation with strict avoidance of enjoying the fruits of labor resulted in the initial formation of capital.
- Consumption vs. production. While Sombart attributes the genesis of capitalism to changes in the forms of consumption, Weber focuses on changes in the pattern of production.

However, the fact that Weber and Sombart explore capitalism from two different perspectives, production vs. consumption, suggests that their theories are actually not mutually exclusive. The possibility of combining them may be found in the uniqueness of economics as an exact science of humankind. The fascination in economics with the exact sciences has led to some questionable notions, notably, the neoclassical idea of an unequivocal model for human action. Yet economics is distinguished from other sciences of humankind by the use it can make of the indubitable fact that every purchase is at the same time a sale. This basic economic fact has led macroeconomics to surprisingly rich results (Krugman 1994: xii). To follow this intuition, a perspective on capitalism from the side of consumption must comply with a perspective from production. Weber and Sombart may actually illustrate two parts of the same picture, where what is produced in ascetic devotion is consumed in promiscuous sin. Or from an ascetic production perspective, the consumption of what was produced appears sinful. The concrete significance of this parallel is evident in the attitudes of Weber's and Sombart's typical agents in relation to money.

Weber identifies the spirit of capitalism not just with the desire for riches that characterized also the traditional economy. Rather, his calculating manner distinguishes the capitalist entrepreneur from his predecessors. The capitalist spirit is "an attitude that seeks profit rationally and systematically" (Weber 1992: 27). The mirror image of that spirit lies, for Sombart, in luxury consumption. The nobility, which set the tone for luxury consumption, had an aversion to calculation, according to Sombart: "Money, and all that was associated with money, was looked upon with contempt. To be concerned with money matters, to balance expenses and income, was considered vulgar and left to the care of stewards. . . . The steward receives his instructions. It is then up to him to worry about from where the money is to come. Whether or not the steward pays the merchant is not a gentleman's concern" (1967: 87). These diametrically opposed mentalities—endless rational profit calculation on the side of production, set against aversion to calculation on the side of consumption—drained wealth from the aristocracy to the rising bourgeoisie. A specific type of object, the luxury good, mediates this process, and defines the subject positions of the entrepreneur and the courtier. The luxury consumer is an economic agent who suspends monetary calculation when confronted with goods, while the entrepreneur is a subject who prefers money over goods. His conduct is defined by calculating profit along with abstinence from enjoying the fruits of labor. Both positions are colored by luxury. The suspension of calculation marks consumption as luxury. But in parallel, the entrepreneur is the subject for whom every good is suspected of being a luxury.

The category of luxury is significant in that it allows us to conceive of the economic subject as defined in terms of attitudes toward objects and more importantly by different relations between objects: different relations between the commodity object and the money object. Weber's entrepreneur disavows the enjoyment of goods, whose practical result is the accumulation of money, while Sombart's courtier is infatuated with goods through a suspension of monetary calculations.

Luxury as a Historical Object

The more familiar view of capitalism, which focuses mainly on production, situates it in a relatively defined sphere of human activity. It allows us to consider how goods are made, but is indifferent to the goods themselves. It has less to say regarding the possibility that capitalism involves its own everyday experience of the world of goods. In theoretical terms, this view is lacking when it comes to the question of the historical persistence of capitalism. This weakness is most evident in Weber. Addressing the question of persistence, Weber coined the famous metaphor of the "iron cage," which denotes how the capitalist spirit becomes embedded in economic reality, independently of its religious origins. But we should keep in mind that this is no more than a metaphor and does not come close to the rich social and historical analysis of his account of the emergence of the capitalist spirit. His explanation for persistence consists of one sentence: "This order is now bound to the technical and economic conditions of machine production which to-day determine the lives of all the individuals who are born into this mechanism, not only those directly concerned with economic acquisition, with irresistible force" (1992: 123). Strangely enough, he jumps from being suspicious of materialist accounts of capitalism's emergence straight into the most vulgar type of materialism, suggesting that machines can determine social and human reality by themselves.

A perspective from consumption encourages us to consider how capitalist economy is inscribed in the everyday presence of certain goods and in how they confront people in their everyday lives. It allows us to consider how subjective attitudes are entailed in certain goods. It suggests viewing goods as a horizon for the subject, involving moods, expectations, behavior, aspirations, fantasies. By producing goods, a capitalist organization of production also produces the subjects who carry it through time.

This point is particularly relevant to luxury. It has always troubled the economic mind, and it is hard to define it. Its Latin etymology suggests that luxury is based on some form of excess. One basic definition used by Sombart is that luxury includes more than what is absolutely necessary. Luxury goods are based on refinement, which is "any treatment of a product over and above that which is needed to make it ordinarily useful" (Sombart 1967: 59–60). Turning to Veblen, who made luxury fundamental to his economic theory, we can add a social dimension to the excess that defines luxury. Luxury in Veblen is related to the basic form of ownership, and is grounded on social comparison, or on having more than others (ibid.: 61). Sombart implicitly echoes Veblen's basic idea that luxury involves the gaze of others, something destined to be looked at, when he dwells on its contagious nature, its trickling down from the circles of aristocracy to the bourgeoisie. A more basic feature may lie behind these various forms of excess: the luxury good is an excessive object because it contains something of the subject (as suggested by the popular luxury advertising formula: "you deserve more"). Luxury implies an intense subjective attitude. The everyday usage of the term is never neutral and often implies a complex attitude charged with ambivalent sentiments: contempt alongside jealousy, denunciation alongside desire. As Jane Guyer shows in this volume, in the context of luxury money most explicitly becomes "food for thought." Looking into contemporary advertising she shows how luxury confronts us as a puzzle, as a source of an ethical imperative ("a must-have"), and as a tool for individuation.[3]

That is what renders luxury crucial to a materialist historical account. Because it invokes intense subjective attitudes, luxury is one way in which objects shape subjectivity. So although Sombart, like Weber, emphatically rejected Marxism, his work can be read as a historical-materialist approach. It goes beyond the vulgar sense of materialism, as the idea that material things shape human reality, into a deeper sense: the idea that some aspects of human reality are embedded in objects, confront people in the guise of objects.

Luxury and Sex

Let us proceed one step further with Sombart's thesis. It promises an intriguing connection between economy, sex, and society. We have seen how it presents luxury as mediating new economic goods and practices with consumer subjectivity and with social relations. But Sombart goes further, and attributes luxury not just to social imitation but also to sexuality and to a transformation in gender relations. This is the aspect of his book that is hardest to accept literally. Sombart introduces it in a mechanistic approach to sexuality: "Indubitably the primary cause of the development of any kind of luxury is most often to be sought in consciously or unconsciously operative sex impulses" (1967: 60–61). This goes with attributing the rise of luxury to the growing influence of women—one subchapter is titled, without irony, "The triumph of woman"—and makes it easy to dismiss Sombart's book as a wild fantasy, a misogynistic expression of anxieties over capitalism.[4]

However, approaching the book from the question of historical persistence, rather than that of origins, provides a more plausible reading. The issue is not one of cause but of expression. In attempting to prove that sexual desire motivated the rise of luxury, Sombart demonstrates something else: how the rise of luxury involved new ways of articulating desire and gender relations through goods and money.

Thus, with regard to the new retail stores, discussed above, Sombart notes the emergence of merchants of trinkets and novelties. "These shops," he writes, "became the meeting places for the world of fashion, particularly the gentlemen who came to select presents for their lady-loves," and quotes a contemporary observer, Louis Sebastien Mercier, who claims that these gifts "were presented to respectable women who would not accept cash money" (ibid.: 133). Now, even if we accept these observations as purely factual, they do not affirm Sombart's speculation that luxury originates in sex impulses. Yet, they are no less important if we read them as partly imaginary in that they reveal how commodities and money carry gendered meanings. They do not show that consumption is motivated by sexual impulses, but rather that commodities express sexual meanings—how commodities are eroticized. In this erotic meaning of commodities we see how marriage and extramarital love are related to two different economies. To the extent that it is as an economic arrangement, marriage is conceived in terms of utilitarian calculation. Love acquires an economic aspect through the luxury gift that upsets utilitarian calculation. It upsets calculation in a double sense: first, in the form of the transaction, as a gift that demands no reciprocity, at least not explicitly. It is the upsetting of reciprocity that associates the gift with love in contrast to marriage. Second, calculation is upset by the object itself as a luxury good. The articulation of the economy of love in the gift object highlights the theoretical potential of Sombart's thesis, which shows how goods, in the specific form of luxury goods, may encode intersubjective relations.

This reading of Sombart is both much less and much more than he intended. It is less because it loosens the focus on the origin of capitalism. It is more because it presents capitalism as being entangled with its own gender identities, gender relations, and eroticism. It shifts the focus of attention from the question of history, as process or narrative, to the question of historicity, the state of being in history. In this reading, Sombart's claim makes it possible to conceive of basic economic objects, money and commodities, as being entangled with gender and sexuality. In other words, it promises an outline of the sexual economy characteristic of capitalism.

I will first point to its presence in the early capitalist imagination, and later to its usefulness for understanding contemporary capitalism.

Literary Parallel: Zola

The presence of Sombart's erotic economy in capitalist imagination finds a prominent example in Emile Zola's novel *Ladies Paradise*. The story is set in a department store during the 1860s, which Zola modeled on the real department stores *Bon Marché* and *Louvre*.

Like Sombart's book, Zola's novel combines two ostensibly remote contexts: business and money, on the one hand, and love, sexuality, and desire, on the other. The department store *Au Bonheur des Dames*, founded by the young widower Octave Mouret, demolishes the business of all its neighboring traditional small shops. Any new department it opens foretells the crash of a related shop. The shop owners' bitter attempts to resist invariably result in more catastrophic breakdowns. Behind Mouret's success lies a simple business principle, to increase inventory turnover as much as possible, using a sophisticated commissions system for sales personnel. As Mouret explains to the literary figuration of Baron Haussmann: "You will understand, Baron, that the whole system lies in this. It is very simple, but it had to be found out. We don't have a very large working capital; our sole effort is to get rid of our stock as quickly as possible to replace it by another. . . . In this way we can content ourselves with a very small profit" (Zola 2013: 70). In that way Mouret can turn over his capital four times a year—in contrast to his bitter opponent across the street, the traditional draper Baudu, who believes, "The art was not to sell a large quantity, but to sell dear" (ibid.: 25).

This basic business principle is accompanied by a comprehensively new social experience, which suddenly makes traditional shops appear stale and obsolete. It goes without saying that a part of this is the experience of the crowd, and mostly the feminine crowd. This is but the social counterpart of the department store's business principle. But there is more to it. *Au Bonheur des Dames* radiates with an inexplicable seductive power. Even the hostile shopkeepers cannot take their eyes off its glittering windows, and rich and lustrous displays. Most important, a sense of promiscuity and radiating sexuality surrounds the department store. It is manifested in various ways: the male clerks' flirtatious service to female customers, their liberal leisure habits, the rumors they spread and their conversations about love affairs among themselves and between Mouret and some female workers. Even the experience of the crowd is erotic. Mouret, a notorious womanizer, combines in his business conduct a constant flirtatious courting of high-society women with the implicit misogynistic intention of turning women into the raw material of his department store. "Mouret's unique passion was to conquer woman. He wished her to be queen in his house, and he had built this temple to get her completely at his mercy. His sole aim was to intoxicate her with gallant attentions, and traffic on her desires, work on her fever" (ibid.: 215). And indeed, this passion translates into an erotic "shopping experience." Thus, on the opening day of a grandiose sale:

> The ladies, seized by the current, could not now go back. As streams attract to themselves the fugitive waters of a valley, so it seemed that the wave of customers, flowing into the vestibule, was absorbing the passers-by, drinking in the population from the four corners of Paris. They advanced but slowly, squeezed almost to death, kept upright by the shoulders and bellies around them, of which they felt the close heat; and their satisfied desire enjoyed the painful entrance which incited still further their curiosity. (ibid.: 220)

Compare this fiction, based nonetheless on meticulous research, with Sombart's mixture of historical evidence and fantasy. He cites Johann Wilhelm Archenholz on eighteenth-century England:

> If a chastity committee, such as existed in Vienna, could function in London, it would depopulate this city . . . innumerable food businesses, to which half the population owed their sustenance, even their existence, would be ruined and London would be turned into a desert. If further proof is desired, one only has to ask the owners of the thousands of small shops who their most frequent buyers and best customers are. The profit, which is reaped in one single night by this large class, is brought to the shopkeepers on the following day, because the personal tastes of these unfortunates are quite moderate; in fact, they are inclined to starve in order to spend their entire income in finery. Without them the theatres would be empty. (Sombart 1967: 111)

We can hardly accept as a historical fact that prostitution propelled the whole of London's economy. Yet in the movement between fantasy and reality, a certain truth emerges about the way commercial spaces of emerging capitalism are imbued with sexuality.

To untangle this articulation we turn to the two central narrative lines of Zola's novel. Both narratives involve business, love and sexuality, but they take place on the opposite sides of the street, representing the old and the new economy: Mouret's and Denise's love affair developing in the department store, and Colomban's engagement with Genevieve, the daughter of Baudu, in the traditional shop.

In the main narrative, Denise, Baudu's orphan niece, starts working in *Au Bonheur des Dames* due to the economic hardship of her uncle's shop. Mouret gradually falls in love with her, but the obstacle to the fulfillment his love has to do with business. He is afraid that breaking his reputation as a womanizer would destroy his business. He is sure that his promiscuous reputation is one of the secrets of his store's success. In order to keep feeding his giant machine with a stream of deluded women, he must keep fooling them in his intimate life. It gradually dawns on him that Denise's decency will not let her surrender unless he proposes to marry her. But this raises a further obstacle. Denise is indeed secretly in love with him too, yet the rumors concerning Mouret's special relation to her—promoting her and seeking her advice on every matter—force her to stop working at the store.

At the plot's denouement, Mouret invites Denise to his office, in a last attempt to convince her to stay. A million francs intake from the big sale—the biggest intake he has reached—is lying on the table, but Mouret has lost all interest in money. He asks Denise to marry him, and although she is at first reluctant, she eventually confesses that she loved him all along, and throws herself on his neck. The million francs on the table between them effectuate the strange presence of money in relation to love in this story. It is not precisely that love has nothing to do with money. Rather, Mouret's disinterest in money is the evidence of true love. Love is still characterized in monetary terms, just not in terms of exchange. Love is what money cannot buy. Thus a final obstacle has to be overcome, and it is solved in the most artificial way. The last sentence of the novel reads: "He did not quit Denise, but clasped her in a desperate embrace, telling her that she could now go, that she could spend a month at Valognes, which would silence everybody, and that he would then go and fetch her himself, and bring her back, all-powerful, and his wedded wife" (Zola 2013: 391–392). The artificial one-month break before the wedding is necessary in order to cleanse love of any sign of an exchange. Marriage alone would not achieve this. It would imply the possibility that Denise succeeded in a strategy aimed at winning the big prize: wedding rather than a passing romance. The artificial nature of this solution underscores the unresolvable tension on which the novel is grounded. As opposed to the seducing world of money and luxury goods, love cannot be fully separated from it.

The secondary narrative echoes the central plot in a reversed form. Colomban, the clerk at Baudu's dying shop, is engaged to be married to Baudu's daughter, Genevieve, and in marrying her he will inherit the business, just as Baudu himself inherited it from his own father-in-law.

But the long-planned wedding is postponed because of the shop's deteriorating state. Baudu, who wants to deliver the business to his son-in-law in good shape, keeps hoping that it will recover. Throughout its inevitable collapse we learn that Colomban is secretly in love with Clara, one of the most hedonistic sales girls in the department store. Genevieve suspects this is so, and she falls ill in parallel to her father's demise. On her deathbed Colomban finally abandons Baudu's house, after having spent several nights with Clara.

These two plot lines enact Sombart's basic distinctions in narrative form. The department store, with its rational use of capital, is aided by the dazzling display of luxury associated with love and promiscuity. And across the street, Baudu's shop, "The Old Elbeuf," which takes pride in its traditional commercial practices and products, is where marriage is inseparably entangled with economic arrangements.

Sexual Economy

Zola's novel sheds light on Sombart's association of luxury, illicit love, and capitalism. When the opposition between love and marriage becomes institutionalized—when love, to use Sombart's terminology, is not simply free love, but becomes an "art of love," with its own female masters, "devoting their whole life to its practice"—then love and marriage come to mark two contrasting economies. Marriage is marked by one where ownership and household considerations are integrated with contractual gender relations, represented in Zola by Baudu's and Colomban's marriage arrangement and inheritance of the business. Love, insofar as there is an economy proper to it, is marked by the double disruption of the calculating, pragmatic marriage economy by luxury consumption and luxury gifts.

Zola's novel, however, provides an important supplement to Sombart's thesis. The Ladies Paradise, the locus of luxury economy in the novel, is characterized by both pure love and promiscuity. This strange duality provides a way to reformulate Sombart's thesis as a basic matrix of the sexual economy of capitalism. Bluntly, the basic principle of capitalism's sexual economy is that the purchase of a woman has become traumatic. In The Old Elbeuf, the locus of traditional economy in the novel, such exchanges are respectable: it is perfectly natural for Colomban to exchange lifelong service for a wife and a shop. There is nothing promiscuous in this exchange. It is simply a traditional form of marital economy. What it lacks is love. Across the street, in the department store, love designates a different economy. The various forms of direct involvement of sexuality and commerce are suspected as a form of prostitution, and accordingly love has to be purged from the suspicion of exchange. In this sense, the purchase of a woman can be seen as a traumatic principle, organizing the sexual economy involved with new commercial practices. It is banished from reality in its direct form, but in its absence it keeps exerting influence on practices involving gender and economy. Its contours are visible in their split to love and promiscuity.

To point at the relevance of this sexual economy for contemporary capitalism, we can turn to some examples from the sociology and anthropology of money. Keith Hart recounts a story of a young man from Ghana who spent a night with a foreign Western student. The morning after, as a token of gratitude, he left a small gift on her dressing table, a money note. Her response, of course, was outrage over the insinuation that the intercourse was a sort of prostitution (Hart 2005: 165). This anecdote reflects more than cultural differences in relation to money. It can be read as reflecting different measures of penetration of the capitalist logic into everyday reality. For the Ghanaian, a money note is obviously equivalent to any other object he could have given as a gift—a flower, a book, or a jewel. But this means that his everyday interactions are not yet colored by the function of money in capitalism. In capitalism money is indeed a unique object, distinguished from goods. We usually understand this uniqueness in terms of production. Following Marx, we tend to see capitalism as an economy where goods are produced primarily according to monetary considerations. The incident Hart recounts suggests that the unique status of money informs also consumption and interpersonal relations. For the young woman in the story, money is a unique object, sharply distinguished from all other objects, even in the most intimate interpersonal context. The incident thus demonstrates an erotic underside of the uniqueness of money in capitalism. Capitalist production is defined by a certain relation between money and things. However, in the context of consumption, a mirror image of this relation between money and things outlines an erotic map, where anything but money can be given by a man to a woman. This is basically how money and goods are eroticized in capitalism. In some contexts, an object is an obscene substitute for money.

Viviana Zelizer (1997) makes a similar observation in *The Social Meaning of Money*, where she notes that when money gifts first became acceptable in the United States at the beginning of the twentieth century, they were disapproved in one context: a young unmarried man could not give a money gift to an unmarried woman. For Zelizer this prohibition exemplifies how culture resists the flattening, homogenizing effects of money (ibid.: 71–118). Against the background of Sombart, its meaning may be the complete opposite: it shows how capitalist logic penetrates interpersonal relations. The prohibition of an unmarried man giving money to an unmarried woman is not necessarily a social norm set against economic practice, but can be seen as an economic principle informing gender relations. The consequences of this distinction for sociological and anthropological studies of money may be considerable.

Zelizer's work has set a major paradigm for the sociological study of money, informed by an opposition to its conception in orthodox economics. According to this paradigm, the economic concept of money as an impersonal means of rational calculation is inherently blind to the complex involvement of money in social life. Focusing on social contexts that from a mainstream economic perspective would appear marginal—gifts, household management—Zelizer shows how everyday practices extract money from its homogeneity and inscribe social differences and meanings on it. The drawback of this approach, however, is that it poses sociological knowledge of money as noneconomic. What escapes it is the possibility that the idea of money as homogenizing, neutral means is wrong already as an economic idea—that it fails to account for the unique economy of capitalism. Indeed, outside the narrow scope of orthodox economics, money is not conceptualized as neutral, homogenizing means. In Marx, money, in its form as capital, is not just means, but means that have become ends. As money that begets money, it cannot be subsumed within the framework of homogeneity either. Sombart's emphasis on luxury supplements this view of money in the realm of consumption.[5]

Obscenity and History

We tend to say that in capitalism everything is up for sale. Commoditization makes this idea indispensable. But it only highlights the peculiarity that, when it comes to marriage, capitalist societies are actually the historical exception. In precapitalist societies marriage settlements often have an explicit economic meaning. Sometimes they involve the purchase of a wife. Elsewhere they are framed by the wide context of household economy. Capitalist societies abhor the idea of marriage as an economic settlement.

The rise of liberal civil societies together with capitalism would probably be our immediate explanation for this peculiarity. However, it would be too quick to see liberal civil society simply as a counterweight to the commodifying pressures of capitalist economy. The exclusion of gender relations from exchange also had an economic meaning for capitalism. This is evident from the fact that gender exchange was not simply banished from reality but retroactively acquired an obscene meaning. Patriarchal as it obviously was, the conception of marriage as exchange was not obscene before capitalism. Its obscenity is the key to how it keeps informing capitalist economy through substitute practices and objects and the imaginings that surround them. That is how it becomes the secret key to the eroticization of the economy.

But that is the correct reading of the idea that in capitalism everything is up for sale. This idea is so powerful not because it suggests that money in capitalism makes everything commensurate. It is rather in precapitalist economies that money makes things commensurate. In such economies everything is up for sale in the simple literal sense: everything within the confines of economy is up for sale, and money makes everything within these confines commensurate. Capitalism is distinguished as an economy where things that should not be sold and bought are nonetheless suspected as involving an exchange. A common critique attributes the moral problems of capitalism to the expanding scope of things included within the realm of economy. But the idea that in capitalism everything is up for sale actually refers to a topology unique to capitalism. It points to a certain margin of the world of commodities, to things of ambivalent status, things that should not be for sale yet nonetheless motivate economic activity. The exclusion of gender relations from the sphere of exchange is the most explicit manifestation of these margins.

This topology also marks capitalism as an economy grounded in desire. The familiar idea that money makes all things commensurable actually runs in contrast to our most basic intuitions on desire. We are accustomed to think of an object of desire as consisting of a surplus that makes it incommensurable with other things. It is because in capitalism gender relations are excluded from exchange that it can be seen as an economy managing desires, rather than needs. That is the reason for the ubiquitous use of images of women in advertising. Commodities are eroticized by being associated with the ultimate representation of what cannot be bought.

Precapitalist economies can more easily be seen as social systems managing the customary lifestyles of various classes. In capitalism such a notion becomes impossible: the very idea of a "customary lifestyle" makes no sense.

A Parallel in Weber

Our reading of Sombart has taken us far from common conceptions of capitalism that emphasize production for profit. Yet this view of capitalism from the perspective of consumption points to one more parallel between Weber and Sombart. Weber also links the rise of capitalism to the emergence of something that cannot be bought, namely salvation.

The ingenious core of Weber's thesis, which survived the objections of historians, is the link between the doctrine of predestination and the capitalist spirit. A naïve set of mind might imagine that predestination should result in nihilism: if people's deeds are not relevant for their destiny in the afterlife, why should they not indulge in the pleasures of this world? Weber's ingenuity lay in pointing out the opposite effect: predestination led to harsher forms of devotion, and when this devotion was expressed in worldly activity, it resulted in the ascetic work ethic of the capitalist spirit, in an unconditional devotion to work.

As with consumption, the historical transformation associating predestination with a new work ethic results from a banished economic transaction. The immediate occasion for the protestant reformation, we should recall, was the systematic selling of indulgences by the Catholic Church. Thus Weber's narrative may be read as showing how the banishment of a certain transaction retroactively renders it traumatic: its banishment restructures the field from which it is banished. When salvation is no longer sold, it does not disappear from economic life, but propels it in a different way, which is more intense precisely because it can no longer simply be bought. Salvation cannot be bought, but in some conditions wealth may be a sign for it: "the attainment of [wealth] as a fruit of labour in a calling was a sign of God's blessing" (Weber 1992 [1967]: 116). Taken together, Sombart and Weber outline what is historically unique about capitalism: it is an economy organized around what cannot be bought.

Noam Yuran is a research fellow at the Edmond J. Safra Center for Ethics and at the Minerva Humanities Center at Tel Aviv University. He specializes in political economy and economic philosophy. His latest book is *What Money Wants: An Economy of Desire* (2014).

NOTES

1. Marx also problematizes the relation between money and commodities. For him, money is not simply external to the world of commodities, as implied by the orthodox means-ends distinction. Rather, money is a commodity abstracted from use value. Thus in the *Grundrisse* Marx writes that "the exchange value of the commodity is its immanent money-property; this separates itself from it in the form of money, and achieves a general social existence separated from all particular commodities and their natural mode of existence" (1973: 147).
2. The study of media and technology provide a way to pose the question "what is X" in relation to artifacts. Both McLuhan and Heidegger show that the question is meaningful insofar as differentiated from its instrumental equivalent "what do people do with X." As regards the latter we usually have ready-made yet trivial answers. The question becomes meaningful when we can distinguish between "what people do with X" (mobile phone, car, television or money) and "what X has done to human beings." As regards money, which we should keep in mind is a medium and a technology, there is an easy way to go beyond the instrumental perspective. When inquiring what is capitalist money we can approach it from the reverse perspective. Instead of asking what people do with money we can start from the opposite question: what people do not do with money?
3. Strangely enough, these various aspects of luxury were explicitly explored at a significant moment in early economic thought, only to be abandoned with its celebrated beginning in Adam Smith. Luxury occupies a fundamental place in Bernard Mandeville's *The Fable of the Bees*. It is conceived, paradoxically, as both an excess over economic essentials and as the very substance of economic life. The prosperous beehive in this fable is inflicted with all kinds of vices, but as these are miraculously abolished, its economy quickly disintegrates. The inhabitants learn in retrospect that "Envy itself, and Vanity / Were Ministers of Industry; / Their darling Folly, Fickleness, / In Diet, Furniture and Dress, / That strange ridic'lous Vice, was made / The very Wheel that turn'd the Trade" (Mandeville 1988: 25). As the reference to envy attests, luxury in Mandeville is intersubjective, and involved with the thick fabric of social life. But when Smith reformulated the idea that self-love contributes to economic prosperity, he recoils from vices such as envy. What we find instead in his idea of "invisible hand" is an individual who "intends only his own gain," who thereby promotes the wealth of the community (Smith 2007: 351–352). Envy could not be included within this framework, simply because it is not egoistic enough. It involves a too intimate experience of others in one's self-perception. In this shift from Mandeville to Smith we can already find an origin of the rift between economy and society, of the blindness of economics to the social.
4. Warren G. Breckman (1991), for example, reads it as part of a long tradition of fears over the effeminizing effects of luxury consumption in Germany.

5. Luxury's primary status in capitalism finds affirmation in the contemporary consumer economy, dominated by brand names. Brands are akin to luxury in that they are more costly than mere products, and are often associated with notions of social prestige. A contemporary paradox is that in most categories of goods consumers have no choice but to buy branded items. In this sense, all consumer goods are now in the form of luxury. A brilliant commercial expresses this paradoxical situation for something branded "Second Cheapest Wine." The tone and imagery of this parody perfectly mimic real commercials. We see a man ordering wine on a date, a woman arriving at a party with a bottle of wine etc. But the name of the wine discloses the economic principle that must be suppressed to take effect: to take part in the social world we must buy, at least, the "Second Cheapest Wine." A minimal form of waste, the cheapest form of luxury, is an entry ticket to society.

REFERENCES

Breckman, W. G. 1991. "Disciplining Consumption: The Debate about Luxury in Wilhelmine Germany, 1890–1914." *Journal of Social History* 24(3): 485–505.

Hart, K. 2005. "Money: One Anthropologist's View." In J. Carrier (ed.), *Handbook of Economic Anthropology*. Cornwall: Edward Elgar.

Ingham, G. 2000. "'Babylonian Madness': On the Historical and Sociological Origins of Money." In J. Smithin (ed.), *What is Money?* London and New York: Routledge.

Krugman, P. 1994. *Peddling Prosperity: Economic Sense and Nonsense in the Age of Diminished Expectations*. New York: W.W. Norton.

Mandeville, B. 1988. *The Fable of the Bees, or, Private Vices, Publick Benefits*. With a Commentary Critical, Historical, and Explanatory by F. B. Kaye. Indianapolis, IN: Liberty Fund.

Marx, K. 1973. *Grundrisse*. New York: Vintage Books.

Smith, A. 2007. *An Inquiry into the Nature and Causes of the Wealth of Nations*. New York: Cosimo.

Sombart, W. 1967. *Luxury and Capitalism*. Ann Arbor: University of Michigan Press.

Veblen, T. 2007. *The Theory of the Leisure Class: An Economic Study of Institutions*. Oxford: Oxford University Press.

Weber, M. 1992. *The Protestant Ethic and the Spirit of Capitalism*. London and New York: Routledge.

Zelizer, V. 1997. *The Social Meaning of Money*. Princeton, NJ: Princeton University Press.

Zola, E. 2013. *The Ladies Paradise*. London: Sovereign Classics.

Part III
The Evolution of Money Today

CHAPTER 5

 The Future of Money is Shaped by the Family Practices of the Global South

SUPRIYA SINGH

Many of the exciting changes affecting how we experience money today originate in the global South. Conversations addressing two-fifths of the world's people who are unbanked—and more women than men are excluded—are South-South conversations. When central bank governors from the global South meet, they want to know how they can adopt for their own countries the successes across cultures elsewhere in Africa, Asia, the Pacific and Latin America. Kenya's M-PESA has become the point of reference for mobile money. Mexico's Oportunidades and Brazil's Bolsa Familia (Ballard 2012) and its banking initiatives offer templates for direct cash transfers attempted in India and the Philippines. And many in the global South are watching how India's unique identification system, Aadhar, will help the unbanked.

The future of money is being shaped by the growing economic and political influence of the global South. In this vision of money's future, personal and market dimensions of globalization and money are intertwined. The unbanked and especially women are a major part of this story. The picture that emerges when seen from this perspective differs markedly from one that looks at globalization primarily in terms of interconnected markets, where electronic information about money whizzes instantaneously around the globe.

The global South is trying to bring financial services to the poor and the unbanked through new methods of payment and banking (Maurer, this volume). These include microfinance in Bangladesh, and mobile money in Kenya. In India, KGFS (Kshetriya Gramin Financial Services) is experimenting with new ways of branch banking, with the rural customer's wealth management at the center. These initiatives have met with setbacks and have had to be modified many times. The challenge is for new forms to be sustainable and scalable, while addressing the needs of poor women and men that have hitherto not been served by banks. Payment innovations like M-PESA go beyond what is being attempted in the global North. In the case of KGFS, the end result parallels digital aggregator initiatives such as Simple in the United States, but via local branches rather than online.

As the economies of the global South grow and people move, "mainstream" approaches to money and the family are shifting. At present, economic policy, banking practices, and theories of money management and control in the United States, United Kingdom, and Australia are based on the Anglo-American pattern of money management by the neo-local nuclear family. Money flows one way, from grandparents to grandchildren and parents to children. In many parts of Asia, Africa, and Latin America, however, money is often shared within varied patrilineal, matrilineal, or bilateral versions of the extended family. Money is the medium of relationships and gifts. It flows two-ways across generations. The idea of money as an impersonal quantity opposed in principle to giving, sharing, and caring is becoming blurred. Money has always been both personal and impersonal (Hart 2007), but with the global South moving to the center, this will become more obvious. Family practices in the global South combined with migration generated $436 billion[1] in remittances to developing countries in 2014. This interplay between the local and global, family practices and remittance infrastructure illuminates the social dimensions of the human economy (Introduction, this volume).

The new information and communication technologies (ICTs) are central to addressing financial exclusion and improving the efficiency and reducing the costs of international remittances. The new ICTs affect the reality of how we pay, save, borrow, transfer, and give money in our everyday lives; how we use money as a medium of relationships, often in multigenerational transnational families and kin groups; and how money changes character when it crosses borders as remittances (Pedersen, this volume).

Money will remain intensely personal while becoming more mobile and virtual. Multiple channels and forms of money, and at times multiple currencies, will continue to be used as vehicles for cultural meanings and activities. It will require different ways of calculating gifts, relations within and across borders, and purchases in interconnected markets. The challenge is to get money's gender right.

This chapter draws primarily on my multidisciplinary research bringing together anthropology, sociology, history, media, and user-centered design in studying money, banking, migration, and the family in India, Southeast Asia, Australia, and recently in the Pacific. In moving from the micro to the macro, I use the "sociological imagination" (Mills 1959) to link issues such as globalization and money, financial inclusion, migration, and remittances to family norms and practices, money as a gift, and my experience as a woman and a migrant twice over—first from India to Malaysia and then to Australia. I focus on money and family practices that are seen as being mainstream in different societies, in that they are embedded in law, in how a country collects data on household, family, and migration, and the design of economic policy. Beneath the attempt to analyze global aspects of money lies the immense complexity and diversity of family and household structures, banking, and the characteristics of money within individual societies and cultures in South and North alike. I try to reignite anthropology's "comparative endeavor (Guyer 1999: 233) to make visible global patterns amid the cultural distinctiveness of money, the family, and use of technologies.

In what follows I will focus on three issues that are central to conversations about money and its future in the global South: the unbanked and money's gender; empowering poor women and men through new ways of making payments and banking; and money as a medium of relationships within the family and across borders.

The Unbanked and Money's Gender

Irene, 30, in a remote village in the Morobe province of Papua New Guinea, is one of the 1.1 billion women who are unbanked. There is no bank or microfinance institution in her village. When she has 100 kina to spare for the journey to Lae, six hours away, she says she will open a mobile bank account. But for the present, she hides the money she saves in the walls of her pandanus hut or in a hole in the ground. She is saving to educate her four boys. She cannot save much for she controls the small amounts of money she makes by growing and selling taro, fruit, and greens every two weeks in the market. The main income of the household, about $500 a year, comes from betel nut. But as it is grown on her husband's land, he controls that money. Her father and brothers help her when they can.

Irene lives in the East Asia and Pacific (EAP) Region, which has one of the smallest gender gaps in financial inclusion among the developing countries (Demirguc-Kunt et al. 2015). In Irene's case, it means that both the men and women in her village have no bank accounts.

The central story of globalization and money in the global South is that 38 percent of the world is unbanked. Poor men and women living in rural and remote areas are more likely to be without secure ways to pay, save, borrow, or insure their goods and their future. Even in the high-income countries in the West, the underbanked are coming into more open view; the United States for example recognizes that more than a quarter (28 percent) of its population is ill-served by formal financial providers (Burhouse et al. 2014). In the European Union, more than a third of the population (35 percent) in 2010 did not have a credit card, overdraft facility, or outstanding loan (European Commission 2010).

The Cultural and Institutional Context of Exclusion

Having a bank account or access to credit is in itself not a recipe for financial inclusion and empowerment. Women's financial exclusion translates as lower access to and control over money within the household and marketplace. This economic inequality has its roots in women being valued less than men in many societies. This rings a personal bell for me, as I heard my mother tell of her childhood during the 1910s–1920s in a middle-income family in Rawalpindi in undivided India. She was a girl and always ate last. She was not only given less to eat compared to her brothers, but she was educated less. It is a story that changed for my mother because of the upheaval of gender norms that accompanied the Partition of India in 1947 (Singh 2013). However, it continues in many parts of India. In 2010, the female to male death rate for children aged 1–4 was 1.55. Of the adults, aged 24 years and above, 27 percent of women had a secondary education compared to 50 percent of men (Drèze and Sen 2013).

We must identify and address the factors contributing to women's greater financial exclusion. These include the gender of money, women's unequal pay for the same work, legislative barriers to women owning property, and men's control over money management. Women also have lower access to the new information and communication technologies. Banks historically have not seen women as important customers.

The design of financial accounts also has to be customer-centered. These accounts should better serve the poor's need for flexible savings, credit, and insurance. In India, providers' focus on ticking regulatory boxes in the last few years led to about 80 percent of new bank accounts lying dormant (Keshri 2014). Granting more access to credit without considering ability to repay can lead to women feeling more anxious. The example of Chile is instructive since easy access to unsustainable credit worsened women's well-being there, instead of lending more dignity to a life with choices (Han 2012).

An important characteristic of money's gender is that women across cultures and generations spend more of their money on the household and children than men do (Zelizer 2011b). Though most women deal with money in their everyday lives, they are socialized to feel more comfortable with money in the domestic context (Papanek and Schwede 1988; Rabow et al. 1992; Wolf 1993; Singh 1997). Women's work at home and in the marketplace is valued less than men's work. At home, women's work is seen in terms of caring and a gift. It is not measured or valued in the marketplace and so does not count (Waring 1988). Women continue to get paid less for the same work as men. Occupations dominated by women often attract lower rates of pay (Boserup 1970; Reskin and Roos 1990). Women are often in the worst-paid and most informal occupations generated by economic globalization. This means that they have less wealth than men. In the United States, nearly one in three single women has no wealth or has more debt than assets. Single women own 36 cents for every dollar owned by single men (Chang 2010).

Women seldom own land in the patrilineal societies in South Asia and East Africa. Weakening the legislative barriers to women's ownership of property in some Latin American countries, Vietnam, and Ethiopia has had a positive influence on women's land rights (Kabeer 2012). However, in other parts of Asia and Africa, men can still prevent women from exercising control over property (Agarwal 1994; McAuslan 2010). Women in India and sometimes overseas choose to keep up their relationship with a brother rather than an uncertain hold on ancestral land to which they are entitled (Kishwar 2005; Basu 2005a, 2005b; Misra and Thukral 2005; Singh, Cabraal, and Robertson 2010).

The gender gap in financial inclusion also connects with male control of larger sources of household finance in the global South. In Kenya, among the Kikuyu, men and women control separate but unequal sources of money (Johnson 2004, 2012). I found the same pattern of separate and unequal gendered finances in Morobe, a southern province in Papua New Guinea (Singh and Nadarajah 2011). In India, where only 43 percent of women have bank accounts, money in most patrilineal joint families is controlled by men. Unlike in the West, male control is prevalent among middle, lower-middle, and "struggling" households, particularly in nonmetropolitan Delhi and in the small town that we studied (Singh and Bhandari 2012).

Women lack resources, so that banks do not see them as important customers. This is true of many of the patriarchal societies of the global South, just as it was in Britain and Australia in the nineteenth century. Until 1870, a married woman in the United Kingdom did not have the right to hold property in her own name or to open a bank account without her husband's authority. Australia followed the British pattern in terms of women's property and banking rights. Women in Australia in the 1960s were routinely asked to have their husband or a male guarantor sign for a loan, even when they were the sole earner (Summers 1994; Singh 1994). Even in the early 1990s, I heard women tell how they had to get their loan application guaranteed by a husband or brother, even though they were earning more of the income that justified the loan. At the same time, it was usual for banks to ask women to guarantee debts by the men in their family, even when the women did not personally gain from the loan. This was so widespread in the 1990s that it was termed "sexually transmitted debt" (Lawton 1991).

Women's lower rates of mobile phone ownership affect their access to new ways of making payments and banking. An Indian woman is 14 percent less likely than a man to own a mobile phone. This gender gap mimics banking and is the highest in South Asia at 38 percent (GSMA Connected Women 2015). In Uganda and Papua New Guinea, women often acquire the second handset in the household. But in Egypt and India, the woman is third in line, after her sons, brothers, or brothers-in-law (GSMA 2012).

The pattern has changed in Kenya, the Philippines, and Thailand, for women and men own mobile phones equally there (Gillwald et al. 2010; Samarajiva 2011; Zainudeen and Ratnadiwakara 2011). A 2012 survey in Kenya showed no gender difference in mobile phone usage at the base of the pyramid (BOP), except for mobile Internet usage. This is partly because women in these countries control at least part of the money in the household. The Kenyan government's removal of value-added tax (VAT) in 2009 reduced the cost of acquiring a mobile phone. So women, even with their lesser resources, can now afford a phone. Gender equality in ownership of a mobile phone comes despite mobile services costing more than a fourth (27 percent) of monthly income in Kenya (Crandall et al. 2012).

The barriers against women's financial inclusion as equals are daunting. However, an effectively designed account with a financial institution is a necessary condition for addressing gendered disadvantage. If women, who are often the main caregivers in their families, do not have their own account, they find it difficult to save formally, insure, or to receive money from family abroad and government payments (Saiag, this volume). It also prevents a woman from asking for or receiving credit. Female-owned microbusinesses in Vietnam for instance have less access to credit compared with male-owned microbusinesses (MCG Management Consulting 2013). Ensuring women's financial empowerment would also increase the well-being of children. Macro- and micro-level evidence shows that "resources in women's hands have a range of positive outcomes for human capital and capabilities within the household" (Kabeer 2012: 4).

Empowering Poor Men and Women

Measurement of financial inclusion is essential if policy is to be based on evidence. But the movement for financial inclusion is driven by passion too, since it offers men and women the freedom and capacity to choose the kind of life they want to live. Amartya Sen, in *Development as Freedom* (1999), argues that this freedom is an essential aspect of development, as well as a means to development. There is a deep complementarity between individual agency and social progress. His focus is on the "capabilities of people to do things—and the freedom to lead lives—that they have reason to value" (ibid.: 85).

Some of the most innovative approaches to empowering poor men and women have come from the global South. Many of these are a response to banks' historical disinterest in the poor as clients. Traditionally the poor were thought to have too little money to enter financial life and were unprofitable and undesirable.

Daryl Collins et al. (2009) focused empirically on how the poor in South Africa, India, and Bangladesh actively manage their small, uncertain and irregular flows of money to connects them to their family, kin, and neighborhood. For example, meet Nomsa, 77 years old, in the village of Lugangeni in South Africa. She lives with her four grandchildren. Nomsa has a monthly income of $120. She has kept up the repayments for loans to help rebuild her traditional round hut and to pay for her daughter's funeral. She saves $40 every month—$9 in a savings club with other women in the neighborhood, and $31 in a RoSCA, a rotating savings and credit association, where three close friends are members (ibid.).

Collins et al. argue that the poor have three key needs when it comes to organizing their money. The first is help in "managing their money on a day to day basis." Second, they need help to "build savings over the long term," and third help to "borrow for all uses" (ibid.: 178).

Mobile Money: New Ways of Making Payments

M-PESA is the world's most successful mobile money—that is, money deposited, transferred, and paid via mobile phones. M-PESA was launched in December 2007 by Safaricom, the dominant mobile network operator (MNO) in Kenya. The success of M-PESA has led to the spread of mobile money in sub-Saharan Africa, is increasing access to financial services. In 2014, 12 percent of adults in sub-Saharan Africa had a mobile money account, compared to 2 percent worldwide (Demirguc-Kunt et al. 2015). The role of mobile money in financial inclusion and payments will increase as regulators and providers begin to address the challenges of competitiveness, regional interoperability, and a clearer route to international remittances.

Mobile money works with or without a bank account. Half the people in sub-Saharan Africa use it without one through cash-in and cash-out agents. A person pays cash to a mobile money agent. This cash is deposited in the sender's mobile money account who can then send money to the mobile number of the recipient. It is instantaneous. The recipient receives the cash from a cash-out agent or can use it as e-money.

Mobile money has become a new kind of money. It is immediate, interpersonal money that strengthens relationships. It is embedded in the reciprocity of giving and receiving among a wide range of family and nonfamily relationships. It is a kind of money that blurs the distinction between the medium of communication and the communication itself. In Kenya, it is a verb, "to M-PESA" money. The activity of sending and receiving money, the meanings of that communication, and the channel of money is M-PESA money.

Though some of the mobile money transmitted remains electronic, the larger part as yet is delivered and taken out in cash. The immediacy of the transfer or payment is empowering and strengthens relationships. M-PESA, like other variants of mobile money, is a different kind of money gift for it separates presence and giving. Before M-PESA, you needed to attend a ceremony to be able to give, so that you could mark the relationship. Now the M-PESA number is given on invitation cards. You are expected to contribute, even if you cannot attend. So failing to give, rather than to attend, discontinues the relationship. This separation of giving and attending can be sometimes exploitative.

In the euphoria of this huge breakthrough, it is easy to overlook problems with M-PESA in particular and mobile money in general that still lurk below the radar. Maurer (2012) directs our attention to a move to privately owned networks from payment networks like the Automated

Clearing House (ACH) that aimed to serve the public good. Payment by cash or check through the ACH are free. No fee deducted. But with new payments such as cards and mobile money, the network owners overlay charges on a free public infrastructure. Now customers pay for services that used to be free.

New Ways of Banking

The global South has had to invent new ways of banking like microfinance and KGFS, because banks preferred to lend money to people who already had some rather to those who had little or none.[2] The challenge in banking the poor is to focus on the social aim of financial empowerment, while keeping to a sustainable business model that is scalable. The difference often lies in what is seen as an acceptable level of profit.

These new ways of banking have to be customer-centered, providing accessible savings mechanisms for small amounts of money and flexible credit. Services must be designed iteratively for daily management and control of money in the household and family within a specific cultural context. Technology often plays an important part in making the service efficient, but it usually operates behind the face-to-face transaction.

Microfinance, like many other banking innovations in North and South, specializes in products and services designed to facilitate management and control of money within the household and family. Microcredit programs are seen as being friendly to women, enabling the borrowing and saving of small amounts of money in a given cultural context. They replicate to some extent the social interactions and relationships that bind Rotating Savings and Credit Associations (RoSCAs).

Grameen Bank, the leading microfinance innovator in Bangladesh, achieved some of these aims when it began to lend to the poor, particularly poor women, to help them set up a microenterprise. When Muhammad Yunus tells the story of the Grameen Bank's success, it is inspirational. The stories most often told are of women who bettered the fortunes of their household through borrowing and were empowered as a result.

Microfinance has spread widely. At the same time, anthropological studies have challenged this "public transcript" of microfinance, by showing that the majority of women handed over loans to their husbands to control. Male violence against women increased. Women who had borrowed from Grameen said the loans allowed to negotiate greater management and control over some parts of household finances (Johnson 2004). Participation in microfinance groups in West Bengal has also shown that it led to women's increased agency and social capital (Sanyal 2009).

Microfinance is going through different stages of redesign. Grameen Bank, like other microfinance institutions (MFIs), is remaking itself. The second version of microfinance concentrates on providing broad banking services, including savings (Saiag 2015). Its loans are more flexible responding to using credit as a way of evening out cash flows and responding to emergencies. The program is positioning itself to provide comprehensive money-management services to poor households (Collins et al. 2009).

The microfinance model's rapid growth, when accompanied by unregulated competition for business, led to a nightmare scenario in 2011 in Andhra Pradesh, India. It was alleged that farmers indebted to multiple MFIs committed suicide. In India this has led to increased regulation of MFIs through capping interest rates and a national licensing system (2013). Regulators are looking for ways to build on the strengths of this alternative finance channel. Confidence has returned to the sector of late. Bandhan Financial Services, the largest microfinance company in India, began operating as a commercial bank, Bandhan Bank, in August 2015. Other MFIs have applied to become "small banks." Others are looking at tying up with large banks as banking correspondents.

Another initiative that has succeeded, at least initially, is the branch-based KGFS, which started in 2008 in three areas of South India. KGFS works with banks, nonbanking finance companies, insurance companies, remittance providers, and pension funds, and plays the role of a financial aggregator. It has a local branch model that operates in areas where there are no or few formal financial services.

The branches are painted green and orange with an open front. There are rows of wooden benches and a teller window. Two online computers and three uniformed staff complete the picture. The staff come from neighboring villages. They know the culture, but are not part of money-related networks in the village. The branch staff seek to enroll all households within a five-kilometer radius.

The focus is on wealth management and helping a household achieve its financial goals. Information about the household's financial situation and its aspirations are the starting point for advice about products, services, and strategies. When customers enroll, they are asked about their wealth-management goals. A detailed financial profile is recorded using the latest technology and becomes part of a computerized database. But customer interaction is with the tellers at the branch. The tellers also go for home and field visits in the afternoon, when the pace of transactions slows. Staff members visit village households when they establish the branch and then every six months to update their reports and financial advice. KGFS employees are evaluated according to how well they fulfill customers' wealth-management goals. This detailed personal knowledge backed up by the database enables KGFS to offer routine loans in ten to fifteen minutes. KGFS in July 2014 had 220 branches in India serving 500,000 rural customers.

Pudhuaaru, its first region of operation—named after the river that flows through Thanjavur—became profitable within four years. Sushila, 40, the owner of a shop in Pudhuaaru, says the opening of the first Kshetriya Gramin Financial Services branch was transformative. Her husband fell ill eighteen years ago. His illness led them to borrow from money lenders. She says, "With Pudhuaaru KGFS, we moved from 10 paisa to 2 paisa." The interest rate with the money lenders was 10 paisa a month in every rupee (one rupee has 100 paisa), 120 percent a year. With Pudhuaaru, she moved to 24 percent a year.

With this credit, then insurance and pensions, has come a sense of empowerment. Their eldest daughter is doing her second year of engineering. The other two girls are in private school. They have been able to buy "money back" insurance for their daughters so that in fifteen to twenty years they will get one lakh (100,000) rupees. She has been putting Rs 1,000 a year for the past four years into a pension fund. Though the house remains half built, it is on land that her husband put in her name.

Money as a Medium of Relationships

Money is a marker of intergenerational relationships, a "memory bank" (Hart 2001). With language, it is one of the two most important means of communication (Introduction, this volume). Money is a medium of relationships and care. It can also be a medium of coercion and control. If personal money has so far been contained within narrow nuclear family households, these are now being widened to include extended and transnational families. The family boundaries of money in much of Asia, Africa, and parts of Latin America are broader than the couple-based money management typical of the North Atlantic societies. In the global South, money moves two ways across the generations, rather than one way from parents to children.

Two-way money flows across generations in extended and transnational families are changing the way we think of money, families, and morality. These everyday practices shape how people do their banking in terms of joint accounts, separate accounts, and nominees in a human economy. Money management within the family involves control of money across the generations. The duty to give money to parents and family has led to migrant remittances in the South becoming one of the largest international flows of funds.

The Broader Boundaries of Family Money

It was a given in my life in India and Malaysia that parents helped children with money and children returned the service. When parents received money from their children, they knew their children had internalized filial piety. Studying money transactions in Melbourne during the 1990s made me realize that this two-way flow of money was not universal.

In Australia, among middle-income married families, the domestic financial unit is the couple. Money is private to the married couple. Money flows one way down the generations (Singh 1997). This is less about caring than the medium of care. Children in Australia show their care through what they do and how often they communicate. They take their parents to the shops or doctor, and help with the gutters, gardening, and home maintenance.

The uses and meanings of money in the global North are diverse. The growing importance of middle-income Asian migration to Australia over the last ten years has also led to more two-way flows of money within transnational families. In many European families, gifts of money for weddings and special occasions remain important. The Aboriginal Ngukurr community in Australia's southeast Arnhem Land (Senior, Perkins, and Bern 2002) distributes money within a fluid cluster of households. This may "vary in composition from a couple, nuclear family, extended family through to one based on a set of siblings or other close relatives" (ibid.: 5). Gifts, mainly of money, absorbed an average of 16 percent of the income of a household cluster.

In New Zealand, among the Maori, there is an accepted moral obligation to share money up and down generations in the family. Money is offered as a gift not only by grandparents and parents, but also by younger people who give to "parents, grandparents or others in their parent's generation as well as to brothers, sisters or cousins" (Taiapa 1994: 33). Money is donated to the *whānau* for ritual gatherings that mark crises in the lives of members. The obligation to give money for the funeral meeting at the *whānau* takes priority over everyday household expenses.

In charting the broad brush differences between the global North and South, I do not suggest that money is always treated the same way within these divisions. In the global North, however, Anglo-American norms concerning money and family are often embedded in the design of public social and economic policy.

In the global South, moral behavior usually treats money as a medium of caring and sharing within the extended family.[3] Stephanie Riak Akuei's study of the southern Sudanese Dinka refugees in the United States shows how extensive these boundaries of care can be (Akuei 2005). She writes of Joseph and his family resettled in San Diego in 1998. In the United States, two of his wife's siblings stay with them. He also has obligations to his transnational family and lineage. Within the first two years, he "became directly responsible for 24 male and female extended family members and indirectly 62 persons displaced" (ibid.: 7) across Egypt, Libya, Kenya, and Uganda. Joseph also periodically helps four unrelated friends in Egypt who helped him in the past. He also has responsibilities for his wife's parents in Khartoum.

His financial obligations include remittances of nearly $400 a month plus contributions toward bride price for members of the immediate three generations of his father's lineage. He also has to contribute to compensation to victims' families for crimes (e.g., adultery) committed by a family member. Remittances are also expected when a relative is evicted or dies. This wider limit to financial obligation is difficult to manage on his annual income of $28,000. But fulfilling these family and kinship obligations is central to how Joseph sees himself as a "moral person" (ibid.: 3).

The monetary obligations of a Dinka family are broader than most, for they cover both the husband's and wife's kin. In India, the normative dominance of the patrilineal joint family means that when family units migrate, it is the man who sends money to his kin in the source country. Adult working children, particularly sons, including those not living at home, recognize an obligation to help their parents, even when their parents can do without. This obligation is couched in terms of "duty" (*dharma*) on the children's part and as a "right" (*haq*) on the parents' part (Singh and Bhandari 2012).

This two-way morality of money in the Indian family means that parents acknowledge an obligation to help their adult children. In my study of recent Indian migrants to Australia, transnational families, and money, I heard how middle-income parents would empty out their superannuation funds, take bank loans, and mortgage their property to send their children to Australia for higher education and to increase their own chances of migration. Parents also spoke of sending money for housing and businesses, framing it as part of their duty as parents to see their children settled. You must give the money when it is needed, they said.

There was an unspoken faith that once the sons are settled, they will look after the parents (Singh 2016; Singh and Gatina 2015). At times this faith is not justified and morals falter.

Money as a Gift

Money as a medium of care is closely connected to its use as a gift. In Asia and Africa, money is often the only acceptable form of gift to mark celebrations and different life stages. It is not possible to think of Chinese New Year without the red *ang-pow* gift packet for children and younger unmarried men and women.

Among the Simunul Bajaus of Sabah, Malaysia, cash is the most appropriate gift given by most of the guests at a wedding or funeral. Among the Anglo-Celtics in Australia, it is acceptable for a grandmother to put some dollars with a birthday card for her grandchild. But to give money instead of a material present is thought in other situations to show a lack of thought and care . Though cash is becoming a preferred gift in Australia for couples that have lived together in de facto relationships or couples that have been married before, there is still a lingering sense of discomfort about these cash gifts.

At Indian weddings you don't say you want money, you just write, "No packaged gifts," and everybody knows that means you want the *"shagun,"* the mandatory cash gift. It is a delicate calculation. You need to take into account relationships, often spanning generations, the history of reciprocity, and inflation. Some families have a written record of who gave how much at the last wedding, so that you know how much more to give. I learned that in Vietnam this calculation of relations through the money gift is even more routinized. The gift money is put into the envelope of the wedding invitation. It means the giver's name and address are marked already, so that the amount may be noted for the record.[4]

Remittances and the Transnational Family

Family money and gift money sustain the largest international flows of funds today, remittances, showing how personal and market dimensions of money are intertwined with globalization (Pedersen, this volume). The study of remittances also reveals how global money transfers involve different kinds of calculation from money that flows within national boundaries. A dollar sent is not always a dollar received.

Formal remittances to developing countries in 2014 were estimated at $436 billion. This is more than official development assistance. For many countries, they exceed their most important exports or foreign direct investment. Indian and Chinese migrants send the most money home—$70 and $64 billion, followed by the Philippines, Mexico, and Nigeria (Ratha et al. 2015).

These figures relate only to money sent through formal money-transfer organizations. Total remittances could be 50–80 percent higher than formal remittances (Buencamino and Gorbunov 2002). It is difficult, however, to estimate how much money is taken by hand, sent with friends and family, or through customary circuits of mercantile and family credit and transfers such as *hawala* or *hundi*. Often termed "informal," there is a whiff of illegality, tax evasion, and money laundering surrounding these customary money-transfer organizations, particularly after 9/11 when they were deemed to be intrinsic to terrorist finance. One such circuit, *hundi*, during the British colonial period in India, adapted customary practice to new laws in interestingly flexible ways (Martin, this volume). The social sanctions ensuring the reliability, credibility, and flexibility of *hundi* are particularly important (Rahman and Yeoh 2008). These customary money-transfer networks, rather than being demonized as socially dangerous, should be encouraged since they enable fast and cheap transactions for people who are otherwise inadequately served.

Policy-makers now see remittances as an important way for countries to alleviate poverty and reduce the cost of borrowing through securitization of these dependable money flows (Pedersen, this volume). There is much evidence supporting the view that remittances lead to increased expenditure on health, education, and housing, which in turn aid well-being and development (Ghosh 2006). But, for migrants and recipients, remittances are family money. One of the reasons people send money home is that they want to ensure family well-being. They wish to continue belonging to their family, kinship group, and community.

The importance of regular remittances was brought home to me when, while researching the history of the Central Bank of Malaysia, I interviewed a Chinese corporate executive there in the mid-1980s. The conversation moved to remittances, an important function of Chinese banks in Malaysia, especially in the 1930s and 1940s. During the Japanese Occupation, communications were disrupted and remittances stopped. This is now just a footnote in banking history. Forty years later, the executive sobbed at his desk when he recalled that his mother and four brothers and sisters starved to death in Canton during those war years (Singh 1984).

It is a challenge to bring down the cost of international remittances. Sub-Saharan Africa remains the most expensive destination for remittances, with an average cost of just under 10 percent of the sum transferred. This compares with an average cost in the second quarter of 2016 of 7.6 percent worldwide (World Bank 2016).

International remittances via mobile phones are in their early stages. This is partly due to worries about money laundering, exchange controls, and problems of interoperability between national networks. Financial organizations do not in any case design products and services for this very important flow of money (Ratha et al. 2014). There is hope of enabling regulation, interconnectivity, and interoperability among some of Africa's communication companies.[5] Bitcoin may yet contribute to lowering the cost of remittances (Dodd, this volume). At present, BitPesa's successful use of Bitcoin in Africa has already reduced the cost of cross border business-to-business (B2B) payments by bypassing correspondent banks (Shin 2016; SaveOnSend 2016).

Transnational flows of remittances differ from family money within national boundaries. Both are a medium of relations and care. But transnational money for purposes of caring within the family contrasts with the physical care that siblings and other family members offer in the home country. As with other "special monies" and "social payments," remittances become a qualitatively different kind of family money as a kind of gift money, balanced ambiguously against financial contributions and face-to-face care given by members of the family who remain in the home country. The value of money is interpreted rather than calculated.

Money earned overseas is sometimes seen by stay-at-homes as "easy money" like "windfall income" (Kurien 2002; Wong 2006). Migrants in Persian Gulf countries generally make five to fifteen times what they would have earned locally. This "windfall income" is at times spent in ways that the senders would not have contemplated for themselves or could have afforded for their own nuclear family where they now live. Research over a wide area confirms that receivers often undervalue the sacrifice made by senders in sending remittances (Wong 2006; Akuei 2005; Lindley 2009; Horst 2006). This is particularly true when communications flow one-way from migrants to the transnational family (Singh 2016).

This discrepancy between valuations of remittances and physical caring can spill over into legal disputes. Then conflict is not only "over who gets what but also over structure and meaning" (Zelizer 2005: 225). Issues of inheritance can be particularly messy and protracted when agricultural land is passed on to the second generation of migrants (Singh, Cabraal, and Robertson 2010).

Money in the Future

Money in the future will be different and yet the same. It will be different in that a new world of banking, payments, and insurance will open up for the large minority that is now unbanked. Money will become more mobile and virtual. Money at a personal level will become more global in that it will move across national borders. This will change calculations of its value when measured against care, well-being, and the quality of life.

Despite changes in the technology of transfers, money remains a constant. Trust remains at the center of what defines money. Money is valued only when it is used in networks of trust and shared meaning.

Money will remain personal and impersonal, local and global. It could be impersonal in some payments and market relationships, but intensely personal as a medium of family and kin relations. It is also personal when individuals gain access to credit rather than buy something and walk away with it. At the same time money increases the reach of impersonal financial institutions. Money will remain a marker of the morality inherent in family relations across borders, while at the same time generating huge international flows of funds.

Banking, Payments, and Insurance for the Unbanked

The world of banking, insurance, and pensions will open up for millions of households who do not have access to formal financial institutions now. Putting money in the bank will be a big change from the slats of a pandanus hut.

In this vision, while David Pedersen and I may differ in emphasis, the poor will have access to flexible credit to navigate the ups and downs of irregular money flows. They will have access to insurance in case of illness or tragedy, so that they don't have to go to money lenders charging exorbitant interest. They will have a card to withdraw money from a banking correspondent, a branch, or an ATM. Benefits and pensions will come straight to the bank account rather than being diluted and sidelined by intermediaries.

It may be utopian, but India launched in 2014 a national mission to ensure a bank account for every household and to "integrate the poorest of the poor with bank accounts". This goes much further than just opening a current or savings account (the CASA model). This account will receive government benefits. It will come attached with a debit card, financial literacy education, an overdraft of Rs 5,000 ($82), and insurance of

Rs 100,000 ($1,640). Between 31 January 2014 and 20 July 2016, 226 million new accounts were opened in India, accompanied by 183 million debit cards. Although a quarter percent of these accounts have a zero balance, the new accounts amount to a net total of Rs 406 billion ($6.1 billion) (Department of Financial Services, Ministry of Finance, Government of India 2016). Implementing this vision has been a challenge. It involves different levels of government, technology, and banking infrastructure. The cultural changes entailed in the management and control of money in the home are also forbidding. However, having a vision for inclusion that goes beyond opening an account is an important step forward.

Being part of formal payments systems and having a savings account, credit, and insurance are not ends in themselves. The hope is that financial inclusion leads to empowerment. It is important that many more women and men should feel they have choices in their lives and can ask themselves what they want and then seek it.

Use of Multiple Channels, Forms of Money, and Currencies

The mobile phone will transform money as a channel for payments, banking, and remittances. This is already happening in sub-Saharan Africa. It will only increase in importance. However, there will remain a mix of forms of money corresponding to the social meanings of people's activities and relationships. The balance will change. People and governments are watching the cashless Lagos experiment and India's demonetization push, for cash remains the most used form of money in the global South. Multiple currencies will increase in importance as national currencies lose their monopoly. Just as the precolonial Tiv would not use a brass rod to buy food (Bohannan 1959), I will not give a gift of gold to an acquaintance. Discretionary valuations of money forms have always been with us (Guyer this volume, Hart 2005), but we may be on the verge of a Cambrian explosion of money.

Multiple currencies have long been normal. Money followed the routes of empire and trade. Cowrie shells circulated as money across Asia, the Middle East, Oceania, and Africa. Coins from Greece, Rome, and the Islamic empires spread across many countries. Trade carried Indian coins to Central Asia, Iran, Iraq, and Ethiopia. Indian coins entered Tibet from Nepal in the sixteenth century (Eagleton and Williams 2007; Basham 1954). The use of multiple currencies is enhanced when there is little certainty that the official currency will retain its value. In Zimbabwe hyperinflation led to the Zimbabwe dollar being declared "moribund" by the country's minister of finance. It was suspended as legal tender on

12 April 2009. The country now operates with a mix of different currencies, the most important being the US dollar (Noko 2011).

In Vietnam today, payments of different kinds are made in Vietnamese Dong, US dollars, and gold. In Cambodia, the US dollar is often preferred to the riel. Ceremonial payments and gifts still take the form of shell money and pigs in Vanuatu, as they did long ago of cattle and *tugudu* cloth among the Tiv in Nigeria.

Is Global Money Different?

Money now flows swiftly across borders, not just for banks, corporations, and international traders, but for the ordinary migrant working in a semi-skilled job in the Middle East or in the software industry in the United States. Money not only shapes social relationships and cultural values, but is itself shaped by them (Zelizer 2011a). We need, therefore, to ask how its characteristics have changed in a globalized world. The concept of "global money" draws attention to how money crosses borders and changes its forms and value when it moves across national boundaries.

Global money has to deal with different currency regimes and money-transfer organizations. It is not a frictionless flow, when the relatively high costs of remittances carve away an average 7.6 percent of a transfer's value. This is one of the main differences between global money and local/national money. The latter is place-based, bounded by national borders. Global money has to deal with formal and informal money-transfer operators (MTOs) and exchange rates. Of course since the 1970s many national currencies compete in the foreign exchange market and these are both local and global. The contrast between "hard" and "soft" currencies is still with us.

Both kinds of money are mediated by payment systems that may involve online and mobile technologies. Global money becomes virtual at some part of the formal MTO transaction. Only when money is carried by hand, does it have the same face-to-face characteristics of local/national money.

A dollar of global money does not translate into a dollar's worth of local money. The dollar is earned in a different environment from the context in which it is spent. But calculations of the value of remittances are not limited to the face value of the dollar, but are measured against relationships, the caring it represents, and care that is remote, not physically present.

Changes in the value of money sent and received are reflected in a shift from calculation to interpretation of number as a key aspect of money. This is important for global money as it moves between local, national, and global registers of value. The anthropology of money shows that number may be ambiguous and multiple monies must be interpreted in social and cultural context. Number allows for approximation, for dealing with asymmetry, for nonequivalence, for "enclaving" a particular kind of money for specific uses, and for moving from one scale of valuation to another (Guyer 1999, 2004). The approximation of number is particularly important when we see money as a social payment (Maurer 2007 and this volume).

Getting Money's Gender Right

When dealing with the unbanked, are we getting money's gender right? There are challenges ahead even for well-meaning policy-makers who want to keep gender in mind. In Bangladesh's Rana Plaza tragedy, most of the 1,200 people who died were women. Failure to redress the unequal position of women is most apparent at the intersections of national, regional, and global policy.

Until now connecting the economic to the social has not figured prominently in the concerns of central bank governors, ministers of finance, bankers, and economists. Gender and the management and control of money in the household have not been at the forefront of policies dealing with inequality and exclusion. Thomas Piketty (2014), when discussing inequality in his *Capitalism in the Twenty-First Century,* in 700 pages mentions gender only once (Hart, this volume).

The 2013 Nachiket Mor report on financial inclusion in India has been influential in shaping the contours of the country's future banking system. It does not mention "gender" once in its 247 pages (Reserve Bank of India 2013), this despite the fact that gender is an everyday reality in Mor's involvement with banking innovations like KGPS.

Gender issues occupied a central place in the Indian prime minister's Independence Day speech on 15 August 2014. Yet policy announcements cannot settle on whether the aim is to have one or two bank accounts per household. Within the wider context of gender inequality in India and male control of money, for many women in India an overdraft facility of Rs 5,000 ($75) in their own account remains an unattainable dream.

Supriya Singh is professor of sociology of communications at RMIT University. Her latest books are *Money, Migration and Family: India to Australia* (2016), *Globalization and Money: A Global South Perspective* (2013), and *The Girls Ate Last* (2013).

NOTES

This chapter is based on the keynote lecture given to the Pretoria conference, "Money in the Making of World Society," from which this book is derived.
1. Unless otherwise noted, all figures are in US dollars.
2. In the last decade or more, this situation has changed radically, at least in the more affluent Anglophone countries. The subprime lending boom in the United States showed that banks could make more from charging fees on bad loans to the poor than from interest on loans to "reliable" customers.
3. Parry and Bloch (1989) assemble case studies from the global South where money is part of many social relations that are thought to be contaminated by it in the North. This power of money to transform relations reflects a moral economy based on a sharp contrast between paid work outside and unpaid sharing within the home. This is largely absent from traditionally non-capitalist societies (Hart 2005, Introduction, this volume).
4. Personal communication, Dr. Thai Thi Ngoc Du, director, Gender and Society Research Center, Hoa Sen University, Ho Chi Minh City, Vietnam, 6 June 2014.
5. Three East African countries—Kenya, Uganda and Tanzania—have already launched a common telecommunications system. Here too the region is pioneering innovations in money and communications that are blocked in the interest of national capital elsewhere.

REFERENCES

2013. "Microfinance in India: Road to Redemption." *The Economist*, 12 January.
2014. "Full text of Narendra Modi's I-Day address." *Sify News*, 15 August.
Agarwal, B. 1994. *A Field of One's Own: Gender and Land Rights in South Asia*. Cambridge: Cambridge University Press.
Akuei, S. R. 2005. "Remittances as unforeseen burdens: The livelihoods and social obligations of Sudanese refugees." In *Global Migration Perspectives*. Geneva: Global Commission on International Migration.
Ballard, R. 2012. "Geographies of development II: Cash transfers and the reinvention of development for the poor." *Progress in Human Geography* 37: 811–821.
Basham, A. L. 1954. *The Wonder That Was India*. New York: Grove Press.
Basu, S. 2005a. "Haklenewali: Indian women's negotiations of discourses of inheritance." In S. Basu (ed.), *Dowry & Inheritance*. New Delhi: Women Unlimited.
———. 2005b. "The politics of giving: Dowry and inheritance as feminist issues." In S. Basu (ed.), *Dowry & Inheritance*. New Delhi: Women Unlimited.
Bohannan, P. 1959. "The Impact of Money on an African Subsistence Economy." *The Journal of Economic History* 19: 491–503.
Boserup, E. 1970. *Woman's Role in Economic Development*. London: Allen and Unwin.
Buencamino, L., and S. Gorbunov. 2002. "Informal Money Transfer Systems: Opportunities and Challenges for Development Finance" [Online]. United Nations. Available: http://www.un.org/esa/esa02dp26.pdf (accessed 5 May 2005).
Burhouse, S., et al. 2014. *2013 FDIC National Survey of Unbanked and Underbanked Households*. Washington, DC: Federal Deposit Insurance Corporation (FDIC).

Chang, M. L. 2010. *Shortchanged: Why Women Have Less Wealth and What Can be Done About It.* Oxford: Oxford University Press.

Collins, D., et al. 2009. *Portfolios of the Poor: How the World's Poor Live on $2 a Day.* Princeton, NJ: Princeton University Press.

Crandall, A., et al. 2012. *Mobile Phone Usage at the Kenyan Base of the Pyramid: Final Report.* Nairobi: iHub Research and Research Solutions Africa.

Demirguc-Kunt, A., et al. 2015. *The Global Findex Database 2014: Measuring Financial Inclusion around the World.* Policy Research Working Paper 7255. Washington, DC: World Bank.

Department of Financial Services, Ministry of Finance, Government of India. 2016. *Pradhan Mantri Jan-Dhan Yojna* [Online]. Available: http://pmjdy.gov.in/account-statistics-country.aspx (accessed 31 July 2016).

Drèze, J., and A. Sen. 2013. *An Uncertain Glory: India and its Contradictions.* London: Allen Lane.

Eagleton, C., and J. Williams. 2007. *Money: A History.* London: The British Museum Press.

European Commission. 2010. "Financial exclusion in the EU: New evidence From the EU-SILC Special Module" [Online]. Available: ec.europa.eu/social/BlobServlet?docId=6709&langId=en (accessed 15 May 2014).

Ghosh, B. 2006. *Migrants' Remittances and Development: Myths, Rhetoric, and Realities* Geneva: International Organization for Migration (IOM).

Gillwald, A., A. Milek, and C. Stork. 2010. "Gender Assessment of ICT Access and Usage in Africa." Research ICT Africa.

GSMA. 2012. "Striving and Surviving: Exploring the Lives of Women at the Base of the Pyramid" [Online]. GSMA mWomen Programme. Available: http://www.mwomen.org/Research/striving-surviving-exploring-the-lives-of-women-at-the-base-of-the-pyramid (accessed 17 October 2012).

GSMA Connected Women. 2015. "Bridging the Gender Gap: Mobile Access and Usage in Low and Middle-Income Countries" [Online]. GSMA. Available: http://www.gsma.com/mobilefordevelopment/programmes/connected-women/bridging-gender-gap (accessed 18 June 2015).

Guyer, J. I. 1999. "Comparisons and equivalencies in Africa and Melanesia." In D. Akin and J. Robbins (eds.), *Money and Modernity: State and Local Currencies in Melanesia.* Pittsburgh, PA: University of Pittsburgh Press.

Guyer, J. I. 2004. *Marginal Gains: Monetary Transactions in Atlantic Africa.* Chicago, IL: University of Chicago Press.

Han, C. 2012. *Life in Debt: Times of Care and Violence in Neoliberal Chile.* Berkeley: University of California Press.

Hart, K. 2001. *Money in an Unequal World: Keith Hart and His Memory Bank.* New York: Texere.

———. 2005. "Money: one anthropologist's view", in J. Carrier (ed) *Handbook of Economic Anthropology*, Edward Elgar, Cheltenham, 160–175.

———. 2007. "Money is always personal and impersonal." *Anthropology Today* 23: 12–16.

Horst, H. A. 2006. "The blessings and burdens of communication: Cell phones in Jamaican transnational social fields." *Global Networks* 6: 143–159.

Johnson, S. 2004. "Gender Norms in Financial Markets: Evidence from Kenya." *World Development* 32: 1355–1374.

———. 2012. "The Search for Inclusion in Kenya's Financial Landscape: The Rift Revealed" [Online]. Bath: Centre for Development Studies. Available: http://fsdkenya.org/wp-content/uploads/2015/08/12-03-29_Full_FinLandcapes_report.pdf (accessed 19 August 2012).

Kabeer, N. 2012. *Women's Economic Empowerment and Inclusive Growth: Labour Markets and Enterprise Development*. London: School of Oriental and African Studies.

Keshri, G. 2014. "Right-wingers peg cost of Modi's financial inclusion plan at over Rs.100,000 crore" [Online]. Available: https://www.swiftpage2.com/speasapage.aspx?X=2U0WGLOGIDWHZ5W800YWWW (accessed 19 August 2014).

Kishwar, M. 2005. "Dowry and inheritance rights." In S. Basu (ed.), *Dowry & Inheritance*. New Delhi: Women Unlimited.

Kurien, P. A. 2002. *Kaleidoscopic Ethnicity: International Migration and the Reconstruction of Community Identities in India*. New Delhi: Oxford University Press.

Lawton, J. 1991. "What is sexually transmitted debt?" In R. Meikle (ed.), *Women and Credit: A Forum on Sexually Transmitted Debt*. Melbourne: Ministry of Consumer Affairs.

Lindley, A. 2009. "The Early-Morning Phonecall: Remittances from a Refugee Diaspora Perspective." *Journal of Ethnic and Migration Studies* 35: 1315–1334.

Maurer, B. 2007. "Incalculable payments: Money, scale, and the South African offshore grey money amnesty." *African Studies Review* 50: 125–138.

———. 2012. "Payment: Forms and Functions of Value Transfer in Contemporary Society." *Cambridge Anthropology* 30: 15–35.

McAuslan, P. 2010. "Personal reflections on drafting laws to improve women's access to land: Is there a magicwand?" *Journal of Eastern African Studies* 4: 114–130.

MCG Management Consulting. 2013. *Final Report—Access to Finance Program—Gender Borrower Survey in Vietnam*. International Finance Corporation, World Bank Group.

Mills, C. W. 1959. *The Sociological Imagination*. New York: Grove Press.

Misra, S., and E. G. Thukral. 2005. "A study of two villages in Bihar." In S. Basu (ed.), *Dowry & Inheritance*. New Delhi: Women Unlimited.

Noko, J. 2011. "Dollarization: The Case of Zimbabwe." *Cato Journal* 31: 339–365.

Papanek, H., and L. Schwede. 1988. "Women are good with money: Earning and managing in an Indonesian city." In D. Dwyer and J. Bruce (eds.), *A Home Divided: Women and Income in the Third World*. Stanford, CA: Stanford University Press.

Parry, J. and M. Bloch (eds.). 1989. *Money and the Morality of Exchange*. Cambridge: Cambridge University Press.

Piketty, T. 2014. *Capital in the Twenty-First Century*. Cambridge, MA: The Belknap Press of Harvard University Press.

Rabow, J., et al. 1992. "Women and money: Cultural contrasts." In P. A. Adler and P. Adler (eds.), *Sociological Studies of Child Development*. Greenwich, CT: JAI Press Inc.

Rahman, M. M., and B. S. A. Yeoh. 2008. "The social organization of Hundi." *Asian Population Studies* 4(5): 29.

Ratha, D., et al. 2014. "Migration and Remittances: Recent Developments and Outlook." *Migration and Development Brief*. Washington, DC: The World Bank Migration and Remittances Team, Development Prospects Group.

———. 2015. *Migration and Development Brief 24*. Washington, DC: The World Bank.

Reserve Bank of India. 2013. *Committee on Comprehensive Financial Services for Small Businesses and Low Income Households: Report*. Mumbai: Reserve Bank of India.

Reskin, B. F., and P. A. Roos. 1990. *Job Queues, Gender Queues: Explaining Women's Inroads into Male Occupations*. Philadelphia, PA: Temple University Press.

Saiag, H. 2015. "Money for a Human Economy: A Reflection from Argentina" in K. Hart (ed) *Economy For and Against Democracy*. New York: Berghahn Books, 182–200.

Samarajiva, R. 2011. "Mobile at the Bottom of the Pyramid: Informing Policy from the Demand Side." *Mobile Telephony Special Issue* 7: iii–vii.

Sanyal, P. 2009. "From Credit to Collective Action: The Role of Microfinance in Promoting Women's Social Capital and Normative Influence." *American Sociological Review* 74: 529–550.

SaveOnSend. 2016. "Does Bitcoin make sense for international money transfer?" [Online]. SaveOnSend. Available: https://www.saveonsend.com/blog/bitcoin-money-transfer/ (accessed 4 August 2016).

Sen, A. 1999. *Development as Freedom*. Oxford: Oxford University Press.

Senior, K., D. Perkins, and J. Bern. 2002. "Variation inmaterial wellbeing in a welfare based economy." Unpublished manuscsript, University of Wollongong, South East Arnhem Land Collaborative Research Project.

Shin, L. 2016. "Elizabeth Rossiello Describes How BitPesa Slashes International Payment Fees" [Online]. Women@Forbes. Available: https://www.forbes.com/sites/laurashin/2016/06/15/elizabeth-rossiello-describes-how-bitpesa-slashes-international-payment-fees/ (accessed 4 August 2016).

Singh, S. 1984. *Bank Negara Malaysia: The First 25 Years, 1959–1984*. Kuala Lumpur: Bank Negara Malaysia.

———. 1994. "Marriage, Money and Information: Australian Consumers' Use of Banks." PhD dissertation, La Trobe University.

———. 1997. *Marriage Money: The Social Shaping of Money in Marriage and Banking*. St. Leonards, NSW: Allen & Unwin.

———. 2013. *The Girls Ate Last*. Eltham, VIC: Angsana Publications.

———. 2016. Money, Migration and Family: India to Australia, New York: Palgrave Macmillan.

Singh, S., and M. Bhandari. 2012. "Money management and control in the Indian joint family across generations." *The Sociological Review* 60: 46–67.

Singh, S., A. Cabraal, and S. Robertson. 2010. "Remittances as a currency of care: A focus on 'twice migrants' among the Indian diaspora in Australia." *Journal of Comparative Family Studies* XXXXI(2): 245–263.

Singh, S., and L. Gatina. 2015. "Money flows two-ways between transnational families in Australia and India." *South Asian Diaspora* 7: 33–47.

Singh, S., and Y. Nadarajah. 2011. "School Fees, Beer and 'Meri': Gender, Cash and the Mobile in the Morobe Province of Papua New Guinea" [Online]. Irvine, CA: Institute for Money, Technology and Financial Inclusion. Available: http://www.imtfi.uci.edu/files/imtfi/blog_working_papers/working_paper_singh.pdf (accessed 20 September 2012).

Summers, A. 1994. *Damned Whores and God's Police*. Ringwood, VIC: Penguin.

Taiapa, J. T. T. 1994. "'Ta Te Whanau Ohanga': The economics of the whanau—The Maori component of the Intra Family Income Study." Unpublished manuscript, Massey University, Department of Maori Studies.

Waring, M. 1988. *Counting for Nothing: What Men Value and What Women are Worth*. Wellington, NZ: Allen & Unwin and Port Nicholson Press.

Wolf, N. 1993. *Fire with Fire*. New York: Random House.

Wong, M. 2006. "The gendered politics of remittances in Ghanaian transnational families." *Economic Geography* 82: 355–381.

World Bank. 2016. "An analysis of trends in cost of remittance services." *Remittance Prices Worldwide*. Washington, DC.

Zainudeen, A., and D. Ratnadiwakara. 2011. "Are the poor stuck in voice? Conditions for adoption of more than-voice mobile Services." *Mobile Telephony Special Issue* 7: 45–59.

Zelizer, V. 2005. "Culture and consumption." In N. J. Smelser and R. Swedberg (eds.), *The Handbook of Economic Sociology*. Princeton, NJ, and New York: Princeton University Press and Russell Sage Foundation.

———. 2011a. *Economic Lives: How Culture Shapes the Economy*. Princeton, NJ: Princeton University Press.

———. 2011b. "The gender of money." *The Wall Street Journal*, 27 January.

CHAPTER 6

 Remittance Securitization in the Hemisphere of the Américas

From Wall Street to Calle Principal *and Back*

DAVID PEDERSEN

On the face of it, this chapter is about a practical outlook shared by some government officials, private bank administrators, and members of development organizations, namely that international migrant remittances should be treated like regularized payment streams suitable for developing into securities to be bought and sold in financial markets. Most of the recent scholarly and professional literature on the subject treats remittance securitization as a technical problem requiring an appropriate mixture of empirical measurement, formal modeling, and coordination of government policies and private-sector initiatives. Remittances are a fairly fresh phenomenon, joined with new discursive categories and doctrinal codifications, as well as the practices, infrastructure, and institutions required for their securitization and marketing. Taken together they yield a nascent project of social structuring.

The central challenge addressed here is how to study critically and make sense of this growing project. I place it in the context of the historical development of capitalism and as a discrete instance of migration and remittance transfer between El Salvador and the United States (Pedersen 2014). In this way, I hope "to connect minute field observations to world society and history" (Hart and Ortiz 2014). In their review of the anthropological literature on money and finance, Keith Hart and Horacio Ortiz suggest following forms of money and digital electronic media in a "trans-disciplinary and transnational" way to explore connections and real variations across different contexts. In what follows I seek to show what is entailed in this sort of analysis.

This chapter contributes to the human economy approach by pursuing the insight that money does not just have the capacity to take one beyond any particular here and now. Money relations entail "the mutual determination of the abstract and the concrete" (Introduction, this volume). I explore here several concrete contexts, showing how particular money relations constitute them. By literally following the money, these seemingly separate domains taken together participate in a more general process, much the way that multiple symptoms relate to an overall disease. The effect is to upset some hierarchies, illicit fissions, and fusions, showing how "centers" like Wall Street in the United States not only rely on, but hide relations with their peripheries. This relationship is highly uneven and in part maintained as a feature of the overall process of dissimulation. This claim and the sort of critical analysis it is predicated on are unconventional. But I take seriously Hart's point that opposites are mutually determined.

Following money and media requires not only moving across multiple places and times of inquiry, but also varying the content under study and the geo-historical scale of the analysis. Academic disciplines tend to fix for us the relevant places, times, objects, and scales of analysis. Varying all of them at once may seem to be undisciplined, but this sensibility allowed Hart (2000) to recognize money as a "memory bank" for both visible aspects of its national history and its less visible, but larger and more open-ended social dimensions. A similar perspective informs the Human Economy Programme (Introduction, this volume).

I am concretely concerned here with an important change in capitalist relations between El Salvador and the United States. Over the past thirty years, these two nation-states have been redefined by the migration of over one million Salvadorans to several major urban centers in the United States, the concentrated work of Salvadoran migrants in the expanding service sectors of these US cities, their annual transfer of over $4 billion back to family and friends in El Salvador (contributing a sixth of the country's GDP), and the remarkable variety of new productive activities, capitalist ventures, and government policies that these remittance practices have generated (Brown and Patten 2013). Although fairly exotic in the early 1980s, especially from the vantage point of metropolitan areas like El Salvador or a US suburb, these quotidian connections extending into personal and familial relations across both countries are now well-recognized by researchers, media reports, and political and business leaders in each of them.[1]

A mixture of study, celebration, and cashing-in on this new transnational circulation (Singh, this volume) now characterizes not just El

Salvador and its relations with the United States, but is a global phenomenon throwing light on capitalists, governments, and institutions devoted to diffusing capitalist relations across the hemisphere of the Americas and beyond.[2] In 2012, The United Nations Development Program (UNDP) published an important report entitled "Innovative Financing for Development" that identified securitization of migrant remittances and debt-based instruments more generally as among the four most important mechanisms for generating development capital (Hurley 2012). In fall 2014, the World Bank released a report announcing that global migrant remittances were approaching a half-trillion dollars annually (World Bank 2014). These reports announce that there are profits to be earned from a giant untapped global payment stream, in principle no different from other kinds of regularized transfers like mortgages and credit card payments.

The remittance securitization project, as it developed in the Americas since the 1990s, congealed out of a much larger and longer history, some of which can be seen in its figurative appearance. However, the project also conceals much of its own formation, especially those aspects that deny what it seems to promise. The project tends to obscure how it helps to perpetuate these relations that contradict what it purports to do and say on the surface. A "transdisciplinary and transnational" approach here leads not only to a more inclusive, dynamic, and interactive account, in the spirit of the Human Economy Program, but also to one that discloses contradictions, rather than presupposing overall functionality or completeness.

Wall Street in the News

I begin with a television program recorded on 25 July 2012 for the US cable news service MSNBC, located in Hoboken, New Jersey. I place the online recording of this event within the perspective of something like a worldwide digital media sphere.[3] The show is called *Squawkbox* and takes its name from the traditional intercom system that investment analysts, traders, and brokers use for trading. The hosts that morning were Rebecca Quick, Joe Kernen, and Andrew Ross Sorkin, and their guest was Sanford "Sandy" Weill, the former CEO of the banking and investment conglomerate Citigroup. Weill was famous on Wall Street for championing, indeed bringing about, with his allies there and in Washington, DC, the end of 1930s-era banking regulations that prevented speculative investment banking being combined with retail lending in a single firm. Citigroup under Weill was the first of its kind since the 1920s in the United States and he was widely referred to as "the man who smashed Glass-Steagall" (Langley 2003).

Rebecca Quick opened the discussion by asking Weill if he thought that the current financial crisis was related to the existence of huge financial combines (like Citigroup), which were thought to be "too big to fail." Weill swiftly replied by reframing the spatiotemporal scope implied by Quick's question: "Let me start by saying that I think in the two decades before the problem, the big banks really led the growth of the world by creating capital markets in all these countries, converting communist countries to the capitalist system; really helping over a billion people come from abject poverty to the middle class as defined in [their] parts of the world." Weill emphasized the importance of what he called the banking system as the primary cause of these transformations since at least the 1990s. He then identified three conditions or tendencies that had led to the crisis beginning in 2007 and suggested that they should be averted in the future: (1) "too much concentration of investments"; (2) "way too much leverage"; and (3) "very little transparency with lots of off–balance sheet things that didn't really count." He then immediately returned to his larger vision and projected it forward a bit: "Even after the problem, there is really no other country in the world to be the leader of the world yet. So it really falls on the United States to still be the leader. And if we are going to be the leader, we have to have a financial system that can help us be the leader and that is not happening right now." Weill continued to talk, offering a suggestion immediately picked up by hosts and viewers worldwide: "What I think we should probably do is go and split up investment banking from [retail] banking and have banks be deposit takers, have banks make commercial and real estate loans. And have banks do something that will not risk tax-payer dollars. And that ... will not be too big to fail." As he concluded this statement, the hosts jumped in and vociferously urged him to clarify what appeared to be a radical proposal for splitting up the big banks. In near real time, this moment in the interview generated tremendous excitement worldwide. Multiple commentaries soon flooded print and television media, especially through online discussion boards. The principle focus was on the idea that one if not *the* leading proponent of the "lender-trader" model of banking now appeared to be calling for their institutional separation.

Weill made two other major claims in the interview that had no echo in popular coverage and discussion. The first linked his call for ending the lender-trader model to one to restore the legitimacy of the US financial sector, its global dominance, and by extension the United

States' ability to stand as the dominant political and moral world leader. Second, the three problems that Weill acknowledged—overconcentration of particular investments, deep leveraging of capital, and a relative lack of transparency—also provoked only modest discussion. By blithely admitting the three problems and emphasizing a longer heroic phase of US world leadership, Weill deflected deeper inquiry into these issues, although he was himself a significant cause and beneficiary of them.[4]

The casualness of Sandy Weill's admissions and his US-centrism, together with the issues overlooked by hosts and online discussants, are key features of a kind of capitalist common sense. As it circulated around the digital media, primarily in the Americas, Asia, and Europe, this composite participated in a broader process of instantiation. What then is this story?[5]

What went unremarked upon was that three sets of practices that flourished since the 1990s had been good for people around the world because they gained some new wealth in the form of money and commodities. The three tendencies got a little out of hand, but now with some restraint and reform, the overall project of US leadership through the same general practices could and should be continued. The only part of the story that attracted attention was the debate about amounts and concentration. "Too much" or "too little" were Weill's words, with reference also to the relative size of the banks themselves. The larger rhetorical frame fades into a background of aesthetic, ethical, and logical common sense: it feels nice, it seems, to contribute to good things and it also looks reasonable, even true. Although Weill and *Squawkbox* authored this story, it has many echoes and inflections, including the growing body of new work at the intersection of finance and development, especially as it is promoted by US organizations like the Clinton Global Initiative and the Bill and Melinda Gates Foundation. As such, its apparent ubiquity offers our first telling symptom.

Inside the Symptom

When Weill referred to "too much concentration in investments" as a cause of the crisis, he was making a vague claim that may be applicable to many financial crises. But if we ask what historical conditions made his claim plausible, a specific pattern comes into view. Since the mid-1980s the major Wall Street investment banks had expanded their proprietary trading activities relative to the traditional practice of earning profits from the fees charged for trading on behalf of clients.[6] This new kind of trading entailed using the bank's own funds to invest in shares and securities as well as in other trading entities like hedge funds and private equity groups. Both the banks and other trading groups followed various strategies oriented to making bets on relative price differences and shifts in various markets. Technically known as arbitrage, this entails simultaneously buying and selling assets such as bonds, stocks, derivatives, commodities, or currencies to take advantage of price imbalances across different markets.

As one trader described his approach:

> "Quantitative" prop traders like me have a systematic view, meaning I build strategies and then trade them longer term on the market. . . . I will have an idea about a pattern in the market, say, if the share price of two English banks with a broadly similar outlook diverge, they will most likely converge again very soon. . . . Or I might look at the ways unusual rainfall in Argentina translates into higher wheat prices.[7]

What were some of the broader conditions that made this expansion of speculative arbitrage possible? Centrally, the practice was facilitated by domestic financial liberalization in the United States (such as the act that repealed Glass-Steagall) and by opening up other countries' financial systems to US banks and investors. Part of this was what Weill referred to heroically as "creating capital markets" throughout the world.

When Weill mentioned the second issue, "way too much leverage," he was gesturing specifically to the mobilization of huge sums of money for speculation on and actually to influence price movements in various markets. Through a variety of novel mechanisms, banks increased their ability to borrow without altering their reserve requirements. Among the most important means for this was the so-called repo-market, where banks could borrow against presupposed asset growth. Banks also could use the collateral of a hedge fund in which it had invested to back its own borrowing.

Finally, Weill's cryptic reference to "very little transparency with lots of off-balance sheet things that didn't really count" may be understood to refer in part to the rise of what has been called a "shadow banking system" and its many innovations, like special-purpose vehicles (SPV), special investment vehicles (SIV), collateralized debt obligations (CDO), and credit default swaps (CDS).[8] These are financial instruments traded in fairly unregulated markets by nonbanking private companies often incorporated in offshore locales free from regulation. The notable failures of the hedge fund Long-Term Capital Management in the Asian and Russian financial crises of 1997–98 and of the energy trading company

Enron in 2001 (Jorion 2003) shed light on this sector. Taken together, the three general tendencies and their conditions of possibility characterize the development of the US-dominated financial system that Weill wanted to restore.

The general trends that Weill wanted to keep going, in however tempered a way, describe a largely New York- and London-centered world as it evolved since the beginning of the 1980s. As mentioned earlier, a key part of the rise in proprietary trading and speculative arbitrage was the opportunity for major US banks, investment funds, and corporations to make bets on and within other newly liberalized national economies, especially in Asia, Eastern Europe, and Latin America. From the perspective of Wall Street, this as a liberating and lucrative endeavor of "creating new capital markets." This opening up actually was a fairly coercive project of social engineering.[9] Of course, it yielded the possibility for a prop trader in front of a screen in midtown Manhattan to make huge amounts of money for his firm by betting on shifts in Argentinian weather and wheat prices with quantities of borrowed money and great confidence, but what were the other consequences and how was the overall transformation experienced in Latin America, for example?

For the region of Latin America as a whole, the past three decades have entailed systematic privatization of public services and institutions, deregulation of private activities, promotion of nontraditional export production through preferential trade agreements, and overall fiscal austerity. Although the stated goal was to stimulate economic growth and efficiency, the effect was to wipe out much existing social protection for the poorer sectors of the country, decrease domestic agriculture and food production, expand commercial imports and the private financial sector, while ultimately yielding modest growth.[10]

One significant side effect of this restructuring was that a growing number of people left regions of Latin America and moved to live and work in the United States, regularly sending money home to support family and friends. Countries throughout Latin America became increasingly reliant on this remittance transfer as a source of national wealth, none more than El Salvador. Indeed, by shifting analysis to El Salvador, it becomes possible to identify more precisely what sustained the three trends mentioned by Weill. Whether it was called structural adjustment, globalization, or neoliberalism, a specific mix of processes and events shaped El Salvador's transformation over the past thirty years. At the center of these changes was the country's twelve-year civil war (1980–1992). The conflict developed as popular protest movements and diverse guerrilla forces challenged the Salvadoran military, paramilitary "death squads," and their private right-wing supporters during the 1970s. Although a reformist military-civilian coup in late 1979 sought to resolve the tension, full-scale civil war erupted at the beginning of 1980. The revolutionary forces combined to form the Frente Farabundo Martí para la Liberación Nacional (FMLN) and received significant civilian support throughout the country. After some initial FMLN gains, El Salvador seemed poised to become like Nicaragua, where popular revolutionary forces had overthrown the Somoza dictatorship in 1979 and began to reorganize the country. Against this backdrop, the US government directly intervened with a counterinsurgency strategy resurrected from the Vietnam War, eventually spending over $6 billion in support of the Salvadoran government and its armed forces. With training, weaponry, aid, and a limited number of US troops, Salvadoran government forces reversed some of the initial FMLN advances, though the conflict then settled into a violent stalemate during the late 1980s and early 1990s. In 1992, the war was resolved through a negotiated settlement overseen by the United Nations that led to a substantial reduction of the Salvadoran military and the transformation of the FMLN into a legitimate political party.

Part of the context for the war was the general collapse of the country's export agriculture that had begun in the 1970s, driven by a perfect storm of OPEC petroleum price hikes, a worldwide drop in agricultural commodity prices, and the phenomenon of stagflation. With the onset of the war in 1980, leaders of El Salvador's export sector, especially coffee interests, moved several billion dollars out of the country. Part of this capital flight included the Regelado-Dueñas family's investment of $9 million in Mitt Romney's new Bain Capital enterprise (Tanfani, Mason, and Gold 2012). Besides investing in new hedge funds and equity groups abroad, the dominant business interests in El Salvador also recognized that migrant remittances and US expenditure were driving a commercial and financial boom in the country that was outstripping the old agro-export sector. With the election as president of Alfredo Cristiani of the Alianza Republicana Nacionalista party (ARENA) in 1988, a particular subset of relatively diversified capitalists less narrowly tied to the export sector came to power, poised to carry out the full bevy of neoliberal reforms stipulated by the so-called Washington Consensus. They were highly motivated to end the war through a negotiated settlement for the sake of new business opportunities beyond coffee exports. One complication is that this impulse went directly against hard-liners in the Pentagon, the White House, and the Salvadoran military, as well as some agro-export elites who wanted full military defeat of the FMLN.

The Cristiani-led fraction worked to carry out the privatization of the country's financial sector, which had been nationalized by a coalition of reformist military officers and social democratic party members that had taken over the government at the outset of the war. By the mid-1990s, the country was dominated by a private financial oligopoly comprised of six major banks and financial organizations, each held by different major family groups in the country, many of whom had dominated the country since the 1880s.[11] Cristiani, together with members of the Llach, Bahaia, and DeSola families, controlled the largest financial conglomerate in El Salvador, Banco Cuscatlán, as part of their larger Panama-based holding company. During this financial consolidation, El Salvador's domestic agricultural system was effectively abandoned, dramatically transforming rural life and contributing to increased migration from these areas to the United States as well as to the rural population's overall reliance on remittances for their survival.

Approaching the Disease

Although I have summarized this transformation as a nearly antiseptic flip of a switch, it was a gradual and difficult process that included many conflicting forces and influences both within and beyond the immediate context of El Salvador. One of these historical actors was actually a representational system that played a direct role in the privatization and liberalization of the financial sector. By considering this discursive codification in particular and then inquiring into some of its less visible historical content we move a little further from symptom to disease.

In 1996 the World Bank released a country report on El Salvador that made the general claim that remittances were a novel though likely long-term influx of hard currency that went primarily into "household consumption" in El Salvador and were essentially not productive. The report drew on the economic model known as "Dutch Disease" to explain the consequences of the remittance influx. This takes its popular name from the Netherlands' experience in the 1970s when it exploited North Sea oil reserves and experienced a dramatic influx of hard currency. The model describes the effects of this influx of new revenue and its tendency to drive up a country's currency, putting pressure on its export sector while stimulating imports of commercial goods and the expansion of commerce and services (non-tradable goods) within the country, whether this be public or private (Cordon and Neary 1982). The report used the model of reality in El Salvador to justify its argument that the

Salvadoran government should not use resources for fiscal expenditure or government-led investment and instead should pursue an even tighter fiscal policy. This effectively ensured that the remittances would circulate through the newly privatized financial sector as well as in commerce, both of which were fully controlled by the wealthiest family consortia in El Salvador.

The report also emphasized the newness and uniqueness of the remittance flows, making two important claims: (1) the flow is long-term and structural, and (2) people in El Salvador use remittances to purchase mostly non-tradable consumer goods. The first claim is just an assertion without any supporting evidence: "As long as emigrant workers remain in the US, and the US economy continues growing, remittances will continue. However, they should not increase much beyond current levels, remaining at 8–10 percent GDP" in the receiving country (Grandolini 1996: 16). The second claim regarding the use of remittance monies is substantiated with reference to a report written by the policy research center FUSADES (Fundación Salvadoreña para el Desarollo Económico y Social), which was founded in 1983 with support from the United States Agency for International Development. The latter was known for its steady production of neoliberal policy reports and support for the Cristiani-led faction of the ARENA party. The FUSADES report referred to by the World Bank report is the *Economic and Social Bulletin* of January 1994 called "Salvadoran emigration and its economic and social impact" (FUSADES 1994). It is short and contains four sections. In the third, the authors refer to "studies completed by CEPAL" (the Economic Commission for Latin America and the Caribbean, or ECLA in English) showing, according to them, that remittances are principally used for "family consumption."

There is no more reference to the CEPAL reports, but it seems likely that the FUSADES authors had in mind a report issued in June 1991, "El Salvador: international remittances and family economics", that drew on a wealth of survey research, interviews, and a review of government documents (CEPAL 1991). One of the cases included was the well-known town of Intipucá with its history of migration to the Washington, DC, area (Montes Mozo and García Vásquez 1988).

I had been living in Intipucá on and off since 1993, learning about its ties to Washington, DC, and why it provided such an attractive case study of migration and remittance circulation in El Salvador. Its appearance as a data point embedded in the World Bank report confirmed its role as an exemplar of El Salvador's restructuring around migration and remittances. The argument that remittances were used for family consumption in the town was accurate in a general way, but this understanding also short-circuited their actual trajectories and effects. This occlusion of the fuller story did play a role in substantiating the Dutch Disease model as a plausible and seemingly rational way to understand remittances in El Salvador and to support the World Bank's argument that the country should reduce fiscal expenditure.

Calle Principal in Intipucá

Briefly, the story of remittances in Intipucá is about the town's reorganization around a kind of a subaltern service sector as people in the town (including many who recently moved there from other parts of El Salvador) worked for remittance recipients there. It is a tale of the journey from low-wage farmworker to low-wage service-worker and a fairly brutal account of increased, not reduced poverty, in contradiction of the World Bank project which hid how it sustained this exploitation.

It is true that remittances arrive and are used by people to support their households and for the purchase of consumer goods, including food. But this household consumption also includes using the money for the work capacities of servants who produced the appearance of wealth in the town through the well-kept homes and capabilities freed up by their work for the residents who live there. Remittances also stimulated the development of a collection of food stands in the town center where residents with access to cash, primarily sent from US relatives, could purchase meals, snacks, and drinks (including prepared drinks, soda, and beer). In the immediate aftermath of the war, the number of stands grew rapidly as Salvadoran migrants in the United States returned to visit relatives and friends, spending money at the public stands. This expansion also reflected the overall collapse of rural agriculture in the region, which had fostered new political dynamics as well as growth in the number of people who were in a position to become stand operators.

One woman who ran a popular stand recognized that she could earn more money in the aftermath of the war from the general growth of remittances to town residents during the mid-1990s. She obtained a modest loan from a wealthier town resident known for such micro-loans and purchased a metal "kiosk" from which she could sell cold drinks and snacks. She obtained a refrigerator from the national brewery and bottling company *La Constancia*, which offered them for free in return for regular sale of its products. Besides the loan, her other main cash expense was the electricity needed for the drinks cooler. She also purchased ice from a servant who used his home's refrigerator/freezer to run an informal ice cube business, in defiance of the development economists' assumption that domestic consumption fueled by remittances was "nonproductive" investment. The stand owner explained that almost everyone in the town recognized how the flow of former town residents returning for visits and the general flow of remittances into the town had stimulated the spread of food stands there. She was solely responsible for raising her daughter and had calculated that operating a stand would be a greater and more reliable source of income than her previous work as a *curandera* (healer).

Such healing practices remain common throughout El Salvador and among Salvadoran migrants in the United States. Typically patients pay a modest fee for treatment by the *curandera* that could include herbal and plant-based drinks and poultices as well as incantations and other actions meant to cleanse and heal. Some treatments are specifically oriented toward the health of a newborn child or freeing individuals from bad luck or curses. Often the treatment would entail a kind of ritualized repurposing of Christian religious idioms and iconography. One popular treatment involved surreptitiously obtaining fresh communion wafers from the Catholic Church, dipping them in oil, and applying them to the temple region of the face.

One evening at the woman's stand in the late 1990s, she appeared visibly upset, weeping and loudly lamenting that she was poor and in debt (for the stand) and would remain poor, despite long hours of working at the stand every day of the week. One man comforted her with a hug and stressed that everyone in the town was poor and everyone worked extremely hard. This man, in fact, was from one of the wealthiest land-owning families in the area and was known to have ample cash sent from relatives in the United States. She knew him as a regular customer and looked out for his patronage. Gradually her mood lifted and the typically playful banter of such evenings in the park returned for the group sitting at her stand.[12] In a teasing manner, many people called her *La Bruja* (witch), in reference to her previous vocation.

From Wall Street to Intipucá's Main Street

This brief account of market life in Intipucá and the pseudo-medical symptom-to-disease investigation began with Weill's interview and ended in Intipucá's central park area. The journey was not one of lineal temporality, from past to present, nor was it based on the convention of examining the function of discrete parts in a closed set. By modulating the locus, focus and scope of analysis in a way that moved through immediate formations to show some of their hidden logics, content and context—like relating symptoms to disease—I tried to suggest a way of inquiring critically into capitalism that could better show its unevenness and heterogeneity, while also pointing to broader tendencies and forces of change. There is one more symptom to be examined, however, which leads to a better sense of the overall affliction and at least to the potential to overcome it.

When the market woman expressed her sadness and sense that she could not fully appropriate her world, but rather it, in the form of her debts, controlled her, she was criticizing the same world that Weill had evoked from a different vantage point. She was angry and hurt at being reduced to being trapped in money and commodity relations from which there seemed no escape. It is possible to recognize that, although the most generic quality of her efforts that night (what she cursed as the relentless unfreedom of 'work') mediated the other particular, personal, and inter-subjective qualities of her life, these latter dimensions still included asserting her autonomy relative to the abstract aspects of her life. That relative autonomy could spring forth and potentially disrupt the overall tendency of mediation at any moment. I believe this potential was recognized by the wealthier customer when he consoled her. His was a representational practice structurally akin to Weill's talk on *Squawkbox*, as our journey from Wall Street to Intipucá has sought to show, even if each gesture occurred within different representational systems, most obviously those defined by language. With this image of the contradictory whole under consideration, while recognizing that the composite of representational practices literally coproduces the vast opposites of Weill and the market woman, we can now look forward from this moment to gain a sense of where the whole ungainly process might be going.

From Disease to Cure

A decade after the 1996 report on El Salvador that used the Dutch Disease model to account for US dollar remittances in El Salvador, thereby justifying pushing the Salvadoran state away from its use and administration, the World Bank developed a completely new perspective. Drawing on the work of senior economist Dilip Ratha, the Bank argued that remittances were crucial to grassroots development and poverty reduction and should be encouraged, even leveraged, for greater benefits in receiving regions worldwide (World Bank 2006). This view of remittances as cure rather than disease has spread since then and now undergirds the work of the United Nations and a host of national governmental and nongovernmental organizations too.[13] Intipucá has made a modest appearance in some of the literature on remittance-based development, now cast as an important example of grassroots remittance-led development (UNDP 2006; Itzigsohn and Villacrés 2008). Remittances are no longer defined as the cause of end-use consumption and a problem to be managed through neoliberal reforms. Instead, they are a novel kind of direct, non-state contributor to poverty reduction. In just a decade, the meaning of remittances, and also of Intipucá itself, were completely transformed, at least according to the development institutions.

This new development agenda includes an understanding that remittances may be treated as a payment stream similar to any kind of long-term regularized debt payment flow. It then becomes possible to buy and sell the flow in the form of an "asset-backed security," much like mortgages or credit-card debt payments. Remittance securitization rests on the central role that the transferring institutions, usually banks, play with regard to money and its movement. Turning what seems like a technical challenge into a financial product hinges on the distinction between a bank's receipt of remittances and its payout to the recipients. In what is called a future-flow securitization, a bank may effectively sell its control of the regular stream to an offshore entity known as a special-purpose vehicle (SPV). Weill referred to the unregulated trade in such instruments as "off–balance sheet things." The SPV may be rated by international agencies, which attracts investors who are guaranteed a steady return. The SPV then passes on its income from investors to the bank, which the latter effectively has earned in exchange for selling on its "first right to receive" the remittance flow.

Proponents tout the overall practice as a key way for banks to raise funds, especially if they find it difficult to borrow in international markets. Remittance-backed SPVs are promoted to long-term "buy-and-hold" investors working on behalf of institutional endowments such as pension funds. At the same time, legal interpretations of the practice recognize that these financial deals are structured so that the least-protected participants are the remittance receivers. In order to make the SPVs attractive to investors, the remittance payment stream itself must be pledged as collateral. Hypothetically, if remittances were to dramatically decrease, banks would have to cover the payments out of their own funds. In the event of a significant collapse, the recipients are legally defined as the last to get paid.

One well-known example of this novel financial practice involves Banco Cuscatlán in El Salvador and its successful issuance of future-flow remittance-backed securities in 1999. This was made possible in part because it had opened offices in the greater Washington DC area, the second largest concentration of Salvadorans in the United States. However, with the passage of the Central American Free Trade Agreement (CAFTA) in 2003, US and Salvadoran national banking laws were coordinated and it became possible for banks to open fully owned and controlled offices in any member country, or even buy banks in member countries outright.

In 2004 Cuscatlán made another successful issuance, receiving the letter grade of 'BBB' from Fitch Ratings. At the time, Cuscatlán was El Salvador's second largest bank, owned by the Cristiani-led holding group. After assisting Cuscatlán with its 2004 issuance of remittance–backed bonds–Citigroup recognized the money to be made in the whole endeavor and purchased the bank and its subsidiaries throughout Central America as well as its US offices. The bank's name, Cuscatlán was not altered. Now visible as a contradictory whole, a small portion of Citigroup's profits come from remittance-backed securities, whose relative worth rests on the poverty of rural El Salvador and the necessity of migration and remittance transfer for survival.

Among the main challenges faced by future-flow remittance securitizations is that there must be agreements among all the banks involved with the flow of remittances and some guarantee that there will not be any sovereign intervention or disruption of the deal. With the passage of CAFTA and Citigroup's purchase of Cuscatlán, the flow was effectively controlled fully by one single bank. However, the distinct national governments of El Salvador and the United States still sit as two separate sovereign authorities across the circuit. Among SPV investors, one distant risk is that the deals could be affected by the intervention of a particular government, perhaps through nationalization, as occurred in 1980 in El Salvador.

In 2012, the US State Department signed an agreement with representatives of El Salvador and Honduras, stipulating that the three governments and their respective private-banking sectors would work together to better coordinate and build the market for remittance-backed securities. This effort coincides with US support for the broad program of "innovative financing for development," a growing worldwide agenda that brings together governments, international organizations, researchers, international donors, and activists. A US State Department official told me about the agreement: "it has kind of lost momentum, you know, after Wall Street and all." Although there seems to be a momentary pause in the project of transforming Salvadoran migrant remittances into asset-backed securities, the broader project of innovative finance for development continues apace. "Banking the unbanked" is the refrain in what amounts to an effort to scour the globe for regularized payment streams to be transformed into financial instruments to be bought and sold on world markets (Singh, this volume).

Spin the Dial

As these seemingly disjunctive stories come together at the end, linking Wall Street with main street kiosk activity in Intipucá, I hope it becomes clear that my unconventional approach helps to disclose some of the disparate practices that are both a product of and contribute to an overall tendency. From this symptom-to-epidemic journey, it becomes possible to appreciate better that Intipucá remittances and their securitization are hardly part of a process that is "lifting a billion people out of poverty." This claim of Weill's is made by proponents of innovative finance for development and their concern for the "bottom billion" (Collier 2008).

Methodologically, the project rests on a capacity to "hold" at once facets and qualities of social life according to multiple and varied loci, foci, and scales, informed by, but also unencumbered by, any single set of disciplinary coordinates. Although these tendencies are not absolute, the typical discipline that would consider everyday life in Intipucá is anthropology, or perhaps the subfield, rural sociology. In anthropology, inquiry typically would have begun and ended within a single cultural group chosen for study as defined by its members. Its considered foci could be *curandera* practices, perhaps in relation to so-called Western medicine and capitalism, each understood as separate and discrete entities coming into contact and interacting. Indeed, this is a well-trodden line of inquiry in the anthropology of medicine and healing (Strathern and Stewart 2010).

Now anthropologists also study Wall Street, especially figures like the trader as a member of a relatively distinct Wall Street sub-group. Of course, economics has much to say about the models used by traders and in World Bank reports, while scholars working in science studies have inquired critically into the science of economic modeling. Communications and media studies certainly could have interrogated Weill's interview and its online circulation. Historians of El Salvador have focused on such topics as rural productive systems and land use, nationalism, and social memory. There is a superb tradition within El Salvador of studying critically state formation, elites, and the reconfiguration of political and economic sectors. Political scientists have also addressed these themes. Finally, bank leadership and malfeasance is well covered in a growing body of English-language scholarship, usually written for a nonacademic audience.

The problem with all these discipline-specific considerations is not that any one of them is true or false and subject to empirical refutation. The difficulty arises when the content or objects of analysis are erroneously assumed to be fundamentally discrete and different in kind. To substantiate a specific discipline often means to keep inquiry within a pre-set place and time, focus on specific kinds of evidence, and maintain a delimited spatiotemporal scale of analysis. In this regard, disciplinary fundamentalism comes from the relative stability and widely shared nature of these kinds of settings. Instances of academic border control often occur through tacit enforcement of them. Similarly, changing intellectual concerns within a discipline may be understood in part as attempts to recalibrate some of the dominant settings as well as justifications for them. Finally, the relative strength and influence of particular academic disciplines rests on their capacity to universalize their particular settings and what is gleaned from them.

Despite the apparent naturalness and almost eternal quality of varied settings and, for example, the current movement in anthropology to recalibrate its settings back to small-scale others, we should note that the life of disciplines is shorter than that of Lehman Brothers!

David Pedersen is associate professor in the Department of Anthropology at the University of California–San Diego. He is the author of *American Value: Migrants, Money and Meaning in El Salvador* (2014). His current research focuses on money, violence, and belief.

NOTES

1. My book *American Value: Migrants, Money and Meaning in El Salvador and the United States* (Pedersen 2014) examines the asymmetrical reorganization of El Salvador and the United States in terms of migration, remittances, and service work.
2. "Transnational" here indicates that the congealed and meaningful domain of this circulation comprises multiple locales spread across more than one nation-state. See Roger Rouse's (1992) definitive essay.
3. According to International Telecommunications Union (ITU) estimates, this group currently comprises about 2.7 billion people worldwide. The terms "commons" and "public sphere" seem appropriate, but the Internet is fully

mediated and shaped by private corporations and many states, especially the United States through its National Security Administration.
4. I thank Bill Sewell for pointing out how Weill embodied this contradictory position, mainly through a large dose of self-delusion.
5. The images and text considered here are the digital records of an event that initially reached a small subset of this group, probably about 135,000 people, according to Squawkbox's official tally. The potential reach of this video event and its aftermath is the audience of 2.7 billion with digital access to it and its diffusion by other means to the 4.4 billion people who do not have direct Internet access. As an Internet user, my most inclusive locus of analysis is a vantage point concentrated in Asia, Europe, and the Americas (with 88 percent of world Internet users).
6. For the historical content hidden in Weill's words, I rely on the late Peter Gowan (2009).
7. http://www.businessinsider.com/a-prop-trader-explains-his-work-his-salary-and-why-everyone-is-wrong-about-his-kind-2012-4#ixzz3RDUk3K2W.
8. See Tett (2009).
9. Sub-Comandante Marcos (1997) of the Zapatista National Liberation Army offers a counterpoint to Weill's perspective in a famous article entitled "The fourth world war has begun" (published in *Le Monde Diplomatique*, September 1997): "Unlike the third world war, in which conflict between capitalism and socialism took place over a variety of terrains and with varying degrees of intensity, the fourth world war is being conducted between major financial centers in theaters of war that are global in scale and with a level of intensity that is fierce and constant. . . . Thanks to computers and the technological revolution, the financial markets, operating from their offices and answerable to nobody but themselves, have been imposing their laws and worldview on the planet as a whole."
10. See Hershberg and Rosen (2006).
11. Friends in El Salvador during the middle 1990s shared a rueful joke that the settlement of the war was a crude stereotype of Marx versus Weber. The oligarchy got the economy while the FMLN gained political representation.
12. From a more extensive account of food-stand operators in Intipucá (Pedersen 2014: chapter 8).
13. The Global Forum on Remittances and Development brings together the United Nations, World Bank, host government agencies, and nongovernmental organizations to promote migrant remittances for development globally. See their tremendous clearinghouse of information at http://www.remittancesgateway.org.

REFERENCES

Brown, A., and E. Patten. 2013. "Hispanics of Salvadoran Origin in the United States, 2011." Washington, DC: Pew Research Center.

CEPAL. 1991. "El Salvador: Remesas Internacionales y Economia Familiar." Mexico City.

Collier, P. 2008. *The Bottom Billion: Why the Poorest Countries are Failing and What Can Be Done About It*. Oxford: Oxford University Press.

Cordon, W., and J. Neary. 1982. "Booming Sector and De-Industrialization in a Small Open Economy." *The Economic Journal* 92(368): 825–848.

FUSADES. 1994. "La Emigracion de Salvadoreños y su impacto economico y social." *Boletin Economico y Social* 98, enero de 1994. San Salvador.

Gowan, P. 2009. "Crisis in the Heartland: Consequences of the New Wall Street System." *New Left Review* 55.

Grandolini, G. 1996. *El Salvador: Meeting the Challenges of Globalization*. Washington, DC: World Bank.

Hart, K. 2000. *The Memory Bank: Money in an Unequal World*. New York: Texere.

Hart, K., and H. Ortiz. 2014. "The Anthropology of Money and Finance: Between Ethnography and World History." *Annual Review of Anthropology* 43: 465–482.

Hershberg, E., and F. Rosen. 2006. *Latin America after Neoliberalism: Turning the Tide in the 21st Century?* New York: The New Press.

Hurley, G. 2012. "Innovative Finance for Development: A new model for developing finance?" United Nations Development Programme Discussion Paper.

Itzigsohn, J., and D. Villacrés. 2008. "Migrant Political Transnationalism and the Practice of Democracy: Dominican External Voting Rights and Salvadoran Home Town Associations." *Ethnic and Racial Studies* 31:4.

Jorion, P. 2003. *Investing in a Post-Enron World*. New York: McGraw-Hill.

Langley, M. 2003. *Tearing Down the Walls*. New York: Simon & Schuster.

Montes Mozo, S., and J. J. García Vásquez. 1988. *Salvadoran Migration to the United States: An Exploratory Study*. Washington, DC: Center for Immigration Policy and Refugee Assistance, Georgetown University.

Pedersen, D. 2014. *American Value: Migrants, Money, and Meaning in El Salvador and the United States*. Chicago, IL: University of Chicago Press.

Rouse, R. 1992. "Making Sense of Settlement: Class Transformation, Cultural Struggle and Transnationalism among Mexican Migrants in the United States." *Annals of the New York Academy of Sciences* 645: 25–52.

Strathern, A., and P. Stewart. 2010. *Curing and Healing: Medical Anthropology in Global Perspective*, Ethnographic Studies in Medical Anthropology Series. Durham, NC: Carolina Academic Press.

Tanfani, J., M. Mason, and M. Gold. 2012. "Bain Capital started with help of offshore investors." *LA Times*, 19 July 19.

Tett, G. 2009. *Fool's Gold: The Inside Story of J.P. Morgan and How Wall St. Greed Corrupted Its Bold Dream and Created a Financial Catastrophe*. New York: Free Press.

UNDP. 2006. *Informe sobre Desarrollo Humano de El Salvador 2005 Una Mirada al Nuevo Nosotros. El Impacto de las Migraciones*. San Salvador: Programa de las Naciones Unidas para el Desarrollo.

World Bank. 2014. "Migration and Remittances: Recent Developments and Outlook." Development Brief 23, Washington, DC.

———. 2006. "Global Economic Prospects: The Economic Implications of Remittances and Migration." Manuscript, Washington, DC.

CHAPTER 7

Cross-Border Investment in China

HORACIO ORTIZ

In the last thirty years in Europe, the United States, and many other jurisdictions, the finance industry expanded its role in the distribution of monetary resources, legitimized by a narrative derived from liberal philosophies, according to which the organization of supposedly efficient markets would generate an optimal allocation of resources for world society. During roughly the same period, after the end of the Cultural Revolution, with a policy called "reform and opening," the Chinese finance industry, nonexistent in the early 1980s, became one of the biggest in the world. This was accompanied by a legitimizing narrative that combined the liberal discourse above with nationalism, anticolonialism, socialism, a call for economic development, and, lately, sustainability. These two processes are intertwined today, as the Chinese territory has become a center of global manufacturing, affecting not only the United States and Europe but also the rest of the world. This has important implications for the approach adopted in this book, and in this chapter, that takes world society and the issue of inequality in the distribution of monetary resources as analytical starting points.

Financial flows connect people in different areas of the globe, concretely establishing interdependencies and hierarchies among them, across and beyond the juridical and symbolic borders established by states. In that sense, they are a powerful driver of the constitution of world society, as they create a global space of hierarchy in the distribution of money. The meanings of these hierarchies are multifarious and evolve over time. Changing them may eventually allow for establishing a clearer global agenda setting the political issue of resource distribution at the center of debates. The meanings currently proposed by the finance industry and its regulators (i.e., by the institutions in charge of collecting and distributing money on a global scale) are nowhere near this aim.

Understanding them is thus a necessary step to changing them. This poses conceptual and methodological challenges that can only partly be addressed by one piece of research.

From a methodological point of view, this chapter aims to highlight some of the concrete practices whereby these two historical processes come together in the finance industry today. It does so based on research carried out, through interviews and participant observation, with people working for companies in charge of cross-border investment inside the Chinese territory, who use money coming from Europe and the United States to purchase companies based in China and/or money from China to purchase companies in Europe and the United States.[1] These activities imply the conjuncture of different institutional and legal settings, as employees and companies have to comply with rules that are differentiated by the border crossed by the transactions. Through these activities, employees also redefine the meanings of their professional and nonprofessional lives and the moral and political imaginaries that come with them.

From a conceptual point of view, this chapter attempts to tackle the issue of unequal monetary distribution by following approaches that show that money can have multiple meanings and uses. In her work on West Africa, Guyer (2004) explored a historical process whereby different monetary organizations, with specific scales of measure and moral and political references, came together in creative ways, both shaped by and reshaping social relations of power (Hart and Ortiz 2014). This approach contrasts with others claiming that one main monetary organization, be it "Western," "colonial," or, more recently, "neoliberal," characterized by both homogeneity and political power, imposes itself on a myriad other weaker but resisting practices (Parry and Bloch 1989). Analyses of everyday transactions (Zelizer 1997), of the activities of central banks (Hart 1986; Holmes 2013) or of political and administrative agencies, when they determine the monetary value of love (Zelizer 2005) or of nature (Fourcade 2011), remind us that the so-called West is not a social space with homogeneous monetary practices. Within that often-undefined category (Trouillot 2003), multiple, contradictory, disconnected, labile, and shifting practices of money and finance take place (Dodd 2014). From this theoretical perspective, the same can be said of the institutions associated with what is designated, often also in very vague ways, as "China."

I consider the border to be both constituted by and constitutive of everyday financial practices. The act of "crossing" itself is generated by two sides of a divide. At the same time, crossing, in this context, as we will see, challenges the border and transforms its regulatory and institutional meanings. I show that employees make sense of their everyday lives through their technical, moral, and political understanding of their place in a professional milieu and of the balance of power in commercial transactions. Conflicting narratives of universality evoke cultural and nationalist views organized around the centrality of states as the main foundation and horizon of future transformations. This chapter shows the importance of institutional arrangements and legitimation in the everyday practices of financial professionals and how these shared meanings are reproduced and transformed. These practices are responsible for the everyday production of global hierarchies. Analyzing them is important for understanding how world society is being made today (i.e., the imaginaries and practices that connect the seven billion of us through the money managed by the financial industry). This analysis aims to contribute to a critique of current financial imagination, practices, and institutions. This is the concrete ground from which alternatives must be explored and proposed.

I will first review the main institutional features and political imaginaries of cross-border investment in China, Europe, and the United States. I will then show how employees make sense of their financial activities in a professional, bureaucratic setting with standardized procedures and how they make sense of the power relations implied in financial transactions by mobilizing the political and moral references of the institutional setting of which they are part. Finally, I will show how this limited set of common references is produced and reproduced in multiple and labile ways by each employee. I will explore this through the specific example of three interviewees.

Global Financial Flows, Macroeconomic Relations, and Legal Frameworks

Since the mid-1980s, in the United States and Europe (Abdelal 2007; Krippner 2011), the financial industry has taken an increasingly central role in the distribution of money. Privatization and the growing use of stocks and bonds to finance economic activity have brought to prominence investment funds, brokerage houses, rating agencies, and insurance companies, alongside the banks, which have reshaped their own activities to partake in these new developments (Couppey-Soubeyran, Plihon, and Saïdane 2006). The rules of the financial industry have become increasingly important for how states and companies are managed (Fligstein 2001; Sinclair 2005). In the United States, a reshuffle of the financial system in the 1970s was linked to the break-up of the Bretton Woods agreement and to a new balance of power between trade unions, companies, and governments. This ensued in a new organization of the pension system, increasingly run by the finance industry, contributing to exponential growth in the exchange of bonds, listed stocks, and other financial securities (Clark 2000; Montagne 2006). In Europe, the finance industry did not occupy such a central role. Regulatory changes in the 1980s aimed to capture some of the money held as savings by the middle classes, as well as to channel part of it to financial securities in the United States. Yet, the growth of an autonomous and privatized finance industry did change how states were managed, given their increasing reliance on bonds (Lemoine 2016).

Since the end of the Cold War and of the bloody conflicts and dictatorships that it sustained, the finance industry's expansion was fostered by the International Monetary Fund (IMF) and the World Bank in vast areas, such as Latin America, the former Soviet bloc, and Southeast Asia (Blyth 2003; Pedersen this volume).[2] This process ensued in the privatization of public services and production of more financial securities to be held by what was now deemed a "global" finance industry (Stiglitz 2006). This latter came to occupy an increasingly political role, officially legitimized by a liberal narrative whereby "technical" changes in the organization of credit, through "markets" where "investors" would meet, would result in an "optimal" allocation of credit thanks to market "efficiency" (Lee 1998; Ortiz 2014a). This discourse was linked to one emphasizing the protection of US and European social security and the idea, inherited from colonial times and reinforced after the Cold War, that Europe and the United States remained the geopolitical centers of the world (Eichengreen 1996).

At the same time, after the Cultural Revolution, the government of China, through the Chinese Communist Party network, created a banking sector that, following China's integration into global commercial circuits, ranks today among the biggest in the world by assets, market capitalization, and profits and constitutes the main source of money production and distribution in China (Zhu 2009). Bonds and stock markets that did not exist thirty years ago have today attained volumes that equal or surpass Europe's. The overwhelming majority of the finance industry belongs, in one way or another, to the state (Hsueh 2011). Its top managers are part of the ninety million members of the Communist Party, as are much of the administration and the economic elite. Many of these companies are listed in stock exchanges in China, Hong Kong, and the United States, a transformation that has been called the "corporatization" of state-owned enterprises as opposed to their "privatization." With marginal exceptions, nonresidents cannot invest in bonds and stocks within the Chinese territory and residents can only invest small amounts abroad. The Chinese finance industry thereby holds most middle-class savings, investing them in major infrastructure projects managed by state-owned or state-backed companies.

This process, starting in the 1980s, has been central to wealth distribution within the Chinese territory, reducing poverty and contributing to redrawing inequality and power relations in access to money with the emergence of a richer middle class, composing around 20 percent of the population and of a small super-rich elite almost invariably related to the Communist Party (Davies and Wang 2009). This is today legitimized by several narratives. At the end of the nineteenth century, the creation of a financial system joining "national" private capital and state-backed administration was justified by the importance of using "economic development" to build a "Chinese nation" conceived of in republican fashion against the colonial powers (Wu and Ma 2003; Cheng 2003). These narratives were retained by the Communist Party when it took over in 1949, conjugating them with a discourse about "socialism" and, since the 1980s, the liberal narrative about "markets" evoked above (Hertz 1998; Bell and Feng 2013). In the last few years, the notion of "sustainable" development became increasingly important without displacing the other discourses.[3]

Since the 1990s, cross-border investment around the world has expanded partly through purchases of bonds and stocks listed in exchanges, as part of regulatory transformations legitimized by and often imposed through institutions such as the IMF and the World Bank. Within the Chinese jurisdiction, the rules concerning the right to purchase bonds and listed stocks, as indicated above, have channeled cross-border investment toward the purchase of companies that are not listed in exchanges. This belongs to what global accounting standards call "foreign direct investment." Thus, the transactions analyzed here are defined as being part of the constitution of national borders and global rules of the distribution of money in its various forms. "China," "Europe," the "United States," like other categories, are partly constituted by these borders, which are in turn determined in part by financial regulations and their appropriation and transformation in specific practices.

China is the second largest receiver of "foreign direct investment" in volume after the United States, with about $150 billion coming in a year, a similar amount going out, and one trillion dollars of compounded investment having entered the territory since the early 1980s. This might be compared to the outstanding amount of around $7.7 trillion levied in bonds in China or to over $20 trillion in assets held by banks, an amount that has more than doubled since 2008. In spite of the relatively small amounts of cross-border investment, it occupies a particular place in the macroeconomic organization of credit by central government. Since most Chinese banks tend to lend to big companies and since foreign investment companies are virtually barred from purchasing listed stocks, cross-border investment appears as one way for small Chinese companies to find funding outside the banking system. It is also an important way for big Chinese companies to purchase companies abroad.

Companies, Employees, and Procedures

The people I met worked for companies who specialized in purchasing, partly or in whole, small and medium enterprises (SMEs) based in China, with money coming from the United States and Europe, or purchasing SMEs based in the United States and Europe, with money coming from China. Some companies specialized in both types of transaction, called "inbound" and "outbound" investment. This is done through two types of organization. Investment funds in private equity and venture capital look for small companies that can be reorganized and can use the investment to expand and eventually become big enough to be sold to others, usually in the form of an Initial Public Offering (IPO) on a stock exchange. These investment funds collect money from other financial institutions and usually only purchase a part of the company, but one big enough for them to exert control over management. Private equity funds tend to buy already-established SMEs, while venture capital funds concentrate on start-ups. The other type of organization consists of consultancy companies for mergers and acquisitions (M&A), which serve as intermediaries when one company buys another, usually for the purpose of integrating its operations, patents, client base, or other "assets" into its own. I will concentrate on "inbound" investment to China, because this is what most of my interviewees worked on at the time of the research presented here, between 2011 and 2015.[4]

Even though their aims may be very different, these companies often operate in similar fields. "Target" companies of a private equity fund can also be interesting for a bigger company working in the same sector. And private equity and venture capital funds can attempt to resell the company they purchased a share of to a bigger company, through M&A instead of the stock exchange. The sectors and sizes of companies are similar for all these transactions. In China, they concern companies considered to have growth potential linked to the future evolution of the Chinese economy, in particular in sectors linked to the growth of middle-class consumption, such as health, education, leisure, and high technology. In the United States and Europe, purchased companies usually operate in high technology, which Chinese companies are interested in importing to expand within China and worldwide.

The methodologies of valuation and investment are also similar. In all cases, employees are expected to conduct a financial valuation of the company according to the same standardized methods taught in business schools and finance departments, formalized as the mainstream financial theory that has become dominant in the United States and Europe in the last forty years (Whitley 1986; MacKenzie 2006). Employees are expected to do this from the point of view of an investor seeking to maximize returns, according to commercial and labor contracts that specify that this is how clients' interests (either the selling or purchasing company or investment funds) are best represented. Not applying these techniques can lead to losing one's job or even to legal suits and jail. The career trajectory, income volume, and prestige of each employee is in great part defined by his[5] ability to apply these procedures and increase revenue for his company. This revenue usually comes in the form of a fee, calculated in two ways. In all cases, "operating fees" are charged along the way, ensuring a minimum return that pays salaries, and "success fees" are charged once the transaction is concluded, from which bonuses are distributed among employees. Success fees are calculated as a proportion of the transaction, in the case of M&A, and of the profits of the resale, in the case of private equity and venture capital. While investment fund employees are pushed always to buy cheap and sell high, those working for M&A consultancy firms may try to buy cheap, if their client is a purchasing company, or to sell high, if the client is a target company.

As happens elsewhere in the finance industry (and not only there), within a single financial company employees develop relations of complementarity, competition, and hierarchy (Abolafia 1996; Zaloom 2006; Godechot 2007; Ho 2009; Ortiz 2014b). They have to work together on specific projects, but they also must compete against each other, inside the company and within the financial industry, since the next step up may be to a competing company or in a related sector. In that sense, the skills demanded for employees in private equity, venture capital, and M&A may not always be too different, and employees can move within these structures in their careers. In all cases, even if these companies are small, they are bureaucratic structures, bound by financial regulations and the fact that often they themselves belong to bigger financial companies, of which they are a subsidiary created to develop this particular activity. The diversity of situations may be explored through three specific cases.

Mr. Jones[6] was the head of a venture capital fund, in a major city on the eastern coast of China. He oversaw investment in very small companies, which would eventually be sold to other companies or through IPOs after five years, during which he and his team would contribute to their growth with investment and consulting services. He obtained a diploma in engineering in Western Europe, where he was born, and continued his studies in China in the early 1990s, later obtaining a PhD in physics in the United States. He had spent the last eleven years in China, when I interviewed him in 2014. The fund he directed had money coming from different institutions, in particular from the municipality where the fund was based, and from state-owned investment funds in the Middle East. His everyday working life mainly consisted of looking for companies to purchase, through formal and personal networks, and negotiating the price to be paid, according to the standards he had learned when he was living in Silicon Valley. An important part of his job implied participating in the management of companies already purchased, providing them with access to commercial networks, technology, and further funding. His income was split between a fixed salary and a variable bonus that depended on the profit made by selling the companies he invested in. He spoke of his company as "we" and planned to work in this field in China in the coming years.

Ms. Li was born and grew up in China. She studied finance at one of the most prestigious Chinese universities in the 1990s and obtained the US-based, internationally recognized diploma of Chartered Financial Analyst, given by the relevant professional association, which is very active in establishing regulatory and professional standards in the United States.[7] She worked as a chief financial officer for international companies in China and, when I interviewed her in 2013, she was a partner for one of the four major auditing companies in the world, whose global base was in the United States. As a top manager, she oversaw many mergers and acquisitions, in which she worked as a consultant, in particular for the valuation of assets bought and sold by her clients. Most of her daily professional life involved overseeing financial accounts, industrial sites, and documents that made up the tools to provide a price range that could be used by her clients either to sell or buy. As a partner, she was also expected to bring new clients to her company and part of her professional life also implied engaging in social relations that could help her meet potential clients and convince them to work with her. Her income was composed of a fixed salary and a bonus linked to how well her company was doing and to the income she brought in by attracting new clients. Like Mr. Jones, she spoke of the company as "we" and planned to stay in it for the foreseeable future.

Mr. Martin was the chief financial officer of Steel Inc., the Chinese subsidiary of a midsized industrial group established in Western Europe. A citizen of a European country, he had spent most of his life working in the financial departments of industrial companies in different European countries. When I met him in 2012, he had been working for five years in China and was about to retire. One of his last major operations as an employee was to purchase Stone Inc., a subsidiary of a company owned by the municipality of a major city on the eastern coast of China. Steel Inc. produced similar but higher-quality products to Stone Inc. and the acquisition would serve multiple purposes. It allowed the European company to set foot in China, using the commercial network already established by Stone Inc. It also allowed it to propose a wider range of products, with different qualities and prices. The mother company of Stone Inc. was interested in selling its subsidiary, according to Mr. Martin, because it was concentrating on its main activities, of which Stone Inc. was not a part. Mr. Martin's salary was not going to vary with this transaction and this kind of operation was simply part of his normal job. He had to use the services of a renowned consultant for valuation of the assets and his own expertise in financial analysis to influence the Europe-based top management of his mother company, itself bound to the rules of the stock market where it was listed. Since Mr. Martin was about to retire and the operation had already taken place, he spoke about it with some distance. Unlike Ms. Li and Mr. Jones, he did not identify with his company, which he was about to leave and where he had spent a relatively small fraction of his adult life.

These three examples hint at the diversity of cross-border transactions when seen through the organizations that carry them out, the aims of the transactions themselves, and the trajectories of the employees, who can develop very different emotional relationships with their everyday work. At the same time, for these employees, the diversity is articulated with common methods of valuation and investment, which they share from their education and the professional standards they have to comply with. These methods determine what information is and how it should be treated through standardized forms of reasoning and mathematical formulas. They are fundamental if employees wish to retain their jobs and advance in their careers, and are supposed to organize how money crossing the border is distributed through investment operations. These transactions imply negotiation of the rights and duties of interested parties, including the price that is paid for an exchange of ownership. For these employees, the balance of power in these negotiations made sense as part of an institutional, political, and moral setting.

Financial Transactions as Power Relations

The purchase of companies occurs within particular temporalities and regular forms of interaction. The process is usually marked by important moments when parties sign contracts and agree on the next step, before the actual exchange of money for property rights. This exchange calibrates tension between the parties, since all employees agree that they have a common interest in realizing the transaction and share official mistrust, since each side may want to manipulate or hide things. According to all interviewees, in M&A operations less than half of those officially started come to a conclusion. In private equity and venture capital, less than one in ten prospected companies end up being bought. The balance of power can favor either side and change sides during the transaction. The purchaser may bring money that the seller company is looking for, but the latter may have assets that are hard to find elsewhere. Usually, the purchaser wants as much information as possible about the target company before the transaction is concluded, but this may only be negotiated at the latter's own rhythm. It may demand proof of engagement by the purchaser, for instance by agreeing on a "target price," before disclosing information that could be used for other purposes, especially if the transaction breaks down. Confidentiality clauses, exclusivity periods, target prices, and the rights and duties of each party are specified in contracts that constitute important landmarks in a process lasting between three months and more than a year.

The employees I met stressed that transactions are always marked by negotiations concerning at least two interrelated topics: the legal rights and duties of each party during and after the transaction and the price. SMEs are usually located in one place and can develop close connections to local political and legal authorities, in particular if the managers are members of the Communist Party. The relationship can be even closer if the SME is a subsidiary of a larger state-owned company. Interviewees stressed that, if the purchase of an SME distances its previous managers from the company, the latter may actually not only lose its commercial connections, but may have to face renegotiation of licenses and even property rights of the land on which it stands. These potential tensions are intertwined with discussions about how to calculate the price of the SME. The interviewees' professional norm is based on standardized methods taught in business schools and the finance departments of universities in the United States, Europe, China, and many other places. These methods are multiple and do not lead to similar results. They can define the "market value" of a company's assets, considered as the sum of the sale price of its assets or as the cost of replicating the company, for instance by buying the land, machinery, patents, etc. They may consider the "relative value" of the company, comparing it to similar companies that have either just been sold or are listed in stock exchanges and who therefore have a "market price" for their shares. Finally, a third, more legitimate method holds that the price of a company must reflect the value of the future revenues an owner should obtain from operating it. These revenues should be discounted at an interest rate "reflecting" the "cost of funding" the investment and the "risk" that it may not work. This is called the "discounted cash flows" method of valuation (Ortiz 2014b).

Interviewees assert systematically that in most transactions, the sellers of SMEs in China do not accept the discounted cash flows method and prefer valuation according to assets and by comparison. Discussion of the price to be paid is of course concerned above all with the purchaser's attempt to buy cheap and the seller's to sell high. Valuation methods, then, work partly as a common language for exploring the investment potential of the target company, involving the current market value of assets, the prices of other companies, and the money that could be earned in future. These items would be raised through using common formulas for calculation and rationales of analysis that orient the explicit outlooks of the two parties. Yet, according to my interviewees, this opposition is made harder to manage in many cases by the failure of the two parties even to agree on how to discuss the price (i.e., on the method of valuation that defines the object of the transaction). This tension about methods of valuation becomes particularly important for companies that are legally bound by regulations concerning investment in the United States and Europe. Discounted cash flow methods may be considered by a judge in the United States as a legitimate way to dispose of shareholder's money. An employee or a company may be brought to court for having conducted the transaction through the wrong use of method.[8] In China, this is not the case. Besides, the State-Owned Assets Administration and Supervision Commission (SASAC), the agency managing state-owned assets in China, even though it recognizes all mainstream methods of valuation in its statutes, tends to insist on valuation of sales according to the price of assets, reinforcing what appears to be the legitimate professional standard.

The balance of power would be described differently depending on the aims and position of the company in a transaction. These, in turn, made sense for the employees depending on where the transaction is in the macroeconomic, legal, and political space in which they are operating.

Mr. Martin explained that in the purchase of Stone Inc. he was dealing with the managers of the parent company as well as with those of its subsidiary. Both were vying to present the operation as a great sale, to foster their careers in the company and within the Communist Party, to which most of them belonged, as do many top managers of state-owned companies. Besides, since they were under the supervision of SASAC for the sale, they also had to comply with that administration's specific rules. This meant, according to Mr. Martin, that the price was only partly negotiated with the managers of the selling company. The latter insisted that valuation be made according to the market value of the assets of the company, which comprised land and factories. He explained that this was problematic since his company, Steel Inc., was listed on a European stock exchange and financial analysts would examine the details of the deal. So he had to justify a high price through the methods of valuation that he favored. Mr. Martin remarked that he found part of this approach "incomprehensible" and in particular he considered that the land on which the company was based was only partly an asset for the purchaser, because it was never too clear how that land had been acquired by the target company, since this was often done half-legally, when the municipality changed the status of agricultural land into land available for industrial purposes in the 1990s. Permission to stay on that land would only hold for as long as there was a good relationship with the municipality. This, according to him, explained why the purchase was actually a joint venture, in which the former management stayed in place. Yet, this meant that there were two CEOs in the company, Chinese and foreign. The Chinese CEO would hold meetings closed to employees who were not members of the Communist Party, where things would get decided that the foreign employees, including the foreign CEO, had little say on.

Ms. Li's employer, one of the "Big Four" auditing and consultancy companies in the world, was officially one of the major sources of global standards for valuation, accounting, and management. For her, the conflict between methods of valuation was mainly cognitive. While some companies' management had learned them, others had not. Her job was partly to provide her expertise in applying the right methods. This did not preclude power differences, but oriented them toward the concrete distribution of rights and duties when money is exchanged. For her, this meant that in China, any transaction "normally" required the counterparties to understand each other's political backing: "normally . . . before you choose the partners you are dealing with, you definitely need to look at or check their background, right? . . . You can't just go blindly into the market, without knowing who your partners are and how powerful they are, because all these things will affect your bargaining power when you are dealing with them."

In the profession, it is accepted that valuation methods for venture capital are extremely uncertain, because the bet is that the business of the purchased company can expand dramatically in a short time. For Mr. Jones, strength in negotiations when purchasing a small company's shares depended on how much money and support he could offer. In his case, negotiating power was high, thanks to state-owned funds backing particular sectors, such as renewable energy and clean technology that were targets of official government policy. He explained that the municipality's support went beyond the money invested in companies, since it also secured for start-ups a wide range of offices and labs next to a major technical university. This would foster interaction between scientists and the start-ups and enhance the latter's creativity. He considered that his model of investment used the best practices of Silicon Valley, which he knew from studying there, with significant funds provided by Chinese state authorities for strategic targets. He compared this to the European country of his birth: there "the state" intervened "too much" in this kind of investment, since it demanded that people working for start-ups with municipal backing employ only its own nationals. In contrast, the start-ups he invested the fund's money in could employ people of any nationality. He thought that this Chinese city could attract young people from Silicon Valley, offering better conditions for their start-ups and the thrill of being in China, a place with much better prospects for economic growth in the future and also one that could be more fun than most small cities in the United States, especially for scientists in their twenties.

The balance of power in the transaction was shaped by the distribution of rights and duties and the price. Technical aspects of valuation were mixed with legal and organizational issues with which employees were more or less acquainted or comfortable. These tensions made sense in terms of the legal and regulatory border that divided China from the rest, in particular from the United States and Europe, often bundled together as the "West." This border became a technical financial issue, but one that made sense only in connection with moral and political understandings of finance.

Finance, Identity, Morals, Politics

Mr. Martin, Ms. Li, and Mr. Jones use the same references as other professionals that I interviewed, but in different ways. These can also be found in the official discourses of institutions such as the People's Bank of China and the IMF, in professional financial reports, and in the popular and specialized media. Different understandings of power relations and the role of professional standards of investment and valuation in negotiating the rights, duties, and price of a transaction were shaped by an employee's position in the process. They involved expressing more or less explicit and consistent moral and political interpretations of the financial practices themselves, where the border the money was crossing became a focal point, which defined the global space where that border was situated.

For Mr. Martin, the conflicts before, during, and after a transaction showed that the "Chinese" were marked by "socialism" and "Leninism" and could not be trusted, unlike the respect for the rule of law and transparency typical of "the West." He thought valuation procedures had been shaped by rationales imposed on him, without any respect for what he considered the correct way to conduct them. He had had to struggle with the top management of his company in Europe, who did not understand the conditions of work in China and still had to "learn" to adapt to the new environment, in particular because he did not expect the "Chinese" to change. Elaborating openly on his own political conservatism concerning debates in Europe about how to deal with the financial crisis, he worried about the decline of Europe in contrast to China's geopolitical growth.

Ms. Li spoke of China as "we," but distinguished between different Chinese companies and professionals. On the one hand, the "international" Chinese companies were no different from other non-Chinese multinationals: they followed the same standards of valuation and investment that she applied as consultant in her job. These companies were much more "sophisticated" than smaller companies that did things "from a local perspective." For her, the former had learned to adopt international standards as their experience abroad grew. This was an inevitable process that would eventually encompass the whole of China. According to her, the standards of valuation and management that she upheld in her job were indeed "universally applied."

For Mr. Jones, the money mobilized by his fund signaled the superiority of a Chinese approach to long-term investment, innovation, and sustainable growth that would propel China to a more powerful position internationally. He was happy to be part of this process. He explained that when he left China to do a science doctorate in the United States, he did so "as a Chinese," since at the time, the United States was not a pole of attraction for European students, but he learned from his student friends in China to be fascinated by it. After that, he went "back" to China. He has remained there ever since and expects to stay at least for the rest of his professional life.

Conflicts about methods of valuation and investment were partly understood as the opposition between different technical definitions of the transaction's object. These tensions were also usually related to the participants' "national" or "cultural" identities, with distinctions between the "West" and the "Chinese" or between the "sophisticated" and the "uneducated" (sometimes "old") "Chinese." The supposed technical superiority of these standard professional methods of valuation was incorporated into moral and political interpretations of the institutional settings where they were applied. The idea of "efficient markets," "states," "socialism," "sustainability," and "economic development" articulated these contrasts. Financial methodologies were thus understood as markers of identity, themselves related to the propositions of nation-states, within imagined futures where the two sides of the border would clash, mix in a hybrid, or be eventually unified by the victory of one side over the other.

These narratives were elaborated in interviews, where the participants explored meanings in different registers—of authenticity, justification, established narratives, deceit, and concealment—in a professional milieu where there is a consensus about not "disclosing" sensitive information, especially concerning deals that are ongoing. Their references do not constitute a coherent whole; on the contrary, they are fragmented, contradictory, and labile. But in all cases, the meanings explored help employees to make sense of their operations, for themselves and others, thereby making sense of their own life trajectories as they pursue them.

Interviewees may be contradictory; as when Mr. Martin complains about the failure of the "Chinese" to use mainstream formulas and claims at the same time that his "European" management should learn to deal according to their rules. Ms. Li claims that SMEs do things "from a local perspective," but the methods she upholds are "universally applied"; and Mr. Jones says that European states intervene "too much" in venture capital operations, unlike the state-backed project that he works in. Their notions of identity, of "China" and the "West," of the institutional settings in which they work, are fragmentary and labile, shifting according to a moment of the conversation. What Mr. Jones refers to when he says he went to the United States "as a Chinese" may not be what Mr. Martin has in mind when he evokes "socialism" or what Ms. Li designates by "we." But these notions themselves can shift in the course of an exchange and financial methodologies play an important role in stabilizing their meaning. Thus, financial valuation for investment purposes is a potential marker of identity in the professional and nonprofessional trajectories of the employees in charge of cross-border investment. By making sense of their everyday operations in these multiple ways, employees both reproduce and transform the idea of a border; the imaginaries of finance are at once technical, moral, and political (Ortiz 2013).

In spite of their diversity and plasticity, these narratives explore similar references and remain within the limits of ideas about nationality, state, market, professional standards, and the globalization of finance. They situate financial operations within emotional and rationalizing repertoires that are technical, moral, and political, being concerned with the soundness of operations, the moral value of participants, and the fairness of the outcomes of transactions, both where they occur and in the world at large. This locality can be a small city, a province, a whole country like "China," or an even bigger and undefined geographical area like the "West." In all these cases, the border crossed by the transactions that these employees oversee is a marker helping them to make sense of their activity. Other examples would show different results, while mobilizing very similar narratives. These employees appropriate and thereby reproduce, transform, and disseminate these particular imaginaries, both rendering them more complex and preventing other meanings from entering the space of possibility.

Conclusion

I have explored how employees carrying out cross-border investments in China make sense of their everyday practices, combining narratives about their own personal trajectories, about financial techniques and controversies, about organizational rules within their companies and between companies, about macroeconomic relations, about states and regulatory frameworks, and about a global space understood to be in a process of being unified, but with different horizons. Narratives that are formalized by political and regulatory institutions mostly encompass how these employees give meaning to their own activities. Yet employees are not merely repeating official discourses as if these are simply the echo of formal professional milieus. These discourses are multiple, fragmented, and contradictory, and employees, like official reports, combine them in varying ways. An interview is one moment to rework them in labile ways. In most such discourses, "states" are opposed to "markets" and "national" and "cultural" identities are mobilized to problematize the technical, moral, and political meanings of cross-border investment. The borders are appropriated and recreated, in a movement where crossing both reasserts their existence, but also appears to challenge them. For these employees, allocating money to clean technologies, retaining power within the network of the Communist Party, or adopting international standards are all technical, moral, and political at once. As in the West African cases reported by Jane Guyer, employees redraw the definitions of what is morally and politically right in financial terms, reaffirming the fairness of social hierarchies that result from their professional practices.

This kind of research reveals the complexity of the production of world society through financial interdependencies in the everyday of the financial industry. On the one hand, the observation of everyday practices and discourses shows both the importance of grand narratives about financial globalization, and the fact that these discourses do not operate as they are meant to when they are presented as formal consistent wholes. On the other hand, what these observations highlight is that other imaginaries about a fairer distribution of monetary resources are excluded. The integration of the Chinese financial system comes with official discourses about socialism and sustainable development in an institutional space that, in Europe, the United States, and many other places, is articulated around the liberal narrative concerning the centrality of markets for social justice. Yet, this is made within nationalist discourse and the status quo about the current concentration of power in the distribution of resources in Chinese territory. This shows both the contents and the limits of the financial imagination proposed in the financial industry.

This raises the question of the status of the main narratives mobilized by these employees in anthropological discourse. Using the talk of "states," "markets," "investors," and "value"; of "national" and "cultural" identities such as "Chinese," "Western," "European," or "American"; and conducting analyses of political systems and macroeconomic policy, they mobilize terms that echo the analytical categories of anthropology and of disciplines with which anthropologists must converse in order to study cross-border investment—macroeconomics, political science, history, and sociology. Anthropological reflexivity implies not using these categories analytically, but understanding them as how the people we study make sense of their own practices. This would be a precondition for proposing critical forms for imagining the global and the fair distribution of the money that could constitute it.

Horacio Ortiz is associate professor at the Research Institute of Anthropology, East China Normal University, Shanghai, China, and researcher at Université Paris-Dauphine, PSL Research University, CNRS, IRISSO, Paris, France. He is an anthropologist specializing in finance, and author of *Valeur financière et vérité. Enquête d'anthropologie politique sur l'évaluation des entreprises cotées en bourse* (2014).

NOTES

1. This chapter is based on approximately forty interviews with financial professionals working in Shanghai, Beijing, and Hong Kong, most of which were directly concerned with cross-border investment; as well as on short-term participant observation between 2011 and 2015 with two consulting companies, based in Shanghai, conducting mergers and acquisitions between China and Western Europe. This is part of broader fieldwork-based research on the financial industry, first carried out in the early 2000s with stock brokers, hedge funds, and fund managers in New York and Paris and continued by obtaining a diploma as a financial analyst and doing research in business schools in Paris and Shanghai between 2008 and 2014.
2. See Müller (2006) for Brazil, Reddy (2009) for India, and Amyx (2004) for Japan. In 2011, when the United States and European banking systems were in serious difficulties and Chinese banks were untouched by the crisis, the IMF issued a report saying that the latter still needed to "reform"–i.e., to privatize and come closer to the neoliberal ideal espoused by the institution (International Monetary Fund 2011).
3. See for instance the official declaration published after the Third Plenum of the Chinese Communist Party in 2013, where all these references are repeatedly bundled together.
4. The amount of outbound investment has been growing in recent years and in 2015 it could eventually surpass that of inbound investment, but most of my observations occurred before this change.
5. Since most positions of power in global finance are held by men (Fisher 2012; Ho 2009; Roth 2006), I use male pronouns when speaking of employees in general. Using female pronouns could indeed have the counterproductive effect of erasing this gender bias.
6. As agreed with the interviewees, all the names of persons and companies have been changed to preserve their anonymity. I only use quotation marks for the words that I want to highlight, since these examples draw on quotations throughout.
7. This diploma may be obtained by passing exams in China.
8. Cf. the decision of the Court of the Chancery of the State of Delaware, 8 July 2013, in the case of Merion Capital L. P. et al. vs. 3M Congent Inc.

REFERENCES

Abdelal, R. 2007. *Capital Rules: The Construction of Global Finance.* Cambridge, MA: Harvard University Press.
Abolafia, M. 1996. *Making Markets: Opportunism and Restraint on Wall Street.* Cambridge, MA: Harvard University Press.
Amyx, J. A. 2004. *Japan's Financial Crisis: Institutional Rigidity and Reluctant Change.* Princeton, NJ: Princeton University Press.
Bell, S., and H. Feng. 2013. *The Rise of the People's Bank of China: The Politics of Institutional Change.* Cambridge, MA: Harvard University Press.
Blyth, M. 2003. "The political power of financial ideas: Transparency, risk, and distribution in global finance." In J. Kirshner (ed.), *Monetary Orders: Ambiguous Economics, Ubiquitous Politics.* Ithaca, NY: Cornell University Press, pp. 239–259.
Cheng, L. 2003. *Banking in Modern China: Entrepreneurs, Professional Managers and the Development of Chinese Banks, 1897–1937.* Cambridge: Cambridge University Press.
Clark, G. L. 2000. *Pension Fund Capitalism.* Oxford: Oxford University Press.
Couppey-Soubeyran, J., D. Plihon, and D. Saïdane. 2006 *Les banques, acteurs de la globalisation financière.* Paris: La Documentation Française.
Davies, D., and F. Wang (eds.). 2009. *Creating Wealth and Poverty in Postsocialist China.* Redwood City, CA: Stanford University Press.
Dodd, N. 2014. *The Social Life of Money.* Princeton, NJ: Princeton University Press.
Eichengreen, B. 1996. *Globalizing Capital: A History of the International Monetary System.* Princeton, NJ: Princeton University Press.
Fisher, M. 2012. *Wall Street Women.* Durham, NC: Duke University Press.
Fligstein, N. 2001. *The Architecture of Markets: An Economic Sociology of Twenty-First-Century Capitalist Societies.* Princeton, NJ: Princeton University Press.
Fourcade, M. 2011. "Cents and sensibility: Economic valuation and the nature of 'Nature.'" *American Journal of Sociology* 116(6): 1721–1777.
Godechot, O. 2007. *Working rich, salaires, bonus et appropriation du profit dans l'industrie financière.* Paris: Editions La Découverte.
Guyer, J. I. 2004. *Marginal Gains: Monetary Transactions in Atlantic Africa.* Chicago, IL: University of Chicago Press.
Hart, K. 1986. "Heads or tails? The two sides of the coin." *Man* (New Series) 21: 637–656.
Hart, K., and H. Ortiz. 2014. "The anthropology of money and finance: Between ethnography and world history." *Annual Review of Anthropology* 43: 465–482.
Hertz, E. 1998. *The Trading Crowd: An Ethnography of the Shanghai Stock Market.* Cambridge: Cambridge University Press.
Ho, K. 2009. *Liquidated: An Ethnography of Wall Street.* Durham, NC: Duke University Press.
Holmes, D. 2013. *Economy of Words: Communicative Imperatives in Central Banks.* Chicago, IL: University of Chicago Press.
Hsueh, R. 2011. *China's Regulatory State: A New Strategy for Globalization.* Ithaca, NY: Cornell University Press.
International Monetary Fund. 2011. "People's Republic of China: Financial System Stability Assessment." Country Report No. 11/321, Washington, DC.

Krippner, G. R. 2011. *Capitalizing on Crisis: The Political Origins of the Rise of Finance.* Cambridge: Harvard University Press.
Lee, R. 1998. *What is an Exchange? The Automation, Management, and Regulation of Financial Markets.* Oxford: Oxford University Press.
Lemoine, B. 2016. *L'ordre de la dette. Enquête sur les infortunes de l'état et la prospérité du marché.* Paris: Editions La Découverte.
MacKenzie, D. 2006. *An Engine not a Camera: How Financial Models Shape Markets.* Cambridge, MA: The MIT Press.
Montagne, S. 2006. *Les Fonds de Pension. Entre protection sociale et spéculation financière.* Paris: Editions Odile Jacob.
Müller, L. 2006. *Mercado Exemplar: um estudo antropológico sobre a Bolsa de Valores.* Porto Alegre: Editora Zouk.
Ortiz, H. 2013. "Financial value: Economic, moral, political, global." *HAU Journal of Ethnographic Theory* 3(1): 64–79.
———. 2014a. "The limits of financial imagination: Free investors, efficient markets and crisis." *American Anthropologist* 116(1): 38–50.
———. 2014b. *Valeur financière et vérité. Enquête d'anthropologie politique sur l'évaluation des entreprises cotées en bourse.* Paris: Presses de Science Po.
Parry, J., and M. Bloch (eds.). 1989. *Money and the Morality of Exchange.* Cambridge: Cambridge University Press.
Reddy, Y. V. 2009. *India and the Global Financial Crisis: Managing Money and Finance.* London: Anthem Press.
Roth, L. M. 2006. *Selling Women Short: Gender and Inequality in Wall Street.* Princeton, NJ: Princeton University Press.
Sinclair, T. J. 2005. *The New Masters of Capital: American Bond Rating Agencies and the Politics of Creditworthiness.* Ithaca, NY: Cornell University Press.
Stiglitz, J. 2006. *Making Globalization Work.* London: Penguin Books.
Trouillot, M. R. 2003. *Global Transformations: Anthropology and the Modern World.* New York: Palgrave MacMillan.
Whitley, R. 1986. "The Transformation of Business Finance into Financial Economics: The Roles of Academic Expansion and Changes in U.S. Capital Markets." *Accounting, Organizations and Society* 11(2): 171–192.
Wu, J., and C. Ma (eds.). 2003. *Modernization and Internationalization of finance in Shanghai.* Shanghai: Shanghai Ancient Books Editing House.
Zaloom, C. 2006. *Out of the Pits, Traders and Technology from Chicago to London.* Chicago, IL: University of Chicago Press.
Zelizer, V. 1997. *The Social Meaning of Money: Pin Money, Paychecks, Poor Relief, and Other Currencies.* Princeton, NJ: Princeton University Press.
———. 2005. *The Purchase of Intimacy.* Princeton, NJ: Princeton University Press.
Zhu, M. 2009. "China's Emerging Financial Industries and Implications." In: M. Zhu, J. Cai, and M. Avery (eds.), *China's Emerging Financial Markets: Challenges and Global Impact.* Singapore: John Wiley & Sons (Asia) Pte Ltd., pp. xxiii–lviii.

CHAPTER 8

 # Value Transfer and Rent
Or, I Didn't Realize My Payment Was Your Annuity

BILL MAURER

Samsung, the Korean mobile phone giant, announced in 2015 that its phones would come equipped with a new technology that mimics the magnetic stripe on the back of plastic payment cards. It had begun using a different technology between 2005 and 2008, so-called chip-and-pin cards, with an embedded microchip that transmits payment information to a point-of-sale terminal. When Apple released its new iPhone with its own mobile payments service, Apple Pay, it relied on a similar technology but one that does not require physical contact with the point of sale. Apple was making a bet on the United States' eventual adoption of the newer European-standard technology; Samsung seemed to be assuming that change would come more slowly, and created a payment tool that will work with existing infrastructure—the magnetic stripe terminals that were still in use all across the United States.

Just dip into new payment technology, however briefly, and you realize that you are pulling on a string that leads to a tangle of ever-bigger balls and knots: devices built to work with other devices, bets on new infrastructure or assumptions about the slowness of change, connections to this or that networked system, overlays on top of other systems, flows of data and electricity, and corporate interconnectedness that quickly become almost impossible to map. The payments industry—the collection of public and corporate entities designed to assist us in transferring value to one another, denominated (usually) in state-issued currency but also and increasingly in private tokens (coupons, points, or credits)—is a vast and variegated territory. Payment is obviously about money. It's about how we get money from here to there, how we exchange money between ourselves, with businesses and governments.

If, as Keith Hart suggests, money is a mode of extending the local into the global and vice versa; that money links inner subjectivity to the outer object world; that money can "build bridges between all levels of association" (Introduction, this volume), then money itself is an infrastructure. It is a "bridge that delimits a landscape, facilitates a passage, and forestalls a loss"; it "ensures that some medium endures—that words won't fade, that goods won't spoil, that personas won't wither" (Kockelman 2010: 206).

This chapter focuses on money's infrastructures—not money itself as the means to forestall loss (of value, of social connection, indeed, of human economy) but the infrastructures that facilitate money's own endurance, money's transit without decay or transformation. For what is most interesting about money's infrastructures is how they route money through other economies. The infrastructures and technologies of payment, of money's transit, are interesting because even when they facilitate capitalist, market-based exchange they, themselves, do not solely depend on such market principles. At every point from payment device to terminal to independent operator to network to bank, a fee is collected. Understanding those fees is complicated for merchants, consumers, regulators, and all participants in the payments industry, to say nothing of academics. And those fees show that in its routing, something else is going on with money that complicates the story of it as "the historical manifestation of capitalism" (Introduction, this volume).

Take interchange fees. These are usually the biggest fee assessed on merchants who accept electronic payments. Interchange was originally a term from transit engineering referring to a system of routes around an intersection that permits the smooth flow of traffic through it. It is used in the payment card industry, but this was virtually unknown elsewhere until several antitrust lawsuits involving the card networks in the late 1970s. The industry has historically gotten its profits from fees on transactions. That fee makes a transaction "non-par," the value of the money paid and the good being exchanged being unequal. In classic liberal and critical approaches to markets, interchange is hard to figure.[1] It is not the only fee involved in electronic payments, but it is usually the most significant for merchants.

Interchange and other such fees are generally invisible to a consumer when using a credit card or other payment technology that is not cash or a paper check: a gift card, a prepaid card, a telephone airtime card or airtime itself, American Express points, or Apple Pay. Seminars promote events where you can "Join us and 1,000+ innovators in the new money community!"[2] And interchange may soon be supplanted by the mining of consumers' transactional data, not just the fee on the movement of funds from a bank to a merchant via a card network activated by a piece of plastic and magnetized tape in my wallet.[3]

Under its entry for "interchange," the *Oxford English Dictionary* (*OED*) lists a host of meanings all related to reciprocity, in which one thing substitutes for another within the system of relations that enmeshed the first thing.

> The act of exchanging reciprocally; giving and receiving with reciprocity. . . . The change of each of one (or more) thing, condition, etc. for the other . . . the taking by each of the place or nature of the other.[4]

The use of the term "interchange" in the payments industry makes sense given the history of clearing houses, where paper slips were "interchanged" for one another to settle credit transactions. If relations of interchange are becoming more generalized in early twenty-first-century economies, it is not surprising that new business models based on service fees also borrow this language of reciprocity: the Silicon Valley–inspired platforms that allow people to connect with each other to harness their "excess capacity"–unused parking spaces, residential rooms, or automobile rides newly available through the "sharing economy" of Uber, Lyft, and Airbnb.

This chapter brings out a neglected side of money–the infrastructures and revenue for moving money around in the act of payment. Payments can help us see that there is more to money than credit and debt. It may be a "two-sided balance sheet operation" (Bell 2001: 151), in that it is created when a creditor accepts it from a debtor. "Everyone can create money," says Hyman Minsky–that is, everyone can offer a means of payment as an IOU for credit or a product or service. The problem "is to get it accepted" (quoted in Bell 2001: 150). Indeed, it is not "money" until someone actually does accept it (ibid.: 152). Determination of who will accept your IOU is based on the hierarchies in which you are embedded, with the state at the top. The state's money is thus the only one accepted for final settlement of debts.

For many people in the payments industry, however, this argument is beside the point. What they are interested in is not "who will accept my IOU," but what value can be mined from the act of transferring and settling it. Although they inquire into money and many think they are remaking it, their main concern is with this value chain in payments, in clearing and settling others' debts and not in the credit/debt nexus itself. In fact, from the beginning, it was understood that the business model would not be about credit at all, but about tolls on settlement. As Dee Hock, founder of the Visa network, recalls, "It was a revelation then.

We were not in the credit card business.... *We were really in the business of the exchange of monetary value*" (quoted in Stearns 2011: 45, emphasis in original).

My first point is Minsky and Bell's, about getting your money accepted and the changing nature of the social hierarchy of money. Some people want to reorganize that hierarchy, replacing the state with private actors. My second point is that, by introducing tolls on settlement, payments bring to light the excess inherent in any straightforward "monetary" transaction. That excess defines payment as the work involved in settling an exchange. There's a lot of money in that, which inspires the industry to remake the hierarchy of money itself. And that money, garnered through a kind of rent seeking, is becoming a general condition. Scholars as diverse as Nobel laureate Jean Tirole (Rochet and Tirole 2003) and the Italian critic Carlo Vercellone (2008) have identified such developments as "market failure" or as a transformation of the relationship between rent and profit, respectively.

When anthropologists investigate finance and capitalism, we often become exchange-centric, drawing inspiration from Mauss, Marx, or Simmel. We need to refocus on payment. Exchange and equivalence, commensuration and value calibration stand to one side of payment. Payment refers to the act and infrastructure of value transfer, not the creation of that value itself. Payment is orthogonal to exchange. There may be a pyramid of money, but there is scaffolding and infrastructure holding it up. My focus, as professionals put it, is the portals, rails, and plumbing, and the fee-based business of relaying value through that plumbing.

Payment is a hot area. But, because it relies on that tangle of infrastructures and services, it is incredibly variegated: people developing some new mobile phone applications rely on the latest distributed, peer-to-peer ledger systems like Bitcoin's blockchain (Dodd, this volume), while others are still selling to traditional merchants "value add" packages that bundle credit- and debit card–acceptance services with data management tools catering to specific lines of business.

The stakes are shifting rapidly, too. The payments industry is fracturing. Mobile telecommunications network operators, Internet start-ups, mobile phone airtime distributors, social networking services, and search engines all issue various types of prepaid products. Legal tender from one source (a bank account or physical cash) is surrendered to a third party who converts the cash into some kind of electronic value. That value is then available for transfer to another at the point of sale, online, or over the wireless network. Regulatory changes in the United States and the

European Union, meanwhile, are cutting into the fees levied by the traditional networks. Revenue from interchange is dwindling for the major card networks just as hundreds of new mobile and computing start-ups enter the game. These are discovering other potentials in payments.

Is It "Money" When . . . ?

Scholars of money may object that I am mistaking the nature of money in Aristotelian terms (Noko, this volume): the classic "functions of money" issue. This often turns on the bundling of different functions into one currency object on subsequent conundrums posed by that object's ability to signify "value." This is a familiar anthropological problem.[5] Others argue that the nature of money lies not in its functions of exchange, payment, or storage, but rather as a unit of account for final settlement with the state (Ingham 2004a) and as credit relationships whose final settlement, though warranted by the state, is perpetually deferred. Credit and state theories of money constitute an alternative tradition connecting Defoe and Keynes, which tempers the "bewilderment" of credit (Ingham 2004b: 213) with a pragmatic understanding that the "identification of money as coin, or any other commodity, is a conceptual category error"; the focus should be on the "hierarchy of credibility and acceptability by which money is constituted" (ibid.). Still, "practical metallism" (ibid.: 212) has powerfully shaped our understanding of money. This oscillation between money as commodity and as credit warranted by a political community shapes the design and regulatory conundrums of new means of payment.

We need to get into the technicalities of money, credit, and payment to get at value forms in practice.[6] Certainly, cash is still king, and deposits in bank accounts underpin the money that makes the world go around; the current crisis signals finance's centrality to the global economic order. Perhaps we should be writing about finance, derivatives, abstraction, and the complex market devices that brought the world to ruin. Yet prepaid instruments occupy a growing share of the payments industry, especially in the wake of the global financial crisis, and as online and mobile computing transform purchase and payment around the world. You can't have finance without value transfer—payment, the little technicality that sets finance into motion.

Industry specialists refer to themselves with pride as "payments geeks," and no doubt their products and services do seem obscure. And yet almost every day each of us is likely to make use of a payment instrument other than cash or checks: we buy coffee with a prepaid card, receive loyalty points at the supermarket, pay online with a credit card, or use World of Warcraft's virtual "gold" to purchase a sword.

Some readers may remember Facebook credits. What happened when someone sent Facebook credits to a merchant to purchase a mobile phone game? What happened when someone else used Facebook credits to purchase a voucher she then printed out and used to buy a "real" good? Facebook credits were discontinued in 2012. But uses like these posed definitional and regulatory questions. And similar services have been modeled on Facebook credits since.

"Is it money, or is it a value-add?" This was an informant's question to me. At first, it sounds nonsensical. How could one thing be substitutable for the other? Money—the commodity version—is a means of exchange. "Value-add" is the difference between production cost and sales price or, in the Marxist tradition, surplus value. In a marketing context, it refers to the differentiating features of a product. This question came up repeatedly when professionals and regulators decided how to treat use of an electronic currency on a mobile device during the early days of mobile payment and things like Facebook credits.

The scale and significance of revenue collected from value transfer generally goes unrecognized. Payment systems law has been called "perhaps the most esoteric topic in the already esoteric world of commercial law" (Porter 2008: 1168). However, according to estimates, the payments industry now surpasses in size biotech, Hollywood, and global venture capital investment, as well as airlines and lodging (Levitin 2008: 1323–1324, Brown 2009: 130).

Size apart, what makes payments interesting is that the value chain in value transfer—the market in payments—confounds conventional accounts of money and finance. Payments exist almost as Mauss (1967 [1925]) described for the commonplace exchanges (*gimwali*) that occurred alongside *kula*. There is a double parallelism here. Payment is to *kula*, as money and finance are to *gimwali* alongside *kula*: both payment and *kula* seem to operate outside the market, in a realm of obligation, rent, fees, and tolls rather than supply, demand, and price. In symbolic importance, however, payment is to *gimwali* as money/finance are to *kula*: the latter pair being supposedly where the action is, the former pair a sideshow.

With online payments and social media currencies, however, we have to stop and ask: what are we seeing, making, doing? "What *is* it?" "*When* is it . . . money?" And, again, "Is it 'money' when you. . . ." These questions arose when the purchase of "virtual" goods with an online "currency" was compared with buying "real" goods. The context was financial monitoring: how can regulators get a handle on the volume of payments through new technological devices and channels? In terms of monetary policy: how can a financial regulator know the volume of money in circulation, if "money" is found in virtual coupons exchanged outside the mainstream banking structure, when airtime minutes are transferred from one mobile phone to another and Facebook credits move from "friend" to "friend" in an online game? This problem invokes the trust in the entire system that supposedly derives from knowing that it is not being used for fraudulent purposes or hijacked by anyone who wants to disguise the origin and movements of their funds by using channels outside the regulated financial sector.

So, the question is, is it money when you purchase a game or ringtone for your phone? And is it money when you purchase a physical-world good or "cash out" your credits somehow—licitly, illicitly, informally, however? In a directive circulated globally, the European Union decided: "The definition of [electronic money] should cover all situations where the payment service provider issues a pre-paid stored value in exchange for funds, which can be used for payment purposes because it is accepted by third persons as payment" (Directive 2009/110/EC, section 7).

This harks back to the hierarchy of money. But it is not always regulators who bolster that hierarchy. Under pressure from the mobile telecommunications industry, the European Union also *exempted* "money" used to purchase certain "digital goods" from the definition of electronic money:

> this Directive [does] not apply to monetary value that is used to purchase digital goods or services, where, by virtue of the nature of the good or service, the operator adds intrinsic value to it. . . . This is a situation where a mobile phone or other digital network subscriber pays the network operator directly and there is neither a direct payment relationship nor a direct debtor-creditor relationship between the network subscriber and any third-party supplier of goods or services delivered as part of the transaction. (Ibid., section 6)

Mobile network operators wanted to be exempted from the definition of money to escape added regulation. In the process, though, they opened the door to a "money" that is not money. It is "monetary value," separate from "money." The electronic value adds value—constitutes value-add—to an existing device or service. Only when it comes out of the system and off the device does it become money. State and credit theorists might remark, "Naturally, as long as the value remains in the system, it can never exit to serve for final settlement of a claim with a creditor or the state, so it is not money." Ethnographically, however, confusion over commodity versus credit money inspires conversations about and the design of new payment systems. And politically, some system designers imagine a world where the value never leaves the system at all, deferring indefinitely any settling of accounts, collecting rents along the way, becoming the final arbiter of payment and thereby privatizing payment and money.

First, we have a payment that is not a payment: I buy Facebook credits with funds from my bank account. When I then purchase items in Farmville, a Facebook game, for use on my mobile phone, a value-added service is added to my Facebook service, and to my mobile device. This is not money, and it is not a payment. It is outside relations of money and payment. So what is it?

Second, when I exchange funds in my bank account for a virtual currency, for electronic value, where and how is that value stored? The regulations are clear in the European Union, the United States, and countries with mobile money services. The funds backing electronic value are pooled (from different clients mingled together and not separated or registered by individual account holders), and segregated from the issuer's operating capital. In the European Union:

> The issuance of electronic money does not constitute a deposit-taking activity . . . in view of its specific character as an electronic surrogate for coins and banknotes, which is to be *used for making payments*, usually of limited amount and *not as means of saving*. Electronic money institutions *should not be allowed to grant credit* from the funds received or held for the purpose of issuing electronic money. Electronic money issuers *should not, moreover, be allowed to grant interest* or any other benefit unless those benefits are not related to the length of time during which the electronic money holder holds electronic money. (Ibid., section 13, emphasis added)

The string of negatives is striking, yet a positive definition is hard to set. The funds I use to buy an online currency or airtime do *not* constitute a deposit; the funds cannot be used as savings and I get no interest.

So, it is not a deposit nor a store of wealth, for me or the issuer, who cannot intermediate the funds or use them for operating expenses. It is not, therefore, capital—for anyone. If I am the user, I get to buy online games, ringtones, or airtime. I might buy physical goods, too, and my electronic value undergoes a miraculous transformation into money. But what is in it for the issuer?

On Payment

> Historically, private property rights have not attached to the infrastructure of exchange. Nobody owns the system of making payments by writing, presenting, and clearing paper checks. Nobody owns the apparatus of paper currency as a medium of exchange. Nobody owns the general concept of paying and selling by means of a payment card system.
> —Robert Fram, Margaret Jane Radin, and Thomas Brown, 1999

Consider an everyday purchase. You go to a market. You offer money to a vendor in exchange for goods. You provide an amount of money equivalent to the price demanded. If you disagree, you can haggle, you can compare prices with those offered by other vendors. Demand, supply, the price mechanism—this is the stuff of Robinsonades. The transaction is the line between M and C in Marx's classic formula.

But if you use a credit card, what happens then?

The exchange of goods or services for money often does not occur at par. Merchants generally bear the cost of accepting alternative forms of payment besides cash or checks. For the $100 I offer a merchant, he receives net around $97 after paying a discount, a fee with several parts, the largest being usually interchange, with an additional ad valorem component based on the purchase price. Merchants pay the merchant discount in exchange for enhanced sales and convenience.

In the case of online credits, a fee is levied on merchants, too: for iTunes, the portion taken by the electronic-value issuer is 30 percent. The 30/70 split in revenue for online and mobile prepaid credits is becoming the industry standard, though it was arbitrarily set by Apple at first. When Facebook was still offering credits, from a dollar's worth of purchased items in a game from Zynga (Farmville's developer), Zynga gets seventy cents. And Facebook still takes its 30 percent cut from game developers for transactions made through its payments platform. *This is where the money is.* This is not news to the payments industry, but others should pay attention to it too. As with interchange in card networks, a toll generates a huge revenue stream. It is a toll on the means of value transfer, on payment, that renders it a non-par transaction, non-equivalent to the market price of the good purchased.[7]

Par clearance during exchange was once a monumental technical and political achievement. A slow victory of the United States Federal Reserve was to chip away gradually at the non-par clearance of paper checks, that is, the practice of deducting exchange charges from checks' face value. Non-par check clearance created a value chain within the act of payment.

Fees were levied not on float or the leveraging of bank paper as capital, but rather for the act of clearing. Non-par banks argued that the expense of clearing checks from more distant US states justified charging exchange fees. But exchange charges on checks could not be justified, economically or pragmatically, in the wake of the Federal Reserve (Stearns 2011). With the centralization of Federal Reserve Banks throughout the country, the costs of transporting currency and paper were diminished and absorbed by the Reserve banks themselves. The Fed—in effect, creating a public infrastructure for check clearance and currency reserves—eliminated the justification for interchange. Par clearance was instituted by the political decision asserting the nonownership of the means of value transfer. No one would own payments; the value chain in payment was cut. Even today, payments industry professionals refer to cash and checks as "virtual" payment systems because no one "owns" them.

The early charge card systems—Diners Club in 1948, Carte Blanche, American Express and BankAmericard by 1960—were the first privately owned payment systems last century (Swartz 2014). Only when the major card networks, Visa and MasterCard, arrived in the 1970s did non-par clearing of payments catch the attention of merchants and regulators. Claiming to recoup the costs of clearing paper credit slips between receiving and issuing banks, the card networks assessed fees on card transactions, including "interchange."

Credit and debit interchange fees have largely escaped scholarly attention (Evans and Schmalensee 2004: 3). No one knew the term outside Visa and MasterCard before 1979, when a major antitrust lawsuit (the *NaBanco* case) was filed against the card networks. Visa won the first case and interchange again faded from view. The "topic languished in obscurity until around the turn of this century" (Evans and Schmalensee 2004: 3). By then, the use of credit and debit cards, online payments using cards, and payment cards had become one of the fastest growing expenses for businesses (Levitin 2007: 429).

Interchange was interesting for another reason. As James Evans and Richard Schmalensee note, "understanding their determination and effect is *intellectually challenging*" (2004: 4, emphasis in original). Why is it so challenging? Because in classic liberal and critical approaches to markets, it is hard to figure out these fees. Both in litigation and academic writing, lawyers and legal scholars have pondered the peculiarities of payment cards. This is a "two-sided market," where card networks face both merchants and banks as their customers and the network provides a *platform* more than a specific product, an infrastructure that brings players together in a new, networked market.

The banks are of two kinds: banks that issue a card to a consumer and the acquiring bank that processes card transactions for a merchant. The platform facilitates settlement between the acquirer and the issuer. The merchant and the consumer pay the cost of the transaction, the merchant through interchange, and the consumer through the passed-on cost of interchange plus whatever other fees the platform or its client, the issuing bank, might charge (an annual membership fee, for example). The platform's customers are neither the merchant nor the consumer, but the banks.

If interchange is a price, then of what is it the price? Who is selling what here? The issuing bank is selling access to the consumer's account. The merchant is buying access to this via the acquiring bank. But how is the price of access determined? The platform or card network sets the price. And who is the card network's customer? The issuing bank. (Look in your wallet at your credit card: the bank named on the card is the network's real customer, not you.) If the issuing bank does not issue the card, then the card network does not receive any revenue in fees. In short, then, the card network sets the price that its customer—the issuing bank—will receive from the merchant via the acquiring bank. Let's now imagine a lot of issuers competing for business. Every bank wants to issue me with a credit card. What does the card network do to attract issuers to its product? It raises the price paid by merchants. "Competition for issuance *raises* prices," I was told, it does not lower them. The merchant, who actually pays that price, cannot bargain or negotiate. If the merchant wants to accept payment cards, the merchant has to agree to this arrangement. So, the network sets the price that the issuing bank receives, not the price that it will pay for the service.

Private card–network rules govern payment card transactions. Among these is the "honor all cards" rule, which states that if a merchant accepts one payment card he or she must accept all co-branded cards: the merchant cannot choose only to accept cards for which lower interchange is being assessed. This has been challenged several times in antitrust lawsuits. But the "honor all cards" rule helps prevent competition among cards based on the price paid at the point of sale. This helps issuers avoid "commoditization"—"where sellers compete solely on the basis of price for the sale of individual products" (Levitin 2008: 1360).

Some question whether such a platform can properly be considered a private commodity. Platform owners ask the same question and come up with the same answer: no. But they do not favor public infrastructure or the idea of card networks as common carriers. What they provide is neither a commodity nor a public good. It is another kind of beast entirely, sitting athwart money alongside and constituting the market economy.[8] Since the *NaBanco* case, from 1979 to 1986, the card networks have generally opted to settle lawsuits rather than fight claims in court. The settlement in the so-called *Wal-Mart* case was telling.[9] Wal-Mart and other merchants argued that the card networks practiced anticompetitive price fixing; that the "honor all cards" rule was collusion; and that differential interchange for debit and credit cards was unjustified given the risks and costs of each. Use of debit cards increased dramatically in the late 1990s and early 2000s.

Credit cards involve risk of credit loss, obviously: some cardholders will default. Interchange does not make up for this loss: the courts and card networks insist that credit loss should not be passed on as a cost of doing business via interchange. Rather, interchange compensates for the "cost of funds" (COF) or the time-value of money. In a credit card transaction, the issuing bank pays the merchant the next day. But it does not receive payment from the cardholder for thirty days. The issuer bets that the cardholder will not pay off the balance at the end of the month, but will pay an installment, incurring an interest charge that more than compensates for the loss of the funds. But when a cardholder pays off the balance in full at the end of those thirty days, the issuing bank has lost the use of the funds for thirty days and has no opportunity to earn interest. In effect, "credit" never made its appearance: the money extended to the cardholder never contributed to the bank's ability to leverage debt. This "cost of funds," therefore, is included in the interchange calculation. Or so the card networks argued.

Wal-Mart and other merchants noted, however, that COF was also included in the interchange calculation for debit. Unlike credit, there is no risk of credit loss with debit—it is linked directly to a person's bank account balance. And debit payments settle either within seconds (for PIN debit) or within one to three days (for signature debit). In other words, there is no COF. Wal-Mart demonstrated this, and Visa settled out of court. Subsequently, the US Congress and the European Union's Single Euro Payment Area (SEPA) took up the issue of reducing interchange on debit card purchases, as they became a major growth industry, accounting for almost 25 percent of all payments in the United States by 2009.

Again: what kind of relation is interchange?

Interchange, Rent, and Annuity

My research partners and I are participating in a webinar—a live seminar over the Internet sponsored by the Electronic Transactions Association. It is about Independent Sales Organizations (ISOs) in the United States, and how to become one. ISOs act as intermediaries between merchants and acquiring banks—the banks that process electronic payments for the merchants. Instead of the bank sending agents out to every shop owner in town, an ISO establishes a relationship with a bank, and does this work on its behalf. ISOs work indirectly for the card networks. Their job is to make it easy for merchants to start accepting electronic payments (and, increasingly, mobile payments). They also explain to merchants the fee structure of electronic payments. Often, they bundle other services into a package, so that, instead of only facilitating card transactions, they also supply and maintain point-of-sale devices and may offer the merchant tracking software, regulatory compliance services, online payment options, and varying degrees of customer support. ISOs levy fees, and are assessed fees in turn by the acquiring banks and payment card networks.

ISO agents are required to disclose these fees to merchants. Our webinar instructor insisted that these fees are not "Visa or MasterCard fees." Visa requires disclosure of which party in the payments chain is levying which fee. "It now has to indicate that it is a 'processing fee for Visa transactions.' And the reason is Visa is not the one imposing this fee; the sponsors [acquiring banks] do that." For ISOs, and for merchants, this quickly becomes murky, since there are so many components of the fee structure for different kinds of electronic payments.

As noted earlier, the *OED* does not (yet) record the payments industry sense of "interchange." Rather, it lists a host of meanings related to reciprocity. In particular, interchange refers to a reciprocal exchange in which one thing takes the place of another thing, and thereby shares a relation to things around it with the object for which it was exchanged. One thing substitutes for another within the system of relations that enmeshed the first thing. The transit metaphor is a good one for payments: in transit contexts interchange refers to engineering routes for vehicles to permit the flow of traffic through or around junctions.

The acquirer and issuer do what two railcars do. They cross without touching the M-C-M equation: they allow a pass-through to take place. According to its critics (e.g., Levitin 2008), the card network fixes a price for the pass-through. It is not based on market price being rather an arbitrary levy on passage. A bridge toll collected by private entities on what was heretofore—at least since the consolidation of national currencies—a public infrastructure.[10]

Interchange has no place in classical or critical accounts of modern political economy. In the *Wealth of Nations*, Adam Smith (1843) briefly mentions fees charged by the city of Amsterdam for opening bank accounts, transferring funds, and other services. He noted that the amounts collected were considerable, but it was an "accidental" revenue stream that, though profitable, was incidental to the bank's main operations. Levying such fees was supposed to serve the interests of "public utility," to help facilitate clearance and settlement for the bankers. This revenue accrued to the public coffers, not to the bank.[11]

Alexander Hamilton (c. 1756–1804) was the architect of the first Bank of the United States and coauthor of the *Federalist Papers*. Federalist 44 says that the federal state's establishment of a public means of payment is crucial to the republic's functioning. The section of *Capital* on the "Means of payment" lays bare the credit relations at the heart of commodity exchange. Not all payments settle when they are promised.

> The quantity of money in circulation no longer corresponds with the mass of commodities in circulation during a given period, such as a day. Money which represents commodities long since withdrawn from circulation [i.e., those "paid for" on credit in the past] continues to circulate. Commodities circulate, but their equivalent in money does not appear until some future date. Moreover, the debts contracted each day, and the payments falling due on the same day, are entirely incommensurable magnitudes. (Marx 1901: I, 237)

In a lengthy footnote, Marx quotes an anonymous author on the workings of deferred payment that create a "mass of liabilities," all due to settle on indefinite dates in the future. Marx proceeds to discuss the perturbations of the credit system created by varying settlement dates: "The development of money as a means of payment also makes it necessary to accumulate it in preparation for the days when the sums which are owing fall due" (ibid.: I, 239). Chapter 33 of *Capital* III similarly takes up the effects of credit for money as a means of payment. He does not mention fees collected for clearance and settlement. What mattered to him was deferred payment generating more money in circulation than the sum total of commodities at any given time. Thus was labor power transformed into capital, and capital into accumulation. This is consistent with the credit theories of money mentioned earlier.

Famously, Marx wrote:

> The consumption of labour-power is completed, as in the case of every other commodity, outside the limits of the market or of the sphere of circulation. Accompanied by Mr. Moneybags and by the possessor of labour-power, *we therefore take leave for a time of this noisy sphere*, where everything takes place on the surface and in view of all men, and follow them both into the hidden abode of production. (Ibid.: I, chap. 6, emphasis added)

We must pay attention the whole world alongside, underneath, and extending below the M-C-M formula, astride credit, never touching it so as to interrupt its flow but channeling it and other payments and collecting tolls along the way. For Marx and other nineteenth-century analysts of political economy, it was important to understand the relationship between money as specie and bills of exchange and bank notes as methods of payment. Bills of exchange were dominant for long-distance trade, after all. Marx was writing before the consolidation of national currencies (Helleiner 2003) with many coexisting forms of money, not all of which entered into the credit nexus (from tobacco, to leather, to specie, lottery tickets, nonbank issued notes, etc.; Nyquist 1995). But surely the rise of capitalism rendered those other forms of money marginal to the main act, if not articulated in some way to capitalist processes of accumulation broadly defined.

The consolidation of the money form was a state project, however. In the United States, clearance of bank checks at par represented a huge political and economic accomplishment of the Federal Reserve, which made Marx's account of the credit system truer by eliminating much of the noise accompanying it. Defenders of non-par banking had to go through contortions to come to its aid, arguing that it was not hidden interest, but a legitimate fee for a service, even after it became clear that the service was unnecessary.

But today, with interchange and the proliferation of new payment options, these subterranean relations can become visible again, can reassert themselves, can grow to the point where interchange expenses take up 50 percent of the profits of certain classes of merchants (Levitin 2007),[12] where the payments industry becomes a sector in its own right, and when cash purchases are overtaken by plastic, so that new, privately owned means of value transfer can assess a 30 percent toll on transactions while removing themselves from the realm of public money.

Remember too the recent phenomenal growth of debit cards, instead of credit cards, and of prepaid instruments, where there is no cost of funds and payment is settled immediately or the next day. The credit system's day of reckoning so colorfully described by Marx has not come for debit. The difficulty of explaining in standard economic terms the pricing of debit interchange is further evidence of the oddity of interchange itself.

Conclusion: Alternative Interchanges

What people make money from in payments is not money as a "store of wealth." This is not capital, credit, or debt. "Stored value" has even been regulated away in the United States. Regulations often prohibit intermediation or leveraging of funds along the payment-processing chain. In emerging mobile money services in Kenya and Afghanistan, the float is held in a trust account—sometimes several trust accounts, spread over a number of banks in case of bank failure or corruption—and is segregated from the service provider's operating capital. What people make money from in payments is rent, a toll, a fee that does not reflect market price. Profit comes from money-in-exchange, as "soft currency" (Guyer 2012), for everyday payments.

There is by now a body of ethnographic work on financial professionals, techniques, and settings (Maurer 2005b; Hart 2012). But some of them overstate conventional claims. Annelise Riles notes that critical perspectives on finance "play to" popular conceptions of "virtual" money, "infinite circulation," "gambling," and "acceleration" (2011: 795). Janet Roitman (2013) writes that the conceit of "crisis"—borne of a theoretical commitment to teleological determinism or to a crude dialectic—is an oxymoron. One cannot claim that capitalism is permanently in crisis without denaturing the very term, sucking it of analytical purchase.

Roitman notes a theoretical contradiction. Riles sees an ethnographic opportunity. Getting away from trading room floors, from the dazzling technological devices even as we try to open their black boxes, she urges us to inspect "the margins—collateral to—the trading room" (ibid.: 796). This collateral knowledge includes the humdrum legal practices of contract and regulation. For me, they include the payments geeks. In a related argument, Guyer (2012) points out that the focus on money as a store of wealth participating in long-term temporal cycles of credit and finance understates the means of exchange and payment function and money's multiplicity in the short-term, as in cash economies. There are 180 national currencies currently in circulation, and only a handful serve as reserve currencies warranted by strong states. This handful has provided the models of money, including for critics capital, finance, abstraction, and fiction. Empirically, the world is more complicated, a place of "soft currencies" used in unstable contexts, short time horizons, and constant fuzzy conversion into other forms of "cash" (ibid.).

"Cash" refers to the material practices of storing and exchanging short-term moneys. It originally indicated the cashier's box where money was placed for short-term storage. The money had to be held safe; it need not be stored for all eternity. With a receipt, one would exchange paper for a currency note out of the cash box, "cash" a check (Maurer 2011b). Collateral knowledges and soft currencies care about the contexts of their enactment and use. Far from being the virtual fictions of popular and critical imagination, they are always linked to positional differences of subjects, currencies, objects (Guyer 2012); their uses unfold in different contexts.[13]

In a footnote to the section on Hindu law, Mauss wrote:

> Nous ne voulons pas lire non plus que le contrat n'ait eu dans l'Inde que cette origine, partie réelle, partie personnelle et partie formelle de la transmission des biens, et que l'Inde n'ait pas connu d'autres formes d'obligations, par exemple le quasi-délit. Nous ne cherchons à démontrer que ceci: la subsistance, à côté de ces droits, d'un autre droit, d'une autre économie et d'une autre mentalité. (Mauss 1923–1924: 142)

The English translator abbreviates the last sentence: "We seek only to show the existence, beside these laws, of another system" (Mauss 1967: 123). A more literal translation might be: "We seek to demonstrate this: the persistence, alongside these laws, of another law, another economy, and another mentality." A more significant passage comes in the section on the *kula* gift-exchange system. For Mauss *kula* provides the occasion for more mundane exchanges: "All the *kula* provides the occasion for *gimwali*, commonplace exchanges" (ibid.: 27). And these are "extremely diverse in scope" (ibid.).

Another meaning of interchange from the *OED* is: "Alternate or varied succession in time, order, or space; alternation, vicissitude." For Mauss the alternatives that sit beside gift exchange are central; and alongside our market economy runs another, an economy of regard and relationships. A human economy, Keith Hart argues in this volume, connects these levels of association and money can be a bridge for crossing over to them. Attending to the infrastructures moving money, seeing their literal and figurative (and fee-oriented) interchanges opens up the possibility of alternatives lying right in front of us. As Mauss opened out a myriad alternatives—times, orders, and spaces that are integral to the forms and functions of all value exchange in contemporary society—so, too, the wires, routers, chips, and networks of payment. These actually existing alternatives may be far more significant, analytically and politically, than the fictions of finance that have received so much critical attention since the crisis. These are the mundane, subterranean practices of payment. And they are engaged in battle with each other: private players against each other and against the public goods of cash, check, and par clearance. In the world of private payments, money-as-exchange is subject to a toll. In the world of public payments, cash still passes hand to hand. One might imagine an alternative world where money-as-wealth is levied by a similar toll or massive exchanges of money-as-capital are assessed a fee. A "Tobin Tax" (Tobin 1978) would represent a new set of relations in place of the old: inter*change*, indeed.

Acknowledgments

This is a much modified version of a paper originally published as Maurer (2012b). It has been presented in several places. I would like to thank Ute Tellmann, Sven Opitz, José Ossandón, and Ariel Wilkis. Thanks too to Tom Boellstorff, Julia Elyachar, Jane Guyer, Keith Hart, Stefan Helmreich, Katherine Porter, Janet Roitman, Hillel Schwarz, Maryon McDonald, and Lloyd Constantine. Jenny Fan, Scott Mainwaring, Sean Mallin, Taylor Nelms, Stephen Rea, Elizabeth Reddy, Nick Seaver, Lana Swartz, and Melissa Wrapp have been my fellow travelers in the payments space. Research has been supported by National Science Foundation, Law and Social Sciences Program (SES 0960423 and SES 1455859). Any opinions, findings, and conclusions or recommendations expressed in this material are those of the author and do not necessarily reflect the views of the National Science Foundation.

Bill Maurer is a professor of anthropology and law at the University of California, Irvine. He is the author of *How Would You Like To Pay? How Technology is Changing the Future of Money* (2015), as well as other works on money, payment technologies, and finance.

NOTES

1. By "liberal," I refer to the classical economic and liberal traditions; by "critical," I refer to the Marxist tradition but also the related moral arguments from Aristotle to Appadurai.
2. Email to author from Money2020 organizing committee, 1 June 2012.

3. This chapter concerns the retail payments industry: consumer-facing mechanisms for making everyday retail payments at a point of sale, online, or via other electronic devices. The only other anthropological discussion I know of the wholesale payments industry is Riles (2011). See Maurer (1999). An excellent account of the payments infrastructure is Stearns (2011).
4. Oxford English Dictionary, "interchange, n." Second edition (1989); online version, September 2011, http://www.oed.com/view/Entry/97600. First published in *New English Dictionary* (1900).
5. From Bohannan (1959); see Maurer (2006); and Guyer (2004), Foster (1999), Hart (2000), Graeber (2011).
6. I thank Janet Roitman for this phrasing.
7. If the high margin for using such credits is just for access to a distribution channel *as well as* or *incidentally* a payment service, then there is nothing necessarily interesting here. But when the aim of system designers is to become the primary means of payment for physical goods, services, and accounts settlement, we do have something different. If the goal is to forget about interchange and focus on the transactional data in every real-world purchase, bridging the gap between actual and virtual economies and societies will have been achieved (Boellstorff 2012).
8. Helmreich (2009: 23).
9. In re Visa Check/Mastermoney Antitrust Litigation, No. 96-CV-5238, 2003 WL 1712568 (E.D.N.Y. Apr. 1, 2003).
10. Riles notes that market participants had to be made to understand and act as if the market were a public good (2011: 234). This was Alexander Hamilton's aim, and finds expression further back in eighteenth-century debates about credit and speculation: with honesty, trust, and open account books, there was no reason to fear credit (Pocock 1985). Daniel Defoe's pragmatic realism concerning paper credit underscores the *political* foundations of the current situation, and the need for honesty to mitigate epistemological uncertainty (Sherman 1997: 328) rather than seek to abolish uncertainty with the seemingly substantial commodity money, abolition of speculation, or unfettering "the market." Honesty, and not reputation (Sherman 1997: 343), should militate against credit's fantastic and fatalistic specters, according to Defoe. Thanks to Julia Elyachar and Tomaz Mastnak here.
11. "The city of Amsterdam derives considerable revenue from the bank. Besides what may be called the warehouse-rent above mentioned, each person, upon first opening an account with the bank, pays a fee of ten guilders; and for every new account three guilders three stivers; for every transfer two stivers; and if the transfer is for less than three hundred guilders, six stivers.... Public utility and not revenue was the original object of this institution.... The revenue which has arisen from it was unforeseen and may be considered as accidental" (Smith 1843: 198).
12. The United States and the European Union have recently sought to rein in interchange fees through legislation and regulation. A new shift may be on the horizon. "Over the 5–10 year term as interchange and similar fees approach zero, transactional advertising will be a major source of payment

profit. If you haven't been an advertising person yet, you will be" (industry professional, 2012). So from float and credit to fees to . . . data mining.
13. See Appadurai (2011). Payment is not "external to and prior to any and all of its distinctive devices" (ibid.: 519) and payment stream revenues are not "gambles" at all (ibid.: 521)—there is little "spirit of uncertainty" (ibid.: 522) when you know you can collect 30 percent on every transaction. Hence, perhaps, the strenuous resistance from financial professionals to a similarly certain revenue stream generated by a toll on large-scale transactions—a Tobin Tax—not just on everyday small-scale transactions. Neither interchange nor Tobin Tax would have "risk at its very heart" (ibid.: 522).

REFERENCES

Appadurai, A. 2011. "The ghost in the financial machine." *Public Culture* 23(3): 517–540.
Bell, S. 2001. "The role of the state in the hierarchy of money." *Cambridge Journal of Economics* 25: 149–163.
Boellstorff, T. 2012. "Rethinking 'digital' anthropology." In H. A. Horst and D. Miller (eds.), *Digital Anthropology*. London: Berg, pp. 39–60.
Bohannan, P. 1959. "The impact of money on an African subsistence economy." *Journal of Economic History* 19(4): 491–503.
Brown, T. P. 2009. "Keeping electronic money valuable: The future of payments and the role of public authorities." In R. E. Litan and M. Neil Baily (eds.), *Moving Money: The Future of Consumer Payments*. Washington, DC: The Brookings Institution, pp. 127–139.
Evans, D., and R. Schmalensee. 2004. *Paying with Plastic: The Digital Revolution in Buying and Borrowing*. Cambridge, MA: The MIT Press.
Foster, R. 1999. "In God we trust? The legitimacy of Melanesian currencies." In D. Akin and J. Robbins (eds.), *Money and Modernity: State and Local Currencies in Melanesia*. Pittsburgh, PA: University of Pittsburgh Press, pp. 214–231.
Fram, R., M. Radin, and T. Brown. 1999. "Altered states: Electronic commerce and owning the means of value exchange." *Stanford Technology Law Review* 2. https://journals.law.stanford.edu/stanford-technology-law-review/online/altered-states-electronic-commerce-and-owning-means-value-exchange.
Gad, C. 2012. "What we talk about when we talk about sailor culture." *Culture Unbound* 4: 367–392.
Graeber, D. 2011. *Debt: The First 5,000 Years*. Brooklyn, NY: Melville House.
Guyer, J. 2004. *Marginal Gains: Monetary Transactions in Atlantic Africa*. Chicago, IL: University of Chicago Press.
———. 2012. "Soft currencies, cash economies, new monies: Past and present." *Proceedings of the National Academy of Sciences*. www.pnas.org/cgi/doi/10.1073/pnas.1118397109.
Hart, K. 2000. *The Memory Bank: Money in an Unequal World*. London: Profile Books.
———. 2012. "A Note on Arjun Appadurai's 'The spirit of calculation.'" *Cambridge Anthropology* 30(1): 18–24.

Helleiner, E. 2003. *The Making of National Money: Territorial Currencies in Historical Perspective.* Ithaca, NY: Cornell University Press.
Helmreich, S. 2009. *Alien Ocean: Anthropological Voyages in Microbial Seas.* Berkeley: University of California Press
Ingham, G. 2004a. *The Nature of Money.* Cambridge: Polity.
———. 2004b. "The emergence of capitalist credit money." In R. Wray (ed.), *Credit and State Theories of Money: The Contributions of A. Mitchell Innes.* Cheltenham: Edward Elgar, pp. 173–222.
Jensen, C., and P. Winthereik. 2012. *Monitoring Movements: Building Partnership through Aid Infrastructures.* Cambridge, MA: MIT Press.
Kockelman, P. 2010. "Enemies, parasites, and noise: How to take up residence in a system without becoming a term in it." *Linguistic Anthropology* 20(2): 406–421.
Levitin, A. 2007. "Payment wars: The merchant-bank struggle for control of payment systems." *Stanford Journal of Law, Business and Finance* 12: 425–486.
———. 2008. "Priceless? The economic costs of credit card merchant restraints." *UCLA Law Review* 55: 1321–1406.
Marx, K. 1901. *Capital: A Critique of Political Economy,* 3 vols. New York: The Modern Library.
Mas, I., and O. Morawczynski. 2009. "Designing mobile money services: Lessons from M-PESA." *Innovations: Technology, Governance, Globalization* 4(2): 77–91.
Maurer, B. 1999. "Forget Locke? From proprietor to risk-bearer in new logics of finance." *Public Culture* 11(2): 365–385.
———. 2005a. "Finance." In J. Carrier (ed.), *Handbook of Economic Anthropology.* Cheltenham: Edward Elgar, pp. 176–193.
———. 2005b. *Mutual Life, Limited: Islamic Banking, Alternative Currencies, Lateral Reason.* Princeton, NJ: Princeton University Press.
———. 2006. "The anthropology of money." *Annual Review of Anthropology* 35(1): 15–36.
———. 2011a. "Note from IMTFI–Mobile money regulation: A story of best practices and emerging realizations." *USAID Microlinks* Note, 6 December 2011. http://www.microlinks.org/learning-marketplace/notes/note-imtfi-mobile-money-regulation-story-arc-best-practices-and-emerging-.
———. 2011b. "Regulation as retrospective ethnography: Mobile money and the arts of cash." *Banking and Finance Law Review* 27: 299–313.
———. 2012a. "Mobile money: Communication, consumption and change in the payments space." *Journal of Development Studies* 48(5): 589–604.
———. 2012b. "Payment: Forms and functions of value transfer in contemporary society." *Cambridge Anthropology* 30(2): 15–35
Maurer, B., T. Nelms, and S. Rea. 2012. "'Bridges to cash': Channeling agency in mobile money." *Journal of the Royal Anthropological Institute* 1: 52–54.
Mauss, M. 1923–1924. "Essai sur le don. Forme et raison de l'échange dans les sociétés archaïques." *L'année sociologique* 1.
———. 1967. *The Gift.* Introduction by E. Evans-Pritchard. Translated by I. Cunnison. New York: Norton.
Miller, M. 1949. *The Par Check Collection and Absorption of Exchange Controversies.* Cambridge, MA: Bankers' Publishing Company.

Nyquist, C. 1995. "A spectrum theory of negotiability." *Marquette Law Review* 78: 897–971.

Pocock, J. 1985. *Virtue, Commerce, and History: Essays on Political Thought and History, Chiefly in the Eighteenth Century*. Cambridge: Cambridge University Press.

Porter, K. 2008. "The debt dilemma." *Michigan Law Review* 106: 1167–1192.

Riles, A. 2010. "Collateral expertise." *Current Anthropology* 51(6): 795–818.

Riles, A. 2011. *Collateral Knowledge: Legal Reasoning in the Global Financial Markets*. Chicago, IL: University of Chicago Press.

Rochet, J., and J. Tirole. 2003. "An economic analysis of the determination of interchange fees in payment card systems." *Review of Network Economics* 2(2): 69–79.

Roitman, J. 2013. *Anti-Crisis*. Durham, NC: Duke University Press.

Sherman, S. 1997. "Promises, promises: Credit as contested metaphor in early capitalist discourse." *Modern Philology* 94(3): 327–349.

Smith, A. 1843. *An Inquiry into the Nature and Causes of the Wealth of Nations*. Edinburgh: Thomas Nelson.

Stearns, D. 2011. *Electronic Value Exchange: Origins of the VISA Electronic Payment System*. London: Springer.

Swartz, L. 2014. "Gendered transactions: Identity and payment at mid-century." *Women's Studies Quarterly* 42(1–2): 137–153.

Tobin, J. 1978. "A proposal for international monetary reform." *Eastern Economic Journal* 4(3–4): 153–159.

Vercellone, C. 2008. "The new articulation of wages, rent and profit in cognitive capitalism." Queen Mary University School of Business and Management, London. *HAL Archives Ouverts*. Halshs-00265584.

Zhan, M. 2012. "Worlding oneness: Daoism, Heidegger, and possibilities for treating the human." *Social Text* 29(4): 107–128.

CHAPTER 9

The Politics of Bitcoin

NIGEL DODD

I examine here the view that Bitcoin is a form of money that transcends social life and politics. This is the image that tends to be put forward by those who celebrate Bitcoin as a mechanized monetary system that can solve classic problems of monetary governance by relying on technology rather than trust. This very belief has to be seen in a political context, not least as a response to the perceived failures of states and central banks to manage the global economy effectively since the 1970s. In practice, Bitcoin appeals to a diverse range of political interests, from libertarians and anarchists who want to free the monetary system from state interference, through people who oppose the power of banks over the production of money and its consequences for rising debt, to those who fear that the development of electronic payment systems has increased the opportunities for public and private surveillance over our everyday economic lives. Seen in this light, Bitcoin is a highly politicized currency whose prospects are tightly bound up with a number of other developments in the world's monetary landscape. Consequently its future cannot be viewed in technological terms alone.

There is a paradox at the heart of the Bitcoin phenomenon: the currency relies on that which the ideology underpinning it seeks to deny, namely, the dependence of money on politics, social relations, and trust. Insofar as Bitcoin has been successful up until now as a form of money—and it is a moot point whether it has—this has been in large part because of the community that has grown up around it and the political beliefs that sustain it. Ironically, this community is underpinned by the commonly held belief that Bitcoin has *replaced* social and political relations—the trust on which all forms of money depend—with machine code. This belief is a fiction. Bitcoin has thrived despite, not because of, its reliance upon machines. If ever there was a form of money that validates Georg Simmel's (2005) description of money as a claim on society, it is Bitcoin, the very currency that was set up in denial of that conception. In this chapter, I will first examine the claim that Bitcoin is politics-free money and then challenge that view. I will conclude with some very brief reflections on the potential significance of Bitcoin for the future of money.

Bitcoin as Antipolitics

Bitcoin was launched in January 2009, using open-source software, as a peer-to-peer payment network. Monetary claims are created within the network, and their creation is strictly controlled without being governed by a central issuing authority. Bitcoins are created through dedicated rigs (PCs), which mine for new coins through a series of tasks that require considerable computational power. The network is designed to produce a fixed number of Bitcoins per unit of time: twenty-five new Bitcoins will be generated every ten minutes until 2017, and that number will subsequently be halved every four years after that. The more people (or rigs) there are mining for coins, the harder they will be to produce; now, only the most powerful rigs (i.e., several computers working together) are able to create new coins.

So what makes Bitcoin special and why is it alleged to be politics free? According to Nakamoto (the anonymous individual or collective from whose paper the Bitcoin project was derived), the key problem with most conventional forms of money is their reliance upon trust:

> The root problem with conventional currency is all the trust that's required to make it work. The central bank must be trusted not to debase the currency, but the history of fiat currencies is full of breaches of that trust. Banks must be trusted to hold our money and transfer it electronically, but they lend it out in waves of credit bubbles with barely a fraction in reserve. We have to trust them with our privacy, trust them not to let identity thieves drain our accounts. Their massive overhead costs make micropayments impossible. (P2P Foundation 2009, 2015)

Nakamoto proposed bypassing monetary governance altogether, first, by employing a computer network to control the rate at which coins are produced, and second, by using a blockchain (shared by all computers or nodes within the network) through which the transaction history of each coin would be publicly known. Privacy would be maintained, meanwhile, by encrypting the public keys, ensuring that the history of every "coin" is anonymized.[1]

In one sense, the idea that the need for trust can be removed from a monetary system is complete nonsense. For example, money *always* requires trust in order to work, simply for people to accept it as payment (Dodd 1994). But Nakamoto was specifically referring to two things: first, the trust we place in the monetary policy-makers—central bankers, for example—to act responsibly; and second, in the specific context of digital currency, the trust we need to place in one another not to double spend. These are critically important aspects of Bitcoin today; indeed they point to two separate development trajectories in Bitcoin's future. The first relates directly to money. Although it is open to debate whether—as Nakamoto alleges—trust in fiat monetary systems has been undermined, he was surely right to criticize a system that enables banks to "lend [money] out in waves of credit bubbles with barely a fraction in reserve." In this sense, Bitcoin is in tune with political sentiments that emerged after the 2008 financial crisis. The second trust issue points to wider applications of blockchain technology beyond money. The idea of keeping failsafe records through a distributed network that does not rely on trusted (but potentially inefficient, corrupt, or incompetent) intermediaries is perhaps the most radical aspect of Bitcoin, and will be pivotal to a future much broader than money alone.

Nakamoto's project rests on four basic ideas: first, the Bitcoin network is decentered and flat—with no hierarchy and no single point of authority; second, Bitcoin offers technological solutions to conventional problems of monetary governance, such as inflation; third, Bitcoin dispenses with the need to trust others, whether they are experts, politicians, or ordinary people; and fourth, Bitcoin is debt-free money, just like gold. Of course, like all other forms of money, Bitcoin implies assumptions about the organization of society, and the role that money plays within it. But in one crucial respect, Bitcoin is unique, because it seeks to achieve its aims by technological means alone. Some of these aims are purely technical; so for example, while it is usually up to institutions like central banks and the IMF—or in the case of a local currency, a board of trustees—to protect the value of money, Bitcoin delegates the task to a distributed network of machines. But Bitcoin's genealogy can also be traced back, *beyond* money, toward projects that grew up alongside the Internet itself, which were primarily concerned with using technology to deal with the emergence of digital society and its myriad challenges for governance and participation. This was a response to the "datafication of everything" (Clippinger and Bollier 2014: xii), that is to say, the growth of a new ecology of data in which almost anything—identities, currencies, contracts, genome, goods and services, etc.—could become a digital asset. In such a world, the capacity of the Internet to transcend extant regulatory boundaries—as defined by national borders, for example—is fraught with risk, as failures of security and privacy can have a direct and serious impact on critical infrastructure. According to John Clippinger and David Bollier, existing—largely centralized, physical, and human-dependent—solutions to such problems no longer seem to work in the face of such risks: "it is not possible, indeed, even necessary, to make such processes digital, algorithmic, autonomous, transparent and self-correcting" (ibid.: xiii).

There may be many and varied reasons for using (and supporting) Bitcoin. Such variety inevitably makes for some intriguing and seemingly contradictory political and ideological alliances around cryptocurrency in general. In wanting to divest banks of the right to create money, Bitcoiners (and other cryptocurrency enthusiasts) share common cause with movements such as Positive Money in the United Kingdom, which follows the Chicago Plan first conceived by Frederick Soddy during the 1920s (1926, 1933, 1943) and subsequently advocated by Irving Fisher (1935, 1936) and Henry Simons (Simons et al. 1933) in the aftermath of the Great Depression (for more recent investigations of the merits of this plan, see Benes and Kumhof 2012; and Jackson and Dyson 2012). But there is a crucial issue that sets Bitcoin apart from the arrangements envisaged by advocates of the Chicago Plan and Positive Money. Whereas those who support Positive Money argue that money's creation should be placed in the hands of a politically accountable central bank committee, Bitcoin is premised on the belief that only technology can be trusted to do such an important job.[2] In this sense, the broader appeal of Bitcoin is not simply that it takes money away from the control of banks and states, but that it removes politics from the production and management of money altogether. It is in this sense, particularly, that I would refer to Bitcoin as techno-utopian.

Bitcoin is underpinned by beliefs about the efficacy of technology per se as a means of bypassing politics altogether. This makes it sociologically interesting and problematic, because as sociologists of science and technology will tell you, technological artifacts cannot simply enact organizational forms—for example, a monetary system—on their own. Human, social, and political factors inevitably emerge as those who interact with and use these artifacts both shape and are shaped by their practical use (Winner 1985). This, specifically, is where a gulf opens up between the ideology behind Bitcoin and the practical reality of its operation.

As a technology, the Bitcoin network actually does two things, which are sometimes run together in debates about cryptocurrency. First, it produces coins according to schedule (specifically, a decreasing supply algorithm that mimics what happens when mining for a commodity like gold) that will—by design—have run its course by a fixed date. Second, the network listens for transactions, collectively verifies them, and records them onto a block, which rolls forward to form a chain—rather like a rolling spreadsheet. In both senses, Bitcoin is meant to be—and many of its advocates seriously believe it to be—politics free. In the first sense, it is by producing money automatically that the Bitcoin network is held to transcend the usual pressures that would be experienced by governments and central and commercial banks in relation to the production of money. If money is produced according to a fixed schedule, there is no scope to increase its supply for political expediency. In the second sense, the idea of recording every Bitcoin transaction onto a collectively verified database carries with it an implicit expectation that no payment or exchange—ever—needs to be doubted or contested again: if something is recorded on the blockchain, it is fixed in time and space, once and for all.

Arguably, the notion of distributing power throughout the network of computers that are responsible for producing the currency—and, just as importantly, distributing the record of transactions throughout the network by means of the blockchain—is perhaps the most important of its utopian aspects. Herein lies one important aspect of Bitcoin's significance that has both political and financial implications, because curiously, the theory behind the currency attracts interest as *both* a (quasi-anarchist) monetary means of escaping state surveillance *and* as a financial asset (or store of value) that has the potential not only to rival but to surpass gold.

Public discourse about Bitcoin often focuses on the idea that this is money created out of nothing—virtual rather than real money.[3] But as even a casual glance at the specialist monetary literature will tell you, there is nothing unusual about this—*all* money is "virtual" in the sense that it relies upon the series of claims and obligations in which it is embedded (see Dodd 1994, 2014; Hart 1986, 2001; Ingham 1996, 2004; Graeber 2001, 2011; Desan 2014; Neiburg, this volume). But although Bitcoin is certainly no exception to the argument that all money is "virtual"—for it, too, relies on honoring generalized claims to payment—the theory behind it relies on a form of reasoning derived from the opposite theory, namely, that money gains its value from its material form as a medium of exchange. Indeed, arguably the key aspect of Bitcoin's appeal to its advocates and supporters qua money—and an important reason for its rising price up until recently—is that the currency mimics gold. Bill Maurer, Taylor Nelms, and Lana Swartz (2013) characterize the philosophy behind Bitcoin as a form of "digital metallism" that relies on the semiotics of metallic money, with its language of mining and rigs. One of the most striking aspects of Bitcoin is the material infrastructure on which it rests, and the materialistic language that gets used to describe its virtues. It seems as if Bitcoins are being dug up from the ground. As Henrik Karlstrøm notes, Bitcoin is a materially embedded network: a complex chain of technology has to be in place before even the first Bitcoin transaction can be undertaken, consisting of "computers, fiber-optic cables, and all the other kinds of physically grounded machinery that underlie the wrongly assumed-to-be nonphysical internet" (2014: 30).

In monetary terms, the arguments of the goldbugs rest on the idea that the gold supply is subjected to natural limits of supply, meaning that governments or banks are unable to increase the supply artificially. As Maurer and his colleagues point out, it was this philosophy that led Locke to associate sound money with liberty, because it emancipated money from government control. With Bitcoin, "nature" is replaced by computer software (i.e., by the inbuilt cap on Bitcoin production) leading some Bitcoiners to claim that the currency is superior to gold because it is not even subject to natural contingencies (i.e., the prospect that new gold might be discovered). The cap on Bitcoin production can be removed, however, through a democratic decision—suggesting that this is no more natural, nor any less political, a monetary regime than the gold standard itself. Or to be more precise, Bitcoin's value is not—ultimately—determined by technology any more than the value of gold is conditioned by nature.

One Bitcoin trader I spoke to accepted that it is quite possible for the cap on Bitcoin production to be removed, yet insisted that such a decision was unlikely because it would undermine the techno-utopian ideals that are so important to Bitcoin, which hinge on the argument that the supply of Bitcoin can *never* be altered. In other words, he suggested that the *belief* that the total number of Bitcoin would never exceed 21 million acts like a socially necessary fiction that holds the network together. Karl Polanyi once argued that the only way of realizing the "stark utopia" (1957: 218, 250) of the self-adjusting market was through the support of a strong interventionist state, wittily describing such a system as planned laissez-faire capitalism: "There was nothing natural about laissez-faire, free markets could never have come into being merely by allowing things to take their course . . . laissez-faire itself was enforced by the state" (ibid.: 145). Much the same could be said of the "utopia" of Bitcoin as a monetary space with built-in—technologically controlled—scarcity: it is a utopia that must be embedded within a set of social practices that are sustained by strong beliefs. One could also compare the "socially necessary fiction" of Bitcoin's finite supply to the fictions that arguably sustain the idea of monetary policy as something largely technical, not political, and of central banks as institutions operating independently of government

(Ingham 2004). In other words, this is a techno-utopia that relies on far more than technology alone. The idea of Bitcoin as technological means of transcending the politics that surround money's production is as misleading as it is naïve. It relies, indeed, on a social and political life that sustains not only Bitcoin, but also *any* form of money (Dodd 2014).

The Politics of Bitcoin

Viewed solely as a form of money—as I discuss later, it has other uses too—Bitcoin needs to be viewed against the backdrop of changes in the global monetary system that have been going on since the Bretton Woods system broke down in the early 1970s. During this period, national governments and central banks have found currency management increasingly difficult in the face of the unprecedented growth of financial instruments being produced by banks and other complex financial institutions operating in a global scale. These were the developments talked about by Susan Strange (1986, 1998) when she warned that states were increasingly powerless to control the circulation of financial instruments that had been developed specifically to deal with risks that emerged once those very same states had abandoned exchange rate controls. Money, which she conceived through Georg Simmel's classic definition of it as a "claim upon society" (Simmel 2005: 177), was being placed under threat by a series of sophisticated financial instruments that were designed to manage global risks. Many of these new instruments, such as derivatives, seemed to operate like forms of money in their own right. Dick Bryan and Michael Rafferty would later argue that derivatives "are a new form of money that now provides an anchor to the global financial system" (2006: 15). Alongside other digital currencies, Bitcoin appears to be an extreme case because it not only operates outside state regulation and control, but also seems specifically designed to undermine the regime of state money. What seems to make Bitcoin unique is that it is produced not by an institution—whether a state agency or a bank—but rather by a computer network that has been programmed to produce a set number of coins up to an absolute limit. In this latter sense, Bitcoin has something in common with gold, and so it is here that we should begin thinking about the implications of the new currency for the Westphalian system of territorial money.

Alternative monies typically involve two kinds of monetary disintermediation: from banks and from the state. Some aim only for one of these, e.g., "one hundred per cent money" (or "sovereign money") as envisaged by the Chicago Plan and adapted more recently by various pressure groups—such as Positive Money in the United Kingdom, Fair Money in Austria, and Gode Penge in Denmark—aims only at disconnecting monetary creation from banks. Friedrich Hayek's (1976) proposals for denationalizing money (echoed more recently by various proposals for "monetary freedom" or "free market money") aimed at disconnecting money's production from the state. Bitcoin aims at both. Far from removing Bitcoin from politics, however, it is Bitcoin's apparent promise of a dual disintermediation for money (from banks and the state) that accounts for a substantial amount of its political appeal; indeed, it could be seen as something of a protest currency. This is perhaps the most important (although not the only) aspect of the politics of Bitcoin.

Bitcoin attracts a range of supporters, not least because both aspects of monetary disintermediation—separating money from both banks *and* the state—resonate with two major axes of political debate about the relationship between finance and the state. It seems obvious that much of Bitcoin's impact is due to the 2008 financial crisis—although, as we will see, its roots long predate the crisis. Public interest in Bitcoin resonates with debates about the nature of money and banking that were triggered by the 2008 crisis. For all their political diversity, Bitcoiners seem to unite around the common view that there are major problems with our existing monetary system, which require radical solutions, not piecemeal reform (see Pedersen, this volume). This is the political conversation that sustains Bitcoin. Bitcoin therefore feeds on the same vein of discontentment as Positive Money, which argues that banks should be deprived of their right to create money through lending. Much of this is related to the problematization of debt, too. Bitcoin therefore appeals to the political sentiments of those who are troubled by the power and influence of the so-called Wall Street System and, more specifically, are critical of the fractional reserve system that enables high-street banks to create money whenever they make a loan. From this perspective, the problem with our current monetary system is the way that it ties the production of money systematically to the production of debt. Like supporters of Positive Money—and like goldbugs (Yang 2016)—Bitcoin thus appeals to those who regard debt as morally, economically, and politically problematic.

Debt has become an increasingly prominent feature of sociological (e.g., Ingham 1996, 2004) and anthropological treatments of money (e.g., Peebles 2010; Graeber 2011), and is consistent with the "claim" theory of money that (contrary to the "commodity" theory) seems to have become the orthodoxy in most social science disciplines outside of economics—and even in heterodox economics, e.g., the French school as represented by Michel Aglietta and André Orléan (1984, 1985, 1998). This is basically the view that money is created as a form of debt, for example as an IOU or credit note (Dodd 2014: chap. 2). For all of its "heterodox" provenance, even the Bank of England recently appeared to subscribe to this view in the first *Quarterly Bulletin* of 2014. Rather than viewing money as a *thing* that gets deposited in a bank and lent out again—with the bank acting merely as an intermediary between a depositor and a borrower—the Bank of England accepted the view that money is a *process* that begins whenever a bank makes a loan:

> Commercial banks create money, in the form of bank deposits, by making new loans. When a bank makes a loan, for example to someone taking out a mortgage to buy a house, it does not typically do so by giving them thousands of pounds worth of banknotes. Instead, it credits their bank account with a bank deposit of the size of the mortgage. At that moment, new money is created. For this reason, some economists have referred to bank deposits as "fountain pen money," created at the stroke of bankers' pens when they approve loans. (Bank of England 2014: 16)

While much was made of the implications of this view for the politics of austerity—for example, David Graeber wrote in *The Guardian* that by publishing this paper the Bank had "effectively thrown the entire theoretical basis for austerity out of the window" (18 March 2014; see also Graeber 2011)—it is also significant in theoretical terms for underlining the social and political relations (in this instance, between creditors and debtors) of which money essentially consists. According to this view, money is not a thing that exists outside its users, after being deposited in a bank for example, but "comes into existence" *through* social relationships such as those between creditors and debtors. Money does not preexist the act of lending it; rather it is created by that very act. The image of money that emerges from this view mirrors that of Simmel (2005), who portrayed money as dynamic and fluid, as a claim upon society—essentially, an IOU whose value rests on the very relationship (between society and the individual) that brings it into being—rather than a thing whose value exists outside (and preexists) the relationship between its users. In explicitly opposing this view of money, Bitcoiners cannot remove politics from money; rather, they politicize it all the more, unwittingly supporting an approach to its governance (favoring austerity) that has cut through the post-2008 economic landscape—not least the Eurozone—like a major fault line. This may not, of course, be a school of thought to which some of Bitcoin's more "radical" supporters feel naturally aligned. This is, however, the unwitting outcome of a false belief that politics can be removed from the governance of money. Or to put it another way, it is the upshot of a profoundly flawed techno-utopianism.

Bitcoiners are not simply opposed to banks. Many of them have major issues with the state, too. Historically, this is Bitcoin's biggest source of public notoriety, and was fueled initially by Silk Road, the website through which one could buy drugs and pornography, free from state regulation. But in more general terms, this explains Bitcoin in a post-2001 world, because Bitcoin operates as a mirror image of the state's increasing use, post-9/11, of the mainstream financial system for security purposes (de Goede 2012). Bitcoin and other forms of cryptocurrency are particularly attractive to those with libertarian and/or anarchist sympathies who want to see money removed from the control of government. According to David Golumbia (2015), Bitcoin's appeal is mainly political, attracting those who sympathize with "the profoundly ideological and overtly conspiratorial anti–Central Bank rhetoric propagated by the extremist right in the U.S. from as far back as the Liberty Lobby and the John Birch Society" (ibid.: 119). It would be mistaken, however, to homogenize Bitcoin politically. While Golumbia's analysis of Bitcoin as a manifestation of "distributed right-wing extremism" certainly captures the politics of some of its advocates, this is an unnecessarily partial view. For example, one might just as easily view Bitcoin in anarchist terms. From this perspective, Bitcoin is a direct descendant of the Cyberpunks, and its genealogy can be traced back through the work of David Chaum in the 1980s, Wei Dai's b-money, and Nick Szabo's idea of bit gold (Dodd 2014: 363–364). As Maurer, Nelms, and Swartz (2013) suggest, Bitcoin has attracted a range of political activists holding a variety of political beliefs that might collectively be called "countercultural." In these terms, Bitcoin consists not of one techno-utopia but myriad potential social utopias, because it appeals to a vast range of interests and concerns about the nature of money and, more broadly, its role in society: "In the world of Bitcoin there are gold-bugs, hippies, anarchists, cyberpunks, cryptographers, payment systems experts, currency activists, commodity traders, and the curious" (ibid.: 2).

We therefore need to be sensitive to Bitcoin's contrasting political sides. While some want the currency simply because they think it is a surefire way of getting rich and are persuaded by freelance business promotion, protest—however diffuse—also seems to be a crucial factor in what nurtures and sustains Bitcoin. One might even say that in this particular sense, Bitcoin is a (diverse) social movement as much as it is a currency. Intellectually, Brett Scott (2013) captures some of what is at stake here when he suggests that Bitcoin embodies a "Rousseauian" approach to finance, which can be contrasted to the old, "Hobbesian" world of central banks. In other words, Bitcoin has replaced the sovereign with the general will: "In place of a centralised, hierarchical group of banks keeping score of the money, a decentralised network of individuals records every transaction on a virtual ledger called the blockchain."[4] From a narrow monetary perspective, the reasoning behind both kinds of antistate support for Bitcoin–libertarian as much as anarchist–is that governments cannot be trusted to resist increasing the money supply when political expediency demands, even if it results in high inflation. At their worst, the argument runs, irresponsible governments use their powers over money creation to fund military adventures. The prominent Bitcoin investor Roger Ver (2014) offers a fairly extreme version of this perspective when he argues that "Bitcoin will prevent governments from being able to just print money at will and then use that to buy tanks and guns and bombs to murder people around the world."[5]

Here again, Bitcoin's connections with arguments about personal privacy and freedom are important. According to Scott, Bitcoin plays an important role as a "counterpower" to the Wall Street System–irrespective of the exact political reasons one has for being supportive of or suspicious toward the new currency itself. One significant reason for this, he argues, is that in the UK for example, while something like 97 percent of money in circulation consists of digital money (not cash) issued by commercial banks, "every single one of your transactions becomes a potential piece of data to be monitored, incrementally building up a database of your personal characteristics" (Scott 2015). In such a world, Bitcoin–like cash–simply offers privacy.

Politically, then, Bitcoin seems to be in tune with the times. It resonates with the post-2008 Occupy movement, not just because it challenges the role of banks in creating money, but also due to its horizontalism. In this context, it is as a means, more than an end, that horizontalism matters. In his book on Occupy and the Arab Spring, the English journalist Paul Mason (2012) describes this in terms of the distinction between network and hierarchy. Social media such as Twitter epitomize a brave new world of the network, governed not by central sources of authority but by the wisdom of crowds. Likewise, David Graeber (2013) has drawn attention to horizontalism as one of the defining features of Occupy's strategy. He also finds evidence of it in Argentina after its 2001 crisis–in which, as he points out, alternative currencies played a key role. Perhaps the ultimate financial expression of the wisdom of crowds is P2P lending, while the fast-growing sharing economy–couch surfing, for example–has taken the principle into the consumer world. Bitcoin seems to belong to this world–the only caveat being that it automates the crowd.

For all of its value as a reading of the potential of Bitcoin as a protest currency, this image of it as a horizontal network that embeds trust into computer code misses some crucial aspects of the reality of Bitcoin's actual operations, which shed a rather different light on the politics behind it. As with all complex technical systems, social practices are crucial. Bitcoin has a strong flavor of punk DIY-ism about it: the idea of rigging up your own machine and creating your own currency. Besides Bitcoin, other cryptocurrencies have been developed, such as Dogecoin and Litecoin, which offer variations on the theme. But in the case of Bitcoin, especially, the argument for its horizontalism is undermined by the way the system incentivizes the most powerful producers of the currency to become even more powerful. Most of Bitcoin mining is carried out through mining pools, which pull together multiple rigs in order to generate a block. Where you might wait years to generate Bitcoin if you operate alone, by joining a pool you stand a good chance of receiving fractions of Bitcoin on a regular basis. Reinforcing the incentives, rewards are scaled: the rewarded block is split according to processing power. Relatively few powerful pools dominate Bitcoin mining. Indeed, it is mathematically possible for one miner (or mining pool) with enormous processing power to monopolize the creation of new coins. If this were to happen, Bitcoin would resemble the most hierarchical monetary system imaginable; indeed, it would make most existing monetary systems (wherein money is created through commercial bank lending) look flat by comparison. In this sense, Bitcoin is potentially more centralized than most hitherto existing monetary systems. Calling Bitcoin horizontalist not only renders it sociologically anemic, but also buys into the false ideology that it is essentially a machine.

Conclusion[6]

I have suggested here that Bitcoin could be seen as something of a protest currency. From the perspective of monetary theory, however, perhaps the most problematic aspect of Bitcoin is its depiction of money as a thing. Arguably the greatest barrier to Bitcoin's success as money is the hoarding that this image of money encourages. Speculation has focused attention mainly on the *value* of Bitcoin, suggesting that its rising price against the US dollar is an indicator of its success qua money. This is nonsense of course: nothing that experiences this kind of price increase — even without the volatility — is going to work well as money. This mentality underwrites the logic of storing money as if it were an asset, not a medium of exchange. Bitcoin was meant to be a form of money that will not lose its value: it is meant to be inflation proof. Technically speaking, as a form of money the danger of Bitcoin, if anything, is not hyperinflation, but hyper*de*flation. Little wonder that Bitcoin is loathed by Keynesians such as Paul Krugman.

One of the most eloquent statements of the hoarding problem came from Sylvio Gesell (2007), who argued that money is "an instrument of exchange and nothing else," whose sole test of usefulness was the "degree of security, rapidity and cheapness with which goods are exchanged." Good money, as Gesell understood it, should secure, accelerate, and cheapen the exchange of goods. By contrast, the introduction of the gold standard to Germany had been a "disaster" because it had "over-improved" money, considering it only from the point of view of its holder. Gesell's proposal was disarmingly simple: make money less attractive to hold on to (demurrage). Money, he argued, should age, just like commodities. It must go out of date like a newspaper, rot like potatoes, rust like iron, and evaporate like ether. Bitcoin fits Gesell's description of a form of money that has been over-improved. When it comes to evaluating its potential as money, Bitcoin's similarity to gold is a huge disadvantage. In other words, the very feature of Bitcoin that renders it attractive as an open and democratic monetary system that is free from asymmetrical power structures—the software that controls exactly how many Bitcoins will be produced—undermines its operation as a form of money. The social and political reality of Bitcoin is somewhat different from the ideology that appears to have fueled interest in the new currency.

So where does that leave Bitcoin? I have two sets of concluding remarks to make: one is about Bitcoin as money, the other—perhaps more significant, in the longer term—is about other uses of the blockchain technology on which Bitcoin depends. As a form of money, sociological features that are directly at odds with the political ideology the theory of money that underpin it are sustaining Bitcoin. These include leadership, social organization, social structure, sociality, utopianism, and trust. None of these necessarily mean that it will work as money: hardheaded analysis suggests that the Bitcoin has far less chance of succeeding as money than the blockchain technology—which is a point I come back to in a moment. And why might Bitcoin fail? If it ever lived up to its ideology it would, not least because of the hoarding problem. Other reasons include rivals that either supersede Bitcoin or crowd it out, volatility, monopoly, regulation, loss of trust, and even technical failure.

Although there is no state in Bitcoin, it is difficult to concur that Bitcoin is an example of horizontalism: in some ways the Bitcoin community mirrors more conventional financial structures—it has its small but wealthy minority, its organized producers, and it is conceivable that there could be a monopoly on Bitcoin production because there are incentives to scale up. There may be no state, but it resembles a fiat monetary system in a number of important ways. Likewise, if the attraction of Bitcoin is that it conquers volatility in the price of money, it has clearly failed. Bitcoin is notoriously bubble prone. Although if the attraction is to see the value of money itself steadily increase—as if it were an asset—then it is difficult to deny that Bitcoin is a success. But that would make Bitcoin successful as a tool of speculation, not as money. And finally to *trust*, to portray Bitcoin as trust free, is clearly wrong. Trust matters to Bitcoin on a number of levels. Bitcoiners clearly place a great deal of faith in the code. Although this isn't directly trust in another human being, it is trust in technology. It is what Anthony Giddens once called disembedded trust. Indeed, it is arguably the shared, collective belief in Bitcoin's efficacy as a technology that underpins it. The community—and the social reality—that exists around Bitcoin sustains this sense of collective belief. Trust plainly matters to Bitcoin, after all.

Ultimately Bitcoin's utopian/dystopian claim to transcend politics has strong parallels with the dogged kind of market fundamentalism that has sustained neoliberalism. Insofar as the idea that money itself can be designed in such a way that it substitutes technology for politics and trust is crucial to Bitcoin, it mirrors one of the most disastrous aspects of the belief system that initiated the Euro—namely, the idea that money can realize political and social forms. Seen in this way, the only real difference between Bitcoin and the Euro is that technology is meant to be doing the hard work with Bitcoin, not money per se. But the underlying conviction is almost identical in both cases, and flawed in the same way. As I have argued in this chapter, neither money, nor any technological artifact that acts as a substitute for money, can enact organizational form on its own. Human, social, and political factors inevitably emerge as those who interact with and use these artifacts and both shape and are shaped by their practical use. Arguably, it was faith in technological solutions to information problems in the economy that enabled people to believe that credit risk could be managed through securitization. This was blind trust. Collateralized debt obligations, like Bitcoin, were underpinned by a trust in numbers that few people who used them actually understood.

Ultimately, although Bitcoin has attracted a great deal of attention as a form of money, its longer-term potential may well be as a database—a distributed ledger—rather than as a form of money. It is important to remember that, in relation to Bitcoin, the distributed network of computers that produces the currency and records all transactions that use it, carries out two tasks simultaneously. First, it mines for coins by solving cryptographic problems every ten minutes. Second, it listens for transactions, which are processed and confirmed by being included in a block, which is then added to the blockchain that is produced every ten minutes. Up until now, most of the attention and debate around Bitcoin has focused on the first of these processes (i.e., the production of coins). Hence the focus on the price of Bitcoin, as well as on the costs of mining and the organizational dynamics of mining pools. The longer-term significance of Bitcoin may well depend on the second process. There are many possible applications of this technology, from the idea that our identities can be validated and secured within the blockchain without being substantively known, through a real-time gross settlement system for clearing payments, to a system of smart contracts used for property transfer or the settlement of debts. Hence blockchain technology (i.e., a distributed ledger jointly maintained across a network) is now being applied to various applications for storing data, recording transactions and agreements, and, if necessary, enacting procedures on the basis of rules on which all participants in the system have agreed in advance. This, essentially, is a smart contract, defined as "computer protocols that facilitate, verify, execute and enforce the terms of a commercial agreement" (Swanson 2015: 15). We have moved from money to law (Byrne 2014).

The idea behind Bitcoin is premised on denying Simmel's most important insight into the social life of money: it treats money as a thing, not a process. This idea cannot withstand close scrutiny. What Bitcoin surely does confirm is that it no longer makes much sense to talk of money as a claim upon society if, by society, we essentially mean something we "belong" to. This is a good reason to read Simmel, because he was careful to avoid such a notion of society from the outset. In his terms, money is a claim, if not on "society," then on varying modes of shared existence and experience. For all of Bitcoin's status as *l'enfant terrible* of the world's monetary landscape, Bitcoin rests on a theory of money that is closer to the politics of austerity than to socially progressive monetary reform. Yet in practice, Bitcoin manifests forms of sociality and creativity that are crucial to money's nature as a process.

Nigel Dodd is a professor of sociology at the London School of Economics. His latest book is *The Social Life of Money* (2014).

NOTES

1. Most Bitcoins are not really coins, of course: this is a ledger-based monetary system.
2. Intriguingly, the possibility that states themselves could be the producers of cryptocurrency has been muted, largely in the form of a thought experiment it would seem, e.g., by Vigna and Casey in the form of a "digital dollar" (2015: 304–305), by the Bank of England in its recent report outlining a research agenda (Bank of England 2015: 31), and by J. P. Konig in the form of "Fedcoin" (see http://jpkoning.blogspot.co.uk/2014/10/fedcoin.html).
3. For examples of this genre of discussion about Bitcoin and other cryptocurrencies, see Patterson (2014) and Tucker (2014)–and there are countless others.
4. See Scott (2013).
5. See Ver (2014).

REFERENCES

Aglietta, M., and A. Orléan. 1984. *La Violence de la Monnaie*. Paris: Presses Universitaires de France.

——— (eds.). 1985. *Souveraineté, Légitimité de la Monnaie*. Paris: Association d'Économie Financière.

———. 1998. *La Monnaie Souveraine*. Paris: Jacob.

Bank of England. 2014. "Money creation in the modern economy." *Quarterly Bulletin* 1. London: Bank of England.

Benes, J., and M. Kumhof. 2012. "The Chicago Plan Revisited." IMF Working Paper WP/12/202. Washington, DC: International Monetary Fund.

Bryan, D., and M. Rafferty. 2006. *Capitalism with Derivatives*. Basingstoke: Palgrave.

Byrne, P (2014) "Smart contract platforms != Law . . . Smart contracts as law?" 25 April 2014, http://prestonbyrne.com/2014/04/25/smart-contract-platforms-law/ (accessed 2 June 2015).

Clippinger, J. H., and D. Bollier. 2014. "Introduction." In J. H. Clippinger and D. Bollier (eds.), *From Bitcoin to Burning Man and Beyond: The Quest for Identity and Autonomy in a Digital Society*. Amherst, MA: ID3/Off the Common Books, pp. x–xxiv.

de Goede, M. 2012. *Speculative Security: The Politics of Pursuing Terrorist Monies*. Minneapolis: University of Minnesota Press.

Desan, C. 2014. *Making Money: Coin, Currency and the Coming of Capitalism*. Cambridge, MA: Harvard University Press.

Dodd, N. 1994. *The Sociology of Money*. Cambridge: Polity Press.

———. 2014. *The Social Life of Money*. Princeton, NJ: Princeton University Press.

Fisher, I. 1935. *100% Money: Designed to keep checking banks 100% liquid; to prevent inflation and deflation; largely to cure or prevent depressions; and to wipe out much of the National Debt*. New York: The Adelphi Company.

———. 1936. "100% Money and the Public Debt." *Economic Forum* Spring (April–June): 406–420.

Gesell, S. 2007. *The Natural Economic Order*. Frankston, TX: TGS Publishers.

Golumbia, D. 2015. "Bitcoin as Politics: Distributed Right-Wing Extremism." In G. Lovink, N. Tkacz, and P. De Vries (eds.), *MoneyLab Reader: An Intervention in Digital Economy*. Amsterdam: Institute of Network Cultures, pp. 117–131.

Graeber, D. 2001. *Toward an Anthropological Theory of Value: The False Coin of Our Own Dreams*. Basingstoke: Palgrave Macmillan.

———. 2011. *Debt: The First 5,000 Years*. Brooklyn, NY, and London: Melville House Publishing.

———. 2013. *The Democracy Project: A History. A Crisis. A Movement*. London: Penguin.

Hart, K. 1986. "Heads or Tails? Two Sides of the Coin." *Man* 21: 637–656.

———. 2001. *Money in an Unequal World*. New York and London: Texere.

Hayek, F. A. 1976. *Denationalisation of Money, The Argument Refined*. London: Institute of Economic Affairs.

Ingham, G. 1996. "Money is a Social Relation." *Review of Social Economy* 54(4): 507–529.

———. 2004. *The Nature of Money*. Cambridge: Polity Press.

Jackson, A., and B. Dyson. 2012. *Modernising Money: Why Our Monetary System is Broken and How It Can Be Fixed*. London: Positive Money.

Karlstrøm, H. 2014. "Do libertarians dream of electric coins? The material embeddedness of Bitcoin." *Distinktion: Scandinavian Journal of Social Theory* 15(1): 23–36.

Mason, P. 2012. *Why It's Kicking Off Everywhere: The New Global Revolutions*. London: Verso.

Maurer, B., T. C. Nelms, and L. Swartz. 2013. "'When perhaps the real problem is money itself!' The practical materiality of Bitcoin." *Social Semiotics* 23(2): 261–277.

Patterson, S. 2014. "Bitcoin is Not Backed by Anything (And That's OK!)." *Bitcoin Magazine*, 21 October. Available at https://bitcoinmagazine.com/17392/bitcoin-is-not-backed-by-anything-and-thats-ok/ (accessed 13 April 2015).

Peebles, G. 2010. "The anthropology of credit and debt." *Annual Review of Anthropology* 39: 225–240.

Polanyi, K. 1957. *The Great Transformation*. Boston, MA: Beacon Press.

Scott, B. 2013. "Riches Beyond Belief: If you want to know what money is, don't ask a banker. Take a leap of faith and start your own currency." *Aeon*, 28 August. Available at http://aeon.co/magazine/society/so-you-want-to-invent-your-own-currency/ (accessed 13 April 2013).

———. 2015. "A Dark Knight is better than no Knight at all." *King's Review*, 24 March. Available at http://kingsreview.co.uk/magazine/blog/2015/03/24/a-dark-knight-is-better-than-no-knight-at-all/ (accessed 13 April 2015).

Simmel, G. 2005. *The Philosophy of Money*. London: Routledge.

Simons, H. et al. 1933. "Banking and Currency Reform." In W. Samuels (ed.), *Research in the History of Economic Thought and Methodology*, Archival Supplement, vol. 4. Greenwich, CT: JAI Press.

Soddy, F. 1926. *Wealth, Virtual Wealth, and Debt*, 2nd American edition. New York: Dutton.

———. 1933. *Money versus Man*. New York: Dutton.

———. 1943. *The Arch Enemy of Economic Freedom*. London: Self-published.

Strange, S. 1986. *Casino Capitalism*. Manchester: Manchester University Press.

———. 1998. *Mad Money*. Manchester: Manchester University Press.

Swanson, T. 2015. "Consensus-as-a-service: A brief report on the emergence of permissioned, distributed ledger systems." Available from http://www.ofnumbers.com/wp-content/uploads/2015/04/Permissioned-distributed-ledgers.pdf (accessed 22 April 2015).

Tucker, J. A. 2014. "What Gave Bitcoin Its Value?" *The Freeman*, 27 August. Available at http://fee.org/freeman/detail/what-gave-bitcoin-its-value (accessed 13 April 2015).

Ver, R. 2014. "How Bitcoin Can Stop War." *Antiwar.com*, 22 July. Available at http://original.antiwar.com/roger_ver/2014/07/21/how-bitcoin-can-stop-war/ (accessed 15 April 2015).

Vigna, P., and M. Casey. 2015. *The Age of Cryptocurrency: How Bitcoin and Digital Money Are Challenging the Global Economic Order*. London: The Bodley Head.

Winner, L. 1985. "Do Artifacts Have Politics?" In D. Mackenzie and J. Wajcman (eds.), *The Social Shaping of Technology*. Buckingham: Open University Press, pp. 28–40.

Yang, S. (2016) "Bitcoin Catches On With Gold Bugs," *Wall Street Journal*, 22 May 2016, http://www.wsj.com/articles/bitcoin-catches-on-with-gold-bugs-1463959897 (accessed 24 August 2016).

Part IV

Money in Its Time and Place

CHAPTER 10

 A South Asian Mercantile Model of Exchange
Hundi during British Rule

MARINA MARTIN

"Hundi," a word of West Asian roots, refers to a financial instrument and institution that had earned a reputation for trust in South Asia for centuries (Subrahmanyam and Bayly 1988; Banarasidas 1981; Ray 1995; Bagchi 2002; Bayly 1983; Habib 1960; Jain 1929; Bagchi 1987, 1997a, 1997b). This indigenous credit system has received no systematic attention in histories of the Indian subcontinent. Poorly understood and ill defined, hundi was a highly negotiable instrument and source of liquid capital. Hundi knitted together the properties of goods, capital, credit, information, and agency, all of which served as the backbone of South Asian merchant networks.

Broadly described, hundi served as a bill of exchange and a method of remittance (i.e., used both to settle debts and to transfer funds). As remittance instrument or bill of exchange, hundi played a major role in the expanding coastal commerce of eighteenth-century India, and helped the early East India Company run its fiscal operations. Indian bankers and traders made frequent use of hundi in forging links between coastal and interior trades, and between merchant settlements abroad and those at home. Even today, a modified version of the instrument does brisk and reputedly large volumes of business in the remittance of funds by migrant workers internationally—a role that has assumed the mantle of controversy for its suspected association with money laundering (Martin 2009).

The enduring survival of hundi owed much to its adaptability. Its use carried a set of contractual commitments that were either outside the purview of formal law, or only partly covered by it, and therefore largely invisible to the outsider. The informality of hundi muddied a proper understanding of the system in government circles, and this is reflected in proceedings and legislative papers during British colonial rule in India (1858–1947) and the postindependence Indian government. Hundi was also systematically subject to the colonial government's attempts to marginalize the system.

Largely understated and dismissed in colonial discourses, hundi was not well understood outside merchant communities, and hence its unique institutional character has been shrouded in obscurity. In many ways, its broader classification as indigenous relegated it to the murky world of the fringe economy. However, hundi represents a unique insight into the tools and financial operations of Indian merchants. It was an important institution that supported economic development in the Indian subcontinent.

Hundi could be likened to private-order contract enforcement institutions such as that used by medieval traders in Mediterranean trade (Greif 2006) – that is, reputation-based and not dependent on the state for coercion, which nevertheless fused with British courts and legislation as early as the period of British East India Company Rule (1757–1858). The struggle to define hundi and legislate around the instrument particularly during the British Raj, post-1858, provides a critical piece of economic and legal history. Two important insights emerge from British Indian legal documentation: first, that hundi should be treated as a legal rather than illegal instrument. We can contrast this with the twenty-first-century attitude of seeing hundi as a largely illegal entity. Treating hundi as a legal instrument motivated the colonial government's pursuit of how best to regulate around hundi. Second, British Indian courts concluded that hundis were not unconditionally negotiable.

Scope: British East India Company Rule and the British Raj

This chapter frames hundi within debates on "trust" in conceptual terms. In addition, it employs two legal cases, the first an 1833 Privy Council court case from the period of British East India Company Rule, and another from the period in which the British Crown formally assumed control, otherwise known as the era of the British Raj or British India. The Privy Council or King in Council courts were first established in India in 1726, and served as the highest court of appeal until its abolition in 1949. These cases were adjudicated by the law lords of the House of Lords. In essence, court systems that existed under the Mughals between the sixteenth and nineteenth centuries were gradually replaced by the common law system as judicial functions of the British East India Company expanded in line with considerable increases in territorial control. This case is consequently important in demonstrating the early and gradual influence of British rule on hundi. Both cases demonstrate British legislators' approach of treating hundi as similar to other contracts (such as English bills of exchange), albeit functioning under unknown, or undocumented, and at times context-specific conditionality. They also illustrate how cultural norms underpinned contract enforcement.

The choice of the time frame as a whole facilitates engagement with scholarship on legal modifications to the institutional foundations of Indian trade during the life span of the British Company Rule and the British Raj. By the early 1800s, hundi embodies an institution that was traditionally enforced through customary rules but that fuses with the British Indian legal courts organically through common law precedent. This period is defining in representing a critical juncture in the status of indigenous institutions such as hundi.

The post-1978 literature treats hundi very differently, as a largely prohibited entity. Ironically, this ancient South Asian banking system, that had earned a reputation for "trust," has in the last two decades been widely regarded as an opprobrious marker of the black market economy. Also known as hawala, havala, or havale, hundi's disrepute is reflected in the many villainous descriptions awash in the international press: "illegal financial transactions market" (Rao 1993), "black money" and "drug money" (Haubold 1993), "system of tax evasion" (Coggan n.d.), "illegal transfers of foreign exchange" (Nadkarni n.d.), "illegal money laundering network," and the Hindi word meaning "providing a code" (Anon n.d.). In a similar vein, the descriptions of hawala and hundi as informal or alternative[1] have developed because they are perceived as both unofficial and lacking in legal accountability. The confusion does not cease there; there is no universal agreement over whether hundi and hawala are in fact the same, and, just as press descriptions have been wildly different, this uncertainty has much to do with divergent opinions of what hundi and hawala respectively are.

We can also speculate that, in many ways, the notoriety collected by hundi and hawala is connected to what Gareth Austin and Kaoru Sugihara correctly describe as the broader "disparaging" connotations of the words informal or "unorganized" (1993: 2). The authors argue that such negative connotations arise from the persisting dominant view that indigenous or traditional banking and its instruments were primitive and inefficient.

Hundi and Primordial Relationships

Hundi's various contractual characteristics that engaged third parties stretched beyond the primordial relations of the family firm. Yet the reputation-centric emphasis suggests that the institution consisted of a dynamic blend of primordial and contractual relationships. In the nineteenth and early twentieth centuries, the fundamental building block of mercantile relations was indeed the family in its extended sense. Credit-worthiness rested on the reputation of the family, which was synonymous with the "firm." Christopher Bayly's Chayanovian approach to mercantile credit provides a description of "the merchant family," which underscores the foundation of reputation: "When merchants claimed that their credit would suffer by showing their books in the ruler's court, they were not simply making a statement about commercial morality, but about the honour of the family" (1983: 380). Unsurprisingly, hundi has largely been viewed within the confines of the vast body of literature on prominent Indian family firms (Subrahmanyam and Bayly 1988) or community and caste as a reinforcing principle of Indian merchant activity (Banarasidas 1981; Rudner 1994; Bayly 1983). This literature is characterized by a strong focus on primordial relations as a defining feature of Indian merchant family firms. However, the complex organization of Indian merchants in far-flung locations outside India creates reasonable grounds for thinking that hundi functioned in such a way as to facilitate both intra- and intereconomy agency relations.

Central to the mechanics of hundi, the word "honor" was used by both Indian merchants and the British Indian courts to describe functioning and nonfunctioning hundi transactions. If a hundi agreement was met by all parties, a hundi was said to have been honored. Conversely, a breached hundi was described as dishonored. There is nothing unique to hundi in this kind of description; even English bills of exchange were described in such terms.

In fact, hundi/hawala was an institution that served Indian merchants particularly well because it embodied economic and cultural sanctions. Seen from this light, it has explanatory power for understanding how mercantile networks have dominated the business world in India for centuries. In his work on one such successful mercantile community, the Marwaris, Thomas Timberg emphasizes the need to "re-examine the functions of traditional commercial and social values and institutions as they are used by trading communities in the transition to *modern* forms of economic activity." He suggests that perhaps these very values and institutions have been responsible for the success of commercial communities (1978: 16).

Hundi was one such institution, more obviously facilitating the mercantile network's access to capital, credit, and goods; but with a second equally important function of building on and even enhancing merchant reputations, in a kind of harmonious loop. Family reputation, as described, directly influenced the extent to which a hundi was circulated; widespread circulation or usage of hundi by influential persons strengthened the merchant network's status, and increased the merchants' access to capital, credit, and goods.

Embodying contractual relations, hundi was capable of reducing transaction costs within mercantile networks. Distances breached by a given merchant community and levels of difficulty involved in obtaining or exchanging either capital or goods, were reflected in hundi interest rates, which allowed merchants to control supply and demand. If a good or currency was in short supply, hundi interest rates are likely to have been correspondingly higher. For instance, in the case of the South Indian merchant group the Nakarattars, David Rudner writes: "Nakarattar bankers made collective decisions about interest rates that standardised the cost of credit" (1994: 95). This kind of calculative rationality pervaded all hundi transactions.

However, cultural sanctions were also strongly in evidence; for instance, more favorable interest rates were usually available for members of the mercantile community (Rudner 1989). This was consistent with the calculative rationality that members of the network would necessarily be the most reliable borrowers or lenders. In such cases, lower hundi interest rates among merchant communities ensured overall liquidity and easy access to capital; as such, borrowing and lending within the network was common. Rudner (ibid.: 429–430) describes how British attempts to limit the access of small Chettiar firms to credit would have been ineffectual since borrowing among Chettiars was so common. In effect, smaller Chettiar firms could always borrow from large Chettiar firms. British considerations of insolvency were quite meaningless within mercantile networks.

Since the late nineteenth century, hundi has been subsumed within the broader classification of indigenous banking. Even the Negotiable Instruments Act (NIA) of 1881 subordinated hundi to the murky world of the indigenous. However, even this category has not escaped its share of problems. Within the context of South Asia, the term "indigenous banking" has always proven notoriously hard to delineate. Lakshmi Chandra Jain touched upon this in 1929 when he said that there was "no legal definition of the term 'indigenous banker' available" (1929: 1). In 1931, the Indian Central Banking Enquiry Committee stated that use of the term had done a disservice to India. Its statement rested on information collected by the various Provincial Banking Enquiry Committees, which demonstrated the eclectic nature of agents falling within this broad category. It reasoned, did the name "indigenous" carry any real meaning if "different types and varieties of bankers and moneylenders engaged in small functions and large functions, mixed up with land, the trade in precious metals, the trade in grain down to peddling" all fell under the single classification? (Report 1931: 100).

In a similar fashion, a definitive understanding of hundi in its functional, linguistic, and institutional senses is bound up with an understanding of its primary agents, namely, the Indian merchants themselves. The hundi in its various forms was used extensively both within and around the Indian subcontinent, but in all cases it was linked to Indian merchants or bankers. Hundi's instrumentality and the mercantile communities that wielded it were largely indivisible. The critical problem remains that Indian merchants themselves have been poorly understood, so it is hardly surprising that their tools and financial operations, and thus hundi, have remained relatively obscure. Here, it is worth citing Stephen Dale, who drew attention to the following approach toward Indian merchants:

> European scholars have generally seen Indian and other Asian merchants as archaic commercial artefacts of the early modern world. The term peddler has frequently been used to categorise and implicitly denigrate the economic effectiveness of Asian merchants in this period. As it is usually used, peddler represents a kind of economic orientalism in which Asian merchants are viewed as quaint and ineffective commercial "other." The implicit standard of comparison is, of course, the British and Dutch East India companies. It has been relatively easy for scholars to hold this view because there is a lack of data on non-western merchants before the twentieth century. (1994: 5–6)

The problem of defining hundi also stems from seeking comparison with European credit instruments and banking facilities. The hundi was rather different to the European bill of exchange, because it was used to remit funds and to raise different forms of credit. There are in fact many types of hundis; the diverse function of each hundi makes it difficult to squarely apply the usual labels of promissory note, bill of exchange, or system of advancing loans. This was compounded by the Indian government's struggle to document hundi usage and enforcement among multiple mercantile communities. This complexity is reflected in the Provincial Banking Enquiry Committee reports of the 1930s, which covered regions as far afield as Bombay, Bengal, Madras, and Burma.

Business Partnerships

In much of the literature on trade, we come across the importance of business partnerships. Responsible for facilitating trade across disparate and extended regions, institutionalized business partnerships were a natural response to growing economies of scale. The 'commenda', a shared partnership and profit structure, is credited with a significant role in the growth of Mediterranean trade (Udovitch 1962). This network is described as one in which "trust is related to expectations about behaviour and has to do ultimately with reputation" (Markovits 2000: 260). The point about such a reliance on reputation is that it was not premised on altruistic trust, but rather on concrete information flows within given mercantile networks. In his work on the medieval Maghribi traders, Avner Greif claimed that the "observed 'trust' reflected a reputation mechanism among economic self-interested individuals" (1989: 858). Maghribi coalition members were able to conduct business with other agents and merchants because of economic as well as social sanctions implicit within the system.

In common with the commenda, hundi embodied negotiability and exchange over long distances within the framework of a contract. Indian merchants in the Turan, for instance, are known to have been heavily capitalized, and to have invested in a variety of ventures both within the host country and within India (Levi 2002: chap. 4); the sheer scale of their operations must have necessitated the use of agents who were not connected through kinship or caste ties. In all of these conditions hundi had the ability to mitigate the risk of using a third party. But how was it able to achieve this? And how effectively did it mitigate such risk? One way of evaluating this is to adopt an economics-centric approach.

Hundi had great reach, particularly when endorsed by merchants with a strong reputation, but how was this reach achieved? It crucially depended on a framework that sanctioned its usage, hence the importance of infrastructure or specialist discounting houses—which are believed to have been well established and vast (Kumar and Desai 1983: 291)—insurance against loss (Bayly 1983: chaps. 11–12), economies of scale and lower transaction costs. Contemporary studies often regard hundi as a system that evolved to alleviate the need for cash; certainly this was one indispensable quality, but its reputation mechanism and liquidity were corollaries of a more complex institutional framework, of which institutionalized networks, or the multilateral reputation mechanism of the commenda, were a part. Douglass North's description of a successful institution, if it is to capture gains from trade, is helpful. Hundi had all of the ingredients that institutional economists regard as necessary for capturing gains from trade: agency, protection of goods, standardized mediums of exchange, economies of scale, and impersonal contract enforcement (North 1991: 98–102). The different interest rates in operation with hundi also demonstrated more specialized forms of transactions costs. The specific nature of business partnerships or the commenda was influenced by the risks and resources provided by the various partners (Pamuk 2000: 83), but this in turn shaped the nature of hundi. So, what of "trust"?

Reconfiguring Notions of Informality, Formality, and Trust

Francis Fukuyama has argued that trust is essentially an outcome of a context in which commonly shared norms generate cooperative and regularized behavior (1995). For Fukuyama, this trust is a cultural characteristic that tends to degenerate when the institutional context widens. State intervention has tended to dilute the norms of the immediate "informal" communal or familistic sphere. An examination of the word "hundi" provides us with some clue as to how we should interpret the words "honor" and "trust." One key reason for this embedded notion of trust must lie in the etymology of the word "hundi," which, as described previously, carries the senses of trust, as well as inclusive agreement or contract. The whole concept of institutional credibility is based on a form of so-called trust. This notion of trust has undergone a great deal of scrutiny and criticism in scholarly literature.

Greif uses the word "trust" liberally in his explanation of the reputation-based mechanism of the Maghribi traders. But evidently, in his account there is an important distinction to be had between calculative trust and altruistic trust, where the latter is decidedly more risky than the former. Altruistic trust involves having faith in a largely unknown quantity, motivated by benevolence or idealism. This form of trust, we may reason, is much more likely to result in oral agreements that have weak or no penalty mechanisms built in. Calculative trust, on the other hand, is premised on weighing up the costs and benefits of a given quantity, and making a decision based on a number of penalties or fail-safes built into the agreement.

Ultimately, given the calculative quality of this concept of trust, one might question whether the term has any utility at all. Oliver Williamson, for instance, argues that "trust is irrelevant to commercial exchange and that reference to trust in this connection promotes confusion" (1993: 469). Calculativeness, though frequently used to excess in the field of economics, is nevertheless useful in limiting usage of the word "trust." For Williamson, calculativeness (rather than trust) is more useful as a way of characterizing agreements between parties because it is ultimately "pervasive" in transactions. He points out that contracts with built in fail-safes are usually only evident if "cost-effective," thus calculation is intrinsic (1993).

Similarly, Russell Hardin has rooted himself in this sense of calculativeness, by describing the trust that frames transactions as "encapsulated interest": "I trust you because I think it is in your interest to attend to my interests in the relevant manner. This is not merely to say that you and I have the same interests. Rather, it is to say that you have an interest in attending to my interests because, typically, you want our relationship to continue" (2002: 4). Hardin also draws a key distinction between "trust" and "trustworthiness." The difference between the two concepts underscores a shift from the subject to the object of trust. In other words, person A will trust person B purely because B has proven herself trustworthy. Thus there is an inherent calculation in both A's trust in B, and B's status as trustworthy.

In analyzing opportunistic behavior, or "finking" as he terms it, Timothy Guinnane, in common with Williamson, suggests that psychological and cultural claims on the nature of trust have some value, but provide less specific answers to the question of why "finking" takes place. Guinnane too subscribes to the notion of encapsulated interest in his understanding of why parties will form agreements. In his analogy, the costs of "finking" will outweigh the costs or indeed benefits of fulfilling an agreement. Collateral in this instance is not merely an extra form of security, but also an information device; individuals who risk their assets possess an encapsulated interest (Guinnane 2005).

There is one important instance when Guinnane suggests that encapsulated interest can fail, and this is where weak incentives provide for weak institutions. Guinnane asks, "what can trust teach us about the success or failure of an institution that the economics of sanctions and information cannot?" (2005: 12). The empirical examples that Guinnane provides of two credit cooperatives operating with similar economic principles, but with ultimately different outcomes, raises a valuable point: if trust in one context leads to institutional success, and trust in another to institutional failure, then we must look at what is informing trust in each context.

This line of thinking brings us back to Greif's notion that cultural preferences may well underpin the foundations of trust espoused within institutions. In common with Greif, Guinnane argues that social context matters, though Greif makes an explicitly economic rather than cultural or moral argument. Can economic rationalizations suffice in understanding institutional trust? Certainly, the previous discussion has demonstrated that within the context of a contractual institution, altruistic forms of trust are very unlikely to be present. What of normative considerations? What social contexts determine the success or failure of institutions, and how should we interpret these contexts? Do normative and not just economic principles inform the cultural incentives that make up institutional trust?

As the discussion so far has indicated, using pure economic rationalizations for understanding the sets of incentives that inform these institutions is reductive. John Harriss, for instance, argues that "trust" is often used in discourse as a means of masking relationships of power (2003: 768). The central thrust of his argument is that hierarchical structures often impact on social networks, thereby either helping to generate trust, or subordinating trust in relationships. As he pinpoints, trust is "polysemic" (ibid.: 764). It must be construed as polysemic because it can espouse "the interplay of habits of thoughts and practice (which is what the idea of culture entails) with formal institutions (defined, conventionally as rules, norms, and conventions—in this case those that regulate economic activity)" (ibid.: 769).

In several respects, hundi provides an insight into working relationships between merchants. In his analysis of court cases involving Sindhi merchants in the late nineteenth and early twentieth centuries, Claude Markovits observed that "breaches of trust" occurred not among equals, but in relationships characterized by differential positions of subordination and superordination (2000).

The following legal case provides an insight into the type of contexts within which hundi was deployed between merchants, and the agreements that were struck in relation to hundi. One way of explaining this is through Richard Crasswell's breakdown of contract rules as "background" or "default" rules, alongside "agreement" rules. Background rules set out the precise substance of each party's obligations, such as the conditions and sanctions governing performance and nonperformance. Agreement rules define those conditions that are "necessary for a party's apparent consent to be counted as truly valid" (Craswell 1989: 503). As Crasswell notes, these categories might also be interchangeable. While Crasswell uses these categories to better illuminate why promises are binding, these categories are a useful way of breaking down the principles governing individual hundi transactions. For instance, they may help us to understand why reputation and honor, which are integral parts of hundi, may encourage reliance on contractual agreements.

This context-rich legal case also usefully underscores instances when hundi transactions broke down. Such occasions in turn reveal examples of customary practice and enforcement mechanisms binding mercantile agreements. Were private-order institutions sufficiently enforceable for long-distance trade? This hundi court case demonstrates that trust needed to be established between parties of equal status or reputation in order for mercantile agreements to be enforced.

Hundi court cases reveal that the parties involved in a hundi transaction were almost always known or reputed persons. Even the *gomashtah* (agent) of a merchant was usually well-known. In the 1837 Privy Council case of Madho Row Chinto Punt Golay v. Bhookun-Das Boolaki-Das (J. and H. Clark, Law Booksellers, Portugal Street, Lincoln's Inn, London 1837), remarkably a person, Kundoo Bucha-jee, had apparently fraudulently conducted transactions with all the authority of the official gomashtah of a particular merchant house—the firm of Chinto Punt. The alleged gomashtah had purchased two hundis in the name of Chinto Punt from the merchant Roop Chund. He had then endorsed and sold them on in Chinto Punt's name to another merchant, Tapi-das Bhookun-das—the respondent of the appeal case. When the respondent presented the hundis for payment, they were dishonored. The respondent in turn sought payment from Kundoo Bucha-jee for the amount due and expenses incurred. Kundoo Bucha-jee is said to have promised payment, but instead absconded.

Even more surprisingly, there is evidence that Kundoo Bucha-jee was so plausible as the gomashtah of the house of Chinto Punt that none of the persons with whom he conducted business doubted his authenticity. In other words, Kundoo Bucha-jee was credible as Chinto Punt's gomashtah even though a direct connection with the merchant had not been established.

How did Kundoo Bucha-jee succeed in establishing himself as Chinto Punt's gomashtah in the eyes of the other merchants? First, we learn that he was conducting transactions outside the usual remit of Chinto Punt's firm. Thus it would seem quite normal for other merchants to carry out business with Chinto Punt's alleged gomashtah, rather than the merchant alone. This circumstance would also have ensured that Kundoo Bucha-jee did not cross paths with Chinto Punt. For the merchants conducting business with Kundoo Bucha-jee, the strength of Chinto Punt's reputation would have underscored any credibility that Kundoo Bucha-jee carried.

If the house of Chinto Punt had established a strong reputation within the merchant world, other merchants would never doubt that his alleged gomashtah would dishonor any transactions. The importance of maintaining one's reputation, and code of honor, is also evinced by the efforts taken by Chinto Punt's firm to clear both its liability and name in the courts. While Kundoo Bucha-jee himself apparently cared little for his name and fled—an action that must be presumed an admission of guilt—the house of Chinto Punt fought the accusations laid at its door.

Given that the gomashtah absconded, a relationship between the appellants and the gomashtah needed to be established for the respondent (Bhookun-das) to gain reparation for his dishonored bills. The Privy Council decided to reverse the two former decrees that had favored the respondent based on the inconclusiveness of the evidence; it could not be established that the person acting as gomashtah for the appellant's firm was indeed the agent of that firm. There is a clear sense that the negligent attitude of the absconding Kundoo Bucha-jee was a consequence of his subordinate position to both Chinto Punt and Tapi-das Bhookun-das.

The literal definition of "dishonor" is the loss of honor, and therefore if Kundoo Bucha-jee possessed no reputation or status to begin with, its loss could not have much value. In other words, if we are to view hundi as an institution constraining risk-averse behavior, according to certain ideals of commercial ethical conduct, then we can understand that one such ideal is honor, of which reputation is a part. Thus hundi transactions were necessarily premised on codes of honor and status. This is all the more apparent if we ask: would the drawer and the eventual beneficiary of the hundis have conducted business with Kundoo Bucha-jee were he not allegedly affiliated with one of the other reputable merchant houses? It seems very unlikely.

So, what was the substance of Kundoo Bucha-jee's obligation to the parties with which he conducted hundi transactions? The hundi in this case provided a promissory assurance to the parties, who were eventually subject to fraud, that payment would be made. This in essence was a core background rule governing performance. The agreement rule consisted of hundi being issued with the full consent of a valid and reputable party. Reputation, which provided the foundation of the various parties' reliance, essentially formed the corpus of the agreement rule. Thus when the agreement rule was breached, here through fraud, the background rules were not enforceable. In this case, one party—Chinto Punt—had not really consented to the transaction, therefore there were no valid agreement rules, and the background rules were moot.

In the case of Pragdas Thakurdas v. Dowlatram Nanuram (Indian Law Reporter 11 [Bom] 1886: 257), the claims revolved around two separate business dealings that were linked because of the parties involved. One claim centered on collection of a debt, the other claim revolved around two dishonored hundis.

The plaintiffs, being the firm of Pragdas Thakurdas, had initiated a suit to claim funds due on a debt by the insolvent firm of Fatechand Kanayalal and Kanayalal Jugalkissan. The insolvents operated in Delhi and elsewhere, while the plaintiffs had business in Bombay, Calcutta, and Cawnpore. After discovering that payment to their firm from the insolvents had ceased on 3 March 1884, the plaintiffs sent their Bombay *munim* (agent) Kapurchand to Delhi to investigate. At this point, the insolvents owed Rs 11,100 to the plaintiffs.

On reaching Delhi, Kapurchand found that the defendant, Dowlatram Nanuram, who had at least two businesses in Delhi, had taken over the assets of the insolvent Delhi firm. The defendant agreed to pay each of the insolvent firms' creditors a composition of their debts amounting to half the amount owed. In other words, the defendant promised to pay a sum equal in amount to one half of the insolvent firm's debts. Upon receipt of such payment, the creditors were to fully discharge the insolvents' debts.

Kapurchand entered into an oral agreement with the defendant to accept the terms of the discharge. Consequently, letters were exchanged between the defendant's munim and Kapurchand; the defendant's letter laid out the terms of discharging the debt, and the plaintiff's letter agreed to accept such terms, and was signed accordingly. The defendant wrote the amount due in hundis and cash on the foot of the plaintiffs' Calcutta and Cawnpore accounts. Even though both parties were in Delhi at the time of writing the agreement, crucially they both addressed their letters to each other at their formal places of business (Bombay and Delhi), as if they were writing the letters from their respective places of business.

The plaintiffs held other accounts with the defendants, so the court regarded it as entirely consistent that the defendant had agreed to remit the funds to Bombay as soon as they received a detailed statement of accounts from the plaintiffs. Soon afterward, Kapurchand returned to Bombay.

Subsequently, the plaintiffs brought a civil suit against the defendant at the Bombay High Court to claim for the sum of Rs 5,550, this being the sum representing half the amount owed by the insolvents. The defendant in turn denied the jurisdiction of the court, arguing that the alleged cause of action—the composition deed—was at Delhi. He further alleged that the plaintiffs had not provided the defendant with any accounts of the dealings between them and the insolvents. The court inferred that the defendant fully intended to remit the funds to the plaintiffs in Bombay had it not been for another matter (see next paragraph) concerning dishonored hundis. Consistent with this idea, the defendant had also claimed that if the plaintiffs suit was held to be maintainable in the Bombay Court, that the amount claimed by the plaintiffs should be offset by an amount owed to the defendant by the plaintiffs through two dishonored hundis.

In determining the facts of that case, the court found that the insolvents had drawn two hundis, valued at Rs 2,500 each, on the plaintiffs, with the defendant as beneficiary. The defendant in turn sold and endorsed the hundis to a Motiram Jamnadas. Motiram sent the hundis to the plaintiffs' Bombay firm for realization on the due date. The plaintiff's Bombay firm also happened to be the agent of Motiram. On 28 October 1884, the plaintiffs received the hundis, and on 30 October 1884, the plaintiffs wrote to the insolvents (the drawers of the hundis) communicating their acceptance as follows: "Further hundis for Rs 5,000, drawn by the people of the piece-goods shop, were received as payable. The same are accepted."[2] Despite this communication of acceptance to the drawer, the plaintiffs subsequently dishonored the hundis, notifying their nonacceptance to Motiram on 3 November 1884. Motiram returned the hundis to the defendant, and recovered his money. The defendant in turn sought to offset the amount paid for the hundis against the claim of the plaintiffs toward the debt owed by the insolvents. However, the plaintiffs stated that there was no proof the hundis had been accepted by them because they had not communicated acceptance of the hundis to Motiram, and they therefore argued that they were not bound to accept the hundis.

English legal precedent had determined that the liability of an acceptor to a bill of exchange attached, not by a person simply writing their name on it, but rather on the subsequent delivery of the bill, or according to directions given by the person entitled to the bill that it had been accepted. This precedent laid out that a drawee's (or acceptor's) communication of acceptance to the holder would bind the drawee to honor a bill. The question of whether communication of acceptance by the drawee to the drawer was binding had not arisen in English law, and ultimately presented the pivotal focus of the plaintiff's claim to legitimately dishonor the hundis. However, the court determined that there was no reason why a communication of acceptance to the drawer or previous holder would not bind the drawee just as much as communication of acceptance to the current holder. It was felt that the primary contract was between the drawer and the drawee in any event, thus the drawee's acceptance must serve to benefit both the drawer (previous holder) as well as the current holder.

The court asked, did the plaintiffs, in their capacity as drawee, actually accept the hundis? The hundis came to the plaintiffs for acceptance on 28 October 1884, and to the court's thinking the plaintiff's communication of acceptance of the hundis to the drawer on 30 October 1884 was clear and unequivocal. Moreover, the plaintiffs had not notified Motiram of the hundis nonacceptance even by 3 November. This was regarded as an unreasonable amount of time to have held the hundis *in dubio* (in doubt). Presumably, the court's decision was based on the length of time that was customary for merchants to issue acceptances or nonacceptances. The court held that the hundis should have been honored by the plaintiffs, and that the defendants were entitled to offset the value of the dishonored hundis plus costs from the amount owed to the plaintiffs on the insolvent's debt.

Reputation and Insolvency

Encapsulated interest could and did change over the lifetime of a given hundi transaction, largely because welfare outcomes were altered by exogenous elements. One such significant element was, as we have seen in the previous case, bankruptcy. If a firm was known to be insolvent, then there was a strong likelihood that other firms would not honor any hundis drawn by the insolvent firm. Reputation was a requisite quality enabling one firm to draw hundis on another. Why for instance, in the above case, did the plaintiffs chose to dishonor the hundis drawn by the insolvent firm after already providing written acceptance of the order? We can speculate that on learning of the drawing firm's insolvency, the plaintiff's firm no longer felt it was worthwhile to honor the original agreement. If sufficient drawer's funds were not already held by the plaintiff's firm, the latter might have subsequently expected to lose funds on the transaction.

Om Prakash notes that while the hundi system worked "remarkably efficiently" (2002: 49) during the Mughal period, there was also a degree of risk involved with the sarraf (or shroff, meaning moneychanger or banker)—on whom the hundi was drawn, or from whom the hundi was bought—going bust. Therefore, the risk of insolvency was not limited to the drawer alone. Thus, in most instances, reputation was essentially a rational calculative quality. Insolvency adversely affected this kind of reputation, and could breach the original contract between the drawer and acceptor.

Bankruptcy was an endogenous and exogenous force that negatively impacted on reputation, and thus enforcement, as well as rupturing the normative quality of honor. The endogenous quality was simply a state bereft of credit, but economic rationalizations fail to sufficiently account for the exogenous dimension because it was cultural. To understand the cultural enormity of bankruptcy, Thomas Safley provides an excellent account of the scandal attached to the phenomenon in early modern Europe. The downfall of a prominent German merchant house emits a particular cultural signal, which interestingly is based on normative principles. Safley shows that during this period, "bankruptcies signalled ethical decay and economic decline to officials, investors, and creditors alike" (2009: 37). Bankruptcy in this account was scandalous because it could, and usually did, damage the reputations of those connected to the bankrupt. What created this scandalous face of bankruptcy was the sense that choices made by individuals on the eventual path to insolvency and indebtedness were inevitably unethical.

This kind of theme on the immorality of unfortunate choices, misappropriated funds, and indebtedness pervades the novels of Charles Dickens, notably *Little Dorrit*. The debtors' prison is a prominent device providing the sense of "moral atonement." This is in contrast to the moral impunity of fleeing one's creditors, or even committing suicide, thus relegating sole responsibility for the consequences of their actions to their families. Overwhelmingly, the die that has been cast in the run up to bankruptcy is portrayed as a decision generating moral evils for a much wider circle than the bankrupt.

An economics-focused approach might view this as simply a question of good and bad welfare outcomes. However, the weightiness of the issue means that bankruptcy has traditionally carried a strong normative implication, which though welfare related, stretches well beyond into the world of "honor." The infamy attached to being bankrupt was the antithesis of acting with honor. Bankruptcy had the effect of breaching moral codes, in particular, that of the "promise" that formed the corpus of agreement rules integral to hundi transactions.

Conclusion

Using legal cases of the period, we see the way in which hundi bound agents together in different contexts. Hundi transactions were conducted within certain frameworks of conduct and agreements between agents. This kind of calculative rationality pervaded the contractual qualities inherent in hundi. Reputation and solvency were decisive matters for the overall health of hundi transactions. However, economic explanations alone cannot account for the institutional foundations of hundi. As the discussion demonstrates, cultural considerations did impact on incentives.

What can we impute to the reasons behind the disputing merchants' recourse to the legal enforcement of the British Indian courts? In all the cases, the merchants had forged agreement rules defining the conditions that were necessary for each party's apparent consent to be counted as valid. In the case of Pragdas Thakurdas v. Dowlatram Nanuram, the rules governing acceptance of the hundi constituted some of the agreement rules. The plaintiffs argued that their communication of acceptance to the drawer should not be considered a valid consent to the hundi transaction where the holder of the hundi (Motiram) was concerned. By contrast, the court served to plug gaps promoting differential consent of the contracting parties, through background rules of enforcement derived from English as well as Indian law. In other words, the background rules of the court provided a coercive element to the agreement rules. We can presume that the background rules of the court were more coercive than the sanctions and conditions naturally attached to agreement rules.

As we have seen, exogenous elements such as bankruptcy, or insufficient knowledge of interests, could disrupt agreement rules in such a way that the background rules or enforcement of the courts may have appeared the only viable alternative. Normative qualities attached to the concept of honor could, through events such as bankruptcy, make adherence to existing agreement rules secondary to the question of encapsulated interests.

Another important dimension of hundi that requires closer scrutiny is the role of legal precedent in connecting and directing hundi's past and future. How far did legal precedent influence the evolution of hundi? What weight did existing legal precedents in English law (on bills of exchange or negotiable instruments) carry, as against custom? In other words, did legal transplants imprint themselves more strongly than custom. This discussion takes a first step toward indicating the centrality of legal transplants to hundi, however it goes beyond the scope of this analysis to assess and articulate the strength of such an imprint. Nevertheless, whenever the courts chose existing English precedent over Indian customary practice, they were essentially placing greater authority on prior decisions made in an English setting, as against Indian customary practices.

Here we can comprehend hundi as an Indian mercantile credit system that was enforced initially through multifarious mercantile customs. This narrative charts a process by which colonial legislation created a formal character to hundi that could not only be recognized outside mercantile communities, but also enforced in the British Indian courts. Juxtaposed against hundi's contemporary position as an "informal" system, and marker of the black market economy in India, this neglected economic history of hundi has even greater relevance.

Marina Martin is a research fellow at Goethe University, Frankfurt. She is interested in the colonial history and legacies of exchanges and encounters between Britain, India, and Africa. She has explored in depth the history of a traditional or so-called informal South Asian credit network known as hundi/hawala, which is forthcoming as a monograph. She is currently writing a social and economic history on the Indian question in South Africa and the creation of British colonial immigration laws.

NOTES

1. Widely used by Interpol, the Financial Action Task Force (FATF), and the Asia-Pacific Economic Cooperation (APEC), for instance.
2. The insolvent firm at Delhi were the piece-goods shop.

REFERENCES

Anon. N.d. "India Cash Market Tied to Burgeoning Scandal: Funds from Abroad Key Hawala Deals." *Chicago Tribune*, sourced from the Associated Press.

Austin, G., and K. Sugihara. 1993. *Local Suppliers of Credit in the Third World, 1750–1960*. London: Macmillan Press Ltd.

Bagchi, A. K. 1987. *The Evolution of the State Bank of India: The Roots, 1806–1876*. Vol. 1, *The Early Years, 1806–1860*. Bombay: Oxford University Press.

———. 1997a. *The Evolution of the State Bank of India*. Vol. 2, *Era of the Presidency Banks, 1876–1920*. Walnut Creek, CA: Altamira.

———. 1997b. *The evolution of the State Bank of India*. Vol. 3, *The Era of the Imperial Bank of India*. New Delhi: Sage India.

———. 2002. *Money and Credit in Indian History from Early Medieval Times*. New Delhi: Tulika.

Banarasidas. 1981 [1641]. *Ardhakathanak*. Jaipur: Rajasthan Prakrit Bharati Sansthan.
Bayly, C. A. 1983. *Rulers Townsmen and Bazaars: North Indian Society in the Age of British Expansion 1770–1870*. New Delhi: Oxford University Press.
Coggan, P. N.d. "The Chronology of Corruption." *The Financial Times*.
Craswell, R. 1989. "Contract Law, Default Rules, and the Philosophy of Promising." *Michigan Law Review* 88(3): 489–529. Available at http://www.jstor.org/stable/1289110.
Dale, S. F. 1994. *Indian Merchants and Eurasian Trade, 1600–1750*. Cambridge: Cambridge University Press.
Fukuyama, F. 1995. *Trust: The Social Virtues and the Creation of Prosperity*. London: Hamish Hamilton.
Greif, A. 2006. *Institutions and the Path to the Modern Economy: Lessons from Medieval Trade*. Cambridge and New York: Cambridge University Press. Available at http://www.loc.gov/catdir/toc/ecip059/2005006468.html.
Greif, A. 1989. "Reputation and Coalitions in Medieval Trade: Evidence on the Maghribi Traders." *The Journal of Economic History* 49(4): 857–882.
Guinnane, T. W. 2005. "Trust: A Concept Too Many." *SSRN eLibrary*. Available at http://ssrn.com/paper=680744.
Habib, I. M. 1960. "Banking in Mughal India." In T. Raychaudhuri (ed.), *Contributions to Indian Economic History I*. Calcutta: Firma K.L. Mukhopadhyay.
Hardin, R. 2002. *Trust and Trustworthiness* New York: Russell Sage Foundation.
Harriss, J. 2003. "'Widening the Radius of Trust': Ethnographic Explorations of Trust and Indian Business." *The Journal of the Royal Anthropological Institute* 9(4): 755–773. Available at http://www.jstor.org/stable/3134709.
Haubold, E. 1993. "Spekulationen ueber die Rolle der indischen Mafia (Speculation over the role of the of Indian Mafia)." *Frankfurter Allgemeine Zeitung GmbH*.
Indian Law Reporter 11 (Bom). 1886. Pragdas Thakurdas v. Dowlatram Nanuram, Bombay Civil.
J. and H. Clark, Law Booksellers, Portugal Street, Lincoln's Inn, London. 1837. Madho Row Chinto Punt Golay, Eswunt Row Chinto Punt v. Bhookun-Das Boolaki-Das, the Judicial Committee and The Lords of the His Majesty's Most Honourable Privy Council on Appeal from the Supreme and Sudder Dewany Courts in the East Indies.
Jain, L. C. 1929. *Indigenous Banking in India*. London: Macmillan.
Kumar, D., and M. Desai. (eds.). 1983. *The Cambridge Economic History of India*, vol. 2. Cambridge: Cambridge University Press. Available at http://universitypublishingonline.org/ref/id/histories/CBO9781139054522 (accessed 22 August 2016).
Levi, S. C. 2002. *The Indian Diaspora in Central Asia and its Trade: 1550–1900*. Leiden: Brill.
Markovits, C. 2000. *The Global World of Indian Merchants 1750–1947: Traders of Sind from Bukhara to Panama*. Cambridge: Cambridge University Press.
Martin, M. 2009. "Hundi/Hawala: The Problem of Definition." *Modern Asian Studies* 43(4): 909–937. Available at http://dx.doi.org/10.1017/S0026749X07003459.
Nadkarni, S. N.d. "Confidence in tatters over hawala fallout." *South China Morning Post*.

North, D. C. 1991. "Institutions." *The Journal of Economic Perspectives* 5(1): 97–112. Available at http://links.jstor.org/sici?sici=0895-3309%28199124%295%3A1%3C97%3AI%3E2.0.CO%3B2-W.

Pamuk, S. 2000. *A Monetary History of the Ottoman Empire.* Cambridge: Cambridge University Press.

Prakash, O. 2002. "System of Credit in Mughal India." In A. K. Bagchi (ed.), *Money and Credit in Indian History: From Early Medieval Times.* New Delhi: Tulika.

Rao, M. R. 1993. "Finance Minister Interviewed on Inflation, IMF, Subsidies." *BBC Summary of World Broadcasts.*

Ray, R. K. 1995. "Asian Capital in the Age of European Domination: The Rise of the Bazaar, 1800–1914." *Modern Asian Studies* 29(3): 449–554.

Report. 1931. *Indian Central Banking Enquiry Committee, Vol. 1, Part 2 Minority Report.* Nehru Memorial Museum and Library.

Rudner, D. 1989. "Banker's Trust and the Culture of Banking among the Nattukottai Chettiars of Colonial South India." *Modern Asian Studies* 23(3): 417–458.

Rudner, D. 1994. *Caste and Capitalism in Colonial India: The Nattukottai Chettiars.* Oakland: University of California Press.

Safley, T. M. 2009. "Business Failure and Civil Scandal in Early Modern Europe." *Business History Review* 83(1): 35–60. Available at http://search.ebscohost.com/login.aspx?direct=true&db=aph&AN=38797382&site=ehost-live.

Subrahmanyam, S., and C. A. Bayly. 1988. "Portfolio Capitalists and the Political Economy of Early Modern India." *The Indian Economics and Social History Review* 25(4).

Timberg, T. A. 1978. *The Marwaris, from Traders to Industrialists.* New Delhi: Vikas.

Udovitch, A. L. 1962. "At the Origins of the Western Commenda: Islam, Israel, Byzantium?" *Speculum* 37(2): 198–207. Available at http://links.jstor.org/sici?sici=0038-7134%28196204%2937%3A2%3C198%3AATOOTW%3E2.0.CO%3B2-O.

Williamson, O. E. 1993. "Calculativeness, Trust, and Economic Organization." *Journal of Law & Economics* 36(1): 453–486. Available at http://ideas.repec.org/a/ucp/jlawec/v36y1993i1p453-86.html.

CHAPTER 11

 Money and Markets For and Against the People
The Rise and Fall of Basotho's Economic Independence, 1830s–1930s

SEAN MALIEHE

Money and markets are integral to the day-to-day functioning of modern economies. They have played a big role in shaping and developing modern society (Hart 2000: chap. 1). How they are conceptualized shifts dramatically between the "good" and "bad" ends of a spectrum. This is because "[half] of the world worships money and the other thinks of it as the root of all evil" (ibid: 7). "Ours is an age of money. If human society has any unity at this time it is as a world 'market.' There is nothing wrong with people exchanging goods and services as equals. Markets are indispensable to the extension of society. The problem is that they use money: some people have lots of it and most don't have enough" (Hart 2007: 12). The human economy idea refers to an economy whose focus is placed "both on what people do for themselves and on the need to find ways forward that must involve all humanity somehow" (Hart, Laville, and Cattani 2010: 2). Money and markets are indispensable to this process. It is therefore important to develop our understanding of, and provide concrete cases to evaluate, the functions of them both in society.

Referring to Lesotho's[1] precolonial and early colonial period (1830s–1930s), this chapter identifies two distinctive functions of money and markets in Basotho[2] society. One was when Basotho's economic independence peaked and then collapsed. From the 1830s to 1870s, money and markets "worked for Basotho." From the 1880s to 1930s, however, money and markets "worked against Basotho." This shift was not as simple as that. The economic history of Lesotho presented here has been constructed from missionary and travelers' accounts, colonial records, laws, and secondary sources. As in many African countries, before the European encounter, there were no written records.

From a precapitalist society, Basotho's territory was transformed into a capitalist economy through the Europeans. The process started with the arrival of missionaries in 1833. It was expanded further by contact with Afrikaners/Boers who migrated from the Cape into the interior of the region in the 1840s—a migration known as the Great Trek or Boer Trek. Basotho's contact with Europeans at this time rejuvenated trade, which had been disrupted by the *Mfecane* wars of the early 1800s (Hamilton 1995). Missionaries promoted commerce alongside their evangelical activities. Various Basotho converts took advantage. On this foundation, Basotho emerged as the main exporter of grain to South Africa's emergent mining towns in the 1870s (Murray 1980). This newfound economic independence collapsed as a result of land appropriation and a colonial policy designed to make Basotho's territory a reservoir of cheap labor, as in neighboring southern African countries (Feinstein 2005: 65). Henri Brunschwig captured this:

> From the African point of view, this long . . . period [1830–1880] entailed an incubation of European influences which took a much stronger hold than any foreign influence in the past. . . . The evolution took place at the pace of the Black, who was free to accept or refuse the novelties: the African did not feel dominated or constrained, in himself being carried away in spite of . . . [the] path which was alien to him. This evolution could have continued. It was interrupted in the last quarter of the nineteenth century. The European conquest did not give a different direction to the path on which the African had now started. The break did not come from the change of direction, but from a brutal thrust which took away from the Africans control over their progress. (as quoted in Amin 1973: vii–ix)

Specific to conditions in the southern African region, Charles Feinstein adds:

> [African economies were] totally transformed by the discovery of diamonds and gold in the late nineteenth century. From that point forward, the economic history of [southern Africa] becomes, in essence, a story of how this unique combination of indigenous populations, European settlers, and mineral resources was brought together in a process of conquest, dispossession, discrimination, and development to promote rapid economic progress. . . . It is this history of the incorporation of the African people that paved the indispensable labour for a modern economy . . . Africans progressively lost the possibility of continuing to farm independently. (2005: 47)

In the transition from a pre-capitalist to a capitalist economy, the commoditization of land, money, and people went hand in hand. In Polanyi's terms, "fictitious commodities" contradicted the organic purpose of economies—that is, to provide people with the economic means of their survival (Polanyi 2001 [1944]; Hart and Hann 2009: 4–5). Basotho's economy saw private claims to land much increased. Also, the economy shifted from one where money was a means to equalize inequality through trade, with money existing as currency and a store of wealth, to one in which money itself became a commodity to be earned in the mines and other cash-money exchanges like trade and enterprise. Similar processes affected people whose economic liberties were undermined in order to turn them into "labor," workers, or proletarians. These three processes engineered social, economic, and political differentiation, which produced both poverty and acute inequality.

At the regional level, the position of Basotho's territory in southern Africa (with its global economic networks) was altered. A regional economy that supported the free movement of goods, people, and money became one in which strict political controls were introduced to restrict and police people within defined territories as a way of creating a regional industrial "dual economy." This was an economy where South Africa became the center, while "black" communities within and outside the country became sources of cheap labor. This changed the regional economic model of free networks to one based on political restrictions and territorial barriers.

This chapter is organized in four sections. The first introduces Lesotho's society and economy before the European encounter, which took effect from the 1830s. The second section explores the rise of Basotho's economic prosperity and independence between the 1830s and 1870s. This was facilitated by Basotho contact with Europeans, particularly Christian missionaries, who encouraged the commercialization of production. The third section explores the fall of Basotho's economic prosperity and political independence in the period between the 1880s and 1930s due to the creation of Lesotho as a labor reserve by colonial and capitalist interests. The last section explores the role and legacy of financial institutions established to support the newly emergent money economy.

Society and Economy before the Europeans, 1500–1820s

The indigenous people of Lesotho, known as Basotho, have their roots in south *Sotho*-speaking groups descended from Iron Age *Bantu* communities that settled in southern Africa in the sixteenth century. Particularly, these were communities that settled in an area known as the Highveld, all the way down to the Mohokare Valley. These areas form part of the modern Free State Province of South Africa and western parts of Lesotho. These groups were organized into small semi-autonomous chiefdoms, which expressed their identity through clan totems (*liboko*) (Mothibe 2002: 3–10).

Economically, *Bantu*-speaking communities depended on crop production and pastoralism. They supplemented these with collecting wild vegetables and hunting—the former being a female occupation and the latter male (Eldredge 1993: 19–21). They engaged in reciprocal economic exchanges within their groups. They also participated in long-distance trade with other communities in the region like the *Nguni*-speaking communities on the east coast (modern Kwazulu Natal and Eastern Cape regions). There was trade in household utensils made from iron and copper, iron hoes, animal skins, cattle, tobacco, and other goods (ibid.).

Beads were used as a medium of exchange for long-distance trade. They could be given different values according to their color. This was because beads were "fungible, could not easily be obtained, and could be given different values according to their size and colours." They were "considered as *money*, to be employed only as medium of trade with distant tribes, and for the purchase of more expensive articles." Additionally, "beads facilitated the relay trade system in which groups who traded directly with one another but did not need each other's trade goods accepted compensation in beads that could be used elsewhere to obtain the goods they did need" (ibid.: 21).

Beads appear to have been introduced in the eighteenth century, at the time of one senior chief, traditional healer, traveler, and sage, by the name of Mohlomi, who died in 1814. Early beads were named after him. They were called "beads of Mohlomi." Oral traditions also recall that beads were earned through trade with communities on the eastern coast. When beads were in short supply, a barter system was also used to exchange commodities among various groups. *AmaHlubi* and *MaZizi Nguni* groups from the east coast "crossed the mountains [into Lesotho] to trade with the *BaKoena* as early as the seventeenth century, bringing knives, spatulas, and hoes to exchange for animal skins, cattle, and tobacco" (ibid.).

South *Sotho*-speaking groups became more centralized in the early nineteenth century. Between 1820 and 1824, Moshoeshoe, a son of a junior chief of the *Mokoteli* lineage of the crocodile clan, accumulated large herds of cattle through raiding weaker communities. Through these raids, he emerged as an impressive young leader who then gathered people around him to form a dominant chiefdom. He was helped by the *Mfecane* wars of the 1820s (Hamilton 1995). He redistributed cattle and land, while providing security to *Mfecane* war refugees. His chiefdom is popularly taken in the country's history to be the origins of Lesotho (Sanders 1975; Thompson 1975).

Moshoeshoe redistributed cattle to his people through socioeconomic and political systems known as *mafisa* and *bohlanka*. *Mafisa* was a patronage system of cattle loans where the recipient took care of animals loaned to them and enjoyed the usufruct. *Bohlanka* was also a patronage system wherein a chief assisted young men to marry by providing *lobola* for them. Their children and labor belonged to the chief. *Lobola* given when marrying girls from such arrangements went to the chief, not to the biological parents. For agricultural production, people also engaged in communal work parties known as *matsema*. These were mainly used to produce food for chiefs' senior wives, orphans, and refugees (Mothibe 2002: 18–20).

These traditional redistribution strategies promoted people's dependence on chiefs. Chiefs were indispensable because they had wealth, which people needed most after the devastations of the *Mfecane* wars. In return, people owed their allegiance to chiefs who provided for them. Again, the wars had disrupted the vibrancy of most of the trading networks that had existed before (Eldredge 1993: 23). Therefore, people's economic means of survival were limited, making chiefs even more central.

Though people could benefit from such arrangements, the rewards were incidental and episodic (Thabane 2002a: 60). They were obliged to participate in long and strenuous work, which mainly benefited the chiefs. In fact, some scholars have argued that these systems were exploitative (Kimble 1978) and were feudal in nature (Thabane 2002a: 77). On top of this, chiefs proliferated, acquired more lands and required people to work on them. Instead of *matsema* being for social and chiefly use, as was traditionally the case, the chiefs exchanged produce from *matsema* in the markets, as will be seen later. There were even episodes when some people who refused to participate in *matsema* were brutally assaulted by their chiefs (ibid.). The arrival of missionaries in 1833 served to expand economic opportunities for individual Basotho. The missionaries challenged traditional Basotho economic and political formations and promoted commerce.

The Rise of Basotho's Economic Independence, 1830s–1870s

In 1833, the Paris Evangelical Missionary Society (PEMS) arrived in Lesotho at Moshoeshoe's request. When they arrived, they observed: "The trade which the natives [carried] on among themselves [was] not worthy to be enumerated as one of their means of existence. It [was] yet a very small matter" (Casalis 1861:169). Though this observation was accurate, missionaries were oblivious of the trading networks that had existed before, only to be disrupted by the *Mfecane* wars. The missionaries promoted commerce by encouraging Basotho to produce for the market; and they tied spreading the "gospel" to commerce. Judy Kimble points out that the missionaries promoted private property and individual rights in an attempt to undermine "evil" Basotho customs, especially *matsema*, *mafisa*, and *bohali* (*lobola*), which increased people's dependence on chieftaincy. She argues that the missionaries "were aiming at the dissolution of the existing social relations [by] encouraging their followers to refuse to participate in the various forms of obligatory labour-service" (1978: 106–108).

As elsewhere in Africa, missionaries operated through what Kimble calls the "trinity of the C's." These were "Christianity," "Civilization," and "Commerce." She notes that the PEMS "explicitly tie[d] the propagation of the gospel to their encouragement of commodity production, particularly wheat, the consumption of European goods, and labour for the white colonists" (ibid.: 102). The missionaries' promotion of commerce offered a means of emancipation from these "oppressive" systems to most converts. Tefetso Mothibe and Maria Ntabeni affirm that: "[these] three decades of the nineteenth century Lesotho [after the arrival of the missionaries] can be seen as transformational because of a number of changes that occurred within Basotho society. During that time, a class of small independent Basotho commodity producers emerged in and around the mission stations as a result of missionary activities" (2002: 35). Better trading opportunities for individual Basotho producers came with the arrival of the Boers from the Cape in the 1840s. Basotho exchanged grain with them (Walton 1958: 14). Eugène Casalis, one of the PEMS missionaries, observed: "Some tribes have recently adopted the culture of our cereals, especially that of wheat. The corn which is brought from the country of the Basutos to the markets of the colony is remarkable for its extreme purity. . . . It is with white men that the natives transact the most profitable business. In this respect the Basutos are particularly favoured by the fertility of their country" (1861: 169–170). Trade increased due to the penetration of Europeans. It was noted in the Annual PEMS

Conference Report of May 1842 that "civilization continues to make great progress ... the inhabitants have strongly applied themselves to the cultivation of European corn, they sell it to the farmers who barter it for cattle, clothes, soap, salt, etc" (as cited in Germond 1967: 441). In May 1854, Thomas Arbousset, one of the PEMS missionaries, observed that the mission station of Morija was a favorite hub for Basotho producers and customers, particularly those from the Orange Free State (ibid.: 451).

Relations between Basotho and the Afrikaners changed, however, and became violent as Afrikaners settled permanently on the territory that Moshoeshoe had allowed them to occupy temporarily. Conflicts between them led to the shrinking of Basotho's territories as they lost most of their arable land in the western parts. Lesotho's territory, all the way from the Vaal River (in modern Free State), was appropriated by the Afrikaners. During the 1850s, in what came to be known as the Basotho-Boer Wars, the two sides fought over land and pastures.[3] Due to Boer aggression, Moshoeshoe successfully negotiated for British protection. Finally in 1868, Lesotho became a British protectorate.

The same year that Lesotho became a British protectorate, diamonds were discovered in Kimberley, South Africa (Shillington 1989: 317). This marked the beginning of industrialization in southern Africa. Basotho took advantage of commercial opportunities that came with the discovery and exploitation of minerals and industrial developments by supplying grain to the populations of the newly emerging mining and industrial towns (Germond 1967: 322–324). Lesotho became the "granary" (Murray 1980) for these South African towns. In the documents he found in Paris while compiling the *Chronicles of Basutoland*, Robert Germond (1967: 322–324) found reports stating: "[In 1873, the] populations which have profited most from the discovery of the diamond beds are those which, comparatively far from them, have assiduously applied themselves to agricultural pursuits. The Basuto of our stations witness the daily influx in their midst of crowds of people, who do nothing else but buy the wheat and other food crops, with the object of selling them again to the mines."

In 1874, Paul Germond, a missionary, also noticed: "Although far removed from the main current of events, the Basuto have nonetheless reaped their share of the general prosperity. The price of cereals has doubled, their flocks are multiplying and wool commands a good price; as money is easily earned, people are better clothed, the traditional hut is being superseded by more comfortable dwellings" (ibid.).

Basotho's trade flourished to the point that they even worried the missionaries. They were scared that the perceived love of gain would turn Basotho away from their religious obligations and beliefs. For example,

Dr. Eugène Casalis, son of Eugène Casalis of the PEMS, commented in May 1873:

> A danger which now threatens our churches and to which we must draw your attention, is the love of gain. Basutoland is traversed in every direction by the wagons of traders who, in exchange for their money and their commercial ware, convey to the diamond fields and the Free State, Europeans and native corn, also the maize which the Basuto grow on a vast scale. The high prices which their cereals command, and the ease with which their produce is sold, tend to favour among them the love of money; material interests are in danger of turning many souls away from spiritual values. (Ibid.: 322)

The decade of the 1870s was a period of economic recovery and rehabilitation after the Basotho-Boer Wars and the economic depression of the 1860s. Basotho responded positively to trading and economic opportunities that came along with the European encounter and the discovery of minerals in South Africa. However, this growth was not to be sustained. The mineral revolutions in South Africa, colonialism "proper" in the latter part of the nineteenth century, the impact of land appropriation, and chiefs' abuse of power and privilege changed the history and fate of many ordinary people. Contrary to the emancipatory role of money and markets described in this section, money and markets were later used against the majority of the ordinary people.

The Fall of Basotho's Economic Independence, 1880s–1930s

Wage labor and increased commercial production in the latter part of the nineteenth century developed simultaneously. The dominant underdevelopment school of thought, mainly championed by Colin Murray (1980), emphasized a radically simplified and linear transition from a self-sufficient society to a disenfranchised labor reserve through external forces. However, the transition was not so straightforward. As I will demonstrate here, internal political and economic forces creating inequality, whereby the majority of the people were pushed to the margins of the economy while the chiefs occupied its upper stratum, is less acknowledged. As well as the well-known factors in the collapse of Basotho's economic independence, internal inequality became more pronounced after the Gun War and forced many Basotho to "voluntarily" respond to labor opportunities in the mines as their main source of livelihood. In this sense the role of money and markets shifted to the far end of the spectrum and worked against the majority of the people.

The discovery of minerals and industrialization in South Africa led to high demand for labor. Neighboring African communities, within South Africa and outside, were seen as sources. Basotho responded to these labor demands. Because of their general economic prosperity and labor competition between industries in South Africa, many Basotho were able to dictate the terms of their employment. They could easily move from one employer to the next in search for better wages or choose what to be paid with. In the economic history of Lesotho, this is known as "discretionary" labor migration (Thabane 2002: 108b). Many Basotho demanded to be paid with guns. They needed guns to replace obsolete weapons, which they used to protect themselves and their country; for since the nineteenth century Lesotho had been characterized by constant militant conflicts (Eldredge 1993: 147). As a result, colonial officials and missionaries described Basotho as a well-armed African society in the 1870s (Ajulu 1979: 30).

Basotho's standing as a prosperous and well-armed society was seen as an obstacle to industrial capitalist development in the southern African region. Colonial officials and missionaries in Lesotho also resented the fact that Basotho were well-armed (Ajulu 1979). As a result, Basotho's autonomy had to be undermined to turn them into wage workers and their territory into a reservoir of cheap labor. European imperialists attempted to achieve this by dismantling the autonomy provided by Basotho's pre-colonial socioeconomic, political formations and trading activities. To that end, colonial laws meant to undermine Basotho's pre-colonial socioeconomic formations were introduced (Thabane 2002b: 104–105).

In 1868, when Basotho's territory became a British protectorate, Lesotho was placed under a high commissioner, Sir Philip Wodehouse. Wodehouse's approach to imposing colonial laws was that they should be introduced gradually in order not to provoke the hostility of the Basotho. In 1871, the country was handed over to the Cape Colony. The Cape government aggressively introduced colonial laws to undermine Basotho's pre-colonial socioeconomic and political arrangements (Thabane 2002b: chap. 5).

The colonial authorities dismantled Basotho precolonial socioeconomic and political formations by ensuring that money became the primary means for securing basic necessities (ibid.). To that end, they introduced a hut tax in 1870. This compelled Basotho to depend on wages from the mines and industry. The authorities insisted that tax should be paid in money, and not in kind, as was usual. The shift to money-based tax payments was so rapid that the governor's agent commented: "As a marked sign of progress in the material wealth of the Basutos . . . in 1870, the *first* year that the Hut Tax was collected, several thousand sheep and as many *muids* of grain were received in lieu of money; *last* year only a few hundred sheep and as many *muids* of sheep were collected; and *this* year I think the Hut Tax will be paid almost entirely in money" (original emphasis, as cited in Theal 2002 [1872]:500). These early attempts to dismantle Lesotho's autonomy coincided with the death of Moshoeshoe in 1870. Succession conflicts following his death provided the colonial authorities with the political conditions they needed to advance their interests. With his death, the friability of Basotho's polity became apparent. Though Africanist historians, like Peter Sanders (1975) and Leonard Thompson (1975), have attempted to represent Lesotho's pre-colonial period along similar lines to those of the Swazi or Zulu kingdom, as "pre-colonial states" with effective political institutions and legitimacy, this was not the case for Lesotho. Lesotho's monarchy was consolidated by the colonial authorities in order to ensure stability, transition, and the launching of colonialism at large.

Though dominant, the *Mokoteli* lineage had not fully consolidated its power as Lesotho's uncontested monarchy before the country became a British protectorate. Two significant events demonstrated this. First, the sons of Moshoeshoe fought over their father's succession. Moshoeshoe had identified his eldest son, Letsie, as his successor. However, within Moshoeshoe's senior family, his two other sons, Molapo and Masopha, found it difficult to recognize their elder brother. Growing up, they had demonstrated keen interest and acumen in their father's political affairs, especially Masopha, while Letsie had proven to be the opposite. They believed that their father had risen to his position by merit and not by birthright (Thabane 2002b: 124).

It was only with colonial intervention that these disputes were "resolved." The colonial authorities were eager to promote the idea that various groups living in a colonized territory were to be put "under one Family," as Henry Barkey, high commissioner and governor of the Cape Colony, expressed it (as cited in Theal 2002 [1872]: 290). To that effect, they established an institution called "the Sons of Moshoeshoe," which was meant to be a central political body. The colonial government then moved to divide Lesotho into three major districts, which were then placed under the three senior sons of Moshoeshoe: Letsie, Masopha, and Molapo (Thabane 2002b: 125).

Second, and linked to the above, some Basotho groups in Lesotho did not consider themselves to be subjects of the *Mokoteli* lineage. At the extreme, these were *Baphuti* of Chief Moorosi, who saw themselves only as allies (ibid.). When the colonial government attempted to create a money economy and introduce colonial laws, Chief Moorosi had been the first to openly challenge these intentions (Ajulu 1979; Thabane 2002b). His position was that the use of money would destroy the traditional social fabric of their society. To support this, speaking to the specific case of the commercialization of traditional beer, he warned: "you know that if people begin selling beer, then travellers will suffer hunger if they don't have money to buy and besides I know it will be extended to bread also and they will be asking sixpence for that" (as cited in Ajulu 1979: 34). The colonial government and the *Mokoteli* lineage considered Chief Moorosi to be an unruly rebel. The *Mokoteli* lineage believed that "he was not always a very obedient vassal."[4] To demonstrate his autonomy, Moorosi openly and persistently considered "himself to be totally emancipated from Moshoeshoe" (ibid.). Moorosi's "rebellious" tendencies posed a problem for the colonial government, which sought to centralize authority under one chief for ease of control. As a result, Letsie was militarily supported by the colonial government in attacking Moorosi in 1878 (Ajulu 1979: 30). Moorosi was defeated and killed. Immediately after that, the colonial government swiftly moved to enforce colonial laws in 1879. Now the *Mokoteli* lineage resisted. As a result, in 1880–1881, Basotho went to war against the Cape Colony in a conflict that came to be known as the Gun War.

Basotho's status as a well-armed society continued to threaten the Cape government's introduction of colonial laws. Accordingly, Basotho had to be disarmed to undermine their potential for resistance. The need for this had been demonstrated by Chiefs Moorosi and Masopha (ibid.: 36). In May 1878, a Disarmament Bill was introduced in the Cape Parliament. In August 1878, the bill received Royal Assent under the title of the "Peace Preservation Act" (Act 3 of 1878). The act was seen as an attempt to "remove an obvious temptation to resist lawful authority and even to rebellion" (ibid.).

On 16 October 1879, Gordon Sprigg, as the new Cape prime minister, held a public gathering in Maseru to inform Basotho that they were to be disarmed. Basotho were dissatisfied with this, the doubling of taxation and the colonial government's intention to alienate *Baphuthi*'s country from the rest of Lesotho and demarcate it for European settlement. Despite this resistance, the colonial government pursued its agenda to disarm Basotho. As a result, in September 1880, Basotho and the Cape Colony went to war. The war lasted for seven months and ended in April 1881. Colonial officials titled the war the "Basutoland Rebellion" (ibid.: 36–42). Basotho defeated the Cape Colony despite the financial and artillery resources it had at its disposal. The Cape colonial government had borrowed more that £1.3 million from Standard Bank, without security, in order to fight the war.[5]

After the Gun War, in 1884, Lesotho was handed back to Britain. As discussed previously, colonial laws were now gradually introduced. With the defeat of Moorosi and support from the colonial government, the *Mokoteli* lineage assumed the status of being the country's uncontested monarchy. Moorosi's territory was appropriated to form the fourth district of the country, Cornet Spruit district. With all this in place, chieftainship became a conduit for the colonial government to control Lesotho more effectively. Chiefs became instrumental in enforcing the payment of hut tax and in labor recruitment for South African mines. In return for their services, the chiefs received a commission from labor recruiting agents and the colonial government, respectively (Thabane 2002b: 123).

The emergent relationship between the colonial government and the monarchy was consolidated by the formation of a National Council in 1903, under Paramount Chief Lerotholi. The Council functioned as a "parliament" and sat once a year. It was meant "to deal with tribal affairs in consultation with the government" (Stevens 1967: 35). It consisted of no more than one hundred members, five nominated by the resident commissioner and the rest by the paramount chief. The resident commissioner was automatically recognized as the Council's president (ibid.: 35–36). The Council was first proposed in 1886 by Resident Commissioner Marshall Clarke. In a letter to Paramount Chief Letsie I, Clarke wrote: "I send a proposal for the making and the work of a council; this is my own suggestion and is not from the Government" (as cited in Stevens 1967: 33).

In talks leading to the establishment of the National Council, tax and its redistribution became one of the central issues of discussion. Apart from national affairs, Clarke proposed that it would be an ideal structure to administer collected tax. He proposed that it would "receive an account of the manner in which hut tax was spent." Letsie I supported this proposal: "I say that this matter of the Council, I find that this will be a work that will show well; that the hut tax of Basutoland will be of use to the whole country" (ibid.: 34).

In practice, the Council became a chieftain-dominated institution. It was criticized by some Basotho as undemocratic since it only represented the interests of the chiefs and colonial authorities; only five commoners, appointed by the paramount chief, formed part of its membership. The majority were chiefs. Josiel Lefela, one of the founders of and a spokesperson of *Lekhotla la Bafo* (League of Commoners), argued that "commoners' voices ... [were] being totally neglected." He accused the "chiefs of cutting themselves off from the ordinary Basotho and abusing their positions" through the Council (as quoted in Nyeko 2002: 140). Lefela was himself a member of the National Council. His activism was well-informed with first-hand participant observation. As a result, he proposed the formation of the Council of Commoners. This, he believed would be an important democratic institution for the ordinary people. However, his proposal was rejected. As a result, he took successful steps to form *Lekhotla la Bafo* in 1919 (ibid.: 140).

Colonial efforts to turn Lesotho into a labor reserve money economy were buttressed by other economic and environmental factors, which also forced Basotho to depend on wages from South Africa. First, the Free State imposed tariffs on Basotho's produce in the 1890s, thereby forcing them to sell at higher prices. As a result, they could not compete with cheaper grain imported from Australia after railway networks were completed into the interior. Second, in the mid-1890s, Basotho's livestock were decimated by the rinderpest epizootic.[6] Last, due to land they had lost to the Boers and the mountainous topography of the country, arable land was reduced further by soil erosion. This undermined Basotho's agricultural productivity (Murray 1980).

The majority of Basotho were hard hit not only by the war itself but also by the postwar political, environmental, and economic changes and interventions outlined above. A greedy, explicitly oppressive and self-serving chieftainship—as compared to the federated form of chieftainship that existed during the reign of Moshoeshoe—acted only to preserve itself and colonial interests. This new character was one of the major factors behind the acute inequality that became even more apparent after the Gun War. Chiefs had more wealth in the form of livestock and land. Instead of redistributing to the people, they used all these for their individual and family advancement (Leys 1981: 90).

Chiefs punitively charged the people in their courts. They demanded more livestock and labor in their fields from them. By the 1930s, court fines were mainly accepted in the form of cash. Chiefs also established a tribute system through which they extracted labor and livestock from the people. The chiefs obligated people to participate in *matsema* for commercial purposes (ibid.: 91). In some cases, more prosperous commoners were targeted in order to be dispossessed. Hugh Ashton observed: "[The chiefs] obstinately opposed economic development that might enrich and emancipate their subjects, and were given, even then, to the practice of 'eating up a person': namely, punishing a prosperous man for some misdemeanour by seizing all or the greater part of his stock" (1967: 220).

Due to lack of records, it is difficult to establish the extent to which inequality existed between the chiefs and the ordinary people. However, the information available indicates a more terrifying picture. In the 1930s, the colonial system, which had given the chiefs a lot of power, started to show signs of deterioration and, for the first time, it was difficult to administer the protectorate due to the financial crisis of the 1930s. One of the dominant discourses at the time was the eventual annexation of Lesotho into the Free State. The colonial government commissioned Alan Pim to survey the financial and economic position of Lesotho in the mid-1930s (1935). The commission prompted a survey of inequality in the district of Qacha's Nek in 1934. The survey revealed that approximately 80 percent of the people, who had been paying tax for the last five to ten years, had no livestock (Leys 1981: 91). In 1936, the colonial government carried another survey in the Highlands of Lesotho. The sample showed that 11 percent of the people had slightly above twenty head of cattle while 50 percent only had small livestock and the rest (30 percent) had nothing (ibid.).

Observers' accounts of wealth and poverty in Lesotho also show how far inequality existed in Basotho's society. On the one hand, Roger Leys (1981: 91) revealed that some observers identified a wealthy group of principal chiefs, village headmen, and a progressive group of commoners who owned extensive tracts of land and stock, with lavish lifestyles consisting of tailor-made suits, cars, capital-intensive farm implements, and children educated in advanced missionary schools. On the other, he saw an impoverished group of commoners without livestock, who could not feed, clothe, and house themselves adequately even in non-drought years. Leys (Ibid: 92) cited an observation, revealing:

> In 1934, one chief, who kindly showed me his books, owned 200 cattle, 1,500 small stock, 90 equines, and 31 large lands, which in a fair year yielded 300 bags of grain; he had also a revenue from his court of about 200 cattle, 225 small stock and 20 pounds cash, and an allowance of 100 pounds (subsequently raised to 300 pounds) from the administration. He was one of the wealthier chiefs, but not as wealthy as the late Chief Jonathan, who died leaving an estate worth over 20,000 pounds.

These observations were made during the 1930s depression, which followed the 1920s economic crisis in Lesotho that was caused mainly by drought. The economic crisis had worsened ordinary people's economic fortunes and even those Basotho who were in business had to close down.[7]

Due to economic hardship, chiefs' abuse of power and the political-economic and bureaucratic restrictions that many ordinary people experienced, the conversion of workers into wage laborers was set in self-perpetuating motion. By 1904, out of a population of some 350,000, there were more than 86,000 Basotho males working in South Africa

(Stevens 1967: 39). These numbers continued to increase after a railway line connecting Maseru, Lesotho's capital, with South Africa was completed in 1906 (ibid.). It facilitated the increased mobility of migrant workers. By the 1920s, many Basotho depended on wages from South Africa. From now on Basotho could no longer be described as an agricultural society (Murray 1980).

Lesotho thus became a renowned wage labor reserve in southern African historiography. This was achieved through coercive taxes, wars, and strategic colonial policies meant to transform Lesotho's pre-capitalist economy into a reservoir of cheap labor for the capitalist economy. To achieve this, Basotho's pre-colonial economic independence was undermined. This is how "money and markets" worked against the ordinary people. In this latter era—colonialism proper—money and markets were strategically and coercively employed to serve colonial and capitalist interests in southern Africa. The next section will explore how money circulated in and out of Lesotho in this new money economy. By these means, the country was merged with the southern African industrial capitalist economy—and asymmetrically with the rest of the global capitalist economy.

The Role and Legacy of Financial Institutions in the New Money Economy, 1870s–1930s

Previous sections have shown how trade and wages (earned in South Africa) facilitated increased flows and exchange of money in Lesotho's economy. To support the newly emergent money economy, a number of financial institutions were established in Lesotho by the colonial government and international private investors. As a result and because of other infrastructural developments at the turn of the century, Lesotho was already seen by colonial officials as "moving into the twentieth century" (as cited in Stevens 1967: 39).

The first institution established by the colonial government to facilitate flows of information and money between Lesotho and South Africa was the Basutoland Post Office Savings Bank in 1891. Its deposits were passed on to the South African Post Office Bank. In 1862, Standard Bank, a British bank, established a branch in South Africa (Thabane 2009: 4). By September 1901, it was advertising its banking services in Lesotho. At the beginning, it operated as an agency managed by Alfred Ellenberger. Ellenberger would travel on horseback between Lesotho and Ladybrand, a neighboring South African town, to make deposits and withdrawals. In

1904, Standard Bank established a branch in Maseru (Ambrose 1993: 91). Around this time, Bloemfontein Board of Executives and Trust Company, an insurance company, also opened a branch in Maseru. It stopped its operations in 1932 during the Great Depression when it went bankrupt. Other Cape Town–based insurance companies, like Mutual Building Homes Limited, also started to advertise their services in Lesotho (Thabane 2009: 3–4).[8]

Commercial banks presented themselves as saving institutions and not lenders of credit, particularly to Basotho.[9] This could be seen in how they advertised their services. First, when Standard Bank opened a branch in Maseru, it advertised that it had done so for "the purpose of all transactions/operations carried out by banks, that is, to receive and save money in its interest" (as cited in Thabane 2009: 6). Second, the Post Office Savings Bank advertised: "if you are paid in cash, you have to save it for the COMING DAYS. Go to the Post Office near you, they will tell you how you can get a savings book and you can start saving" (ibid.: 6–7).

These financial institutions predominantly served an emergent colonial class consisting of civil servants, missionaries, and European traders. Commerce, namely retail and wholesale, was the main business activity. Major trade items were: groceries, clothes, blankets, skins and hides, wool and mohair, as well as livestock and grain. Commerce facilitated the circulation of money within and outside the country. European traders began to establish stores from the 1870s. By the end of the century, led by Frasers Company, they had emerged as a leading commercial group in Lesotho. It was later in the twentieth century that Indian and Basotho traders inserted themselves in colonial commerce. Thus, the commercial community at the beginning of the twentieth century consisted hierarchically of European, Indian, and a few Basotho traders. By the mid-1930s, there were about 194 stores in Lesotho: 175 of these were owned by European traders while 16 were owned by Indian and 3 by Basotho traders (Maliehe 2014).

For Basotho, it was difficult to gain access to credit from commercial banks. So, Basotho established alternative savings and farmers' cooperatives, with assistance from Christian missionaries.[10] They established cooperatives as a way to deal with the economic hardship they had faced since the end of the nineteenth century, as we have seen. Moreover, this was also how they inserted themselves in the new money economy. Part of the money earned from wages and from the sale of produce or livestock was invested in cooperatives as well as in agriculture and small enterprises. Various cooperatives kept their monies with commercial banks.[11] In these cooperatives, people would pool their money together in order to procure farm implements, groceries, as well as to provide credit to members. However, cooperatives consistently faced the problem of default on loans. For example, in 1938, of the £876 that the African Cooperative Society had lent to its members, only £500 had been repaid.[12]

In essence, by the early twentieth century, Lesotho was more connected to the rest of the global money economy, albeit with ordinary Basotho pushed to the margins of that economy.[13] However, from early on, they attempted to insert themselves in the money economy through collective efforts organized around cooperatives and other individual entrepreneurial pursuits.

Conclusion

The economic history of pre-colonial and early colonial Lesotho provides two insights into the role of money and markets in society. Money can be used for anything and there are various types of markets. However, we need to distinguish between when they work for and against the people. The economic history of Lesotho in the period between the 1830s and 1930s illustrates this. Between the 1830s and 1870s, money and markets worked for ordinary Basotho, while from the 1880s to 1930s, money and markets were deliberately used against the interests of ordinary Basotho. This century can aptly be described as the rise and fall of Basotho's economic independence. Rather than empowering Basotho, money and markets were used to turn Lesotho into a reservoir of cheap labor through land appropriation, colonial policy, environmental and economic catastrophes, as well as internal inequality tied to chieftainship's abuse of power and privilege.

Money and markets in Lesotho predated capitalism and the European encounter. We may talk about them as being outside capitalism. Money and markets facilitate "social extension"—a term Hart takes from Georg Simmel (1978). In *The Philosophy of Money*, talking about social unifying and outreaching predispositions of money, Simmel argues: "[T]he convertibility of the most diverse phenomena into one another (money), transform the differences that are apparent at first sight into a general affinity, a universal equality (ibid.: 56).

Groups that came to make up the Basotho were connected in the region through money and markets. It was with European encounter and later colonialism that money among the Basotho society took a different form. Money and markets in Basotho's territory became what money and markets were in Europe when Adam Smith wrote the *Wealth of Nations*

(1776). Exploring conditions under which Smith wrote the *Wealth of Nations*, Hart demonstrates that military landlords in Europe restricted people's use of money and participation in markets. He argues that the ruling class sought to control people's movement and freedom to engage in trade. Unlike socialism, for example, capitalism did not recoil from money-market mutuality; it explicitly aligned with them as the main engines of economic production and distribution of wealth. Missionaries' promotion of individual production and participation in markets among the Basotho in the early nineteenth century emancipated people from the chiefs who had made themselves indispensable to people's economic life after the devastations of the *Mfecane* wars.

Increasingly, Basotho were integrated into the emerging nineteenth-century global capitalist economy. This process was fast tracked by the discovery of minerals in South Africa. Lesotho became the major supplier of grain to emerging mines and industries. However, the demands for cheap labor saw money and markets being used against Basotho through colonial policy aimed at undermining Basotho's precolonial economic independence. Colonialism, proper, in this sense, acted as a form of "primitive accumulation," wherein people were disenfranchised and forcibly removed from their means of production to work for low wages. There were of course other internal factors that set the proletarianization of Basotho men into self-propelling mode. Colonial and chieftainship enforcement of payment of hut tax, and its payment using money, which was to be earned in the mines acted as a coercive catalyst, and Lesotho was effectively integrated into the twentieth-century exploitative global capitalist and colonial order. This was later overthrown by the liberation movement from the second half of the twentieth century.

Despite the "success" of the liberation movement, and not just in Africa, but even in the West, the majority of the people continued to remain marginal to economies that predominantly privilege those with money. The story of Basotho chronicled here builds on the concept of a human economy and illuminates aspirations for a more inclusive world economy. The role of money is better seen as a structure of alliances than as binary constructions of money and markets as "evil" or "good." This allows us to distinguish the emancipatory and oppressive features of neoliberal capitalism today. Neoliberalism is supposed to operate with a narrow and individualistic logic. This logic lacks appreciation for economic pluralism. Hart argues that one of the most important aspects of the human economy is finding new principles of human association. The Basotho case offers many lessons to be drawn for building a human economy.

Sean Maliehe recently acquired his PhD with the University of Pretoria through the Human Economy Program, and Heritage and Historical Studies. He is a postdoctoral fellow in the same program. He works on the economic history of Lesotho, and on money and mobile phones in South Africa and Lesotho.

NOTES

1. The name Lesotho was made official in 1966 to refer to the territory known as "Basutoland" during the colonial era. In this chapter, Lesotho is used to refer to the territory throughout the colonial period. The name "Basutoland" is used in quotes and as a term for laws, institutions, and so on.
2. In colonial orthography, "Basotho" was spelled "Basuto." This is plural, and "Mosotho" (Mosuto), is singular. Here I will use Basotho/Mosotho to refer to the "native" people of Lesotho. Basuto will be used in direct quotes and other official references.
3. For more information on the history, origins and dynamics of the Basotho-Boer Wars, see Mothibe and Ntabeni (2002).
4. John Burnet, (a British Agent) to Secretary of the High Commissioner Aliwal North, 14 February 1857, in Germond (1967: 332).
5. J. A. Henry as quoted in Thabane (2002a: 111). It was no coincidence that, the same year (1879), the British went to war against the Zulus. For the Anglo-Zulu War, Standard Bank had lent the Cape government no less than £400,000 a month.
6. Rinderpest was an infectious viral disease that attacked cattle and other wild animals. Its symptoms included diarrhea and fever, leading to death.
7. *Lesotho National Archives, Trade, S3/26/1/8-11*, letters of the Basutoland Chamber of Commerce, and those of its individual members, to the resident commissioner, Maseru, 1927 to 1932.
8. It was later in 1957 that Barclays bank established a branch in Maseru. Apart from these, other financial institutions came later after independence.
9. This was not a phenomenon unique to Lesotho, even in other parts of the continent; commercial banks presented an image of being saving institutions. See, for example, Onoh (1982).
10. *Report of a Commission of Inquiry into Coop Lesotho*, n.d.
11. *Financial and Economic Position of Basutoland, Report of the Commission Appointed by the Secretary of State for Dominion Affairs* (London: His Majesty's Stationery Office, 1935), pp. 173–174.
12. *Mochochonono Newspaper*, 20 May 1938.
13. The period from the 1930s to independence (1966) was a period in which Basotho strategically and politically sought to strongly assert themselves in the newly emergent money economy. For more information on this, see Maliehe (2014).

REFERENCES

Ajulu, R. O. K. 1979. "The gun war in Basutoland, 1880–1881: Some aspects of the destruction of the natural economy and the origins of articulation." BA dissertation, National University of Lesotho.

Ambrose, D. 1993. *Illustrated History of Maseru*. Morija: Morija Museum and Archives.

Amin, S. 1973. *Neo-colonialism in West Africa*. Middlesex: Penguin Books Ltd.

Ashton, H. 1967. *The Basuto: A Social Study of Traditional and Modern Lesotho*. London: Oxford University Press.

Casalis, E. 1861. *The Basutos: Or, Twenty Years in South Africa*. London: James Nisbet & Co. Berners Street.

Eldredge, E. A. 1993. *A South Africa Kingdom: The Pursuit of Security in Nineteenth Century Lesotho*. Cambridge: Cambridge University Press.

Feinstein, C. H. 2005. *An Economic History of South Africa: Conquest, Discrimination, and Development*. Cambridge: Cambridge University Press.

Germond, R. C. 1967. *Chronicles of Basutoland: A Running Commentary on the Events of the Years 1830–1902 by the French Protestant Missionaries in Southern Africa*. Morija: Morija Sesuto Book Depot.

Hamilton, C. (ed.). 1995. *The Mfecane Aftermath: Reconstructive Debates in Southern African History*. Pietermaritzburg: University of Natal Press.

Hart, K. 2000. *The Memory Bank: Money in an Unequal World*. London: Profile Books Ltd.

———. 2007. "Money is Always Personal and Impersonal." *Anthropology Today* 23(5): 12–16.

Hart, K., and C. Hann. 2009. "Introduction: Learning from Polanyi 1." In C. Hann and K. Hart (eds.), *Market and Society: The Great Transformation Today*. Cambridge: Cambridge University Press, pp. 1–16.

Hart, K., J.-L. Lavelle, and A. D. Cattani. 2010. "Building the human economy together." In K. Hart, J.-L. Lavelle, and A. D. Cattani (eds.), *The Human Economy: A Citizen's Guide*. Cambridge: Polity Press, pp. 1–17.

Kimble, J. 1978. "Towards an understanding of the political economy of Lesotho: The origins of commodity production and migrant labour, 1830–1885." MA dissertation, National University of Lesotho.

Leys, R. 1981. "Some observations on class differentiation and class conflict within the labour reserve of Basutoland." http://sas-space.sas.ac.uk/4099/1/Roger_Leys_-_Some_observations_on_class_differentiation_and_class_conflict_within_the_labour_reserve_of_basutoland.pdf (accessed 16 June 2015).

Maliehe, S. 2014. "An Obscured Narrative in the Political Economy of Colonial Commerce, 1870–1966." *Historia* 59(2): 28–45.

Marx, K. 1970 [1867]. *Capital*, volume I. London: Lawrence and Wishart.

Mothibe, T. 2002. "Early communities of the southern Highveld, 1500–1800." In N. W. Pule and M. Thabane (eds.), *Essays on Aspects of the Political Economy of Lesotho, 1500–2000*. Roma: Department of History, National University of Lesotho, pp. 1–14.

Mothibe, T., and M. Ntabeni. 2002. "The role of the missionaries, Boers and British in social and territorial changes, 1833–1868." In N. W. Pule and M. Thabane (eds.), *Essays on Aspects of the Political Economy of Lesotho*. Roma: Department of History, National University of Lesotho, pp. 35–57.

Murray, C. 1980. "From Granary to Labour Reserve: An Economic History of Lesotho." *South African Labour Bulletin* 6(4): 3–20.

Nyeko, B. 2002. "Resistance to colonial rule and the emergence of anti-colonial movements." In N. W. Pule and M. Thabane (eds.), *Essays on Aspects of the Political Economy of Lesotho*. Roma: Department of History, National University of Lesotho, pp. 131–151.

Onoh, J. K. 1982. *Money and Banking in Africa*. London: Longman.

Polanyi, K. 2001 [1944]. *The Great Transformation: The Political and Economic Origins of Our Times*. Boston, MA: Beacon Press.

Sanders, P. 1975. *Moshoeshoe: Chief of the Sotho*. London: Heinemann.

Shillington, K. 1989. *History of Africa*. London: Macmillan Education, LTD.

Simmel, G. 1978. *Philosophy of Money*. London: Routledge.

Smith, A. 1776. *An Inquiry into the Nature and Causes of the Wealth of Nations*. Edinburgh: William Strahan.

Stevens, R. P. 1967. *Lesotho, Botswana, & Swaziland: The Former High Commission Territories in Southern Africa*. London: Pall Mall Press.

Thabane, M. 2002a. "The nature of social relations in the nineteenth century." In N. W. Pule and M. Thabane (eds.), *Essays on Aspects of the Political Economy of Lesotho*. Roma: Department of History, National University of Lesotho, pp. 59–77.

———. 2002b. "Aspects of colonial economy and society, 1868–1966." In N. W. Pule and M. Thabane (eds.), *Essays on Aspects of the Political Economy of Lesotho*. Roma: Department of History, National University of Lesotho, pp. 103–130.

———. 2009. "Indigenous entrepreneurial initiative and attempts to solve problems of access to credit in Lesotho, 1868–1975." Seminar paper presented at the National University of Lesotho, Department of Historical Studies, Roma, 11 September.

Theal, G. M. 2002 [1872]. *Basutoland Records 1871–1872*, volume VI. Roma: Institute of Southern African Studies.

Thompson, L. 1975. *Survival in Two Worlds: Moshoeshoe, 1786–1870*. Oxford: Clarendon Press.

Walton, J. 1958. *Father of Kindness and Father of Horses—Ramosa le Ralipere: A History of Frasers Limited*. Morija: Morija Printing Works.

CHAPTER 12

 Gender and Money in the Argentinian *Trueque*

HADRIEN SAIAG

It's almost midday on Friday; about one hundred people mass together beneath shady eucalyptus trees in a wasteland on the edge of one of Rosario's western main streets (a working-class, formerly industrialized area).[1] Neighbors and passersby walk without stopping: the place is said to be dirty and dangerous, attended by "ragmen (*cartoneros*), the unemployed and other indigents."[2] Yet, for some years now, this former rubbish dump has been converted into a hot spot of Rosario's popular economy, where people frantically buy and sell almost everything. Women from Rosario's northern suburbs pool their funds to rent small vans in which they carry the many products they buy and sell, most of them from wholesalers; they also carry chairs and tables that make up their stands. Others bring horse- or hand-drawn carts from the surrounding slums; they sell fruits and vegetables they salvaged from wholesale markets nearby, defective manufactured products such as broken biscuits or damaged canned food, or homemade cleaning products. Many others sell used cloth on the ground, along with items they received as payment in kind for daily casual labor (*changas*) or as poverty relief in kind offered by the municipality or some local church.

Beyond the ambient turmoil, this place merits attention for at least two reasons. First, transactions are carried out through the use of bills denominated in their own unit of account, the *crédito*. This local currency lubricates *trueque* (barter networks), because of their historical affiliation to a wider set of monetary experiments. From 1995 to 2002, a broad spectrum of activists, churches, neighborhood associations, and local politicians issued their own currencies "from below" and formed a federated structure, known as *Red Global de Trueque* (RGT), or Global Barter Network: *ferias* clustered in geographical zones and each zone issued its own set of bills denominated in *créditos*, which were accepted in all the RGT *ferias* (Saiag

2013). The number of participants in *trueque* grew rapidly, as low-income populations were increasingly excluded from the national currency (peso) due to rising income inequality and cash shortage resulting from the peso–US dollar exchange rate. It is the world's largest experiment in local currencies to date, with an estimated two million participants (Ould-Ahmed 2010). However, it got into a deep hyperinflation crisis from June to September 2002: since then, it has partially recovered at a more local level, as the federated structure disappeared (Orzi 2012).

In 2009, when the fieldwork on which this chapter is based was carried out, two such currencies circulated around Rosario's urban agglomeration, exclusively at weekly market places (*feria*). The *créditos* in use in the wasteland described above also circulated in two other biweekly *ferias*, located in Rosario's western periphery (in a public square and a neighborhood association). While previously 50 *créditos* were allocated to each new participant, it is now necessary to pay 10 pesos to one of the *feria*'s "coordinators" to gain access to 8,000 newly issued *créditos*. Acceptance of *crédito* bills was taken for granted, since nobody questioned the legitimacy of the nurse who issued them, as the founder of the Santa Fe provincial *trueque* (she contracted a printer to protect the bills from falsification). However, no formal organization runs *trueque* in Rosario, beyond interpersonal ties between the bills' issuers and each *feria*'s coordinator. Other *crédito* bills circulate in three weekly *ferias* located in Capitán Bermúdez, a small town in Rosario's northern suburbs (the agglomeration's most industrialized area, due to the presence of many harbors). *Créditos* are issued by an association created for "the liberation of the poorest," Poriajhú (standing for "the poor" in Guarani), which also runs various other activities, including a radio station, school tutoring, an adult literacy scheme, microcredit programs, etc. Contrary to what happens in Rosario, participants are offered a fixed amount of *créditos* when they first attend a *feria*.

The second striking element about *trueque* is that it is a women's world. Indeed, women are greatly overrepresented: field research reveals that they were more than two-thirds of *trueque* participants in 2000–2002 (see e.g. Gonzales-Bombal 2002: 285; Leoni 2003: 29; Bogani and Parysow 2005). This proportion grew significantly after the *trueque* crisis, reaching 85 percent in 2004 in Buenos Aires's western suburbs (Gomez and Helmsing 2008: 2596; Pereyra 2007). During my fieldwork, no men ever participated in the Poriajhú *trueque*, while only a few did so in Rosario—and if they did, they came with their wives. Moreover, women also managed the *trueque*: in both localities, no male was in charge of the *feria*'s coordination or of issuing money.

I wish to reflect here on the gender of money. I observed the daily financial practices of eighteen households of which at least one member participated in *trueque* and I conducted in-depth interviews with each of them to better understand intrahousehold transactions (interviews were carried out with women, and sometimes also with their husbands). The chapter's aim is twofold. On the one hand, the differences between monetary practices carried out by adult men and women reveal social hierarchies based on gender, since men and women do not enjoy the same rights over income generation and expenditure. On the other hand, I ask how much women's use of local currencies challenges gender norms that we might consider to be oppressive. In this respect, *trueque* is an interesting case study, since its history coincides with a crisis of household financial management among the urban, industrial working class (Absi 2007). Indeed, until the mid-1990s, most of Rosario's working-class male workforce benefited from Fordist wage labor relations, which provided households with a secure and stable source of income. The emergence of *trueque* in the town in 1998 coincided with a transformation in these employment relations, which led women to assume a greater role in financial matters.

The chapter is structured around two main arguments. The first, developed in the opening three sections, is that the use of local currencies by women allows them to contest gender hierarchy in a limited way. *Ferias* are characterized by a specific kind of social relationship, different from relations within households: at a given time and place, status and gender inequalities are suspended, as market transactions require participants to act as if they were interchangeable (first section). Participation in *trueque* also leads to a limited transformation of households' financial organization. On the one hand, incomes obtained in this way tend to contest husbands' monopoly of income and control over their wives' expenditure. On the other hand, participation in *trueque* goes along with redefinition of the frontier between masculine and feminine monies, which does not allow more egalitarian models of household financial management to emerge (second section). Finally, if there is a degree of women's liberation, participation in *trueque* also acts as a source of social differentiation between women, because they do not engage in the *ferias* with the same initial endowments. Indeed, when *ferias* are based on competition between participants, the most mobile of them enjoy privileged access to money, as they can take advantage of price differences between the peso (national currency) and *crédito* spheres, to the detriment of the poorest participants (third section). This conclusion leads to a second argument: in order to grasp the potential of liberation through money, we must focus on the (always contextual) modalities of access to it. Indeed, money is likely to mediate a wide range of social relations, according to the contexts in which its uses are embedded (e.g. Parry and Bloch 1989; Zelizer 1994). If we want money to subvert gender hierarchy, we should treat it as a common good.[3]

A Temporary Suspension of Class and Gender Identities

The most striking effect of women's participation in *trueque* is the creation of a specific social space, the *feria*, clearly delimited in time and space. *Ferias* are usually spaces of socialization for women (González Bombal 2002), where they indulge in a kind of therapy allowing them to escape from the worries of daily life (Bogani and Parysow 2005). Following Michèle de La Pradelle (2006) and Jean-Michel Servet (2009), I argue that *ferias* are constitutive of a specific kind of social relationship, characterized by the temporary suspension of gender and class identities. This stems from the interchangeability in market transactions. La Pradelle, writing about Carpentras market places, claims:

> Market exchange is itself a social relation of a certain type. Whether people are negotiating the price of truffles, artworks, or tomatoes, goods-value exchange defines a situation where, during a given stretch of time, in a particular place, and for that particular activity, *the actors recognize each other as equivalent partners* no matter how unequal they may otherwise be in terms of power and status. All such partners accept the rules of the game, the first of which is that none may claim any kind of advantage or privilege external to the exchange situation. Or course, each "player" has his and her hand (the quality of the merchandise or the art of displaying it to advantage, buying power, acted indifference, and so on), but each is also just as worthy as any other. *In such ephemeral society of buyers and sellers, all are alike and recognized as such. People have no names or qualities, at least in principle.* (2006: 5, emphasis added)

I discovered this long after I experienced difficulty in obtaining interviews with *trueque* participants. Admittedly, during the *ferias* (for a short time), they were very talkative. It was easy to joke and speak about unimportant topics (such as the weather) or even about the products they offered and the products they were interested in buying (participants' answers often exceeded my expectations). I faced embarrassed refusals, however, as soon as I proposed an interview. All avoided this without offering any explanation. The fact that I was a man in an environment characterized by strong conservatism with regard to gender relations may partly explain this. But this hardly explains all my difficulties: even unmarried women (single, widowed, divorced, or too young to be married) refused an interview. My main problem was probably wanting to ask people to reveal their identity (their history, social ties, and activities outside *trueque*). I transgressed the foundational rule of market transactions—individuals behave as if they are interchangeable like the commodities they buy and sell.

The principle of interchangeability between *trueque* participants does not mean that class differences are ignored. Rather, they are neutralized, so they do not interfere with the transactions. This effect is obtained through dramatization of formal equality: during the *ferias*, participants greet each other warmly, despite obvious differences among them (slum dwellers used to come to the *feria* by horse cart). Likewise, each participant makes an effort to treat all others on an equal footing: anyone is likely to buy and to sell to/from a neighbor regardless of who they are (prices are the same for everyone, without distinction). That is how *ferias* bring together people from very different backgrounds who would not be mixed in any other social sphere: small shopkeepers, women who live in a popular neighborhood and run their own home-based informal selling, but also street vendors and marginal people forced to rely on casual labor who live in Rosario's peripheral slums.

Likewise, the prevalence of the principle of interchangeability during the *ferias* does not mean that personal ties are unimportant. *Trueque* participants deploy complex individual strategies to build and take advantage of long-term interpersonal trust in their commercial relationships. Clientele bonds allow cotraders to obtain key information about *ferias* (date, time, and locale of new *ferias*, the prices of commodities, and good deals). They are used first and foremost to secure households' access to food: because food supplies within the *feria* are very precarious, many participants agree on what they will sell to each other or swap during the next *feria* (Drelon 2009); the first preoccupation of participants is to pay off their debts or recover them. Moreover, when traders have already transacted before, sales are often carried out on credit. In this case, a claim is noted down in the creditor's notebook, and the debt is settled during the next *ferias*, through repayment in *créditos* or in kind. However, such personal ties do not challenge the principle of interchangeability itself, since mutual acquaintance is usually limited to the *ferias*. Ignoring almost everything about other participants' identities, it is usual to name them by the commodity they offer ("the one who sells fruits and vegetables," "the one who sells juice," etc.), rather than use their names or surnames. In addition, class and gender identities are certainly suspended because they resurface as soon as the *feria* finishes. During a *feria* people take care not to slander their neighbors, but discourses take another turn when they reach home. The poorest participants, usually mixed-race indigenous people living in Rosario's slums, are the target of a discriminatory speech: their poverty is attributed to their laziness; they are "dirty," "unproductive," and "abuse child labor."

The equality prevailing during the *ferias* could be criticized for its fictitious nature. However, the targets of this discriminatory discourse may experience it positively: the *feria*'s formal equality takes them out of their daily worries into a utopian world of individuals. That is what Andrea[4] (a regular *feria* participant) argues: "Yes, I love attending *trueque*. I really like the *ferias*, because many things happen. I am not thinking 'what the hell, domestic worries!' Suppose that I'm in bad shape, well, *trueque* distracts me. And when the *feria* ends, all [my problems] come back into my head.... But it makes you think about something else, I love it. If there could be other [*ferias*], I would go!" (interview, 24 November 2009). Because of its formal equality, the *feria* contrasts profoundly with the domestic world to which women are usually confined: the latter is made up of hierarchical relations from which it is hard for them to free themselves. Budget management epitomizes this point.

Challenging the Prevailing Normative Model of Budget Management

The participation of women in the *trueque* also challenges gender hierarchies through its impact on households' financial organization. The normative model prevailing among Rosario's working class reproduces gender-based domination, as wives and children are supposed to rely entirely on their husbands' or father's incomes. Indeed, husbands are considered to be the only legitimate purveyors of money in the household. Wives, in turn, are supposed to manage the money they receive from their husbands in their household's name, as Pascale Absi observed among miners in Potosí (Bolivia). This gendered division of household budget management also goes hand in hand with a spatial division of labor: "men work, women stay at home" in charge of domestic tasks (Absi 2007: 357).

Yet the impact of women's participation in the *trueque* on household financial organization is ambiguous. On the one hand, it weakens the two foundations of the prevailing normative model of budget management: husbands' monopolization of monetary income and the lack of differentiation between a wife's and household expenses.[5] In this way, participation in the *trueque* implies greater financial autonomy for women. On the other hand, the significance of such financial autonomy is limited, because *trueque* participation also engenders a redefinition of the frontier between masculine and feminine monies, rather than its eradication. That is why recourse to the *trueque* is said to be a means of "bypassing" (Guérin 2008) gender hierarchies, along with other monetary practices: these practices do not conform to the prevailing normative model of household financial management, but they do not confront it explicitly and are not recognized as legitimate.

Bypassing Husbands' Monopoly of Income

With regard to husbands' supposed monopoly of income, none of the households I interviewed fully conformed to this model. Two elements account for this. First, workers' employment conditions have worsened considerably since the 1990s, as protected wage-labor relations (characterized by long-term employment and social protection coverage) were weakened by lower real wages, greater income inequality, and informal employment (Sosa 2007; Damill, Frenkel, and Maurizio 2011; Rofman and Lucchetti 2006). Access to money became more scarce and irregular. As a result, it is no longer possible for a husband's wages alone to meet the household's financial needs. Second, wives and children resisted patriarchal domination as expressed by his monopoly of income. Children often generate their own sources of income now, sometimes on the sly; many of them sell miscellaneous items (above all, food) on the street or accumulate and sell recyclable goods (such as cardboard or plastic bottles) in order to avoid having to ask for money from their parents to go dancing or to buy a bicycle or beauty products. Wives also contribute to household income. Some of them have begun to help their husband at work without being paid, through home-based car washing and in T-shirt dyeing workshops (on the other hand, children are always paid for such work). All other adult women had their own source of income, in pesos obtained through informal activities – either as wages (mainly for housework and in sewing shops) or self-employment as street vendors, in small home-based general stores: *kiosko*, sewing, home bakery, etc.). In this last case, entrepreneurship goes with women's control over specific short-term financial circuits aimed at managing their working capital. Women's participation in *trueque* reinforces this tendency, as they control all income in *créditos*.

However, the patriarchal model of financial management still shapes household financial organization. First, for women, marriage means exclusion from wage-labor. Indeed, only three women (out of eighteen) had this kind of employment (in a sewing shop, a supermarket, and as a secretary in a transport company); but they all had to abandon their job when they got married, as wage-labor is hardly compatible with housework, which limits wives' mobility. Second, incomes generated by wives are much lower than those generated by their husbands (even if it is hard to obtain precise data[6]), and their contribution to the household budget is usually considered as extra income. Only those women who were not married (being either a widow, divorced, or a single adult) contributed substantial income (in pesos) to their household.[7] Only one interviewee was in this situation while she lived with her lover. Third, and most important, wives' income generation is usually not legitimate in the eyes of their husbands. The latter were skeptical about their wives' chances of success in business: "my husband did not believe I could; he asked me [ironically], 'how long will your business [selling clothes] last? One or two months?'" (Alicia); and "my husband reproaches me for sewing all the day long" (Samanta). In one case, disputes over a woman's income led to divorce:

> When I knew him [her future husband], I was ashamed to tell him that I used to sell [miscellaneous articles in the street]. . . . I told him two years after we began to go out. . . . Every time my boyfriend wanted to come, I said I had to babysit my niece, but it was false: I had to go out selling. When we decided to marry, he told me "when you marry me, you will have to stop selling." . . . That is when the conflicts began. He wanted to manage my life, but I did not go along with it [*me quería manejar, pero a mí no me maneja nadie*]. (Interview with Mónica, Capitán Bermúdez, October 2009)

Women use *trueque* to challenge budgetary patriarchy first by confronting the social norm that only husbands should supply all of a household's income. Through *trueque*, women get to control part of household income that they are not supposed to control; it is the same with their access to other short-term financial circuits in pesos. However, this does not turn budgetary patriarchy inside out, since the women do not call into question the sexual division of labor itself. Wives are still dedicated to household reproductive work (*créditos* obtained through *trueque* contribute almost exclusively to a household's food supply); and men still enjoy a monopoly of formal wage labor. Moreover, even as these practices bypass traditional norms, they go hand in hand with creating new boundaries between masculine and feminine monies, as financial circuits managed by women involve only small amounts and daily or weekly cycles. *Trueque* reinforces this tendency, since women's incomes are in a separate unit of account (*créditos*). This in turn reproduces the idea of the peso as masculine money.

Bypassing Husbands' Control over Expenditure

Women's participation in *trueque* challenges their husbands' control over expenditure made by other household members. But it also reinforces the existing gendered division of money use.

A second difference between masculine and feminine monies may be observed in how husbands' income is partially deindividualized when it is transferred to wives (Carsten 1989). Because incomes are supposed to be controlled by husbands and spending is their wives' affair, transfers are a key element in household finances. These transfers took three forms as exemplified by the following cases:

1. The first and most evident case of a wife's submission to her husband: Elisandra has to ask her husband (a car mechanic) for money every morning. He rarely gives her enough money (in pesos) to pay for the household's daily expenses. So she has to negotiate for any extras and her husband closely controls the household's spending. In addition, Elisandra cannot influence her husband's spending, since she does not know how much he earns.
2. The second concerns Celina, Jorge (her husband), and their three children; it is characteristic of households where the husband earns a weekly wage: expenditures are compartmentalized to adapt to the temporality of Jorge's remuneration. As soon as he receives his income as a self-employed construction worker every Thursday, he transfers 600 pesos to Celina, who immediately carries out her weekly food shopping: she spends 100 pesos on meat, another 100 pesos each on fruits, vegetables, and staples (pasta, rice, tomato puree, flour, etc.) – that is, 400 pesos in all. The remaining 200 pesos are put in a separate envelope to pay for other miscellaneous expenses and monthly spending on electricity, water, taxes, and rent.
3. Husbands commonly transfer part of their income to their wives through a system of envelopes and notebooks. They used to do this when they were paid (usually around the 5th and 20th of each month). Now only part of a husband's income is transferred in this way, since they usually retain a sum of money for their personal expenses (transport to work, lunch, alcohol, games of chance, etc.). Wives immediately put the money (in cash) in a box or an envelope. On the 5th they might put in separate envelopes money for fixed costs (most of them being paid at the beginning of the month). The wives and children use what's left for their daily expenses, but they have to note down each expense in a notebook or in the envelope itself (usually, with the date, item[s] bought, and the cost). When their husbands' monetary needs exceed the sum they did not transfer to their wives, they can usually draw on the envelope or box; in this case, they just note down that this is for their personal expenses.

The money transferred to a wife through these mechanisms is said to be "general" (which may refers to the unity of the household); it is then "divided" by wives when it is spent or assigned to specific expenditures.

Men's and women's monies do not have the same status. In each case, part of a husband's spending escapes from his wife's control: husbands are not expected to transfer all their income to their wives. (In addition, wives hardly know how much their husbands earn, because there is no pay slip and informal incomes fluctuate.) Moreover, while household expenditure is noted down, husbands can withdraw money from the envelope without specifying its purpose: they only have to note that it is for their personal expenses. Yet wives do not have this privilege since their expenses are merged with the household's: all such expenses are made by women and none of the expenses in the notebook are made in their name. In addition, wives' household expenses are subject to their husbands' control: "If Luis wants to know what I spend, he just has to look at the notebook" (Adela). Thus, through the way it is spent, money expresses the respective position of husband and wife within the household (Guérin 2002; Zelizer 1994: chap. 6).

The domestic dimension of wives' money is reinforced by how spending responsibilities are allocated (Johnson 2004) and the gendered basis of saving. Even if women carry out (almost) all of the expenditures related to daily reproduction, spouses distinguish between husbands' and wives' responsibilities.[8] The former look after significant and irregular expenses, such as monthly fixed costs (rent, taxes, phone, gas, etc.) and buying building materials to improve the house. The latter are responsible for smaller but more regular expenditures, such as children's clothing and, above all, food.[9] Likewise, wives' savings and debts fill short-term gaps between income and expenditure. Husbands, for their part, are responsible for accumulating large quantities of recyclable materials (such as iron, zinc, copper, cardboard, plastic or glass bottles, etc.); these can be sold by weight in order to finance lifecycle events (e.g., marriages, funerals, birthdays, and *fiestas de quince*) or to protect households from loss of income and unpredicted increases in financial needs.

Women's participation in *trueque* can thus be considered a way of partially bypassing gender norms of financial management through how *créditos* are spent. Indeed, the *créditos* earned through *trueque* are not added to the envelope or boxes mentioned above. For this reason, wives do not give a public account of their expenses in *créditos*. (In addition, men do not usually understand the *crédito* economy because prices differ from those in the peso sphere.) Therefore, they enjoy a measure of freedom in how they spend their *créditos*, unlike pesos. However, this is only partial, since the gendered pattern of money use clearly identifies the *crédito* as feminine money. Indeed, *crédito* expenses are almost exclusively for the reproduction of domestic units, as the most traded items are food, used clothes, and, to a lesser extent, sewing materials (thread and zips), cleaning products, and small decorating items. In addition, expenses in *créditos* follow a weekly or daily timescale and each of them represents a very small amount of money[10], while masculine expenses are irregular and involve significant amounts of money.

A Degree of Social Differentiation

To some extent, women's participation in *trueque* allows them to free themselves from patriarchy. However, in many cases, it also reinforces social differentiation in the working class. Temporary suspension of gender and class identities does not mean that all participants take the same advantage from *trueque*: each of them participates on the basis of her own productive and commercial endowment. Yet, these resources are not equal. The most important are mobility in the city and access to pesos, since they allow some *trueque* participants to take advantage of the interface between monetary spheres (peso and *crédito*) at the expense of the poorest ones.

In order to understand this point, it is necessary to compare the prevailing price structures in each sphere. Table 12.1 highlights how relative prices vary greatly from one monetary sphere to the other. Two points must be underlined. First, implicit conversion rates between peso and *crédito* fluctuate from one commodity to another.[11] In other words, the relative prices of commodities depend on the unit of account in which transactions are denominated. Second, despite wide variations of *crédito*/peso ratios within the same group of commodities, the mean ratio is much higher for nonperishables (mainly food) than for products derived from subsidies in kind from social assistance, vegetables, and second-hand clothes. Yet, nonperishable foodstuffs must be imported from the peso sphere. There are multiple opportunities for gain when participants can take advantage of the interface between monetary spheres. Yet, this capacity is distributed highly unequally between *trueque* participants.

Three cases illustrate the pattern. The first shows that taking advantage from the interface between monetary spheres can be great for participants who enjoy comfortable peso incomes. It involves Eleonora, Angela (her daughter), and one of Eleonora's friends, Stefani. Stefani's access to pesos is chiefly due to her husband's income (he owns a small

Table 12.1: Comparative prices (crédito/peso): Rosario

Commodities	Créditos	Pesos	Crédito/Peso
Flour (kg)	3,500	1.30	2,692
Sugar (kg)	3,500	2.20	1,591
Salt (kg)	2,000	2.20	909
Soap (piece)	3,500	1.50	2,333
Tomato puree (carton)	3,500	2.00	1,750
Pasta (500 g)	3,500	1.50	2,333
Mean			**1,935**
Subsidies in kind			
Dry milk	8,000	>10	<800
Vegetables			
Tomatoes (kg)	2,500	4.00	625
Onion (kg)	2,000	1.10	1,818
Carrots (kg)	1,000	0.75	1,333
Pumpkin (kg)	2,000–2,500	5.00	400–500
Courgettes (piece)	1,000	1.00	1,000
Mean			**955**
Second-hand clothes			
Various	>1,000		

road-haulage business, has a car wash in a residential neighborhood, and sells part of his fishing catches from the Paraná River). Her daughter is an employee in a mutual insurance company. Stefani also has direct access to the peso thanks to various services she offers to elderly people in her neighborhood (e.g., taking them to the doctor or pharmacy, helping them with administrative tasks, etc.). Angela and Eleonora run distinctive small businesses ("micro-emprendimientos") for which there is a strong demand (chiropody and massage therapy in Eleonora's case; catering, depilation, and makeup services in Angela's). Their access to pesos is complemented by their husbands' income: Angela's spouse works as a truck driver while Eleonora's works in the construction industry.

Eleonora, Angela, and Stefani take advantage of the interface between the *crédito* and peso spheres by investing part of their peso incomes in *trueque*. They charter a small van with about ten neighbors to go to the *ferias*. They use the trip to get their supplies from a wholesaler. During the *feria*, they resell these commodities (mainly nonperishable foodstuffs). With the *créditos* obtained in this way, they buy fruit and vegetables for their own household consumption. The *crédito*/peso ratio of the commodities they sell is much higher than the normal ratio of the commodities they buy. This allows them to buy fruit and vegetables much cheaper than if they had bought them in pesos.

This approach to the *ferias* is not common: only a few people whose peso incomes are comfortable participate in *trueque*. The family formed by Celina, Jorge, and their son shows that it is possible to take advantage of *trueque* without enjoying comfortable peso incomes. The only access they have to pesos, outside *trueque*, is from Jorge selling cardboard picked from garbage. This activity generates very little money, however.[12] Two of their three children also have governmental scholarships, but they only cover part of their schooling costs (notebooks, photocopies, etc.). Most of the couple's income results from conversion between *créditos* and pesos, where Jorge's job in Celina's mother's small general store (*kiosko*) plays a key role. Jorge and Celina's mother jointly manage the *kiosko*, but income generated by sales of Jorge's commodities goes to him. Jorge's work in the *kiosko* dovetails with the couple's participation in Rosario's *ferias*. Apart from second-hand and new clothing (unsold items from the small clothing business that Célina's sister runs), they also offer perfume and aerosol sprays (deodorants, mosquito repellent, etc.) salvaged from the rubbish dump of the firm producing them. At the *trueque*, Celina is in charge of the clothes and seeks out all kinds of food (yogurt, pasta, rice, fruit, vegetables, canned food, various sauces, etc.). Her husband is in charge of what he describes as the "transformation" of aerosol sprays and perfume into food. In this way, peso and *crédito* are juggled through ongoing return trips between *trueque* and their *kiosko*. Incomes generated in this way (denominated in both pesos and *créditos*) are a result of multiple transactions of small amounts but a high commercial margin.

Multiple Small Profits Made at the Interface between Monetary Spheres

In November 2009, Jorge bought three soaps from a supermarket at 1.40 pesos each and then sold them at the *trueque* for 3,500 *créditos* apiece. With 3,000 of the 3,500 *créditos*, he bought three sponges (at 1,000 *créditos* each) and sold them for 2 pesos apiece in the *kiosko*. He explains: "From 1.40 pesos I get 6. And I still have 500 *créditos* left!" Then, thanks to the income generated by selling soap, Jorge bought some biscuits for 2,000 *créditos*. In the *kiosko*, he divided these biscuits between two boxes, selling them at 1.8 pesos apiece. With 1.50 of the 3.60 pesos he bought a bottle of vinegar, which he then sold for 4,000 *créditos* in the *trueque*. Finally, with the profit made through these transactions, he bought an aerosol with missing pieces for 3 pesos. With the pieces he collected, he repaired and sold the aerosol for 15 pesos in the *kiosko*, and so on and so forth. The family's access to pesos and *créditos* relies mainly on their ability to take advantage of price differences between monetary spheres.

However, the household formed by Andrea, Esteban (her partner), and her son shows that the poorest and less mobile of the *trueque* participants are not in a position to do this. They live in one of Rosario's poor neighborhoods; their house, which they built themselves, has only one room. Contrary to the previous example, the couple's peso and *crédito* income are independent of each other. The couple's access to pesos is limited. Esteban's only peso income comes from menial day labor (painting, repair work, etc.), which amounts to only a few hours a week. He is sometimes paid in pesos, sometimes in building materials (for his house extension), and at other times in second-hand clothing. Meanwhile, Andrea cleans the toilets at a factory next to her house for two hours each Saturday. The couple's main income in pesos comes from washing cars, which they do in front of their house (having "equipped" their garden for the job). However, income from this activity is highly irregular and relatively low (approximately 510 pesos per month). Andrea only brings second-hand clothes to one of the *ferias*, near her house; these are either no longer used by them or are donated by relatives. Some clothes come as part payment for Esteban's casual labor (*changa*). Using the *créditos* she earns from these sales, Andrea mostly acquires other second-hand clothes and second-hand domestic products (curtains, mosquito repellent, cheese graters, etc.). Due to the very low sale price of second-hand clothes in relation to other products (table 12.1), she can only occasionally and in restricted circumstances obtain groceries (potatoes, apples, oil, flour, milk, pasta, etc.). Therefore, the couple meet the majority of their food needs by juggling several sources of poverty relief aid. This comes from a neighborhood association (dry milk), the Rosario municipality (for *bolsón* [oil], maté, sugar, salt, pasta, rice, etc.), and from the church (canned tuna, canned meat, sugar, maté). These resources are critical as they are the only regular source of foodstuffs for the household. Even so, the couple's economic situation remains precarious, as shown by their chronic indebtedness.

The social differentiation resulting from unequal shares of the gains from commerce should not be thought to come from the variable ability of individuals to take advantage of interfaces between monetary spheres. Rather, this variability translates and reinforces the structural inequality within the working class of access to pesos and mobility in urban space. Those who take advantage of interfaces can do so only because other *trueque* participants have limited access to the peso and must use the *trueque* to turn payments in-kind from menial labor or poverty-relief aid into money.

This situation contrasts with another *trueque* system, located in Rosario's northern suburbs. This one is based on its own bills, also denominated in *créditos*, but not convertible with the *créditos* circulating in Rosario. To my knowledge, this is the only case where strict parity between peso and *crédito* has been maintained for each commodity. By doing so, *trueque* participants are put on an equal footing, because their gains do not rely on some groups ability to gain from the interface between monetary spheres, even though *trueque* participants are still highly diverse: they include small shopkeepers, women who run home-based sewing shops and other home-based services that are relatively well-remunerated in peso, small clothing sellers who get by thanks to microcredit programs, street vendors, as well as marginalized people relegated to daily casual work. In other words, in this case social inequalities prevailing outside the *trueque* are suspended during the *feria* through relatively equal access to the means of settlement in *créditos*. Yet, this singularity is due to the fact that *ferias* are not ruled by competition between participants: maintaining strict parity between the *crédito* and the peso and the way newly issued *créditos* are allocated translates monetarily into a broader political project, based on collective emancipation of the poor. This project is supported by an organization of local activists who insert the *trueque* into a broader set of militant activities (adult literacy workshops, tutoring, popular music bands [*murga*], microcredit, community radio, promotion of native languages in Amerindian slums, campaigns against domestic violence, etc.) (Saiag forthcoming: chap. 2).

Treating Money as a Common Good

The above analysis argues against simplistic views of money as an instrument either of oppression or domination. True, to some extent, women's use of the local currencies under study provides them with a degree of freedom from oppressing hierarchies based on gender: participation in the *ferias* goes hand in hand with suspension of gender and class identities and *crédito* income allows them to bypass the prevailing normative models of household financial management that deny women the legitimacy to generate their own income and confine them to domestic space.

However, this emancipation from oppressive gender norms is limited by the inertia of the gendered social relationships incorporated in household financial organization and participation in *trueque* can lead to increasing inequality between women, if it is not embedded in a larger political project of collective emancipation.

This dynamic might be better understood if we take Hart's (2007) view that "money is both personal and impersonal." On the one hand, money is personal and intimate as it marks interpersonal relationships within households: in this case, it is about domination, but also protection, if a household is considered as a unit that would protect itself against the dangers of highly irregular incomes, based on patriarchal norms. On the other hand, money stops being personal when it leaves the realm of households and enters the *feria*: in this case, it mediates highly impersonal relationships, characterized by the principle of commutability between individuals and by immediate settlement of debts, which does not allow bilateral relations to be perpetuated over time. Yet, as Hart argues, money cannot be reduced to either side of the personal/impersonal dichotomy; rather, it consists of a dialectical relationship between them. This is how the *crédito*'s contribution to women's emancipation should be understood: it allows women to bypass some of the prevailing patriarchal norms related to household financial management because it opens up to them the world of impersonal exchange where patriarchal norms do not govern; but, at the same time, it remains embedded in household personal relationships, which reaffirm gender hierarchies.

Because of these limitations, we should pay closer attention to the possible transformations of money's infrastructure. Specific attention should be devoted to providing access to money beyond people's participation in market transactions, since market principles (i.e., commutability and competition between individuals) often reproduce inequality. Yet if money (credit in the form of pay) is considered to be the ultimate form of social recognition within an economic order (Théret 1998), any guarantee for each man and woman to have access to and use of money on an equal footing means struggling against inequality based on class and gender.

One method for achieving this end is to promote different ways for people to relate beyond relying exclusively on market transactions. Jean-Michel Servet (2014) and Camille Meyer (2012), extending Elinor Ostrom's perspective,[13] suggest that money should be treated as a common good. At the most abstract level, this means ensuring each person's access to and use of money according to their recognized needs. This approach raises political, social, and economic issues and it requires us to tackle three of them simultaneously. The first is to disclose and challenge the gender hierarchy implicit in normative models of budgetary management. This would denaturalize gendered uses of money. The second is to recognize the legitimate needs of those who are still marginal to it. This means acknowledging women's right to generate income and to spend it in their own name. Those who have been excluded from protected employment should have access to money beyond their subsistence needs, to have a social life with some dignity. This should include financing lifecycle events and having access to money to protect themselves when domestic budgets are destabilized.

Finally, treating money as a common good implies establishing monetary institutions based on sharing. Yet sharing must be based on collective entities that can ensure effective access to money according to each person's needs (Servet 2014). Admittedly, institutions of this kind already exist between working class neighbors. For instance, bingo is often organized to finance specific events for people in a precarious situation, such as healthcare needs, travel for funerals, visiting vulnerable parents, or school trips organized by primary and secondary schools.[14] These events are usually organized by local associations (*vecinal*), churches, and political parties. They can also take a less formal shape when organized among neighbors. School parents' associations, known as *cooperadora*, can also organize such events; parents pay a small fee every month, managed by elected representatives, in order to contribute to school infrastructure or to pay for expenses related to study trips. However, as they rely above all on neighborhood solidarity, they fail to connect people to wider economic processes. Nor do they specifically confront gender issues. Treating money as a common good should therefore also be instituted at other levels. At the national or supranational level, this implies a fiscal system transferring income from the richest to the poorest, a set of measures controlling the remuneration of labor (minimum and maximum income, etc.), and social protection systems with women's emancipation as a goal. Microfinance services adapted to the needs of women and the poorest would help, through revival of organizations based on mutuality or through monetary systems not based on market principles. It is important to make visible existing sharing mechanisms that explicitly tackle gender issues and to invent new ones. More democratic approaches to managing money could reverse gender inequality (Singh, this volume).

Hadrien Saiag is permanent research fellow (chargé de recherche) in economic anthropology at the CNRS, in Paris (research unit IIAC-LAIOS). His research focuses on working-class monetary practices in Argentina and, more recently, on the incorporation of the Argentinian subproletariat into consumption credit. He is the author of *Monnaies locales et economies populaires en Argentine* (2016) and several articles published in the *Revue Française de Socio-Economie* and *Economy and Society*, among others.

NOTES

A previous version of this work was published in Saiag (2015).
1. Rosario, located on the Parana River about 400 km northeast of Buenos Aires, is the third largest city in Argentina with almost 1.2 million inhabitants in 2010.
2. Evelyn Arach, "La postal que resurge con la crisis," *Rosario 12*, 8 July 2009.
3. In this I follow the lead of Jean-Michel Servet.
4. Names have been changed in order to preserve interviewees' anonymity.
5. Wives' expenses are supposedly in the name of the household (see the next section).
6. Indeed, men's and women's incomes do not usually have the same temporality. Men are either paid daily (contingent labor), weekly, semimonthly, or monthly, while women's daily income must be evaluated by a complex calculation of cost.
7. Only one interviewee was in this situation while she lived with her concubine.
8. Women's expenditures use either money from their husband or, when necessary, from income they generated themselves. Men's expenditures draw exclusively on money transferred by the husband.
9. This gender differentiation of spending responsibilities is firmly fixed in people's practices. For instance, grandmothers who benefit from retirement pensions are usually expected to contribute to daily food expenses, while the monthly rhythm of their income fits perfectly with their being exempt from paying fixed costs.
10. *Crédito* bills have very low denominations: during my fieldwork, the highest denomination bill was 500 *créditos*, between 0.25 and 0.50 pesos, while a bus ticket cost 1.75 pesos.
11. Implicit conversion rates are obtained by dividing the price of a commodity denominated in *créditos* by the price of the same commodity in pesos.
12. Cardboard is sold for $0.30/kg.
13. Servet (2014) emphasizes Ostrom's (2005) idea that the use and the production of the commons are characterized by a democratic relationship between stakeholders and by the concern for social and environmental sustainability. He adds that determining one person's access to the commons implies taking into consideration its recognized needs.

14. Money is not the only object treated as a common good within popular neighborhoods. *Vecinales*, for instance, often provide a room for funerals, birthdays, and key life-cycle events at very reasonable cost. Local churches and political parties may practice something similar. Solidarity among neighbors is also important when it comes to rebuilding houses destroyed by fire or bad weather.

REFERENCES

Absi, P. 2007. "Il ne faut pas mélanger les fortunes: travail, genre et revenus chez les commerçantes de Bolivie." In V. Hernandez et al. (eds.), *Turbulences monétaires et sociales: l'Amérique Latine dans une perspective comparée*. Paris: L'Harmattan, pp. 355–393.

Bogani, E., and J. Parysow. 2005. "Perspectivas de desarrollo económico y social para las mujeres pobres y empobrecidas en los Clubes del Trueque. Estudio de caso: 'La Bernalesa.'" In F. Mallimaci and A. Salvia (eds.), *Los nuevos rostros de la marginalidad*. Buenos-Aires: Biblios, pp. 151–173.

Carsten, J. 1989. "Cooking money: Gender and the symbolic transformation of means of exchange in a Malay fishing community." In J. P. Parry and M. Bloch (eds.), *Money & the Morality of Exchange*. Cambridge: Cambridge University Press, pp. 117–141.

Damill, M., R. Frenkel, and R. Maurizio. 2011. "Macroeconomic policy for full and productive employment and decent work for all: An analysis of the Argentine experience." Paper presented at Pro-employment macroeconomic frameworks, sectoral strategies for employment creation and the informal economy. Geneva: International Labour Organization.

Drelon, S. 2009. "Le club de troc de Roca Negra, une expérience particulière du troc en Argentine. Etude des modes de production et de circulation des biens et leur impact sur les rapports de valeur et d'échange." PhD dissertation, Université Paris Descartes, Paris.

Gomez, G., and A. Helmsing. 2008. "Selective spatial closure and local economic development: What do we learn from the Argentine local currency systems?" *World Development* 36(11): 2489–2511.

González Bombal, I. 2002. "Sociabilidad en clases medias en descenso: Experiencias en el trueque." In L. Beccaria et al. (eds.), *Sociedad y sociabilidad en la Argentina de los 90*. Buenos Aires: Biblios.

Guérin, I. 2002. "Le sexe de la monnaie." *Journal des Anthropologues* 90–91: 213–230.

———. 2008. "L'argent des femmes pauvres: Entre survie quotidienne, obligations familiales et normes sociales." *Revue Française de Socio-Économie* 2: 59–78.

Hart, K. 2007. "Money is always personal and impersonal." *Anthropology Today* 23(5): 12–16.

Johnson, S. 2004. "Gender norms in financial markets: Evidence from Kenya." *World Development* 32(8): 1355–1374.

La Pradelle, M. de. 2006. *Market-day in Provence*. Chicago, IL, and London: University of Chicago Press.

Leoni, F. 2003. "Ilusión para muchos, alternativa para pocos. La práctica del trueque en los sectores populares." Bachelor thesis in Social Policy, Universidad Nacional de General Sarmiento, Buenos Aires, Argentina.

Meyer, C. 2012. "Les finances solidaires comme biens communs durables : étude de ca sde la Banque communautaire de développement Palmas (Brésil)." MA thesis, Université Libre de Bruxelles, Belgium.

Orzi, R. (ed.) 2012. *La moneda social como lazo social*. Buenos Aires: Ciccus.

Ostrom, E. 2005. *Understanding Institutional Diversity*. Princeton, NJ: Princeton University Press.

Ould-Ahmed, P. 2010. "Can a community currency be independent of the state currency? A case study of the credito in Argentina (1995–2008)." *Environment and Planning* 42(6): 1346–64.

Parry, J., and M. Bloch. (eds.) 1989. *Money and the Morality of Exchange*. Cambridge: Cambridge University Press.

Pereyra, F. 2007. "Exploring gender divisions in a community currency scheme: The case of the barter network in Argentina." *International Journal of Community Currency Research* 11: 98–111.

Rofman, R., and L. Lucchetti. 2006. "Pension systems in Latin America: Concepts and measurements of coverage social protection discussion." Social Protection Discussion Paper. Washington, DC: World Bank.

Saiag, H. 2013. "Le *trueque* Argentin ou la question du fédéralisme monétaire (1995–2002)." *Revue Française de Socio-Économie* 12: 69–89.

———. 2015. "Une libération impossible? Marché, genre et monnaie dans le *trueque* argentin." In J.-M. Servet and I. Hillenkamp (ed.), *Comprendre autrement le marché. Marchés réels et marché fantasmé*. Paris: Classiques Garnier, pp. 145–169.

———. Forthcoming. *Monnaies locales et économie populaire en Argentine*. Paris: Karthala (Coll. Recherches Internationales).

Servet, J.-M. 2009. "Toward an alternative economy: Reconsidering the market, money and value." In C. Hann and K. Hart (eds.), *Market and Society: The Great Transformation Today*. Cambridge: Cambridge University Press, pp. 5–90.

———. 2014. "De nouvelles formes de partage: La solidarité au delà de l'économie collaborative." *Publications de l'Institut Veblen*, Paris. Available at http://www.veblen-institute.org/De-nouvelles-formes-de-partage-la (accessed 7 July 2014).

Sosa, R. 2007. "El oncepto de trabajo en un cambio de época. Un estudio sobre la restauracion contemporanea del capital y los impactos objectivos y subjectifos en el mndo del trabajo en Argentina (1976–2006)." PhD dissertation, Universidad Nacional de Rosario, Rosario, Argentina.

Théret, B. 1998. "La dulité des dettes et de la monnaie dans les sociétés salariales." In M. Aglietta and A. Orléan (eds.), *La monnaie souveraine*. Paris: Odile Jacob, pp. 253–287.

Zelizer, V. 1994. *The Social Meaning of Money*. New York: Basic Books.

CHAPTER 13

An Imaginary Currency: The Haitian Dollar

FEDERICO NEIBURG

I examine here a singular feature of the Haitian monetary universe: the generalized use of a currency, the Haitian dollar, without any material existence, past or present, as a coin or banknote. In most transactions in Haiti (price negotiations in markets, working out wages and contracts), calculations are made in Haitian dollars, while payments are made in other currencies, principally in gourdes (HTG, the national currency), but also in US dollars, Dominican pesos, telephone cards, and other forms, such as the pieces of plastic or metal that smooth the flow of various commercial circuits of basic goods among the poorest people, like water and coal.

The rate of conversion between the Haitian dollar and the gourde is 1 Haitian dollar to 5 gourdes. After haggling over a bag of mangoes in a street market, for example, the buyer and seller may agree on a price of 3 Haitian dollars: the buyer pays with a 50 gourde note (10 Haitian dollars), the seller keeps 3 dollars for the mangoes (15 gourdes), and gives 7 Haitian dollars in change (35 gourdes, in three notes of 10 and one coin of 5). Or another example: a supermarket bill comes to 234 Haitian dollars (HD). The buyer pays with 1,500 gourdes (300 Haitian dollars); the cashier says, "here's your change: 66 dollars," and gives the buyer 330 gourdes, keeping the 234 Haitian dollars for the purchase.

All travel tips for foreigners (in tourist guidebooks or websites aimed at expats) warn about this "bizarre" way of undertaking transactions. The Haitian government, with the support of public intellectuals, has tried many times to ban use of the Haitian dollar, condemning it as just another sign of the country's barbarity or backwardness.[1] Nevertheless, people continue to calculate in Haitian dollars while they exchange other currencies.

Many dollars circulate in the monetary space of the contemporary Caribbean, including the US dollar, the Jamaican dollar, the Belize dollar, and the East Caribbean dollar—issued by the islands forming a Common Market, like Bermuda, Dominica, and Grenada. From the viewpoint of standard monetary theories, all of these are "normal" currencies: they serve as a unit of account, means of payment, medium of exchange, and store of wealth. They are identified by a symbol (USD, JMD, XCD, etc.) and exist in a physical form, minted and available to be handled. The Haitian dollar also has a symbol (HD), but unlike the other Caribbean dollars, it is an imaginary money, a pure unit of account. Although basically an oral and conceptual phenomenon, the Haitian dollar is also written and objectified in supermarket receipts, restaurant menus, gas station price signs, contracts for international cooperation projects, notebooks recording debts and credits for bets or lotteries, and at banks, where we can find conversion tables like this: 1 USD : 8 HD : 40 HTG.[2]

One of my main aims, then, is to examine the entanglements (rather than oppositions) between materiality and immateriality, the reality and the conceptualization of the Haitian dollar. As we know, this tension traverses the social history of money. On the one hand, we have the materiality of metals (like gold) and other objects that serve as "ballast," the objectivity of the coins and banknotes themselves, and the strength of the states responsible for their stability and trustworthiness. On the other hand, there are symbols and conventions—in the contemporary world, as we know, it has become increasingly common to contrast real currencies (and economies) with fictional currencies (and economies), identified through numbers, indices, financial assets, Bitcoins, and other digital currencies.[3]

Historians and anthropologists have shown that this extreme monetary pluralism is truly widespread, present in everyday monetary transactions around the world (Introduction, this volume). There is nothing exceptional or abnormal in this fact. Convergence between money and sovereignty in the national currencies that perform money's four functions (unit of account, means of payment, medium of exchange, and store of wealth) is situated more at the level of normative ideas than of empirical reality. In the everyday world of transactions, we encounter multiple monies, currencies that perform just some functions, yet are deeply embedded in social life, enabling and facilitating calculation and exchange (with other currencies and with physical and intangible objects), shaping economic spaces, establishing hierarchies of scale and value. Deductive analyses drawn from theoretical definitions of money then have to be replaced by inductive empirical accounts that emphasize multiple monetary practices (Guyer, this volume), the diverse social meanings of currencies, and the historical processes underlying the creation and disappearance of some and the persistence of others, thereby throwing into question the difference between soft and hard currencies and between material and fictitious monies.

The expression "imaginary money" was first proposed by Luigi Einaudi (1953 [1936]) in his exploration of how people dealt with the instability and extreme plurality that accompanied the creation of new nation-states in Europe before the unification and standardization of systems of weights, measures, and currencies.[4] Marc Bloch contributed decisively to our understanding of the multiplicity and articulation of units of account and means of payment in premodern Europe, anticipating contemporary debates that emphasize the calculative dimension of money, its social existence as a calculative device or instrument of commensuration (see, for example, Amato, Doria, and Fantacci 2010; Callon and Muniesa 2005; Maurer 2006). Analyzing why currencies are born, transformed, and vanish, Bloch (1954: 48–49) proposed replacing a priori theoretical definitions of money, "every intention to establish a set of functional criteria that would qualify (once and for all) all currencies," with a "minimalist and pragmatic definition which recognizes that, above all else, currencies (physical and fictitious) are measuring instruments."

Two complementary approaches have lately examined currencies that, like the Haitian dollar, serve as pure units of account. Akinobu Kuroda (2008a, 2008b) shows how the four classical functions of money may appear to become detached and pure units of account possess an integrating function, enabling conversions between means of payment and stores of wealth. Jane Guyer (1995), setting out from a similar premise in order to observe "the currencies of people" (2004, 2011), provides a historical ethnography of monetary practices in West Africa, situating pure units of account within a "monetary interface." For Guyer, fictional or imaginary currencies are entangled with boundaries and thresholds between scales of value; they also "mediate both the memorization of non-reductive transactions and their nature as conversions" (2011: 2016).[5]

Rather than attribute the Haitian dollar's existence to "Haitian-ness," however singular a feature of the country it may be, my interest is in observing ethnographically its uses now and over time.[6] Through this historical pragmatics I wish to show how the Haitian dollar forms part of an extremely diversified, dynamic, and creative space bringing together units of measure and means of payment, currencies, and calculation, all of which modulate the daily economic life of the majority of Haiti's population—particularly in urban slum areas like the Greater Bel Air region, in the center of Port-au-Prince, where I have carried out fieldwork since 2007 and where people literally have almost no money and are extremely concerned about it at the same time. Following Sidney Mintz (1961), I also show how this space of currencies and calculations possesses a historical dimension, constituted by a multiplicity of superimposed chronologies that are ever-present in daily transactions. This historical pragmatics of the Haitian dollar reveals how monetary cultures are deeply embedded in social relationships and in historical formations and how calculative devices (as monies of account) are also deeply relationally productive, providing unique insights into the understanding of everyday socialities through their web of equivalences and conversions. The uses of Haitian imaginary monies, singularly intense in urban slums such as Bel Air, located at the very margins of the global capitalist system, have integrative effects, by providing the texture of an interface across different circuits of various physical currencies. This also reveals an aspect of the human economy (Introduction, this volume) as the entanglement of different spheres and scales of human experience: the global sphere and the local, the impersonal and personal spheres of human experience. Along similar lines, Haitian imaginary money shows a unique entanglement between universality and singularity in "the social life of money" (Dodd 2014).

Links, Detachment, and the Scale of Five

Units of measure are cognitive sociotechnical artifacts that express relations of equivalence, difference, order, hierarchy, and scale. Generalization of the use of a single unit of account or the formation of a determined monetary culture reflect complex historical processes that resist teleological or causal explanation. Links and detachment between units of account and means of payment can be traced showing how the material and immaterial, imagination and reality, concepts and things all combine to inform a preference for the Haitian dollar and the use of the scale of five to fix prices and calculate transactions.[7]

Hans Van Werveke (1934) stated that behind every "fictional currency" there always lies "a link with some kind of real means of payment." In the case of the Haitian dollar, this link is the five gourde banknote, first issued in 1920 with the following inscription (in French): "This note is payable to the bearer in legal money of the United States at the rate of five gourdes to one dollar." The note was part of the monetary reform launched after the start of the US occupation of Haiti (1915–1934), when the new central bank (formally controlled by City Bank based in New York) established a fixed parity system (or currency board) for making conversions between the US dollar and the gourde at a rate of 1:5.[8]

In his compelling studies of Haitian markets, measures, and transactions, conducted between 1958 and 1961, Mintz does not mention the Haitian dollar.[9] Michel Laguerre (1983), on the basis of research undertaken in Bel Air in 1974–1976, likewise never speaks of the currency, even when describing credit systems and lotteries, both of which are today calculated in Haitian dollars. An early 1970s tourist guidebook in English only mentions the gourde and its parity with the US dollar, whereas today, as mentioned earlier, any such publication would forewarn visitors of the complexities of Haitian monetary transactions.

Calculating in the Haitian dollar seems to have slowly become more general, triggered by the end of a fixed parity exchange rate between the gourde and the US dollar in 1979 (sixty years after its implementation), during the dollar crisis and ensuing economic turmoil, which caused the currency to fluctuate, thereby opening up markets to foreign goods, fueling a rural exodus, and massively increasing the number of Haitian migrants to the United States. At the same time that the unit of account lost its primary material connection (the five gourde banknote convertible to one American dollar), other material attachments were created, reinforcing calculations in the scale of five and the use of Haitian dollars. Just after fixed parity ended the central bank issued gourdes on a scale of five: first a 5 coin was created, then 10, 25, 50, 100, 250, 500 denominations, and later 1,000 notes, were issued. The means of payment (the gourde) thereby became a "support" (Weber 2009) for a long-term cultural disposition to make calculations in imaginary monies on a scale of five.[10]

The scale of five has a long history in Haiti's monetary "space of calculability" (Mitchell 2002) that precedes the gourde/US dollar exchange rate when it was first introduced. It is an older colonial legacy, not American but French. The first gourde banknotes circulated in 1813, nine years after the country's independence from France. The incipient national currency joined the Caribbean's very diverse monetary universe, coexisting with currencies of old and new empires, coins minted in the islands and those issued by private companies (such as the Dutch East India Company). In this universe, governed by commerce and crisscrossed by trade routes, Haiti's national currency gained in 1872 a special relationship with the French franc, the currency of the former metropolis, based on a fixed parity system of five gourdes to one franc.[11] In contrast to foreigners who need time (and often calculators) to multiply and divide, Haitians have internalized the scale of five. As Guyer would say (2011: 2018), it has acquired a mnemonic function, serving as a cognitive benchmark. For those who calculate in Haitian dollars, there is a natural and immediate relationship between unit of account and means of payment: they are "indexed" (Peirce 1932 [1897]), so that 5 is 1, 10 is 2, 15 is 3, and so on.

Undisciplined Spaces

In contrast to Witold Kula's (1986) classic demonstration in the case of modern France, the sociotechnical history of measures is not always about the unification and standardization of state systems of measure (including monetary unification). In many places, both today and throughout history, measures resist standardization, people's practices and conceptualizations seem to confront states, and monies and other measures proliferate. Sidney Mintz (1961) brilliantly showed how this proliferation has been constitutive of the formation of Haitian society.[12]

The passage of time since Mintz did his fieldwork in Haiti only seems to have strengthened this entanglement between a proliferation of monies and measures and Haitian markets and sociability, fueled by three processes: urbanization, transnationalism, and the routinization of emergency regimes.

Today the country is predominantly urban: 60 percent of its inhabitants live in cities, whereas in 1950 the figure was below 30 percent. In 1960 Port-au-Prince had 300,000 inhabitants; today more than two million people live there. Most inhabitants of the metropolitan zone come from elsewhere, a movement that intensified in the 1970s and continues today, stimulated by land shortage and a rural economic crisis caused by soil erosion and competition with cheap imports. As people moved to the cities in huge numbers, there was an increasing exodus from Haiti. Today around ten million people live in the country itself, while more than three million Haitians live abroad, mainly in North America.[13] According to some estimates, money and other objects sent from overseas are the top item in the country's GDP.[14] After the end of the Duvalier dictatorship in 1986, an "emergency regime" (Fassin and Pandolfi 2010) became endemic. Characterized by foreign military intervention (either by one country, a coalition of nations, or the UN) and the massive presence of international aid agencies (IAAs) and nongovernmental organizations (NGOs), these emergency regimes distribute services (like medical care), goods (like water and food), and small quantities of money through "development projects" that hire people on unstable short-term contracts.[15] Movement between the city and countryside and between Haiti and abroad, alongside the predominance of humanitarian agencies, drive the contemporary Haitian popular economy, based on small profits, small trade, and small monies, and on the pluriactivity of people.[16]

Bel Air is a privileged place to observe these transformations and mechanisms. It was the city's first black district—according to Laguerre (1983: 167), "one of the oldest black districts in the western hemisphere." By the late nineteenth century it had become a mixture of slums and homes for an incipient middle class of professionals, public employees, and factory workers—a rare occurrence in a social universe with few wages. It gradually turned into something like a complex of favelas, closely in tune with the political and economic life of the country, "swamped" by migrants, becoming stigmatized by violence, the absence of infrastructure and sanitation, and extreme poverty.[17] As in the city's other popular districts, most people survive by doing many different things, following the logic of small profits (*ti benefis*) obtained in small jobs (*ti travay*) and small trading (*ti biznis*). According to some estimates, less than 10 percent of Bel Air's population is employed in the formal labor market, 80 percent of people live on less than US$2.5 per day, and more than 50 percent on less than one US dollar a day.[18]

Located in the heart of the capital, Bel Air merges with the Croix de Bossales region, the epicenter of Haiti's market system, where the main wholesale market is located, the main link between the rural interior, the city of Port-au-Prince, and international trade circuits.[19] Croix de Bossales is next to the port and was originally a market and cemetery for slaves. Today the area covers more than 350,000 square meters and contains four "public markets" and dozens of streets that are totally or partially taken over by commerce that radiates out from Bel Air to every corner of the city.

The capillary nature of this network is reflected in the dynamics of the popular economy: progressive fractioning of products, multiplication of mediations, the amplified reproduction of small gains, and interplay between different units of measure and scales. At one end of the network, large sacks of coal are unloaded at the port or from big trucks arriving from the interior of the country or the Dominican Republic. At the other end, the traders sell small tins with a few lumps of coal that are used to cook lunch (in the poorest regions, coal and plastic from rubbish dumps are used as fuel for cooking). At one end, the import stores sell sacks of powdered detergent weighing twenty pounds or more, while at the other traders sell small bags the size of a marble. The same mechanism extends throughout chains in which products measured in one kind of unit are converted into others, multiplying transactions, distributing small profits, and undoubtedly increasing the final price of what is consumed by the poorest (who can typically only afford one *kob* or coin of detergent).[20] At one extreme, people calculate and pay in US dollars; at the other, they calculate in Haitian dollars and pay in gourdes.

The most recent foreign military intervention in the country (conducted by the United Nations Stabilization Mission in Haiti, MINUSTAH and launched in 2004) began in Bel Air. Even today the zone is classified by the UN as "red," meaning that for security reasons "under no circumstances may civil staff circulate in the area," including employees of UNDP and UNICEF. This has not prevented the UN from participating in "stabilization" and "development" projects through the mediation of local associations and NGOs, distributing resources and small quantities of money. After the January 2010 tragic earthquake, for example, the UN developed large-scale programs in the region such as "Cash for Work"—which paid individuals thirty Haitian dollars (150 gourdes, a little less than four US dollars) per working day, for periods of fifteen days, to remove the rubble left by the earthquake. This also distributed money to a large number of people (hence the fortnightly rotation).

In places like Bel Air, people have to remain pluriactive. Two expressions in creole reveal what pluriactivity means in Haiti's popular districts: *mwen gen plizyè chapò* and *mwen gen plizyè badj*. Someone with "many hats" may be dedicated to various activities simultaneously, or may receive payment from more than one source to perform the same activity. A privileged few may simultaneously participate in a development project financed by an NGO, work as a warehouse guard, participate in small-scale street trading, nurture close contact with a local government body, and so on. The second expression, "I have many badges," sheds light on the multifaceted relations between pluriactivity and the "humanitarian" universe. Badges, which function like ID cards, become part of the social games generating opportunities and small jobs. When worn on a person's chest, they have various meanings: they may signify a boss or a notable person with many resources (social capital and money), or show the "frustration" of someone who was once waged, employed, "a contender," or was trained but is now unemployed[21].

Managing a public water tap, a popular pharmacy, or cyber café, or refurbishing a space for arts and languages courses, workshops, or band rehearsals, or promoting neighborhood festivals—all generate an infinite range of small jobs and small business, in a universe formed by many kinds of collectives at street, sector, and district level, including youth and women's associations, associations of musicians and artists, and even associations of associations. Their names and acronyms (like the Rue

Saint Martin Civic Service Committee, CSCSM) may be seen on badges, in the minutes of association meetings, on posters in head offices, or sometimes as graffiti on their neighborhood walls. This affinity unites the logics of popular economy, local associations, and international cooperation in a specific place.

Associations linked to "humanitarianism," which receive official recognition from the government and cooperation agencies, distribute badges and form part of a much wider universe of groupings that help shape the social organization of Haiti's popular districts. The most general term for designating these groupings is *baz*, or base—a key social form connecting the popular economy with local government.

As we have shown elsewhere (Braum 2014; Neiburg 2017), the base is a location and area of action, a crowd that protects, ensures somewhere to sleep, a plate of food, help in need, and provides the chance for a small job and small monies. Bases bring people together, equalizing and hierarchizing them, creating belongings and animosities, leaders and followers in an unstable dynamic. Bases are segmentary formations that exist in different contexts and at different scales, allowing multiple belongings in tune with the needs of small jobs, which in turn produce and reproduce the bases, serving as channels for the circulation of money. They could involve development work, the promotion of cultural events (especially musical, such as performances by *rara* bands and *band a pye*), illegal trading, armed actions linked to politics, small or large crimes (ranging from theft to kidnapping), and the control—especially near the markets—of rates and flows of money and goods.

In this universe of small jobs, small trading, and small profits, oscillating to the rhythm of the money supply and the opening and closure of one or other channel of intermediation, people cultivate an acute sense of opportunity, while doing—or trying to do—various things simultaneously.

Trading, small jobs, and illegal activities, for their part, are inserted in money flows sustained by credit.[22] Without credit, generating the capital needed for small commerce or small arms is impossible. Sources of credit include loan and payment deferrals given to traders (ranging from big wholesalers to small shopkeepers) and a myriad of credit associations—an endless variety of formats in which the number of people involved, the timescale for repayment, the amount lent, and the interest rates all vary. All, though, tend to converge on the figure of a manager whose bookkeeping is recorded in Haitian dollars.

These financial microcircuits also include pawnshops (which temporarily exchange goods for money) and betting on the lottery, which in many senses also functions as a mechanism for savings and capital formation.²³ Thus, for example, a neighbor from Bel Air spends between 6 and 8 Haitian dollars (30 and 40 gourdes) every day on the lottery, about a third of what she makes from selling juice in the street (around 30 Haitian dollars or 150 gourdes). Each morning she, her two daughters, and a woman friend who lives with them discuss which numbers to choose for the day's bets. At night they discuss why they failed to win anything or, rarely, how to spend their winnings. They always conceive their bets and speak about their success or failure in Haitian dollars.

The imaginary currency can also organize "earmarking" (Zelizer 1998): Madame K. sells food in a busy area of the Portail Saint Josef region, between a corridor linking the interior of the *gueto* with the zone's main road. Her customers can purchase a fried banana at prices varying between one gourde and one Haitian dollar. Madame K. keeps the money she receives in three separate places. Money worth over one Haitian dollar is placed in the first, which is used to buy the raw ingredients for the next day, while the second is her house money (*lajan lakay*). In the third place she stores money worth less than one Haitian dollar, the small money (*ti kob*) that at the end of a working day is used to buy food and water for the next day.²⁴

Relations with numbers, monies, and business also involve questions that relate to politics and magic. At this level even the images printed on the banknotes could become relevant. Some notes are felt to be more positive or favorable to the business, others more dangerous. Some people might declare their preference for the Haitian dollar and disdain the gourde, since for decades gourde banknotes bore images of the Duvaliers – reflecting a mixture of militancy and fear provoked by the still powerful faces of money (Strassler 2009), even if they are not on the notes anymore (Papa Doc and Baby Doc were banned from appearing on the gourde notes after the end of their dictatorship). In this universe of loans and savings, trading, magic, and politics, involving the physical handling of some currencies and the imagining of others, subjects are formed who become enthusiastic experts in numbers – specialists in units of measure and, we could say, in those "games of scales" implied by accounting and conversions.

The Geography of Monies and Calculation

Some years ago, the country's president, René Préval, complained on public radio about his low pay packet, lamenting the fact that he received just 12,000 dollars a month. He was clearly talking about Haitian dollars, then equivalent to about US$1,500. But the Haitian dollar is not used in all transactions or in all calculations. By mapping uses of the different units of measure and means of payment, we can trace the geography of monetary spaces and of spaces of calculation, composed of currencies, measuring instruments, spheres of exchange, units of measures, and scales. As Guyer (2004) has suggested, their interplay and entanglements constitute and reveal social hierarchies and inequalities: not all subjects exchange and calculate with the same units and scales, nor do they all subjects have the same capacity to use one currency or to exchange some currencies for others.

In Port-au-Prince, as elsewhere, these hierarchies and inequalities are projected onto the territory: in the urban islands of foreigners scattered across various regions of the city, the US dollar predominates as a unit of account and means of payment in sectors such as the housing market, as well as in restaurants, hotels, night clubs, and supermarkets (which used to double as currency exchange bureaus) that cater to upper-class Haitians and the legion of expats, relief workers, and consultants. As we move down the social scale, the US dollar begins to be used as a means of payment for transactions calculated in Haitian dollars. Lower down—where the majority of transactions are to be found—people calculate in Haitian dollars and pay in gourdes. And lower down still, among the thousands who literally have no money and perform transactions involving less than one Haitian dollar, people use gourdes, *kobs* (gourde cents), *gouden* (half a gourde), or *penis* (equivalent to five *kobs*). The latter may also be physically represented by US cents. These are not hard to find on the streets, even though the US one cent coin is actually equivalent to almost 50 *kobs*. Imagination of monetary scales is not bound to the nominal value of the money being exchanged.

There are also situations in which people pay with US dollars but calculate in Haitian dollars. In small international trade—involving female sellers who travel to Miami and Panama, for example—people handle US dollars and buy in the foreign currency. On their return to Port-au-Prince, though, the money invested in purchasing goods and the price fixed on the market are calculated in Haitian dollars. The development officers, "facilitators," drivers, translators, and other specialists linked to the NGOs and AAIs negotiate their contracts in US dollars, but frequently refer to their wages in Haitian dollars during conversations with friends or relatives.

I observed negotiations with moneychangers expressed and calculated in dollars (Haitian and American).[25] Sometimes people used calculators to convert and divide by eight. When negotiating with foreigners, the moneychangers count in gourdes, but when the exchange is between Haitians, people calculate in Haitian dollars. In a transaction involving 50 US dollars, for example, a foreigner would calculate the receipt of twenty 100 gourde banknotes as 2,000 gourdes, while a Haitian would calculate the value as 400 Haitian dollars, or simply 400 *dolà*. The adjective Haitian (*aysien*), as in *dolà aysien*, is only used when one of the participants in a transaction is foreign. Among Haitians, when people say *dolà* they always mean *dolà aysien*.

The *dolà aysien* seems to be more present in urban than rural settings, probably due to the more intense presence of currency plurality. Likewise, the *dolà aysien* is more present in the Haitian territorial space than in the diaspora, where hard currencies predominate. But these are not absolute distinctions, and since the Haitian national space is a single social space due to the intense circulation of persons, things, and currencies, the Haitian dollar does not disappear in these settings (rural or diaspora); it continues to be present in certain contexts and conversions, as when people from outside call to their relatives to speak about money and remittances.

The unit of account is used between Haitians, in the markets and small jobs, remittances, and lotteries, in the heart of the popular economy, where people speak in creole and calculate in *dolà*. In some contexts, people differentiate between foreign money (*lajan blan* or *lajan diaspora*) and national money (*lajan kreyòl*). In fact, the Haitian dollar could be said to be a "creole currency," in the sense of being "of the country," born locally, and engaged in struggles of appropriation and autonomy, as with so many other objects and habits to which Haitians attach the adjective *kreyòl*.

Conclusion

In 2007, the government banned use of the Haitian dollar and made it compulsory to set prices in gourdes, forbidding the display of HD prices in supermarkets and gas stations, for example. As I observed at the outset, intellectuals supported the measure, condemning the imaginary currency as just another sign of the country's backwardness, a display of the state's weakness or failure, and proof of its inability to maintain a true currency.

One newspaper article argued that the government's measure had the merit "of inviting a less schizophrenic approach to the calculations in which our compatriots are engaged in every day . . . forever attached to their arithmetical gymnastics." With the condescension typical of social elites who claim to comprehend while simultaneously disparaging the "pathetic practices of the population," the author condemned "this dexterity of our vendors, workers and other scarcely literate economic agents ... who reproduce the automatism of the older generation." She ended by encouraging young people to "practice the gourde" (Manigat 2007: 3).

Even though these attempts to modernize the country's monetary culture failed—since people continue to calculate in Haitian dollars while they exchange other currencies—other preferences may indeed be emerging: some young people use the Haitian dollar but condemn the imaginary currency for being linked to "old people." In fact, as we have seen, teleology has no place in the history of monies and calculation.

Once conventional premises concerning the normality or sickness of currencies are stripped away,[26] the social productivity of imaginary currencies—previously invisible in analyses of the Haitian economy and its markets—become clear to see and explore.

Relations between the different functions of money are embedded in social interactions and their history, modeling ways of conceptualizing and practicing transactions. Indeed stabilization or unification policies are always in dialogue with monetary cultures created over generations and with the concrete economic conditions that, in cases like Haiti, are intrinsically connected to plural, not unified systems of measures and currencies.

Maybe that is why until now (with some exceptions cited in this article) sociologists and anthropologists have given such scant attention to the social and cultural meaning of pure monies of account. From the perspective of monetary theory and policy, a pure unit of account is no more than a passing curiosity or just another symptom of a weak state, unable to govern its systems of measure and its national currency. I have tried here to show how a system of multiple currencies has an "elective affinity" (in Max Weber's sense) with how people live in an environment of extreme monetary scarcity. The Haitian dollar, as a central element in the country's contemporary monetary universe and forms of calculation, offers a pathway to understanding the dynamics of Haiti's popular economy and its history.

Haitian imaginary money allows us to address the reality of money in terms other than the binaries that normally characterize prevailing conceptualizations of money. We are then able, not to choose only one or another monetary form and condemn the rest, but to integrate them within a more holistic and humanistic perspective. Money's ability to synthesize personal and impersonal relations[27] and to produce those relations,[28] is entailed in its multiple, real and fictional existence as monies. Combining small scale activities with a transnational reach, Haiti's monetary space reveals at once the contours of a larger universe along with people's realization and imagination of several currencies, plural socialities, and their own human lives.

As we have seen, this monetary space (which includes both material and imaginary monies) is extremely local and at the same time intensely transnational, integrated with global flows of currencies, people, and commodities, fueled by a singular entanglement of commerce, humanitarianism, and remittances. With its unique blend of noun and adjective, reality and fiction, the Haitian dollar also tells us something about the relationship between money, national currencies, and the public imagination. The Haitian dollar has been transformed into a pure unit of account from a five gourdes banknote convertible to one US dollar at the beginning of the last century that incorporated a scale of five taken from the French colonial period. Perhaps this should be seen as a sort of national affirmation. Like all forms of national affirmation, this is ambivalent: the Haitian dollar associates Haitian identity with the negative, exotic and backward; yet it also produces a distinctive social ambience, connects people in their everyday lives, and synthesizes collective history through a combination of many relations and transactions, monetary forms, and a commons of shared language.

All attempts to extinguish the Haitian dollar have failed so far, as have numerous projects to contain street trading and "formalize" the economy. The streets continue to be filled with crowds selling, buying, and consuming, even late into the night , relying on candles and kerosene lamps in the absence of electricity. For this swarming multitude—which appears to outsiders to be as chaotic as the monetary transactions themselves— theft and violence are as rare as police and soldiers. Rather, a legion of well-known local leaders and networks connect sellers, commercial circuits, and territorial spaces. For local people, these streets and markets are orderly places where they can practice the arts of trading, chatting, and sometimes singing and dancing, live with their families, make friends and lovers, find food and water, imagine individual and shared futures, while they cultivate numeric habits and exchange monies, even imaginary ones. This is a way, to echo the introduction to this volume, for human beings "feel at home" in their world and the world at large.

Acknowledgments

With minor modifications, this chapter started out as a Sidney Mintz Lecture, delivered at Johns Hopkins University in 2010. A version close to this one was published in *Hau: Journal of Ethnographic Theory* (Neiburg 2016). My thanks go especially to the late Sidney Mintz, for his comments and always powerful and inspiring insights. His genius and humanity were matchless. I would also like to thank Giovanni da Col, Benoît de l'Estoile, Jane Guyer, Louis Herns Marcelin, Bill Maurer, Horacio Ortiz, and Viviana Zelizer for their careful reading of previous drafts. Many thanks to Omar Ribeiro Thomas for challenging me to look into the Haitian dollar for the first time. Finally, my considerable thanks to Keith Hart for his encouragement, care, inspiring comments, and suggestions. The English translation and revision of this text are due to David Rodgers.

Federico Neiburg is professor in social anthropology at the Museu Nacional, Universidade Federal do Rio de Janeiro. He is lead researcher for the Brazilian National Research Council and the coordinator of the Center for Research in Culture and Economy (www.nucec.net). His next book in English will be a volume of *The Cultural History of Money*, "The Age of Empires, 1820–1920" (edited with Nigel Dodd, and organized by Bill Maurer).

NOTES

1. "Whatever we do, we seem unable to rid ourselves of a fiction: the Haitian dollar" (Quoi que nous fassions, nous n'arrivons pas à nous défaire d'une fiction: le dollar haïtien), a columnist complained not long ago in one of the country's main newspapers (Boyer 2012).
2. While the equivalence between the HTG and the HD is always the same (1:5), the gourde (and thus the Haitian dollar) fluctuate in relation to the US dollar. The rate of exchange shown in this table (1 USD : 40 HTG) was valid from 2007 to 2013. It is interesting to note that, given all the political commotions, the constant rise in food prices and the turmoil caused by natural catastrophes, the gourde's value in relation to the US dollar has remained relatively stable – somewhat surprisingly to eyes trained in other economies (like my own, educated in the long monetary instability of countries such as Brazil or Argentina; Neiburg 2006). This is a topic – the stability or volatility of real and imaginary monies – that I cannot address here, of course.
3. See Nelms and Maurer (2014). On the modern dichotomy between materiality and immateriality, see Miller (2005). On the dichotomy between real and fictitious economies, see Guyer (2016). On Bitcoin see Dodd (this volume).

4. Bompaire (2000) has shown how the notion of imaginary currency is multiform, covering a variable semantic field, which "is only unified in opposition to the real money used in payment operations." Also see Day (1998) and Lardin (2007).
5. The links between money and memorialization could also be explored through Hart (2001) and Hart and Ortiz (2014). Maurer (2005: chap. 4) has questioned the teleological and lineal trajectory involved in the dematerialization of money, which supposedly starts with barter and material monies and ends with huge trade and meta coins.
6. Trouillot stimulates us to think about Haiti's "oddities" positively and historically: "Haiti is not weird," he says. "It is the fiction of Haitian exceptionalism that is weird" (1990b: 11).
7. Following Taylor (2005), it is important to grasp the modern dimension of the concept of imagination, which has nothing to do with any kind of supposed backwardness of premoderns who handle incomplete currencies and calculate exotically.
8. A few references to monetary management during the occupation period can be found in Chatelain (2005 [1954]: 121ff.), Schmidt (1995 [1971]), Plummer (1988), and Castor (1987).
9. Mintz confirmed (personal communication) that he had never heard of the Haitian dollar during his fieldwork there.
10. This preference for the scale of five echoes the national currencies of Madagascar and Mauritania, which seem to be the only ones based on such a scale.
11. On the complexities of the Caribbean monetary system during colonial times, see Mintz (1964a). On the colonial monetary history of Saint-Domingue, see Lacombe (1956).
12. The expression "undisciplined" is inspired by Trouillot (1992: 20), who uses the term to speak of the Caribbean as a whole. We can connect the idea of indiscipline with his sketch of Haitian social history as a permanent confrontation between society, state, and nation (Trouillot 1990a).
13. Diverse sources (like the UNDP) agree on an emigration rate of around eight per one thousand. However, these statistics fail to count illegal nonregistered migrants and the coming and going of Haitians from the neighboring Dominican Republic.
14. In 2012 remittances to Haiti amounted to just over 25 percent of GDP (UNDP 2013). On contemporary forms of mobile money linked to the mobility of people, see Maurer (2011) and, in relation to Haiti, Taylor (2011). On Haitian mobility and the diaspora as a Haitian trope, see Ulysse (2007) and Handerson (2015).
15. An account of these changes in the "political economy of aid" to Haiti in the 1990s can be found in James (2010), Marcelin (2011 and 2015), and Schuller (2012).
16. The idea of pluriactivity is central to Hart (1973). Comitas (1963) developed the theme of occupational multiplicity for the Caribbean.
17. For a recent history of Bel Air, see Danticat's extraordinary novel (2007), as well as Laguerre (1983), Ribeiro Thomaz and Nascimento (2006), Beckett (2008), Kivland (2012), Neiburg (2017), and Braum (2014).

18. One hundred thousand people lived in the Greater Bel Air area before the 2010 earthquake (Fernandes and Nascimento 2007). According to the WTO (Portes, Itzigsohn, and Dore-Cabral 1994), only 7.7 percent of the workforce was formally employed in 1987. The Viva Rio Census (Fernandes and Nascimento 2007) found that 78 percent of families in Bel Air have a monthly per capita income below US$43 and 38 percent earn less than one dollar per day. This matches the findings of the latest UNDP report (2013), which indicates that 75 percent of the country's population live on less than 2.5 dollars a day.
19. On the Haitian market system, see Mintz (1959, 1960); on the street markets in the country's capital, see Bazabas (1997).
20. Mintz (1964b) showed how profits are made by playing between scales and units of measurement. Along a similar line, Guyer (2004) developed the idea of marginal gains to describe the logic of accruing small profits in West Africa.
21. On the concept of frustration (*fristrasyon*) in the ghetto, see Neiburg (2017).
22. Mintz (1964b) explored the native notion of capital, *manman lajan* (mother money), in his studies of Haiti's rural markets. On capitalization in small-scale popular urban trade, see Sergo (2010).
23. Laguerre (1983) and Baptiste, Heather, and Taylor (2010).
24. The word *kob* has two meanings: as a hundredth of a gourd (a cent) and as a generic synonym for currency. I lack the space here to explore the creole vocabulary distinguishing *monnen*, *lajan*, *kob*, etc., in relation to more analytic distinctions between money and currency, for example.
25. Medieval historians have called attention to the importance of money changers in context of extreme currency plurality and the presence of pure monies of account (for a synthesis, see Ingham 2004: 113).
26. On sick currencies, see Neiburg (2010).
27. See Hart (2007), and the introduction to this volume.
28. Zelizer (2012: 155ff.).

REFERENCES

Amato, M., L. Doria, and L. Fantacci. 2010. *Money and Calculation: Economic and Sociological Perspectives*. Basingstoke: Palgrave.

Baptiste, E., A. Heather, and E. B. Taylor. 2010. "Haitian Monetary Ecologies and Repertoires: A Qualitative Snapshot of Money Transfer and Savings." Paper submitted to the Institute for Money, Technology and Financial Inclusion.

Bazabas, D. 1997. *Du marché de rue en Haïti: Le système urbain de Port-au-Prince face à ses entreprises "d'espace-rue."* Paris: L'Harmattan.

Beckett, G. 2008. "The end of Haiti: History under conditions of impossibility." PhD dissertation, University of Chicago.

Bloch, M. 1954. *Esquisse d'une histoire monétaire de l'Europe*. Cahiers des Annales. Paris: Armand Colin.

Bompaire, M. 2000. *Numismatique médiévale: Monnaies et documents d'origine française.* (*L'Atelier du Médiéviste* 7). Paris: Brepols.

Boyer, J. C. 2012. "Le dollar haïtien: fiction ou réalité?" *Le Nouvelliste*, December 2, 2012. Available at http://lenouvelliste.com/lenouvelliste/article/91318/Le-dollar-haitien-fiction-ou-realite.html (accessed 5 May 2015).
Braum, P. 2014. "Rat pa kaka: Política, desenvolvimento e violência no coração de Porto Príncipe." PhD dissertation, PPGAS, Museu Nacional, UFRJ, Rio de Janeiro.
Callon, M., and F. Muniesa. 2005. "Economic markets as calculative collective devices." *Organization Studies* 26(8): 1229–1250.
Castor, S. 1987. *L'occupation américaine d'Haiti*. Port-au-Prince: CRESFED.
Chatelain, J. 2005 [1954]. *La Banque Nationale. Son Histoire—Ses problèmes*. Port-au-Prince: Les Editions Fardin.
Comitas, L. 1963. "Occupational Multiplicity in Rural Jamaica." *Proceedings of the American Ethnological Society*, 41–-50.
Day, J. 1998. "Naissance et mort des monnaies de compte (XIIIe–XVIIIe siècles)." *Revue Numismatique* 6(153): 335–343.
Danticat, E. 2007. *Adieu mon frère*. Paris: Bernard Graset.
Dodd, N. 2014. *The Social Life of Money*. Princeton, NJ: Princeton University Press.
Einaudi, L. 1953 [1936]. "The Theory of Imaginary Money from Charlemagne to the French Revolution." In F. C. Lane and J. C. Riemersma (eds.), Enterprise and Secular Change: Readings in Economic History. London: George Allen & Unwin, pp. 229–261.
Fassin, D., and M. Pandolfi. 2010. *Contemporary States of Emergency: The Politics of Military and Humanitarian Interventions*. New York: Zone Books.
Fernandes, R. C., and M. Sousa Nascimento. 2007. "Recensement démographique." Unpublished manuscript, Bel Air, Port-au-Prince, Haiti.
Guyer, J. 1995. "Introduction: The currency interface and its dynamics." In J. Guyer (ed.), *Money Matters: Instabilities, Values and Social Payments in the Modern History of Western African Communities*. London: James Currey, pp. 1–33.
———. 2004. *Marginal Gains: Monetary Transactions in Atlantic Africa*. Chicago, IL: University of Chicago Press.
———. 2011. "Soft Currencies, cash economies, new monies: Past and present." *Proceedings of the National Academy of Sciences* 109(7): 2214–2221.
———. 2016. "Is the 'real economy' disaggregating, disappearing or deviating?" In *Legacies, Logics, Logistics: Essays in the Anthropology of the Platform Cconomy*. Chicago, IL: University of Chicago Press, pp. 238–263.
Handerson, J. 2015. "Diaspora. As dinâmicas da mobilidade haitiana no Brasil, no Suriname e na Guiana Francesa." PhD dissertation, PPGAS, Museu Nacional, UFRJ, Rio de Janeiro.
Hart, K. 1973. "Informal Income Opportunities and Urban Employment in Ghana." *The Journal of Modern African Studies* 11(1): 61–89.
———. 2001. *The Memory Bank: Money in an Unequal World*. Knutsford: Texere Publishing.
———. 2007. "Money is always personal and impersonal." *Anthropology Today* 23(5): 12–16.
Hart, K., and H. Ortiz. 2014. "The Anthropology of Money and Finance: Between Ethnography and World History." *Annual Review of Anthropology* 43: 465–482.

Ingham, G. K. 2004. *The Nature of Money*. Cambridge: Polity.
James, E. 2010. *Democratic Insecurities: Violence, Trauma, and Intervention in Haiti*. Berkeley: University of California Press.
Kivland, C. 2012. "'We make the state': Performance, politick, and respect in urban Haiti." PhD dissertation, University of Chicago.
Kula, W. 1986. *Measures and Men*. Princeton, NJ: Princeton University Press.
Kuroda, A. 2008a. "What is the complementary among monies? An introductory note." *Financial Historical Review* 15(1): 7–15.
———. 2008b. "Concurrent but non-integrable currency circuits: Complementary relationships among monies in modern China and other regions." *Financial Historical Review* 15(1): 17–36.
Lacombe, R. 1956. "Histoire monétaire de Saint-Domingue et de la République d'Haïti, des origines à 1874." *Revue d'Histoire des Colonies* 43(152–153): 273–337.
Laguerre, M. 1983. *Urban Life in the Caribbean: A Case Study of Haiti*. Cambridge: Schenkman Publishing.
Lardin, P. 2007. "Monnaie de compte et monnaie réelle: Des relations mal étudiées." *Revue Européenne des Sciences Sociales* 2(XLV): 45–68.
Manigat, S. 2007. "Gourdes, dollars . . . Ça coûte combien?" *Le Matin*, 21 September 2007.
Marcelin, L. H. 2011. "Cooperation, Peace and (Re-)Construction? A Tale of Shanties." *Journal of Peacebuilding & Development* 6(3): 1–15.
———. 2015. "Violence, Human Insecurity and the Challenge of Rebuilding Haiti: A Study of a Shantytown in Port-au-Prince." *Current Anthropology* 56(2): 230–255.
Maurer, B. 2005. *Mutual Life, Limited: Islamic Banking, Alternative Currencies, Lateral Reason*. Princeton, NJ: Princeton University Press.
———. 2006. "The Anthropology of Money." *Annual Review in Anthropology* 35: 15–36.
———. 2011. "Mobile money, money magic, purse limits and pins: Tracing monetary pragmatics." *Journal of Cultural Economy* 4(3): 349–359.
Miller, D. 2005. "Materiality: An Introduction." In D. Miller (ed.), *Materiality*. Durham, NC, and London: Duke University Press, pp. 1–50.
Mintz, S. 1959. "Internal Market Systems as Mechanisms of Social Articulation." In V. F. Ray (ed.), *Intermediate Societies, Social Mobility and Communication*. Seattle: University of Washington Press, pp. 20–30.
———. 1960. "A tentative typology of eight Haitian market places." *Revista de Ciencias Sociales* 4: 15–17.
———. 1961. "Standards of Value and Units of Measure in the Fond-des-Negres Market Place, Haiti." *The Journal of The Royal Anthropological Institute of Great Britain and Ireland* 91(1): 23–38.
———. 1964a. "Currency problems in eighteenth century Jamaica and Gresham's Law." In A. Manners (ed.), *Process and Pattern in Culture: Essays in Honor of Julian N. Steward*. Chicago, IL: Aldine.
———. 1964b. "The employment of capital by Haitian market women." In R. Firth and B. Yamey (eds.), *Capital, Savings and Credit in Peasant Societies*. Chicago, IL: Aldine, pp. 256–286.
Mitchell, T. 2002. *Rule of Experts: Egypt, Techno-Politics, Modernity*. Berkeley: University of California Press.

Neiburg, F. 2006. "Inflation: Economists and Economic Cultures in Brazil and Argentina." *Comparative Studies in Society and History* 46(3): 604–633.

———. 2010. "Sick Currencies and Public Numbers." *Anthropological Theory* 10(1/2): 96–102.

———. 2016. "A True Coin of Their Dreams: Imaginary Monies in Haiti." *Hau: Journal of Ethnographic Theory* 6 (1): 75–93,

———. 2017. "Serendipitous Involvement: Making Peace in the Geto." In D. Fassin (ed.), *If Truth be Told: The Politics of Public Ethnography*. Durham, NC: Duke University Press, chapter 5, pp. 119–137.

Nelms, T., and B. Maurer. 2014. "Materiality, Symbol, and Complexity in the Anthropology of Money." In E. H. Bijleveld and H. Aarts (eds.), *The Psychological Science of Money*. New York: Springer, pp. 37–70.

Peirce, C. S. 1932 [1897]. "Division of Signs." In *Collected Papers*, vol. II. Cambridge, MA: Belknap Press of Harvard University Press, pp. 227–273.

Plummer, B. G. 1988. *Haiti and the Great Powers 1902–1915*. Baton Rouge: Louisiana University Press.

Portes, A., J. Itzigsohn, and C. Dore-Cabral. 1994. "Urbanization in the Caribbean Basin: Social Change during the Years of the Crisis." *Latin American Research Review* 29(2): 3–38.

Renda, M. A. 2001. *Taking Haiti: Military Occupation & the Culture of U.S. Imperialism*. Chapel Hill: University of North Carolina Press.

Ribeiro Thomaz, O., and S. Nascimento. 2006. "Bel-Air: Neighborhood with a Past, Neighborhood with a Future." Unpublished manuscript.

Schmidt, H. 1995 [1971]. *The United States Occupation of Haiti: 1915–1935*. New Brunswick, NJ: Rutgers University Press.

Schuller, M. 2012. *Killing with Kindness: Haiti, International Aid, and NGOs*. New Brunswick, NJ: Rutgers University Press.

Sergo, J. L. 2010. "L'ascension sociale par le commerce de détail: Le cas des marchands de tissus opérant dans les marchés de rues de Pétion- Ville. Université d'Etat d'Haïti, Faculté d'Ethnologie." Unpublished manuscript.

Strassler, K. 2009. "The Face of Money: Currency, Crisis, and Remediation in Post-Suharto Indonesia." *Cultural Anthropology* 24(1): 68–103.

Taylor, C. 2005. "Modern Social Imaginaries." *Public Culture* 14(1): 91–124.

Taylor, E. B. 2011. "Mobile banking and mobile phone aesthetics: Observations from Haiti." American Anthropological Association paper.

Trouillot, M. R. 1990a. *Haiti, State against Nation: The Origins and Legacy of Duvalierism*. New York: Monthly Review Press.

———. 1990b. "The odd and the ordinary: Haiti, the Caribbean and the world." *Cimarron* 2(3): 3–12.

———. 1992. "The Caribbean Region. An Open Frontier in Anthropology." *Annual Review of Anthropology* 21: 19–42.

Ulysse, G. 2007. *Downtown Ladies: Informal Commercial Importing, A Haitian Anthropologist and Self-Making in Jamaica*. Chicago, IL: University of Chicago Press.

UNDP (United Nations Development Programme). 2013. Human Development Report.

Van Werveke, H. 1934. "Monnaie de compte et monnaie réelle." *Revue Belge de Philologie et d'Histoire* XIII: 123–152.

Weber, F. 2009. "Le calcul économique ordinaire." In P. Steiner and F. Vatin (eds.), *Traité de sociologie économique*. Paris: Puf (Quadrige), pp. 367–407.

Zelizer, V. 1998. *The Social Meaning of Money: Pin Money, Paychecks, Poor Relief and Other Currencies*. New York: Basic Books.

———. 2012. "How I became a relational economic sociologist and what does that mean?" *Politics & Society* 40(2): 145–174.

Index

A
advertisements, 53, 54, 55–6, 57
Alianza Republicana Nacionalista party (ARENA), 135–6, 137
antipolitics, Bitcoin and, 190–95
Apple Pay, 167
  interchange fees on, 168–9
arbitrage, 132–3
Argentina
  budget management, 255–60
  class identity, 253–5
  commodities, 254, 260, 261, 262
  common good, treatment of money as, 264–6
  community currency (*crédito*), 250–51, 252–3
  daily casual labor (*changas*), 250
  dominations, gender-based, 255
  exchange, 253, 265
  expenditures, 252, 258, 259, 267n8
    control by husbands of, bypass of, 258–60
    income and, 259
  financial management, gendered norms of, 259–60
  gender and money in barter network, 250–68
  gender identity, 253–5
  gender of money, 252
  gender relations, conservatism of, 253–4
  gendered social hierarchies, 252, 255–6, 265–6
  Global Barter Network (RGT), 250–51
  household budgets, gendered division of, 255
  household finances, transfers for, 258
  household income, 256, 257
  income generation, 252, 257, 262–3
  income inequality, 251–2, 256, 257
  income monopolies of husbands, bypass of, 256–7
  industry (and industrial areas) in, 250, 251, 252, 261
  inequalities of gender and status, 252
  market-places (*ferias*), 250–51, 252, 253, 254–5, 261–2, 263
    gender participation in, 264–5
    interchangeability during, 254
  market transactions, 252, 253, 254, 265
  monetary spheres, 260
    interface between, 262–4
  money use, gendered division of, 258–9
  patriarchy, 257, 260
  peso income, 260, 261, 262, 263
  profit-making, 262–4
  Rosario, 250–51, 252, 254–5, 262, 263–4, 267n1
    comparative prices (*crédito/peso*) in, 261
  saving, gendered basis of, 259
  social differentiation, 260–64
  street vendors, 254, 256, 264
  trueque (barter network), 250–51, 252, 253–4, 255–6, 257, 258, 259, 260, 261–2, 263, 264–5

Index

gendered monies and, 252–3
patriarchy, challenge to, 257
women's world, 251–2, 253, 255–6
US dollar (and peso parity) in, 251
women
  expenditures of, 267n8
  financial control for, 256–7
  household finances, transfers for, 258
  local currencies, use of, 252
  marriage and exclusion from labor for, 256–7
  rights of, 252
  socialization spaces for, *ferias* as, 253–4, 255
  working-class, 250, 252, 255, 260, 264, 266
Aristotle, 13, 44, 61, 63–4, 64–5, 65–6, 67, 69, 184n1
  Aristotelian Concept of Money, 47–8, 62–3, 77

B

Banco Cuscatlán, 136, 142
banking, banks and
  bank loans, 197
  banking system, 70–71, 131, 136
  Lesotho, Basotho people and, 240, 243–4
  new ways of banking, 111–13
  services in Global South, 103–4
  in South Asia, 209, 211, 213–14, 215, 223–4
  for unbanked, 119–20
  value transfer, rent and, 177
bankruptcy, 223–4, 225
barter, origins of money in, 63–7, 77
Basotho people of Lesotho, 229–30, 231, 233, 244–5, 246, 247n2–3, 247n13
  credit, difficulties of access to, 244–5
  economic independence, rise of (1830s–1870s), 234–6
  fall from economic independence (1880s–1930s), 236–43
  savings and farmers' cooperatives, 244–5
Bitcoin, 189–204
  antipolitics and, 190–95
  appeal of, 189, 193, 196
  austerity, politics of, 197
  bank loans, 197
  Bitcoin network, 192–3
  Bitcoiners, 192, 194, 196, 197, 198, 202
  blockchain technology, 170, 190, 191, 193, 199, 201, 203
  cap on production, 194
  Chicago Plan, 192
  cryptocurrency, 192–3
  datafication, 191–2
  debt, 196–7
  digital metallism, 193–4
  digital society, 191
  genealogy of, 191–2
  gold, currency and, 193–4
  goldbugs, 194
  infrastructure, 191–2
  International Monetary Fund (IMF), 191
  Internet, 191–2
  laissez-faire, 194
  launch of, 190
  libertarianism, 189, 198, 199
  long-term potential, 202–3
  material embeddedness, 194
  mechanized monetary system, 189
  monetary governance, 190
    technological solutions to problems of, 191
  money as claim on society, 189–90
  phenomenon of, paradox of, 189
  politics of, 195–200
    politics free, 190, 193
  Positive Money, 192, 196
  power distribution, 193
  public discourse about, 193
  public interest in, 196
  rationale for use of, 192
  society, organization of, 191

society and, 189–90, 191, 195, 197, 198, 203
sociology and, 192
techno-utopian ideals, 194–5
technology and, 192, 194–5
trust, 189, 190–91, 192, 199, 200, 201, 202
utopia (and utopianism), 194–5, 201, 202
virtual money, 193
Wall Street System, 196, 199
Braudel, Fernand, 30
Bretton Woods agreement (1944), 17, 21, 150, 195
bricolage, 49, 50, 57, 58
BRICS countries (Brazil, Russia, India, China, South Africa), 19, 21–2, 35
bureaucracies, 5–6, 8–9, 19, 30, 47, 54, 149, 153, 242–3
    bureaucratic capitalism, 35
    bureaucratic revolution, 16–17, 29
    cross-border investment in China, 149, 153

C

Calle Principal in Intipucá, 138–9, 139–40
capitalism
    ahistoricity, 82
    asceticism, 85
    bureaucratic capitalism, 35
    capital in South Asia, 209, 213, 215
    capitalist economies, transition from precapitalist conditions, 231, 246
    capitalist markets, 5, 6, 16, 25, 131, 133
    capitalist money, 81
        marriage as exchange and, 82–3
    capitalist production, 36, 94
    deep leveraging of capital, 131–2, 133
    gender and, 82, 89, 94
    inequality and, 22–3
    intersubjectivity, 89, 98
    luxury and sexual economy of, 81–99
    mass (or machine) production, 84, 87
    national capitalism, 10–11, 16–17, 19, 21, 29, 30–31, 35, 36, 37
    production, 85–6
        of luxury, capitalism and, 84–5
    retail space, 84, 89, 90–91
    shopping experience, 90–91
    Sombart's thesis on luxury and capitalism, 81, 82, 83–5, 86, 87–8, 89, 90, 91, 93, 95, 97
    spirit of, 86
    subjectivity, 82, 84, 87, 88
    Weber on salvation and capitalism, 97
    Western hegemony, 44–5
    Zola's literary parallel on luxury and capitalism, 90–93
card-acceptance services, 170
Central American Free Trade Agreement (CAFTA), 142
chartalism, 71, 77
chastity, 91
cheapness, 8, 15, 21, 28, 34, 46, 56–7, 99n5, 117, 241, 262, 275
    buy cheap/sell high proposition, 153, 157
    cheap labor, 230–31, 237, 243, 245, 246
    of exchange of goods, 201
Chicago Plan, 192
cities, 5, 6, 19, 30, 35, 91, 154, 155, 159, 162
    Amsterdam, 180, 185n11
    countryside and, movement between, 275–6
    criminal gangs in, 16
    mobility in, 260
    New York City General Assembly, 31
    population of, change in, 23
    Port-au-Prince, 276, 280
    prostitution in, 83
    Rosario, 267n1

trading cities, 4
US cities, 129, 159
from village to, 6, 16, 24, 275
see also urban settings; urbanization
class, origins of money and, 76
class identity, 253–5
class stratification, 74–5
Coase, Ronald, 8
coinage, 64, 67–8, 75, 76, 77n3
Cold War, 12, 150
collateralized debt obligations (CDOs), 133–4
commodities
　Argentina, 254, 260, 261, 262
　commodity theory, 67–70, 77
　sexual meanings and, 89
commoditization, 95–6
Communauté Financière Africaine (CFA), 45
communications, 15, 16, 18, 36, 46–7, 117, 118, 123n5, 143
　telecommunications, 10, 16, 17, 123, 144–5n3, 170, 173
communities, 7, 20, 21, 22, 56, 189, 231, 237
　Bitcoin community, 201–2
　commercial community, 244
　community banking system, 6
　community currencies, 10–11
　community currency *(crédito)*, 250–51, 252–3
　cultural communities, 19
　exchange, communities of, 22
　Iron Age Bantu communities, 231–2
　kinship groups and, 117
　merchant communities, 210, 212–13, 214, 226
　Ngukurr community, 114
　political communities, 171
　social institutions, money and, 21
　trade between, 64, 212–13
　traditional communities, 15
　wealth of, promotion of, 98n3

companies, 150–51, 152–6, 157–8, 159, 160, 162, 164n1
concubines (and concubinage), 81, 82, 83
consumption, 85–6
　capitalism and, 81–2, 87–8
　money and, 94
contracts, 16, 31, 44, 68, 69, 72, 83, 156, 191, 251
　contractual commitments, 209–10
　contractual gender relations, 93
　contractual relationships, 212–13
　debt contracts, 78n10, 180
　Haiti, imaginary monies and, 270, 271, 275, 280
　impersonal contract enforcement, 216
　labor contracts, 153
　primary contracts, 223–4
　regulation of, 182, 211
　smart contracts, 203
　social contract, 33
　South Asian mercantile exchange and, 209–13, 215–19, 223–4, 225
Copernicus, 45
corporate social responsibility (CSR), 8
corporations, 6, 8, 16, 21, 29, 33–34, 121, 134, 144–5n3
courtesans, 83
credit, 106–7, 109, 111, 112, 113, 117, 119, 120
　credit cards, 168, 170, 172, 175, 177, 178, 181–2
　credit default swaps (CDS), 133–4
　family credit, 117
　microcredit programs, 111
　money and, 171
　Rotating Savings and Credit Associations (RoSCAs), 111
　South Asia, 209, 212, 213, 214, 217, 224
　theories of money, 70–73, 77, 173–4, 180

women and, 106–7, 109, 112–13
cross-border investment in China, 147–64
   borders, 147, 151, 163
   bureaucracies, 149, 153
   companies, 150–51, 152–6, 157–8, 159, 160, 162, 164n1
   crossing, 148–9
   Cultural Revolution, 147, 150
   employees, 149, 153, 155–6, 157–8, 159, 160, 161, 162–3, 164n5
   finance, 147–8, 149–50, 151, 153, 154, 157, 159, 164n5
      globalization of, 162
   finance industry, expansion of, 147
   financial flows, connections and, 147–8
   financial transactions as power relations, 156–9
   geopolitical growth, 160
   global auditing companies, 154
   global financial flows, 147–8, 149–52
   global rules for distribution of money, 151
   global space, 147, 160, 162–3
   hierarchies, 147–8, 149
   identity, 161–2
   imagination, 149, 163
   interdependencies, 147–8
   investment, 148, 149, 151–2, 152–3, 154–5, 157, 159–63, 164n1
   legal frameworks, legitimization and, 148, 150–51
   legitimization, 147, 148, 150–51, 157
   macroeconomic relations, 149–52
   monetary distribution, inequality in, 148
   morals, morality and, 148–9, 156, 159, 160, 161, 162, 163
   political issues, 147–8, 149, 150, 156, 158, 159, 160–61, 162–3
   power
      balance in commerce of, 149, 150, 156, 159
      within Communist Party, 163
      differences in, 158–9
      in global finance, 164n5
      social relations of, 148
   power relations
      financial transactions as, 156–9
      investment and, 160
      money access and, 151
   procedures, 149, 153, 160
   social hierarchies, 163
   universality, conflicting narratives of, 149
   valuation, 153, 154, 155, 157, 160, 161, 162
      global standards for, 158–9
   world society, 147, 149, 163

D

Daily Mail, money articles (28 June 2014), 54–5
debt, 3, 19, 30–31, 32, 70–71, 72, 75–6, 77, 78n7, 196–7
   collateralized debt obligations (CDOs), 133–4
   debt contracts, 78n10, 180
   national debt, 33
democracy, 8, 30, 34, 43, 76
   economic democracy, 6, 7, 9, 36
   social democracy, 17, 18, 23, 33
demography, 37, 38
desire
   capitalism and, 96
   luxury and, 89
development, 17, 37, 109, 117, 230
   capitalist development, 34, 128, 237
   development organizations, 128
   development projects, Haitian economy and, 275–6, 277, 278–80
   developmental states, 17, 32–3

economic development, 147,
149–50, 151, 161, 210, 241
finance and, intersection of, 132,
143
Global Forum on Remittances
and Development, 145n13
'human economy' approach to,
9
infrastructural development,
243
interdisciplinary approach to, 12
new agenda for, 141, 142–3
poverty reduction and, 140–41
remittance securitization, 130,
132, 134, 137, 138–9, 140–41,
142–3
sustainable development, 151,
163
trade, money and development
of, 69–70
UN Development Program
(UNDP), 130, 141
underdevelopment, 236
US International Development
Agency, 137
diamonds, 230, 235–6
digital electronic media, 128, 130–31
digital metallism, 193–4
digital society, 191
division of labor, 68, 73, 74, 75, 76
dollarization, 72
'Dutch Disease' (economic model),
136–7, 140–41

E
ecological paradigm, 15
ecology of data, 191
Economic Commission for Latin
America and the Caribbean (ECLA),
137
economics, 4, 8, 9
capitalist economies, transition
from precapitalist conditions,
231, 246
development projects, Haitian
economy and, 275–6, 277,
278–80

'Dutch Disease' (economic
model), 136–7, 140–41
economic democracy, 6, 7, 9, 36
economic development, 147,
149–50, 151, 161, 210, 241
economic independence in
Lesotho, 234–6, 236–43
economic inequality, 75, 106, 147,
251, 256
economic management, 5
money economy in Lesotho, 231,
239, 241, 243, 244, 245, 247n13
new money economy (1870s–
1930s), 243–5
popular economy in Haiti, 276–7,
278, 281–2
principles of, 5
sexual economy, 93–5
world economy and disguise of
inequalities, 4
see also human economy
Egypt, money and society in
antiquity, 73–6
El Salvador
capitalist relations between US
and, 129, 134–6
civil war in (1980–1992), 134–5
new development agenda for,
141–2
remittances to, 136–7, 141–2
state formation, critical studies
in, 143–4
transfers between US and, 128
electronic money, issuance of, 174
electronic value, cash conversion
into, 170–71, 174
embeddedness, 29, 33, 47, 52–3, 137,
167, 169, 216, 253, 265
Bitcoin as politics and, 193–4,
202
capitalism, luxury and sexual
economy of, 81–2, 85, 87, 88
embedded liberalism, 35
family practices of Global South,
money and, 105, 110, 115
Haiti, imaginary monies and,
271, 273, 282

empires, 6, 17, 19, 274
   age of empire, 62
   capitalist empires, 32
   European empires, 26, 37
   Islamic empires, 120
   trade routes of, 120
energy, 6, 15, 23–4, 133–4
   renewable energy, 159
Engels, Friedrich, 24, 28, 30, 34, 36
eroticism, 89, 90, 91, 94, 96
exchange, 82, 92, 93, 94, 96, 98n1, 253, 265
   exchange-centricity, 170
   gender relations and, 82
   medium of, 65, 67, 70, 76
   par clearance and, 175–6

F

Facebook credits, 172, 173, 174
family practices of Global South, 103–23
   Aadhar identification system, 103
   banking, banks and
      new ways of, 111–13
      services in Global South, 103–4
      for unbanked, 119–20
   Bolsa Familia in Brazil, 103
   capabilities, 109
   credit, 106–7, 109, 111, 112, 113, 117, 119, 120
      family credit, 117
      microcredit programs, 111
      Rotating Savings and Credit Associations (RoSCAs), 111
      women and, 106–7, 109, 112–13
   currencies, 120–21
   empowerment of poor people, 109–13
   exclusion, cultural and institutional context of, 106–9
   family practices, 104, 105
   financial accounts, design on, 106–7
   financial inclusion, 105, 106, 107, 108, 109, 110, 120, 122
   freedoms, 109
   gender inequity, 106, 107, 108, 122
   Global South, banking services in, 103–4
   information and communication technologies (ICTs), 104
   inheritance, 114, 118
   insurance, 106, 112–13
   insurance for unbanked, 119–20
   Kshetriya Gramin Financial Services (KGFS) in India, 103–4
   legislative barriers for women, 106, 107
   management of money, 104, 106, 112, 113, 114
   microfinance, 103, 105, 111–12
   mobile money
      gift and, 116
      M-PESA system in Kenya, 103, 104, 110
      new kind of money, 103–4, 111–13
   mobile money, making payments in new ways, 110–11
   mobile phones, 108, 110, 118, 120
   money
      family money, boundaries of, 114–16
      forms of, 120–21
      future for, 103, 105, 119–22
      gender and, 105–6, 122
      as gift, 116
      global aspects of, 105, 121–2
      management of, 104, 106, 112, 113, 114
      medium of relationships, 113–18
      multiple channels (and currencies), 120–21
      personal nature of, 104
      unbanked money, 105–6
   Oportunidades in Mexico, 103
   payments, 105, 108, 109, 110–11, 118, 119, 120, 121

for unbanked people, 119–20
remittances, 104–5, 110, 112, 114, 115, 120, 121
   transnational families and, 116–18
sociological imagination, 105
First World War, 17, 29, 35, 36
functions of money, 272
   relations between, 282
Fundación Salvadoreña para el Desarollo Económico y Social (FUSADES), 137

G

gender, 82, 89, 94
   gender identity, 253–5
   gender inequity, 106, 107, 108, 122
   of money, 252
   money in barter network and, 250–68
gender relations
   conservatism of, 253–4
   exchange and, 83, 88, 95–6
gifts, 81, 82, 89, 93, 94–5
global auditing companies, 154
Global Barter Network (RGT), 250–51
global financial flows, 147–8, 149–52
global rules for distribution of money, 151
global space, 147, 160, 162–3
gold standard, 17, 19, 29, 194, 201
goldbugs, 194
Goody, Jack, 30–31, 32
Graeber, David, 23, 30, 31, 32, 45, 70, 71, 72, 77n6, 78n10, 185n5, 193, 196–7, 199
Greece in antiquity, 43, 44
Greif, Avner, 210, 215, 216, 218
Guyer, Jane, 13, 45, 52, 82, 88, 105, 120, 122, 148, 163, 182–3, 272, 275, 280, 284n3, 286n20

H

Haitian dollar, 270–86
   account, unit of, 271, 273, 274–5, 280, 281, 282, 283
   Bel Air region, 273–4, 276–7, 279–80, 285n17, 286n18
   calculative dimension of money, 272–4, 277, 282
      geographies of money and, 279–81
   circulation of dollars in Caribbean, 271
   commensuration, 272
   conversion rate, gourde and, 270
   credit systems, 274
   creole currency, 281
   Croix de Bossales region, 276–7
   currencies, birth of, 272
   dynamic and creative space of, 272–3
   fictional currency, 273–4
   fixed parity gourde/dollar exchange rate, 274
   functions of money, 272
      relations between, 282
   Haitian society, formation of, 275–6
   imaginary money, 271, 273, 282–3
      Einaudi's proposal for, 272
   international aid agencies (IAAs), 275–6
   links, 273–4
   lotteries, 274
   materiality, immateriality and, 271
   measures, sociotechnical history of, 275
   monetary cultures, 273, 282
   monetary interface, 272
   monetary pluralism, 271–2
   monetary spaces, 271, 280, 283
   money, theoretical definitions of, 271–2
   multiple currencies, elective affinity and, 282
   payments, Bloch's perspective on units of account and, 272
   popular economy, 276–7, 278, 281–2

public markets, network of, 276–7
reality and conceptualization of, 271
scale of five
 mnemonic function, 275
 space of calculability and, 274–5
undisciplined spaces, 275–9
United Nations Stabilization Mission in Haiti (MINUSTAH), 277
units of measure, 273
warnings about, 270
Hanseatic League, 45
Hart, Keith, 62, 81, 94, 128, 129, 148, 168, 182, 183, 185n5, 193, 265, 285n5, 285n16, 286n27
 Basotho people, economic independence for, 229, 231, 245, 246
 capitalism, history of money and, 16, 17, 18, 19, 21, 22, 24, 26, 29, 30, 31, 34, 37
 family practices of Global South, 104, 113, 120, 122, 123n3
 human economy, money in, 3–4, 7, 8, 9–10, 11, 12
 money, 43, 44, 46, 47–8, 52
hedonism, 85
Hegel, G.W.F., 16, 28–9, 35
home, 9, 10, 11, 45, 134, 138–9, 209, 250, 254–5, 256, 264, 283
 family practices of Global South, 107, 114, 115, 117–18, 120, 123n3
honor, 212, 216, 219, 220, 222, 223–4
human economy, 43, 47, 62, 81, 104, 114, 229, 246, 273
 Human Economy Program, 129, 130
 Lesotho, Basotho people and, 229
 money, language and, 43
 money and capitalism in, 3–4, 5, 6, 8, 9, 12–13, 22, 32
 value transfer, rent and, 168, 183
human universal, 3, 5, 9, 15, 18
humanism, 5, 6, 8–9, 11, 282–3

anti-humanism, 9
humanity, 4, 5–6, 7, 9, 11, 15, 18, 19, 22, 23, 30, 32, 37, 46, 229
hundi/hawala in South Asia
 British rule, influence on, 211
 contract arrangements and, 215, 219
 court cases, 218–23, 225
 customary rules, 211
 definition of, problem of, 214–15
 extensive use of, 214
 honor and institution of, 212–13
 law, legal precedent and, 225–6
 literature, post-1978 treatment in, 211
 mercantile credit system, 209–10, 216, 226
 primordial relationships, 212–15
 reach of, extensive nature of, 215
 relationships between merchants, insight through, 218–19
 trust and system of, 216

I
inequalities, 6, 11, 18, 24, 30–31, 37–8, 54–5, 231, 236, 241–2, 245
 communications inequalities, 18
 contract inequalities, 16
 economic inequality, 75, 106, 147, 251, 256
 in energy distribution, 6
 exclusion and, 122
 of gender and status in Argentina, 252
 gender inequality, 106–7, 122, 252, 265, 266
 in Lesotho, 231, 236, 241, 242, 245
 power relations and, 76, 151
 social hierarchies and, 263–4, 265, 280
 unequal monetary distribution, issue of, 148
 unequal society, Rousseau's anthropology of, 23–4, 30–32

unequal things, money and equivalences between, 64, 65–6, 253
world economy and disguise of, 4
Ingham, Geoffrey, 69–70, 171, 193, 195, 196, 286n25
interest, interest rates and, 28, 33–4, 36, 157, 174, 178, 193, 213, 216, 278
   family practices in Global South and, 112, 113, 119, 123n2
International Monetary Fund (IMF), 45, 191
Internet, 11, 12, 18, 22, 46, 108, 144–5n3, 145n5, 170, 179, 191
   Bitcoin, 191–2
   money, language and, 46–7
   value transfer, rent and, 170–71

K

Keynes, John M. (and Keynesianism), 10, 17, 21, 25, 33, 71, 171, 201
Knapp, Georg Friedrich, 71, 77

L

labor theory of value, 35
land, 4, 20, 23, 26–7, 28, 37, 235–6
   appropriation of, 230, 241, 245
   commoditization of, 231
   Eurasian land mass, 30
   family practices in Global South, 105, 107, 113, 114, 118
   monetary land purchase, 48
   property rights to, 156–7, 158
   redistribution of, 233
   remittance securitization, land use and, 143–4
   soil erosion and shortage of, 275
language, 4, 11, 43, 46–7, 48, 50, 53, 58, 113, 140, 157, 193–4, 283
Law, John, 67–8, 69, 77
Lesotho, Basotho people and, 229–47
   African Cooperative Society, 245
   alliances, money and, 246
   banks and banking, 240, 243–4
   Basotho, 229–30, 231, 233, 244–5, 246, 247n2–3, 247n13
   credit, difficulties of access to, 244–5
   economic independence, rise of (1830s–1870s), 234–6
   fall from economic independence (1880s–1930s), 236–43
   savings and farmers' cooperatives, 244–5
Basutoland Post Office Savings Bank, 243
Bloemfontein Board of Executives and Trust Company, 244
capitalist economies, transition from precapitalist conditions, 231, 246
chiefs and chiefdoms, 232–3, 234, 236, 238–9, 240, 241–2, 245–6
colonial authorities, 237–8, 239–40, 241–2, 243
colonial taxation, 239–40, 242, 243
cooperatives, 244–5
diamonds, 230, 235–6
economic independence, 229–30, 234–6, 236–43, 245–6
European traders, 244
financial institutions, 231, 243, 244, 247n8
financial institutions in new money economy (1870s–1930s), 243–5
Frasers Company, 244
Gun War, 236, 239–40, 241
human economy and, 229
hut tax, 237–8, 240, 246
inequalities, 231, 236, 241, 242, 245
labour-service, 234
Lesotho, 234, 235, 237, 238, 239–40, 241, 242, 243–4, 246, 247n1
   economic history (1830s–1930s), 229–30, 245

society and economy before
    Europeans (1500–1820s),
    231–3
liberation movement, 246
markets and money, 229–47
matsema (communal work
    parties), 233, 234, 241
Mfecane wars, 230, 233, 234, 246
mineral resources, 230, 235–6,
    237, 246
missions and missionaries,
    229–30, 231, 233, 234–5, 237,
    242, 244, 246
modern economies and, 229
money, 231, 232, 235–3, 237–9,
    241, 243, 244–5, 246
money economy, 231, 239, 241,
    243, 244, 245, 247n13
money-market mutuality, 246
Mutual Building Homes Limited,
    244
new money economy (1870s–
    1930s), 243–5
Paris Evangelical Missionary
    Society (PEMS), 234, 235
Post Office Savings Bank, 244
society, social extension and,
    229, 245
South Africa and, 230, 231, 232,
    235, 236–7, 241, 242–3, 246
South African Post Office Bank,
    243
southern Africa, economic
    conditions (1870s), 230
Standard Bank, 244
trade, 230, 231, 232, 234–5, 236,
    243–4, 246, 247n7
Lévi-Strauss, Claude, 7, 30, 48, 49, 58
loans, 28, 71, 131, 138, 196–7, 214, 233,
    245, 278, 279
    family practices in Global South
        and, 106, 108, 109, 111–12, 113,
        115, 123n2
Locke, John, 12–13, 15, 20, 24, 35, 48,
    194
love
    promiscuity and, 93

secularization of, 83
seduction and, 92
semi-institutionalization of,
    83–4
luxury, 98n3
    capitalism and, 99n5
    category of, 86
    consumption of, 86
    demand for, 82, 84
    historical perspective on, 87–8
    refinement and, 87–8

M

macroeconomics
    macroeconomic relations in
        China, 149–52
    of morals, 85–6
market-places
    in Argentina (*ferias*), 250–51, 252,
        253, 254–5, 261–2, 263
        gender participation in,
            264–5
        interchangeability during,
            254
    money, language and, 43, 51, 53,
        57
markets, 4, 7–8, 10–11, 12, 13, 17, 20
    capital markets, 131, 133
    capitalist markets, 5, 6, 16, 25,
        131, 133
    currency markets, 37
    financial markets, 128, 145n9
    foreign exchange markets, 22
    market forces, 68, 69
    market transactions, 252, 253,
        254, 265
    money and, 5, 7, 17, 18, 19, 22, 26,
        229–47
    stock markets, 19
    world markets, 19, 26–7
marriage, love and, 83
Marx, Karl, 9, 12–13, 48, 49, 50, 68, 71,
    76, 81, 94, 95, 98n1, 145n11, 180–81
    capitalism, history of money
        and, 15, 16, 18, 24, 26, 28, 29,
        30, 34–5, 36
Marxism, 29, 88, 172, 184n1

Marxists, 25, 28–9
Maurer, Bill, 11, 13, 45, 46, 103, 110–11, 122, 193–4, 198, 272, 284n3, 285n5, 285n14
    value transfer, rent and, 182, 183, 185n3, 185n5
Mauss, Marcel, 10, 13, 18, 22, 44, 170, 172, 183
media
    as market-place, 53–7
    remittance securitization and, 128, 129, 130, 131, 132, 143
Menger, Carl, 65, 68, 69
Mintz, Sidney, 273, 274, 275, 285n9, 285n11, 286n19–20, 286n22
Mitchell Innes, Andrew, 70, 72, 77
mobile money
    gift and, 116
    M-PESA system in Kenya, 103, 104, 110
    making payments in new ways, 110–11
    new kind of money, 103–4, 111–13
monetary value, exchange of, 169–70
monetization, 46, 49, 58
money
    advertisements, 53, 54, 55–6, 57
    African trade, words in, 52–3
    'appetites of the mind', 56–7
    Aristotle on money and wealth, 47–8
    bricolage, 49, 50, 57, 58
    as claim on society, 189–90
    classical inspirations, 47–9
    Communauté Financière Africaine (CFA), 45
    comparative criteria, worth in, 52
    conversations, 46, 47, 53, 54–5, 56–7, 58
    Copernicus, 45
    credit theories of, 173–4, 180
    Daily Mail, money articles (28 June 2014), 54–5
    'elsewhere,' practices of, 44
    exactness, 48
    family money, boundaries of, 114–16
    forms of, 120–21
    future for, 103, 105, 119–22
    gender and, 105–6, 122
    as gift, 116
    global aspects of, 105, 121–2
    Greece in antiquity, 43, 44
    Hanseatic League, 45
    historical and philosophical nature of, 44–7
    human economy, 43
    infrastructures of, 168, 169
    International Financial Institutions (IFIs), 45
    International Monetary Fund (IMF), 45
    Internet, 46–7
    interpersonal relations, money and, 94
    language and, 43–59
    Lesotho, Basotho people and, 231, 232, 235–3, 237–9, 241, 243, 244–5, 246
    management of, 104, 106, 112, 113, 114
    market-places, 43, 51, 53, 57
    media and, 129, 130–31
    medium of relationships, 113–18
    mondialisation, 45, 46, 47, 58
    monetary value and, 173–4
    monetization, 46, 49, 58
    money, historical and philosophical nature of, 44–7
    money economy in Lesotho, 231, 239, 241, 243, 244, 245, 247n13
    money laundering in South Asia, 209, 211
    money-making, stories of, 54–5
    money-market mutuality, 246
    money-object commensurations over time, 51–2
    multiple channels (and currencies), 120–21
    narrative, money and, 52–3
    nature of, 171

new money economy (1870s–1930s) in Lesotho, 243–5
New York Times, value of expensive products, 55–7
news media as market-place, 53–7
newspapers, 53
participation, 43
personal nature of, 104
persuasive power of, 47
pervasiveness of money as discussion topic, 58
prices of luxury goods, 55–6, 56–7
public space, 43
relations of, remittance securitization and, 129
social hierarchy of, 170, 173
social meaning of, 94–5
social theory, money and, 44
state, market and, 44
trade, trust and, 44
unbanked money, 105–6
use of, gendered division in Argentina of, 258–9
value in exchange, worth as concept in use, 50–52, 58
want, desire and, 48–9
words, 46, 50, 51, 52–3
'World Society, Money in the Making of', 45–7
worth, ethnography of, 47, 48, 50–52, 53, 54, 55–7, 58
see also origins of money, ideas about
money management
Anglo-American pattern of, 104, 115
in East Africa, 107, 123n5
family management, 114–16
in India, 103, 105, 106–7, 108, 109, 112–13, 114, 115, 116, 117, 119–20
in Papua New Guinea, 105, 107, 108
by the poor, 106–7, 109–13, 119–20
in South Africa, 109

morality
macroeconomics of morals, 85–6
morals, morality in China and, 148–9, 156, 159, 160, 161, 162, 163

N
national capitalism, 10–11, 16–17, 19, 21, 29, 30–31, 35, 36, 37
natural sensuality, 83
New York Times, value of expensive products in, 55–7
newspapers, 53–4, 201, 281–2, 284n1
  Daily Mail, money articles (28 June 2014), 54–5
  New York Times, value of expensive products in, 55–7

O
obscenity and history, 95–6
Old Regime in France, 30, 31, 35, 38
origins of money, ideas about, 61–78
  ahistoricity, 62, 63
  Aristotelian Concept of Money, 62–3, 77
  banking system, 70–71
  barter, origins of money in, 63–7, 77
  chartalism, 71, 77
  class stratification, 74–5
  classes, origins of money and, 76
  coinage, 64, 67–8, 75, 76, 77n3
  commodity theory, 67–70, 77
  credit theories of money, 70–73, 77
  customary demand, 66–7
  debt, 70–71, 72, 75–6, 77, 78n7
  demand, 65, 66, 71
  division of labor, 68, 73, 74, 75, 76
  Egypt, money and society in antiquity, 73–6
  exchange, medium of, 65, 67, 70, 76
  hyperinflation, 72
  justice, 62, 64–5
  knowledge workers, 73–4

market forces, 68, 69
nomisma, 65, 66
proportionate reciprocity, 64
social justice, 75
state acceptation, 72
state theories of money, 70–73
tax-driven money, 71
temples and temple officials, 71, 72–3
trade, facilitation of, 64–5
trade, relations of, 74
tribute, 72, 73
Wergild theory, 72, 73, 78n9

P

payments
    exchange and, 170, 171–2
    family practices of Global South, 105, 108, 109, 110–11, 118, 119, 120, 121
        for unbanked people, 119–20
    infrastructures for, 168, 169, 170, 175–6, 177–8, 183–4, 185n3
    options for, proliferation of, 181–2
    payment card transactions, 177
    payment systems law, 172
    remittance securitization, 128, 130, 141, 143
        payment streams, 128
    technology for, 167, 168–9
    value transfer, rent and, 175–8
pecuniary canons of taste, Veblen's concept of, 82
Piketty, Thomas, 22–3, 37, 122
Polanyi, Karl, 10, 18, 20–21, 29–30, 33, 35, 47, 71, 77n2, 194, 231
politics
    of Bitcoin, 195–200
        politics free, 190, 193
    cross-border investment in China, political issues, 147–8, 149, 150, 156, 158, 159, 160–61, 162–3
    remittance securitization, political parties and, 135–6, 137

Positive Money, 192, 196
power
    balance in commerce of, 149, 150, 156, 159
    within Communist Party, 163
    differences in, 158–9
    in global finance, 164n5
    power distribution, Bitcoin and, 193
    social relations of, 148
power relations
    financial transactions as, 156–9
    investment and, 160
    money access and, 151
predestination, 97
primordial relationships, 212–15
private property rights, 175
privatization, 134, 136
    of payments, 174
production, 6, 8, 23, 24, 35–6, 85–6
    Bitcoin, cap on production of, 194
    capitalist production, 36, 94
    of luxury, capitalism and, 84–5
    mass (or machine) production, 16, 24, 29, 84, 87
    new forms of, 25
    production costs, reduction of, 27
profits, 4, 23–4, 25–6, 27–8, 33–4, 35–6
    profit-making in Argentina, 262–4
    rent and, relationship between, 170
    small profits, working on, 262–4, 276, 278, 286n20
property, 4, 20, 23, 25, 26, 64, 67, 77n6, 106
    intellectual property, 36
    land, property rights to, 156–7, 158
    private property rights, 175
    state property, expansion of, 29–30
prostitution, 83, 91, 94

R

religions, 4, 8, 9, 15, 26, 30, 31, 75, 83–4
remittance securitization, 128–45
   agriculture, 134, 135, 136, 138
   Alianza Republicana Nacionalista party (ARENA), 135–6, 137
   arbitrage, 132–3
   Bain Capital, 135
   Banco Cuscatlán, 136, 142
   banking system
      financial organizations and, 136
      transformation and, 131
   Bill and Melinda Gates Foundation, 132
   Calle Principal in Intipucá, 138–9, 139–40
   capital, deep leveraging of, 131–2, 133
   Central American Free Trade Agreement (CAFTA), 142
   Clinton Global Initiative, 132
   collateralized debt obligations (CDOs), 133–4
   credit default swaps (CDS), 133–4
   curandera (healer), 139, 143
   development, 130, 132, 134, 137, 138–9, 140–41, 142–3
   digital electronic media, 128, 130–31
   dissimulation, process of, 129
   'Dutch Disease' (economic model), 136–7, 140–41
   Economic Commission for Latin America and the Caribbean (ECLA), 137
   finance, 128, 132, 143
   financial crisis, 131–2
   Frente Farabundo Martí para la Liberación Nacional (FMLN), 135
   Fundación Salvadoreña para el Desarollo Económico y Social (FUSADES), 137
   household consumption, economy and, 136–7, 138
   innovative financing, 130, 142–3
   international migrant remittances, 128
   Latin America, 134, 137
   lender-trader banking model, 131–2
   Long-Term Capital Management, 133–4
   media, 128, 129, 130, 131, 132, 143
   migration, migrants and, 120–30, 128, 135–6, 137–8, 139, 142, 143
   money, media and, 129, 130–31
   money relations, 129
   off-balance sheet dealings, 133–4
   overconcentration of particular investments, 131–2, 132–3
   payment, 128, 130, 141, 143
      payment streams, 128
   petroleum price hikes, 135
   political parties, 135–6, 137
   privatization, 134, 136
   remittance flows, novelty of, 137
   remittance securitization project, 130
   securitization, 128, 130, 141, 142, 143
   special investment vehicles (SIVs), 133–4
   special-purpose vehicles (SPVs), 133–4
      remittance-backed SPVs, 141–2
   structural adjustment, 134–5
   transnationality, trans-disciplinarity and, 128, 129–30, 143–4
   transparency, lack of, 131–2, 133–4
   United Nations Development Program (UNDP), 130, 141
   US centrism, 131–2
   US-El Salvaror-Honduras agreement (2012), 142–3

US International Development
    Agency, 137
Wall Street, 129, 130–32, 134,
    139–40, 142–3
Washington Concessus, 135
World Bank, 130, 136, 137–8,
    140–41, 143
    see also El Salvador
rent, 23, 27, 28, 30, 33, 35–6, 182,
    185n11, 250, 258, 259
    obligation and, 172
    profit and, relationship between,
        170
    see also value transfer, rent and
rent seeking, 34, 35, 36, 170
reputation, 209, 210, 211, 212–13,
    215–15, 219, 220, 222–3
retail space, 84, 89, 90–91
revolutions, 16, 36, 38
    anticolonial revolution, 15, 24, 37
    Bolshevik Revolution, 4
    bourgeois revolution, 16, 23,
        26–8
    bureaucratic revolution, 16–17, 29
    communications revolution, 15,
        16, 18
    Cultural Revolution, 4, 147, 150
    digital revolution, 8, 11, 18, 21, 36
    French Revolution, 6
    industrial revolution, 30, 36
    Italian Revolution, 6
    liberal revolution, 35
    urban revolution, 30
    world revolution and
        counterrevolution, 32–6
Rosario, 250–51, 252, 254–5, 262,
    263–4, 267n1
    comparative prices (*crédito*/peso)
        in, 261
Rousseau, Jean-Jacques, 23, 30, 31

S
sacralization, 85
secularization, 85
securitization, 128, 130, 141, 142, 143
seduction, 83, 92
sex and luxury, 88–90

sexual economy, 93–5
sexuality, 88–9, 90, 91
    commerce and, 93–4
shopping experience, 90–91
Single Euro Payment Area (SEPA), 178
Smith, Adam, 25, 26, 27, 65, 67–8, 69,
    76, 77n1, 98n3, 180, 185n11, 245–6
social differentiation, 260–64
social hierarchies, 61, 163, 170, 252,
    280
social justice, 75
social networking, 170–71
social theory, money and, 44
society
    Bitcoin and, 189–90, 191, 195, 197,
        198, 203
    organization of, 191
    social extension and, 229, 245
    world society, 36
Sombart, Werner, 13, 24, 72
    thesis on luxury and capitalism,
        81, 82, 83–5, 86, 87–8, 89, 90,
        91, 93, 95, 97
South Asia
    bankruptcy, 223–4, 225
    banks and banking systems, 209,
        211, 213–14, 215, 223–4
    British Courts, legal enforcement
        by, 225
    British rule in India, 210–11
    business partnerships, 215–16
    calculation, 217
    capital, 209, 213, 215
    court cases, 210–11, 218–23, 225
        Madho Row Chinto Punt
            Golay v. Bhookun-Das
            Boolaki-Das, 219–21
        Pragdas Thakurdas v.
            Dowlatram Nanuram,
            221–3, 225
    credit, 209, 212, 213, 214, 217, 224
    honor, 212, 216, 219, 220, 222,
        223–4
    indigenous banking, 213–14
    indigenous credit system, 209–10
    indigenous institutions, status
        of, 211

informality, reconfiguration of
    notion of, 216–23
insolvency, 223–4
law, 209–10, 210–11, 218–23, 225
    common law system, 211
mercantile model of exchange,
    209–26
money laundering, 209, 211
Negotiable Instruments Act
    (NIA, 1881), 213–14
partnerships, 215–16
primordial relationships, 212–15
rationality, 213, 225
reputation, 209, 210, 211, 212–13,
    215–15, 219, 220, 222–3
trade and traders, 209–10, 211,
    214, 215–16, 219
trust, 209, 210, 211, 215–16,
    216–18, 219
see also hundi/hawala in South
    Asia
Spengler, Oswald, 63

T
trade
    African trade, words in, 52–3
    European traders in Lesotho, 244
    facilitation of, 64–5
    Lesotho, Basotho people and,
        230, 231, 232, 234–5, 236,
        243–4, 246, 247n7
    relations of, 74
    and traders in South Asia,
        209–10, 211, 214, 215–16, 219
    trust and, 44
transnationality
    trans-disciplinarity and, 128,
        129–30, 143–4
    transnational families, 116–18
transport, 5, 16, 19, 46, 257, 258
trust
    Bitcoin, 189, 190–91, 192, 199,
        200, 201, 202
    encapsulated interest and, 217,
        223
    South Asia, 209, 210, 211, 215–16,
        216–18, 219

U
United Nations (UN)
    Development Program (UNDP),
        130, 141
    Stabilization Mission in Haiti
        (MINUSTAH), 277
United States (US)
    centrism of, 131–2
    dollar, 17, 19, 21, 32, 57, 107, 121,
        123, 130, 140, 200
        Haitian dollar and, 270, 271,
            274, 276, 277, 280, 281, 283
        peso parity in Argentina
            and, 251
    International Development
        Agency, 137
    US-El Salvaror-Honduras
        agreement (2012), 142–3
utopia (and utopianism), 194–5, 201,
    202

V
value transfer, rent and, 167–86
    annuity, 179–82
    Apple Pay, 167
        interchange fees on, 168–9
    banks, 177
    Bitcoin blockchain, 170
    card-acceptance services, 170
    charge card systems, 176
    chip-and-pin cards, 167
    clearance and settlement, value
        in, 169–70
    corporate interconnectedness,
        167
    cost of funds (COF), 178
    credit, money and, 171
    credit cards, 168, 170, 172, 175,
        177, 178, 181–2
    credit theories of money, 173–4,
        180
    data management tools, 170
    deferred payment, 180
    electronic money, issuance of,
        174
    Electronic Transactions
        Association, 179

electronic value, cash conversion into, 170–71, 174
exchange, par clearance during, 175–6
exchange-centricity, 170
Facebook credits, 172, 173, 174
Federal Reserve Banks, centralization of, 176
interchange, 176, 177, 178, 179–82, 183–4
    alternative interchanges, 182–4
    interchange fees, 168–9, 176
Internet, 170–71
metallism, 171
mobile telecommunications, 170–71, 173–4
monetary value, exchange of, 169–70
money
    credit theories of, 173–4, 180
    infrastructures of, 168, 169
    monetary value and, 173–4
    nature of, 171
    social hierarchy of, 170, 173
online credits, 175
payments, 175–8
    card transactions, 177
    exchange and, 170, 171–2
    infrastructures for, 168, 169, 170, 175–6, 177–8, 183–4, 185n3
    online payments, 172–3
    options for, proliferation of, 181–2
    payment systems law, 172
    technology, 167, 168–9
private property rights, 175
privatization of payment, 174
regulatory change, 171
rent, 182, 185n11
    obligation and, 172
    profit and, relationship between, 170
rent seeking, 170
Samsung, 167
Single Euro Payment Area (SEPA), 178
social networking, 170–71
value added, surplus value and, 172
value transfer, value chain and revenue from, 172–3
Wal-Mart, 178

W

Wall Street
    remittance securitization, 129, 130–32, 134, 139–40, 142–3
    Wall Street System, 196, 199
Weber, Max, 13, 24, 25–6, 30, 35, 70–71, 81, 85–6, 87, 88, 97, 145n11, 274, 282
Wergild theory, 72, 73, 78n9
Williamson, Oliver, 8, 217
World Bank, 130, 136, 137–8, 140–41, 143
world society, 36, 147, 149, 163
    'Money in the Making of World Society', 45–7
worth, ethnography of, 47, 48, 50–52, 53, 54, 55–7, 58

Z

Zelizer, Viviana, 10, 94–5, 107, 118, 121, 148, 253, 259, 279
Zola, Emile, 90–93

www.ingramcontent.com/pod-product-compliance
Lightning Source LLC
Chambersburg PA
CBHW070910030426
42336CB00014BA/2354